SEX ROLES AND SOCIAL POLICY

Editorial Board 1979-1982
SAGE Studies in International Sociology

Ulf Himmelstrand President of the ISA, Uppsala University, Sweden
Tom Bottomore Ex-President of the ISA, University of Sussex, UK
Guido Martinotti Chairman, Editorial Board, University of Turin, Italy

Akinsola Akiwowo University of Ife, Nigeria
S H Alatas University of Singapore, Singapore
Erik Allardt University of Helsinki, Finland
Samir Amin African Institute for Economic Development and Planning, Dakar
Margaret Archer Editor, *Current Sociology/La Sociologie Contemporaine*, University of Warwick, UK
Michel Bassand University of Geneva, Switzerland
Manuel Castells Ecole des Hautes Etudes en Sciences Sociales, Paris
Alessandro Cavalli University of Pavia, Italy
Michael Cernea Academy of Political Sciences, Bucarest
Suma Chitnis Tata Institute of Social Sciences, Bombay, India
Jacques Dofny University of Montreal, Quebec
Orlando Fals-Borda Boguta, Colombia
Salah Garmadi C.E.R.E.S., Tunis
Lim Thek Ghee University of Sains Malaysia, Malaysia
Anthony Giddens King's College, Cambridge, UK
Marie R Haug Case Western Reserve University, USA
Peter Heintz University of Zurich, Switzerland
Artur Meier Academy of Pedagogical Sciences, GDR
Gennady Osipov Institute of Sociological Research, Moscow, USSR
Enrique Oteiza Institute of Development Studies, Sussex, UK
Alejandro Portes The Ford Foundation, Rio De Janeiro, Brazil
Peta Sheriff McMaster University, Ontario, Canada
Marina Subirats Autonomous University of Barcelona, Spain
Joji Watanuki Harvard University, USA
Francisco Weffort C.E.B.R.A.P., Sao Paolo, Brazil
Wlodzimierz Wesolowski Institute of Philosophy and Sociology, Warsaw, Poland
Maurice Zeitlin University of California, Los Angeles, USA
Anton C Zijderveld University of Tilburg, The Netherlands

SEX ROLES AND SOCIAL POLICY:
A Complex Social Science Equation

Edited by
Jean Lipman-Blumen
National Institute of Education, Washington, D.C.
and
Jessie Bernard
Pennsylvania State University

SAGE Studies in International Sociology 14
sponsored by the International Sociological Association/ISA

Copyright © 1979 by the
International Sociological Association/ISA

All rights reserved. No part of this book may be
reproduced or utilized in any form or by any means,
electronic or mechanical, including photocopying, recording, or
by any information storage and retrieval system, without
permission in writing from the International Sociological
Association/ISA

For information address

SAGE Publications Ltd.
28 Banner Street
London EC1Y 8QE

SAGE Publications Inc.
275 South Beverly Drive
Beverly Hills, California 90212

International Standard Book Number
0 8039 9870 8 Cloth
0 8039 9871 6 Paper

Library of Congress Catalog Card Number
77-090858

First Printing

Printed and Bound in the United States of America

CONTENTS

Introductory Note
Mary Berry   1

Preface
Jean Lipman-Blumen and Jessie Bernard   3

Introduction
Elise Boulding   7

I THE COMPLEX EQUATION OF SOCIAL POLICY, SOCIAL SCIENCE, AND SEX ROLES

1. The Dialectic Between Research and Social Policy: The Difficulties from a Policy Perspective — Rashomon Part I
   Jean Lipman-Blumen   17
2. The Dialectic Between Research and Social Policy: The Difficulties from a Research Perspective — Rashomon Part II
   Jean Lipman-Blumen   39
3. Where Research and Policy Connect: The American Scene
   Sandra S. Tangri and Georgia L. Strasburg   61
4. Demographic Indicators of the Status of Women in Various Societies
   Nadia H. Youssef and Shirley Foster Hartley   83
5. A Paradigm for Predicting the Position of Women: Policy Implications and Problems
   Rae Lesser Blumberg   113

II THE DELIBERATE USE OF POLICY TO CHANGE SEX ROLES

6. Public Policy and Changing Family Patterns in Sweden, 1930-1977
   Annika Baude   145
7. Women in Eastern Europe
   Hilda Scott   177
8. Social Policy and the Family in Norway
   Harriet Holter and Hildur Ve Henriksen   199

9	The Changing Role of Women in Jordan: 'A Threat or an Asset?' *Nimra Tannous Es-Said*	225
10	Fertility Policy in India *Vina Mazumdar*	249

III WOMEN AS POLICY MAKERS

11	Women as Policy Makers: The Case of France *Claude du Granrut*	269
12	Women as Voters: From Redemptive to Futurist Role *Jessie Bernard*	279
13	Women as Change Agents: Toward a Conflict Theoretical Model of Sex Role Change *Constantina Safilios-Rothschild*	287
14	Policy and Women's Time *Jessie Bernard*	303

IV UNRESOLVED ISSUES: A LOOK TO THE FUTURE

15	Educational Policy for Women: A Look Ahead *Virginia Y. Trotter*	337
16	The Rights of Women and the Role of International Law *Cecilia Marchand*	349
17	Beyond Equality *Judith Buber Agassi*	355
18	The Policy Promissory Note: Time to Deliver *Jean Lipman-Blumen and Jessie Bernard*	363

Subject Index	381
Author Index	397
Notes on Contributors	401

Dedication

*To our sisters
around the world*

INTRODUCTORY NOTE

Mary Berry
Assistant Secretary for Education, US Dept. of Health, Education and Welfare, Washington DC

There is an underlying conflict between the roles of the Federal government and the research community in pursuing their common goal of improving education. As a public policy making body, the Federal government must respond to political and bureaucratic imperatives; as scholars, the research community is and should be more sensitive to scientific imperatives. If the tension resulting from these different forces is to remain creative, researchers must continue to strive, as they have done, for independence in choosing the substance and methods of their work. Somehow, we in the Federal government must respond to public pressure for problem solving without allowing this pressure to cripple scholars in the performance of their unique role, which is to inform and guide the direction of problem solving and applied research through fundamental inquiry and basic research. To be able to do this, however, we depend heavily on you to articulate, represent and support the principle of independent research (Berry, 1977*.)

I wrote those words to describe how the tensions between politics and science affected educational research. The problem is even more pressing in research on sex roles, as this volume testifies. The need for research on sex roles is not universally recognized within either the policy or scientific communities. In fact, sex role research has faced the lack of understanding and support commonly encountered by new

---

* Berry, Mary. 'Educational Research and the Tension Between Politics and Science', *Educational Researcher*, Vol. 6, No. 5, May 1977, pp. 3–6.

areas of scientific investigation. Yet I hope that sex role researchers will not be deterred by the paucity of general support and understanding for this relatively new scientific enterprise; instead, they must always be aware that research which challenges the core concepts of our lives and our society often confronts social and political resistance. And investigations into the impact of sex role stereotypes inevitably will have a fundamental effect on all our lives and on our political, social, and economic institutions. The need for such research is clear, however, if we are to provide to the female majority of our population the opportunities which have traditionally been denied them.

There is no doubt that the tensions between policy and science are exacerbated when the subject at issue is one that cuts across every social institution. Sex roles, which lie at the heart of all social life, are a subject neither scientists nor policy makers can continue to ignore. The current volume initiated by the International Sociological Association and supported in part by the Education Division of the US Department of Health, Education, and Welfare, is an effort to confront this important subject, which addresses one of the most fundamental issues of this century.

PREFACE

Jean Lipman-Blumen
National Institute of Education, USA
Jessie Bernard
Pennsylvania State University

The history of this volume has been relatively long and exceedingly complex. Anyone who has edited a book can glimpse some of the initial problems of trying to create a coherent message from a diverse set of papers. Anyone who has tried to deal with cross-national efforts is aware of another dimension of complexity, wherein different viewpoints, methodologies, political and social structure coalesce to create a multitude of divergence. Anyone who has concerned him/herself with social policy can sympathize with the problems created by the shifting sands of political issues. And anyone who has studied sex roles can appreciate the difficulties of examining an issue both tradition-bound and tradition-breaking. That anyone would undertake such a 'mission impossible' — to edit an international volume on social policy, social research and sex roles — is probably just short of complete insanity. But the basic question the volume poses — what, if anything, can social science research contribute to the formulation of social policy on sex roles? — is too important to allow even such seemingly insuperable obstacles to prevent its exploration.

At the invitation of the International Sociological Association, we attempted to create such a volume, using as its core the papers on sex roles and social policy presented at the 8th World Congress of the

International Sociological Association (Toronto, 1974). Because the available papers did not constitute a book, we requested permission to invite additional papers from scholars and policy makers around the world. Before we began and all along the way, we consulted numerous people in the field in many countries. Some agreed to contribute chapters, and their work is included. Some who agreed were later unable — for either personal or political reasons — to write their chapters. We regret their absence.

Not all countries we hoped for are included. Inevitably, in a volume such as this, it is impossible to have all the pieces of the puzzle. We envision this book as an opening dialogue — not the last word. We trust that the lacunae in this volume — either because we did not know the appropriate people to approach in different countries, or because those we asked were unable to contribute — will be filled by other social scientists and policy makers. We would have liked more representation from countries of different socio-economic and political structures, as well as of different religious and ethnic mixes. Again, that remains for others to fulfil.

This book is a testament, nonetheless, to the increasingly evident bridges among women social scientists and policy makers around the world.[1] Our lines of communication are imperfect but growing as more and more women commit their lives to the exploration and development of the sex roles appropriate for this day and age — through research and social policy. We need the help of our sisters everywhere in developing our knowledge to create sex role equality for people around the globe.

While this book is built explicitly on the efforts of our consoeurs who contributed chapters, it also has been enriched by the efforts of other colleagues, friends, and relatives who helped behind the scenes. We thank but absolve of all responsibility, the people who shared with us their talents, energies, and time: Elinor Barber, Elise Boulding, Katy Brooks, Greta Coen, Carol Crump, Adrienne Germain, Gary Gosnell, Harold J. Leavitt, Levora President, Ann Shultz, Carol Smith, Lynn Warren, and Lauren Weisberg.

We are particularly indebted to the National Institute of Education, the US Department of Health, Education and Welfare, for supporting the editing and international communications necessary in such an undertaking. Without such help, this book could not have been. We believe the publication of this volume serves the goals of the Women's Research Program at NIE, whose mandate is to understand and help remove the internal and external barriers to women's equity.

---

1 After this book was completed. the papers presented at the Wellesley College Conference on women and national development became available in *Signs*, Autumn 1977, Vol 3 (1). They illustrate and document many of the points developed in this volume.

INTRODUCTION

Elise Boulding
*Dartmouth College and University
of Colorado, USA*

The story of this book really begins in Varna, Bulgaria, during the 7th Congress of the International Sociological Association in 1970. Drawn together by common frustration, a group of sociologists were sitting together at supper, lamenting the impossibility of getting a hearing for a new research topic all were involved in — sex roles — during Congress sessions. A couple of papers on this topic had been accepted for a race relations session, but no one was satisfied with that — least of all the race relations scholars, who felt they had all too little time to discuss their own work. The activities set in motion that evening resulted in the establishment of the ISA Research Committee on the Study of Sex Roles in Society. By the next Congress, at Toronto, the new Committee was conducting its own sessions, with overflowing audiences and keen discussions.

It seemed to all of us at the time that publication of some of the papers given at Toronto, and of the ongoing research of Committee members generally, was an important way to stimulate and support each others' activities. Andrée Michel of the Centre Nationale de la Recherche Scientifique, Paris, who served with me as co-chair of the Research Committee from its inception until the Spring of 1977, edited a volume in French entitled *Femmes, Sexisme et Societies* (Presses Universitaires de France, 1977). This collection of papers, largely from the Toronto meetings, consists of cross-national studies of sex discrimination, sex role differentiation and sex-based stratification.

The current volume, the second to appear in connection with the work of Research Committee members, represents an important presentation for the international social science community of the achievements and dilemmas of researching policy issues relating to sex roles.

The book would never have come into being without the untiring efforts of its co-editors, Jean Lipman-Blumen and Jessie Bernard. Their work has been far more than a coordinating and editorial task. They have contributed to the conceptualization of sex role research in a policy context in a way that made it possible for work by scholars in different world regions to be brought together meaningfully. They both took countless hours from already over-busy schedules to produce this book, and every member of the Research Committee owes them a profound debt of gratitude. We also are grateful to the National Institute of Education of the US Dept. of Health, Education and Welfare for financial support for the work of manuscript preparation.

A key concept throughout this book is sex discrimination and its converse, sex equality. This is an inherently difficult subject. As Lipman-Blumen says in her lucid opening chapters on the dialectics of policy-making and research, sex discrimination is a sponge-like concept. Her plea that it is time to move from the descriptive to the analytic, to develop change models and to identify long and short-term intervention points have been well-heeded by her author-colleagues. Lipman-Blumen herself offers a whole series of snapshot paradigms of sex-role processes in her illustrations of how to do impact analysis studies for proposed anti-discrimination legislation. The difficulty of making research match action needs is also borne out by the book as a whole, however. No one can take this book and design a national anti-discrimination policy! Policy makers with a feel for social research, however, will find it extremely useful, as will researchers with a feel for policy issues. Lipman-Blumen recommends as a matter of principle that researchers and policy-makers should know each other's craft, to make their respective needs and findings more translatable. I strongly agree.

Tangri and Strasburg spell out the complex communication mazeways between researchers and policy-makers. The problem of changing social values over time confounds what researchers research, and how policy-makers apply their findings. The sex roles field is probably more vulnerable than most to cultural lag in value changes. Tangri and

Strasburg give an apt illustration of the problem with the example of earlier (and now outmoded) sex role research on the physical capacities of women providing the basis for protective labor legislation which in turn gave the rationale for discrimination against women in hiring. That issue is still in the wings in the US as some women, and many men, oppose the equal rights amendment now before the states. One of the hardest issues to deal with at present in the international human rights field, going well beyond the status of women, is under what conditions do individuals need to be protected, and how can protection be kept from turning into discrimination?

The difficulties of writing about sex discrimination are compounded when the concept is looked at cross-culturally. As scholars we have both an intellectual and a moral commitment to 'internationalize our feelings of self and society', as Trotter puts it. On the other hand, Blumberg has a persuasive point when she tells us that in conceptualizing the position of women in any one country the standard to be applied is the level of the men in that same society, not that of women in other societies. What does that do to international sisterhood? Ultimately the only way out of this dilemma is to put women's rights in the context of the human rights issue, as Marchand advises, and aim for common human standards for people everywhere. From a policy perspective, however, this means little more than a retreat to rhetoric. That puts us back to the task in hand, developing operational criteria for the measurement of the status of women. An impressive contribution is made to this task by both Youssef and Hartley, and by Blumberg, in Part I of this book.

Readers will not fail to note that although the focal concept of the book is sex role equality, in fact much of the research attention is focussed on women, and how women are doing in relation to men. As Blumberg puts it in her historical survey of sex stratification, it is differential power which underlies inequality, and the policy task is to ensure equal access of women to the poker chips of power. The assumption here is that if women can do all the things that men can do this will be social progress. Youssef and Hartley's demographic survey of the status of women also makes a similar assumption. Women's welfare, and therefore social welfare, will be served by policy planning that gives women equal opportunities for choice of occupation with men (a choice made 'real' by equal educational and equal employment opportunities). These assumptions are certainly not incorrect. The fact that the world mean for the proportion of female to male administrators is 10 percent, and that this mean does not vary very much even in occupational areas in which women dominate, points up the almost complete exclusion of women from positions in which the blueprints for social construction are drawn. If there is to be progressive social change, then women must be in positions to help design such change.

This, however, is where the use of the standard of 'what men do' for raising the status of women must be examined. Women might well become partners with men in a power game *no one should be playing*. The best insurance against this trap is along the lines spelled out by Baude: sex role policy must support changes in men's as well as women's roles. It is no accident that it is the contributor from Sweden, the country that has gone the farthest toward equality for women and men, that emphasized men's role changes the most strongly. Public policy that ensures that all boys learn homemaking and child care skills in school, gives preferential consideration to male applicants for pre-school teacher training, that counts home care of children, for both males and females, as practical work experience to be counted on one's work record, and that gives public recognition to parenting as an important social role for women and men alike, is a policy that equalizes and transforms sex roles at the same time.

Role transformation is an important concept that will need more attention in the future. It appears in this book from time to time, sometimes almost tangentially. Safilios-Rothschild, for example, has an interesting proposal that amounts to role transformation though she does not describe it as such. She suggests that mainstream women identify with and become involved with women in current protest movements, such as the liberation movements for ethnic and racial minorities, the handicapped and the old. (I would add children.) While she is treating this identification primarily as an action strategy, such a process would in fact also affect women's self-concepts and have role-transforming effects.

Such an equality-cum-transformation approach to policy is particularly relevant to preparation for the next major human rights year to be supported by the United Nations: the International Year of the Child (1979). Ultimately, the equal rights concept must be applied to the young — and to the old. At present it applies only to persons between the ages of 21 and 65. It is one of the scandals of the United Nations Human Rights Declaration that it does not include age as a category along with sex, ethnicity, religion and race as unallowed bases for discrimination. Children are apt to become a residual category when equal rights for women are addressed, a residual category that must somehow be taken care of when both parents are employed.

Sweden is a pioneer in the promotion of the rights of children, as we learn from Baude's paper. There, children's centers are established in the interest of the well-being of the child, and not as an afterthought to a full employment policy for women. Once sex role equality as a concept becomes rooted in a life-span perspective, a role transformation involving the concept of personhood will have taken place, and policy makers will not make the absurd differentiations they now make.

The countries of Eastern Europe face something of a crisis in regard to their longstanding commitment to equality-cum-transformation in social roles. Falling birthrates, as Scott points out, have opposed public needs to private preferences. The ideological goal of role transformation for both sexes, basic to all socialist policy, is being undermined by the 'need' to have women stay home and have babies.

The idea of role transformation implies an image of a future society. In general, however, policymakers and researchers alike suffer from the lack of an image of what a more sex-egalitarian future society would look like. It is more a subject for jokes than serious discussion. Almost the only serious work on sex egalitarian futures today is being done by women science fiction writers such as Joanna Russ and Ursula LeGuin.

What is the imagination of the future in this book? Sweden appears to come the closest to having an image of a sex-egalitarian future. The socialist countries apparently began backing off when they got some intimations of what that world might look like. Jordan, aiming for a 'progressive' urban sex-segregated society, actually has a sex-egalitarian society in its midst, the 'backward' Bedouins. The amazing gains described by Es-Said for both urban and rural women in education and enumerated labor force participation, in spite of strong urban cultural beliefs about women staying in the home, suggests that the Bedouin egalitarian tradition may be having some hidden effects on the modernization process.

Israel is perhaps the most futurist-oriented society of any represented among the contributors to this book. It is appropriate that Agassi should be the author to look 'beyond equality', and to talk about changing the quality of life of women, not only bringing women up to men. Agassi is also the one who discusses the separatist creation of alternative structures, models for a more humane future society, by women.

Jessie Bernard also looks to the future. She approaches it via an insightful macrohistorical overview of the course of women's roles from the old redemptive homemaker role to the contemporary two-career role that overloads her with responsibility for both the home and the workplace. When men begin sharing with women the dual home and workplace responsibilities, women will be able to take up futures-creating roles. They will shift from adapters to shapers, says Bernard.

In one sense every author in this book is a futurist, since every author is concerned with social change toward a non-discriminatory society. While few authors offer images of that future, everyone identifies possible intervention points in social processes. The family, the labor force and the educational system are generally seen as the most productive areas for intervention, aided by the courts and, more indirectly, by human rights conventions. Holter's thought-provoking analysis of the social consequences of government policies supportive of 'high-function' versus low-function' families provides a new way of looking at alternative futures for women. Du Granrut's discussion of family and work policy in France and Mazumdar's discussion of fertility policy in India demonstrate vividly the extent to which analytic frames of reference do indeed make a difference in actual policy choices that determine social futures. Safilios-Rothschild pinpoints the political process, particularly political participation via minority protest movements. She also suggests concentrating on new occupational and civic areas not preempted by either sex, as a way to 'find, enter, and dominate' the system.

Bernard's suggestion that discretionary time be made a subject of public policy in order to remove what is a nearly universal imbalance between women's and men's command of leisure time, is a striking one. Free time is a key resource for social innovation. Ensuring that working women have the same amounts of discretionary time that men do, which at present they do not have anywhere in the world, will give women as well as men the opportunity for that creative free play from which social inventions emerge. Using the ratio of women's to men's free time as an indicator of the status of women opens up a whole new approach to the conceptualization of status.

For the most part, the intervention strategies proposed are based on a Western view of the development process. Education is considered a precondition for everything else. What I really missed — but you can't have everything in one book! — was a picture of the nonliterate activist woman found in many third world rural societies, as a possible model for the West. Literacy is not the only recipe for egalitarianism. In fact, if anything, the records on educational progress compared with civic and work force participation country by country would suggest that literacy does not necessarily enhance the status of women. A good candidate for a future book to be undertaken by the Sex Roles Research Committee would be one on sex-role policy by third world authors exclusively. This is an important issue, because technical assistance programs are still based on the assumption that rural women in the third world are ignorant persons who need to be taught literacy and hygiene. By ignoring the high skill level with which they produce food and family necessities with the poorest of tools (the modern tools go to the men, as Boserup has noted elsewhere), technical assistance personnel downgrade women's status still further and fail to do the one thing that could help — assist them in getting better tools so they could work on more equal terms with the men.

A missed intervention point that should get more attention in the future is the 38 percent of the world's women who are over fifteen and either never married, or are widowed or divorced. These unpartnered women are all of labor force age, and in most parts of the world they are in the labor force. They are also, except for the over 45s, of childbearing age. While a certain proportion will eventually marry, the figure of one-third or more unpartnered women over 15 is surprisingly constant both historically and at present, from region to region. Public policy rarely deals with them, in any society, although they are usually the poorest and the most exploited. Sex role researchers certainly do not mean to exclude them from consideration, but once age at marriage has been dealt with, this category of persons often slips out of focus.

If we add to possible intervention points that researchers can have some knowledge of, all the conceivable intervention points where no data exist, we would have a very long list indeed. It is one of the ironies of sex roles research that while everyone knows there is serious inequality of opportunity between women and men, good cross-national data on that inequality are still scanty. Since the construction of process models requires data, policy making is hampered by our not being able to provide more figures about processes we all know exist. The production of the relevant numbers will come from a combination of the researcher's desire to know and the policy-maker's need to decide. Since sex discrimination is an international phenomenon, and no country is unaffected by the sex discrimination policies of any other, it is important to keep sex role research an international enterprise.

That a common language to discuss the research and policy issues associated with sex roles should have developed in the relatively short time period since this has become a major public issue (I would date this at about 1970) is impressive. The contributors to this book clearly share the same universe of discourse. The fact that they have more opportunities than most women for international contact and collaboration does not lessen the magnitude of that accomplishment. The international research community of scholars concerned with sex roles is now well launched. I wish it long life and fruitfulness.

I
THE COMPLEX EQUATION OF SOCIAL POLICY, SOCIAL SCIENCE, AND SEX ROLES

1

THE DIALECTIC BETWEEN RESEARCH AND SOCIAL POLICY:
The Difficulties from a Policy Perspective — RASHOMON PART I

Jean Lipman-Blumen
National Institute of Education, USA

The difficult dialect between social research and social policy is documented in the first two chapters by Lipman-Blumen. After warning of the dangers of creating social policy on sex roles without an adequate research base, Lipman-Blumen examines the difficulties inherent in the researcher-policy maker-activist relationship. In the first of two Rashomon views of the social research/social policy picture, she analyzes the disconsonant characteristics of the research enterprise and the policy community that pose special problems for the social policy maker and the social activist.

Lipman-Blumen suggests at least four dangers to which policy ungrounded in research is vulnerable: an ineffective or negative result; replication difficulties; 'blaming the victim;' and fickle or short-term political interest. She then turns the mirror to reflect the structural and attitudinal difficulties of creating social policy on sex roles in an heterogeneous society in which one group's need is another group's anathema. In her analysis of the special difficulties of the policy maker/activist/researcher relationship, Lipman-Blumen suggests that the different

'Rashomon' is a Japanese concept referring to the phenomenon whereby the same set of events is viewed differentially by the various participants involved. See Ryunosuke Akutagawa, *Rashomon*, Tokyo, Alanda Shobo Publisher, 1917.

traditions of these groups create barriers to communication and collaboration, despite consonant goals. The activist is portrayed as the impatient mover, distrustful of the policy maker, who excels as the architect of compromise, and the researcher, who functions as the seeker of truth.

Lipman-Blumen calls attention to the mismatch between the demands of policy and the results of research. Policy makers frequently want answers to unresearchable questions, while researchers commonly attempt and fail to provide relevant responses. In addition, technical language, elaboration of obvious truths, equivocal and sometimes conflicting results, lengthy reports, and political naivete serve as reporting barriers preventing the use of research results by policy makers and activists. In addition, because of the difficulty of judging the quality and validity of research findings for non-researchers, policy makers often avoid relying upon any but the most simple and irrefutable research results.

The first chapter examines two possible roles for the researcher vis-à-vis the policy maker: consultant and social engineer. Consulting and social engineering roles are scrutinized as two possible mechanisms for translating social science findings into social policy. Lipman-Blumen analyzes the special obstacles to implementation and highlights the importance of interdisciplinary implementation teams composed of researchers, policy makers, community activists, and members of the target population. Finally, the chapter delineates the factors that make implementation of social science results particularly arduous. Lipman-Blumen cites the difficulties of identifying and controlling all the relevant variables in social science research.

INTRODUCTION

The women's movement around the world has been largely a call for action, responsive to increased awareness of the inequities faced by women everywhere. This call for action has been translated into social policy in many parts of the globe. As social policy increasingly becomes a significant instrument for improving the status of women, the potential role of social science research as an important basis for informed and effective policy looms larger (Murphy, 1973; Komarovsky, 1975).

The full definition of the role that social science may play in the policy realm remains to be developed. To date, only a relative handful of social scientists qua researchers has engaged in the policy development process. The degree to which social scientists have played a part in the development of social policy has varied both from time to time, and from one culture to another.

Despite the variable influence of social science on policy making in different contexts, certain constraints recur in the social policy/social science research equation. Difficulties exist on both sides of this equation, with policy makers faulting research for its limitations, and researchers reciprocally denigrating the policy making process. In these first two chapters, we shall focus on the juncture of social policy, social science and sex roles. We shall explore the nature of the obstacles that beset the efforts of these dissimilar groups to collaborate in the search for equity between the sexes.[1]

A brief overview of our perspective suggests that the general, long-range goals of activists, policy makers and researchers are essentially the same: equality between men and women. Yet, each group approaches the problem with different perspectives, strategies, and sub-goals. As a result, they often talk past each other and, even more often, they simply do not talk.

Many activists and policy makers,[2] impatient for social change, perceive research as endless, futile, and often irrelevant to social and political realities. In their understandable haste to make the world a better place, policy makers and social activists frequently overlook a fundamental fact: mistakes in social policy cost dearly in human life, misery, time, money, and political opportunity.

Social change — the ultimate purpose of social policy — is a long, delicate, easily jeopardized and arduous phenomenon. It may be seriously undermined when it is initiated without benefit of a solid knowledge base. Such a knowledge base is at the heart of the research enterprise.

Researchers, for their part, commonly misperceive the needs of social policy, pursuing research that does not speak to the problems that policy makers would address. While they recognize the importance of research findings to policy formulation, social scientists commonly present their results in ways that render them useless for policy purposes,

On the surface, this may seem an obvious and, therefore, easily rectifiable problem. The history of the dialectic between social research and social policy on sex roles, however, stands as eloquent witness to its complexities. The very nature of the research process, as we shall demonstrate, does not lend itself easily to the needs of social policy. Some would even argue that there is a fundamental lack of synchronization between the two.

In 'Rashomon Part I' of this chapter, we shall examine the issues, indeed the dangers, involved in creating social policy for sex roles without an adequate research base. We shall then explore the difficulties activists and policy makers experience with social science research. In Rashomon Part II, we shall present the mirror image: the reciprocal difficulties that researchers experience with activists and policy makers. Finally, we shall attempt to answer the bottom-line question, 'Is there any possibility of productive collaboration among activists, policy makers and researchers?'[3] Our answer will revolve around a clarification of several research strategies that can be tailored to the special requirements of social policy.

THE DANGERS OF CREATING SOCIAL POLICY WITHOUT AN ADEQUATE RESEARCH BASE

A. The Consequences of Ad Hoc Policies

Social policy seeks to create solutions to social problems. The better our advance understanding of all the complexities of a problem, the better the solutions we are likely to fashion. Without that initial step, it is impossible to move with any certainty to an assessment of the possible outcomes of various policy options.

When medical science addressed the problem of polio, no one seriously considered generating a vaccine without first isolating the virus. Social policy on sex roles, while it addresses social problems with which nonscientists feel familiar, nonetheless must start with solid knowledge stemming from systematic research. Otherwise social policy formulators find themselves shooting at a target in the dark. Even if, by some good fortune, they hit the target, they don't learn much, and replication (not to mention long-term results) is unlikely.

Social policy that is created on a premature or ad hoc basis can have serious negative results. The likelihood of failure is high. Such failures of poorly planned social policy harm all involved. The needy target population, in this case women, is depressed by having expectations first raised by new promises and then dashed by ineffectiveness. Often, a more serious consequence is 'blaming the victim' for the inadequacy of the solutions. Recent social history in the US, for example, is strewn with the wreckage of poverty and educational programs whose failures were explained by the alleged inadequacies of the target group. Not only are the victims blamed for the policy failures, but they are further punished by the tendency of the policy maker to escape from the scene without spending additional time, effort or funds on adequately designed alternatives. Thus, social problems that loom large on the political horizon one moment quickly slip from view as political opportunity fades.

Ad hoc policy formulation burns both the activist and policy maker and may mean the loss of major political opportunities. The activists who pushed the policy makers to create the legislative mandates for such programs feel they have 'used their chips' on the wrong bet. They sense the damage to their own credibility by program failures. To add to the debacle, policy makers, eager to protect their own credibility, grow impatient with efforts that backfire and are likely to turn their attention to other pressing issues that clamor for their consideration (and which have better chances of winning).

B. Social Policy in a Heterogeneous Society

Competition for political attention among diverse social concerns is particularly important in complex, heterogeneous societies. The dilemmas posed by competing and conflicting constituencies create special problems for the policy maker. Often the best solution for one constituency is the worst for another.

Social policy solutions and strategies are more easily and efficiently evolved in more homogeneous societies, as in the Swedish experience, which Baude describes (Chapter 6). But recently, with increasing social heterogeneity, even Swedish policy makers are finding it far harder to create and implement social policy. The consensus of social attention focused upon Swedish social welfare legislation has begun to fragment, and the legitimacy claims of alternative positions now compete for center stage.

Political interest in specific issues is inherently fragile and fickle, a problem exacerbated by heterogeneous constituencies. Activists and policy makers, therefore, need politically relevant ammunition to make their programs acceptable and effective. A meaningful portion of that ammunition can be supplied by hard data from research.

In most developed and developing countries, women themselves represent a microcosm of the larger society. As the Es-Said paper demonstrates, without serious research on the problems, characteristics, needs, attitudes and resources of the many groups that comprise the 'female target population', we may fall into the trap of perceiving and treating females as though they were a monolithic group. Women span the age, race, socioeconomic, ethnic, political, religious and educational spectra. Without adequate knowledge of the differences and similarities among the affected subgroups, policy is likely to be designed to meet everyone's needs and end up meeting no one's.

The legitimate vested interests within each group often hold strongly different preferences (witness the current anti-abortion vs. pro-choice struggle in the US). To be effective, social policy makers must assess these competing needs, determining which problems can safely be delayed and which solutions can be linked most effectively with which problems. A critical aspect of political 'savvy' is the ability to judge when the time is ripe for the presentation and implementation of previously unpopular, but necessary, strategies. For example, the environmentalist movement in the US received little political support until its perspective gained greater grass-roots popularity.

Although political judgments ultimately may rule the day, such judgments ideally should be informed by a knowledge base developed through research. Research, properly used, can be an invaluable resource to the policy maker in dealing with the demands emanating from a heterogeneous society.

Free heterogeneous societies rarely can count on the type of long-term continuity of any single political party which promotes systematic goal setting and implementation. For the policy maker qua politician, the need to maintain an acceptable (and re-electable) political posture vis-à-vis a highly diverse constituency complicates policy issues. As many astute policy makers know, research can offer potentially valuable knowledge to those who seek to create systematic, effective social policy in heterogeneous milieux.[4]

This is not to suggest that policy unmoored to research is totally trouble-free in more homogeneous societies. As the Scott and Baude chapters both illustrate, the lack of adequate research or the neglect of available research — whether on the effect of day-care centers (Woolsey, 1977) on childhood development or on projections of demographic trends in relation to housing and labor force patterns — can jeopardize the intended outcomes of social policy even in stable, homogeneous contexts. Heterogeneous societies, nonetheless, offer a special challenge to policy makers, a challenge research potentially could help them meet.

PROBLEMS POLICY MAKERS AND ACTIVISTS EXPERIENCE WITH RESEARCH

If research is so crucial to social policy formulation, why are activists and policy makers frequently reluctant to use it? In the language of cost-benefit analysis, the costs often outweight the benefits. Some of these costs stem from 1) the different traditions of activists, policy makers, and researchers; 2) the mismatch between the 'impossible demands' of policy and the 'irrelevance' of research; 3) the reporting barrier behind which research results are obscured; 4) the hazards of evaluating research that may be highly technical, as well as equivocal, in its conclusions; and 5) the pitfalls of the 'researcher as consultant' role.

A. Different Traditions of Activists, Researchers and Policy Makers

The underutilization of research is traceable in part to the mutual suspicion, miscommunication, and misunderstanding that abound among activists, policy makers, and researchers. Many difficulties these would-be-collaborators face derive from the starkly different traditions in which they have been schooled. Their divergent backgrounds commonly result in different time frames (or pacing), disparate sets of values, skills, expectations, sensitivities, perspectives and styles.

Social policy as a process emanates from the hurly burly arena of social and political life. The activist, as the advocate for a special group or issue, approaches the problem bent on rapid and decisive change. In a sense, the activist is the impatient mover — impatient both with research and social policy processes.

The activist as change agent may feel the problem is clearcut and the correct solutions are readily apparent, tailored to the specific requirements of the target constituency. Delays, whether from research or policy realms, exasperate the activist who seeks immediate results.

The researcher, by contrast, is the careful seeker of truth, stressing painstaking, scholarly study of many factors to arrive at an unassailable conclusion. Truth for its own sake — not merely in the pursuit of social change and equity (or more meanly to advance the needs of a special interest group) — is a central scientific credo. Objective and replicable findings are the goal of the researcher — even when the results may take time ('too much time', say the activist and policy maker) and reveal a truth unpalatable to a concerned constituency.

The scientific tradition rejects the efforts of policy makers and activists to redirect and control the focus of research. Social scientists jealously guard their prerogative in selecting and approaching research topics and defend their scientific autonomy as an essential component of academic freedom. Their specialized training makes them doubt the competency — and perhaps the motives — of any nonscientists to interfere in the research process. In the search for objective truth on fundamental issues, the researcher may cast activists and policy people as Philistines, insensitive to the subtle complexities of social phenomena.

The social policy maker is the architect of compromise. The policy maker recognizes the many truths that, stitched together, comprise the patchwork quilt of political reality. The very essence of the policy maker's existence is constant response to the conflicting needs of many constituencies whose problems create daily headlines. The need for workable legislative remedies to pressing social problems creates an urgency that cannot brook long research delays. At the same time, multiple compromises are the hallmark of policy solutions acceptable to diverse political groups, whose impatient, action-oriented leaders are demanding action yesterday.

How does this work in the real world of pressing women's issues (known as 'sex roles' to social scientists)? To take just one current American example, as the Trotter chapter indicates, education is at the heart of a major controversy. Women activists are demanding equal access to educational opportunities. For the leaders of women's groups, this means co-educational classrooms and equal educational programs and facilities, at the very least. They press legislators to create the legislative mandate for such changes, and they urge researchers to generate the data that confirm that co-educational classrooms are the way to go.[5]

Researchers, for the many reasons already suggested, want to understand if, why, and how learning occurs more effectively in co-ed classrooms; they wish to specify the conditions which facilitate learning in the mixed-sex milieu, as well as the necessary antecedents and expected results. They search for comprehensive answers that will permit long-range, effective solutions.

Policy makers, anxious to address their constituents' immediate problems, want 'hard data' on which to base their legislative initiatives.

But they also recognize that co-educational classrooms and equal facilities, while satisfying women's groups, are a storm signal to other interest groups. The athletic and educational communities, concerned about the potential financial hazard of providing equal (and equally expensive) athletic programs and equipment for both sexes, react with alarm and alacrity.

The policy maker needs evidence to bolster and defend the policy decision she/he makes. The policy maker is confronted with the necessity of fashioning a legislative compromise acceptable to the activists from women's groups, the education community, and athletic interests. Immediate research evidence that can point the way to a useful solution is what the policy maker desperately seeks from the researcher. In this and similar real life situations, the in-depth, cautious, and time-consuming approach of social scientists creates understandable impatience and dismay on the part of those who would take rapid measures to heal the world's ills.

B. Irrelevant Research vs. Impossible Policy Demands

Another tributary of frustration and confusion that policy makers and activists feel in their encounters with the research community is the seeming 'irrelevance' and 'uselessness' of research. As intimated earlier, researchers and policy makers rarely agree about the importance of research topics, since their priorities are vastly different. Witness the 'Golden Fleece Award' given monthly by one US senator for research work on presumably irrelevant topics which waste tax revenues. And even when research has genuine policy relevance, it may not be immediately apparent to social scientists unaccustomed to thinking in policy terms. Tangri and Strasburg (chapter 3) suggest that the plethora of research on women's alleged 'fear of success' has policy implications not sufficiently underscored by academic researchers.

While it would be hard to argue with the negative conclusions about research which some policy makers reach, the sources of difficulty are bilateral, emanating from the policy, as well as the research, side. Some policy makers, confused about what research can and cannot do, may pose non-researchable questions. Some researchers, overanxious to assume a role in the development of social policy, may undertake impossible tasks, promising more than they can deliver. Even when the question is appropriately researchable, the overeager researcher may agree to unrealistic research parameters and deadlines.

C. The Reporting Barrier

Policy makers and their aides are confronted daily with the need to digest an endless barrage of information on a wide range of subjects. They complain that researchers compound the problem by creating a reporting barrier, which consists of several parts: 1) the technical language ('jargon') of research; 2) undue elaboration of obvious truths; 3) the equivocal nature of research findings; 4) the length of research reports; and 5) the political naivete or insensitivity of researchers.

Research usually is reported in the language of research rather than the language of social policy and social action. The technical language developed in any field, including research, has special meaning and conveys a wealth of shared understanding to the insider. To the interested outsider, however, it may serve as a barrier to understanding the meaning and implications of the work. The policy maker, frustrated by the research language barrier, commonly dismisses the entire research undertaking as 'jargon'.

Conversely, in attempting to respond to this criticism, the researcher may fall into still another trap: oversimplifying the results for political and general consumption. This strategy may lead policy people to disregard the findings as a simple-minded elaboration of the obvious. If the social scientist expects research findings to command serious attention outside of the academic world, she/he must learn to speak in nontechnical language that communicates to all interested listeners.

To add to this array of incompatibilities, there is still another difficulty: researchers often present findings in their least usable form. Researchers expect to spell out all the nuances of their results, including the many qualifications of their findings. They tend to produce detailed, often technical and seemingly equivocal reports. The policy maker has neither the time nor the inclination to read these elaborate treatises which seem devoid of clean-cut and consistent findings.

The 400-page tomes on integration, women's labor force participation, pollution control devices and other equally important issues are likely to go unread by policy formulators, not from lack of interest, but lack of time. Even voguish 'executive summaries' tend to strain the reading time available to policy makers. Researchers must recognize the necessity of packaging their results in ways that are succinct, clear, and to the point for social policy purposes.

Aside from the unwieldy length and ubiquitous qualifications of research reports, the neglect of policy implications and implementation possibilities (which we shall treat below in greater detail) further serves to impair the policy relevance of research findings. Researchers need to understand the constraints on the decision-maker's time, technical understanding, patience and resources. Only then will researchers begin to present their findings in ways that strengthen the usefulness of research to activists and policy people.

D. Difficulties in Judging Research

The evaluation of research poses problems on at least three counts: 1) quality and validity issues; 2) conflicting results from different investigations; and 3) the failure of researchers to follow through on new questions raised by research.

The language and reporting barriers already discussed can be overcome. But technical issues, difficult even for researchers, present seemingly insurmountable problems that lead policy people to throw up their hands in despair. For one, the validity of research results is linked directly to the quality of the research design. (This involves sample size and selection procedures, the fit between the problem and the investigative techniques selected, the quality of the research instruments, the control of bias, the degree to which the findings are applicable to a broader population than the one studied, and a host of related issues.)

Unfortunately, no quick and easy solutions exist. There is no simple yardstick by which researchers can teach policy makers to measure research. In fact, such evaluations are difficult and open to debate even within the research community.

Another problem that bedevils social policy-research collaboration is the fact that much research presents differences between groups but fails to explain the *reasons* for such differences. Policy makers, impatient to reduce such differences, tend to ignore research that cannot provide definitive explanations for the documented disparities.

The difficulties of judging research are compounded for the activist and policy maker when multiple investigations of the same topic produce conflicting results. The knee-jerk reaction of decision makers may be to 'throw out the baby with the bath water.' Disillusioned decision makers may be tempted to discredit all research on the subject and respond to their own intuitive or 'gut' reactions.

Undoubtedly, conflicting results create serious problems; but, as our experience in medical research aptly demonstrates, the possibility of contradictory findings need not preclude all policy decision making. Even with the most consistent research findings, the policy maker's judgment remains an essential ingredient in policy formulations. Oftentimes, research findings that refute one another point the way for the necessary second-level research needed to clarify the contradictions.

Thoughtful research raises new questions that warrant investigation. Often the follow-through is missing. This leaves policy makers and activists hanging in mid-air, grasping for elusive answers. Researchers, particularly if they undertake a project on the initiative of those outside the research community, may tend to see the research as finished when the commissioned project is completed.

The researcher may feel no stake in following up new questions raised by research undertaken at the behest of 'outsiders' (i.e., non researchers). The decision not to pursue additional, clarifying investigations may be made on pragmatic grounds: this is what the research sponsor wanted; the sponsor is uninterested in funding the pursuit of answers to the newly-raised questions; the funding for such extended research may not be available either from this or other sponsors; the policy maker qua sponsor may be interested in moving in a totally new direction, to a new or more timely issue. Follow-up research may not be pursued unless the researcher can convince the policy maker/sponsor that additional studies will offer an important clarification; and the researcher may not have a sufficient intellectual or ego-investment in the work to be prompted to make the case for its continuation.

What is the solution when no simple guidelines exist by which non-researchers may evaluate research results? One partial solution is the parascientific expertise the policy maker may develop through a sustained dialogue with researchers. Perhaps, social scientists can learn to function effectively as counsellors to policy makers, providing technical judgments about the usefulness, validity, generalizability, and implications of research findings.

E. The Researcher as Consultant

Another serious grievance the policy maker may hold against the researcher derives from the unfilfilled promise of the social scientist's role as consultant. Occasionally, the researcher as consultant has come through with flying colors; more often, however, the researcher has proven a sad disappointment.

The private sector has been the scene of relative triumph for the researcher as consultant. The successful alliance between social scientists and decision makers in the private sector has led to the now taken-for-granted acceptance of marketing research as an integral part of business and industry. The acknowledged success of marketing research has led political candidates to adapt these techniques to political campaigning (and the successful victors to rely on these methods for assessing constituency attitudes). But beyond an isolated policy maker here or there, the use of social scientists as consultants in any broader sense has yet to take hold.

One historical reason for this situation has been the researcher's failure to articulate for the policy maker the different available types of research, as well as the strengths and limitations of each. Before social scientists can be accepted as reliable consultants to policy makers, they must learn to set aside their own special social science prejudices and pet methodologies. They must be able to assess hard-headedly the relevance of research for a given policy problem and be willing to recommend a broad range of research approaches, including those remote from their own specialities and areas of expertise. Perhaps even more important is the ability to recognize and acknowledge readily those situations where research would *not* be the appropriate strategy. Only through such processes can the researcher's and policy maker's expectations of the fruits of their collaboration become sufficiently congruent to hold any promise of meaning in the policy development process.

Aside from those social scientists who serve as staff to policy makers, until recently only a relatively small band of researchers was attuned to social policy issues. Beyond this group, most other social scientists rarely bothered to lay out the social policy implications of their findings. The interface between research and policy formulation has been a wasteland, with few members of either group able to explain their needs or results to the other. As more social scientists become sensitized to the dialectic between social research and social policy, the role of external consultant to decision makers may appear more congenial to them.

As the Tangri/Strasburg chapter indicates, internal research staffs often exist as part of the formal policy-making structure. The inclusion on policy makers' staffs of social scientists who not only do research, but can interpret and evaluate the research findings of others, can help to overcome the judgment dilemmas we have discussed. But the option to bring in external consultants, whose autonomous position outside the formal policy-making system protects their co-optation by the policy community, remains viable. The use of social scientists as external consultants would strengthen the dialogue among activists, policy makers, and researchers and open one avenue for reducing the frustrations and disappointments of mismatched and unrealistic expectations.

F. Implementation of Research Findings Through the Social Policy Process

Implementation of research findings requires several stages. First, there is the 'what if' stage in which assessments and predictions flow from current findings. The next stage is the 'what kind' and 'how best' phase, in which decisions about the most effective implementation strategies must be made.

1. The 'What If' Stage

Disillusionment with researchers has still other well-springs, linked specifically to the implementation of research. Activists and policy makers blame researchers for their frequent failure to provide the link between findings and implementation. That is, researchers rarely spell out the implications of their research. Implications simply may suggest potential sequelae (i.e., the declining birth rate may lead to an increased labor force participation), or they may indicate the differential consequences of the possible uses to which the research can be put, (i.e., contraceptive programs directed at females trained in occupational fields facing labor shortages will promote their entry and retention in those fields).

Implications also revolve around the consequences of *not* acting upon research findings. The implications may lie close to the surface, requiring only minimal effort to bridge the gap from computer printout to community project. Sometimes, however, the translation from research results to policy planning may be considerably complex and arduous.

The research vs. implementation debate often grows intense, particularly when finite resources must be allocated. Some argue that research has its own value, without concern for implementation. Others think that a mediocre finding that can be implemented is more meaningful than a 'superior' research result that cannot be transformed into action. Ideally, however, research and implementation are an interactive process and should be welded together from the outset.

Despite this ideal, many researchers have neither the training nor the inclination to design useful implementation plans based upon their research. But researchers increasingly are recognizing their responsibility at least for laying out the implications of their findings, so that others may design the implementation that translates research into action. Without explicit implications, the building blocks of implementation are missing.

Implications of research findings clarify the options and costs of different strategies. For example, considerable research effort has been spent projecting the marriage, divorce, remarriage and fertility curves for the next decade. If detailed information exists on how many women will remain single, marry, divorce, and head single-parent families, then it is a relatively easy step to estimate what percent of each female age-cohort will seek jobs outside the home, require welfare aid, need additional education and occupational training, seek individual or group medical insurance plans, use day-care facilities, and so on. Once these estimates are derived, the costs of supplying or not supplying these services can be calculated. Granted, unforeseen factors can derail even the most careful projection. Nevertheless, social science does have the methodologies for outlining the options and consequences of different policy and action strategies. It is this 'what if' stage, a necessary precursor to implementation, that researchers often neglect.

At the 'what if' stage, policy implications of research findings may require a form of cost-benefit analysis. What are the advantages or disadvantages of addressing or ignoring the problem's many aspects? For example, research that focuses on the relationships among marriage, divorce and female work patterns should outline the support systems that women will need to maintain themselves and their families. Weighing the consequences of failing to provide such support systems is equally important.

Besides assessing the possible effects of adopting certain policies, social science research potentially can clarify the consequences of failing to accept certain policies. For example, research can clarify the occupational limitations females face when they fail to study advanced mathematics and science (Sells, 1973; Kreinberg, 1976). Research can demonstrate the likelihood of increased divorce in regions that fail to prevent policies aimed at lowering the legal marital age.

As more mothers of young children seek employment, day care centers, adjustable work periods, extended shopping hours, special health care plans, all gain in importance. The social costs of *not* providing these programs also must be calculated. Knowledge of the needs of different female age cohorts is essential to provide flexibility in long-range social planning. The consequences of *not* planning for these needs may be severe.

Contraceptive behavior is another domain which would benefit from a clearer articulation of research and social policy. It is not enough for researchers simply to calculate the number of women using different types of contraceptive devices. They must go beyond that to project the types of medical benefits that most probably will be necessary for users of different family planning methods. Marketing analyses that examine differential rates of acceptance of various contraceptive methods among women and men from different backgrounds are not enough. Methods of providing family planning services and the implications of different provisions for various groups must be considered before programs for disseminating contraceptive information and devices are developed. The rise in the teenage pregnancy rate in the US, for example, suggests that existing family planning programs do not meet the needs of this group. Only when social policy is tailored to the known needs of different target populations can we expect it to be acceptable and useful to the intended recipients.

Part of the problem here is that the researchers who focus on attitudes, motivation, cultural differences and behavior are not necessarily the appropriate ones to lay out the implications. This may be particularly true when some type of cost-benefit analysis is required. Implications of research may be considered best by interdisciplinary teams that include a broad array of scientific disciplines, as well as activists and social policy types who can inform one another's work.

2. The 'What Kind' and 'How Best' Stage

Effective implementation requires a step beyond this. It must move into the 'what kind' and 'how best' stage. Implementation involves a judgment about the clarified options (Rivlin, 1971), a judgment which selects specific action and policy alternatives and creates a plan capable of transforming research into realistic and achievable goals. In this way, social policy becomes part of the implementation process.

In the realm of women's issues, the implementation stage ideally creates the best possible plan for preparing women of different ages, as well as different educational and occupational levels, to enter or reenter the labor force; for providing useful and easily dispensed welfare aid; for offering educational and vocational training programs tailored to the needs of various groups; for dealing with the entire range of women's issues, each spelled out in pragmatic detail.

There is a growing argument that implementation is best left in the hands of those whose lives are to be affected, those groups which are the targets of proposed changes. The proponents of this view even suggest that researchers should have no part whatsoever in the implementation of research findings, particularly if the researchers are not indigenous to the community being studied. But one could turn the argument around to propose that from the outset implementers should be part of the research team. Then, in effect, the researchers are responsible for implementation. Perhaps, the line between researchers and implementers is best left less clearly drawn, if we are more concerned with the results than the rhetoric of social research and action.

Involving indigenous members of a community in research which affects the community is not a novel approach. Public health people have long recognized the importance of using local interviewers and data collectors (Paul, 1955). Worldwide efforts to increase contraception relied heavily on the use of indigenous women who interviewed potential female users and helped to modify the interview schedules and other aspects of the research/action programs.

Activist members of the target population — in this case females — often need the help of trained researchers and policy planners to implement the policies and programs for which activists have lobbied. The argument for leaving the implementation in the hands of the community or group affected flows from the recognition of the emotional, psychological, and cultural dimensions of the implementation problem. But a continuing dialogue among activists, other community groups, researchers, and policy planners can go far toward developing programs based on sound research and pragmatically implementable.

In organizational change, social planners acknowledge the need to stimulate the interest and motivation of those whose environment and lives they would change (Leavitt, 1977). They focus on strategies for involving the participants in the change process from its earliest planning stages. Such participation, while ideally desirable, is possible when the envisioned change involves a relatively limited group. When social policy is designed to encompass a vast group within a large and complex society, involving participants in the planning of research and the implementation of social change may not always be feasible.

Assessing different types of implementation options is a form of applied research. It is one very direct way that researchers have for dealing with problems of implementation. It is a special form of research in which not many researchers are yet engaged. Some would argue that it as far as researchers should take the results of well-designed and reported research; and it should be left to others to design implementation strategies with only minimal, if any, help from the researcher. Some purists might even insist that to eliminate bias, the assessment of differential implementation options should be done by a new set of researchers, rather than the researchers who designed and conducted the first phase.

This is not to suggest that researchers should never participate in the implementation stage. Policy analysis, particularly, should be conducted by researchers with an eye to implementation. Researchers learn much in that feed-back loop from implementation to new research. Some investigators probably bring special insight and expertise derived from their research perspective to bear on implementation problems. And ideally, much can be gained by treating research and implementation as an interactive process. Nonetheless, this ideal is difficult to achieve, and good research can be conducted by some and implemented by others without major catastrophes.

To fault research because it does not take this extra step, which, in some cases, may be taken more expertly by others, is to overlook the substantial contributions that researchers can make in providing the information necessary for implementation decisions. Perhaps the best of all worlds is to combine the expertise of the researcher, activist, social planner, and social policy maker in the translation of research into reality.

3. The Special Implementation Difficulties in the Social Sciences

Implementation requirements differ in relation to the nature of the research problem and results. For example, the results of research may be the development of a new product or technology whose implementation is virtually 'built in' to the development itself. The demand for the product or technology may already exist and, indeed, may have provided the original impetus for the research. More commonly this is the case in the physical sciences, as well as the medical and engineering fields. The polio vaccine, the pill, the laser, television, all represent in varying degrees the products of such research.

In the social sciences, research results commonly are more amorphous, culminating not in a marketable product so much as in potentially useful knowledge. For example, studies of female professionals may reveal their tendency to come from families in which their mothers had high educational levels. How can this type of knowledge be translated into social programs to encourage the entry of women into professional occupations? Studies of birth order of siblings may reveal that the first-born child is more likely than later-born siblings to be a higher achiever. What types of social programs can be designed to 'implement' or use this information?

The possibilities for implementing social science research are not always readily apparent. Frequently new technology or methods must be developed to implement the findings. Computer-assisted teaching is a methodology that made possible large-scale implementation of social science findings which previously were seen simply as an addition to our knowledge base. More often, however, we lack cheap and transferable technologies to implement social science results.

In those cases where no special technology is needed or can help, how can we implement social research findings? Let us go back to our two examples of daughters of highly-educated women and first-born high achievers. In the first example of daughters with highly-educated mothers, it may be important to offer those girls whose mothers have less educational background a substitute or surrogate relationship with other highly-educated women. Daughters whose mothers have less education might be offered an apprenticeship program with women involved in professional careers. Or more informal programs might be developed in which professional women cooperate with these girls in school or community projects. Interaction with women of high educational levels may provide daughters of less-educated women the necessary role models they need to encourage their entry into professional roles.

In the second example of high-achieving, first-born children, later-born children might be offered special enrichment programs. Alternatively, specific programs might be developed for parents to sensitize them to the ways in which they are dealing differently with their later-born children.

Another problem by which social science research is impeded is the difficulty of identifying and controlling all the contributing factors. Public health experiments in developing countries offer numerous examples of such difficulties (Paul, 1955). Even when what needs to be done in order to implement the results of research is clear — which is not always the case — how to ensure that the program is accepted and utilized is problematical. Cultural values, taboos, fears, public indifference, direct and hidden costs, all may serve as barriers to implementation.

While the legalization of abortion in the US may contribute directly to the reduction in maternal mortality, the acceptance of such legalization is resisted in some quarters on religious and cultural grounds. Large-scale implementation is hampered by the heterogeneity of a given society, where almost any social policy acceptable to one group flies in the face of the cultural, political, or religious beliefs dear to another group.

Implementation of research findings requires that the solution suggested represents a demonstrable improvement over the prevailing situation. Research has a definite role here. The recent furor in the US over the flu vaccine program is a timely example of a situation in which the 'cure' involved potentially even greater danger than the original problem. In any event, the available vaccine was not a clearly safer and preferable solution than the risk of disease. In such cases, research, properly used, can be a valuable tool in demonstrating that the suggested policy implementation is significantly more effective, and, in some instances, safer than other possible methods.

4. The Missing Link:
The Role of Social Engineer

Most democratic societies have balked at the concept of the social engineer. The role of social engineer conjures up images of grisly social experiments and irresponsible scientific programs imposed on powerless victims. Sterilization programs have sometimes been described as the diabolical machinations of social engineers concerned with the genocide of certain socially 'undesirable' groups. Recent political history in India attests to the abhorrence with which social engineering efforts may be met even when applied to the entire social spectrum (Landman, 1977).

Abuses of social engineering undeniably have existed. Nonetheless, responsible social engineers — sometimes viewed as implementers — may be, in fact, the missing link between social science research and social policy formulation. Social science theorists and experimenters may not be the most likely candidates for transforming their findings into applied programs. They may need the help of social engineers. For example, Maslow (1954) developed the now well-known concept of 'self-actualization'; however, it took the additional work of Herzberg (1966, 1968) to transform the concept into job-enrichment techniques designed to help workers grow and flourish in their careers.

The question of implementing research results has many complexities whose adequate treatment is beyond the scope of this chapter. The need to confront the issue of implementing research findings is real. This continuing need, however, does not invalidate the genuine contribution that social science research can make to the development of social policy. Researchers increasingly are becoming sensitized to the need to specify the 'real world' implications of their findings and the relative merits of different methods of implementing such results. Simultaneously, social planners and policy makers are becoming increasingly adept at translating research findings into reasonable social programs. But much remains to be done to solidify the necessary collaboration among researchers, social engineers, policy makers and activists. Before researchers can claim to be useful partners in the development of social policy on sex roles, they must seriously address the complaints of their potential collaborators.

NOTES

1. The examples used in this chapter may be taken predominately from the American experience, with which we are most familiar; however, the problems discussed are relevant to many societies around the globe.

2. Although we recognize that activists and social policy makers constitute two distinct groups, there are times when their goals and strategies for reaching those goals are relatively consonant. Taking this into account, there will be places in this chapter where we deal with activists and policy makers as if they represent one general group which may be distinguished from the research community. In those instances where the perspectives of activists and social policy makers diverge significantly, we shall treat them as two distinct groups.

3. The general argument presented applies to most realms of social policy; however, in this chapter we shall use social policy on sex roles as our paradigm.

4. Research used for policy purposes need not be considered any more Machiavellian than the use of marketing and new product research in industry.

5. Six years ago, the US Congress passed Title IX, landmark legislation which addresses sex discrimination in educational institutions. To date, Title IX remains one of the most poorly enforced laws.

REFERENCES

AKUTAGAWA, Ryunosuke, *Rashomon.* Tokyo: Alanda Shobo, 1917.
HERZBERG, Fred. *Work and the Nature of Man.* Cleveland: World Publishing, 1966. 'One More Time: How Do You Motivate Employees?' *Harvard Business Review.* January, 1968.
KOMAROVSKY, Mirra, ed., *Sociology and Public Policy.* New York: Elsevier Scientific Publishing Co., 1975.
KREINBERG, Nancy, 'Furthering the Mathematical Competence of Women,' *Public Affairs Report,* 17 December 1976.
LANDMAN, Lynn C., 'Birth Control in India: The Carrot and the Rod', *Perspectives,* 9(3), May/June 1977, pp. 101-10.
LEAVITT, Harold. Personal Communication, 1977.
MASLOW, A. H. *Motivation and Personality.* New York: Harper and Row, 1954.
MURPHY, Irene L., *Public Policy on the Status of Women,* Lexington, Mass.: Lexington Books, D. C. Heath & Co., 1973.
PAUL, Benjamin. *Health, Culture, and Community: Case Studies of Public Reaction to Health Programs,* New York: Russell Sage, 1955.
RIVLIN, Alice, *Systematic Thinking for Social Action.* Washington, D.C.: The Brookings Institution, 1971.
SELLS, Lucy, 'High School Mathematics as the Critical Filter in the Job Market,' in *Developing Opportunities for Minorities in Graduate Education.* Proceedings of the Conference on Minority Graduate Education at the University of California, Berkeley, May 1973, pp. 47-59.
WOOLSEY, Suzanne H., 'Pied Piper Politics and the Child-Care Debate,' *Daedalus,* Spring 1977, pp. 127-45.

2
THE DIALECTIC BETWEEN RESEARCH AND SOCIAL POLICY:
The Difficulties from a Research Perspective — *RASHOMON PART II*

Jean Lipman-Blumen
National Institute of Education, USA

In this second Rashomon view of the dialectic between social research and social policy, Lipman-Blumen turns to a detailed analysis of the problems researchers confront in their attempts to engage in policy-relevant research. Two complex sets of issues overshadow the research/policy landscape. First, policy makers and activists often overestimate their understanding of social phenomena. Because the grist for social science research is drawn from everyday experience, non-researchers may tend to regard these social issues as easily comprehensible. Policy makers and activists may have difficulty in recognizing the need for systematic social science analysis vs. common sense interpretations. Additional problems arise when contradictory findings become part of a public debate; these obstacles are compounded by imprecise reporting, sensationalizing, and popularization by mass media.

Research on sex roles has special political problems. Recent feminist analyses of sex roles question dearly-held assumptions about male superiority and pose a threat to the vested male interest and established life patterns. Recent sex role research undercuts the traditional biases that perpetuated male privilege and thus calls for serious social change. The political sensitivity of the issues involved in sex role research spells danger to policy makers who prefer to avoid or ignore career-threatening questions, particularly in election years.

The second major set of issues revolves around the misuses of research by policy makers and activists. Both groups often demand research results on an unrealistic timeline. When such time constraints create impossible problems, policy makers occasionally respond by eliminating altogether the research component of social programs. Researchers commonly complain about policy makers' failure to understand the distinction between fact finding and systematic research. To complicate the picture, policy makers and activists frequently are put off and intimidated by sophisticated research techniques necessary to the understanding of social, political, economic and psychological processes. These very techniques of a maturing social science are the ones that allow researchers to make useful predictions. Theory and model building, based upon strong and sometimes complex conceptual frameworks and methodologies, provide a predictive power that offers a meaningful basis for social policy. Fact finding, while perhaps more readily accessible to the non-researcher, is the preliminary descriptive phase of research, which rarely yields reliable predictions about future trends and needs. The denial of the importance of sophisticated social science models and strategies and the reliance upon more straightforward, but less useful, enumeration and fact finding are serious abuses of the potential of research as the foundation for social policy. Activists point to policy makers' substitution of research for significant social action. The call for still another study of a social problem provides the illusion of action, while serious delays exacerbate the unresolved social issues. Commissioning a research undertaking may be a political legerdemain for tabling the question.

Another serious abuse of research by policy makers and activists is the manipulation of women's roles through the use of selected research results. Congenial research findings are used to promulgate and rationalize desired social policy. Child development research has been used to support, as well as to deny, the demand for child care centers. Research findings on contraception and abortion have served both to encourage and discourage motherhood, depending upon the state of key social and economic indicators.

The political determination of relevant and appropriate research topics creates another potential misuse of the research enterprise. Policy makers often perform a useful function by reminding researchers that pressing social issues deserve their immediate attention. Nonetheless, the fickleness of policy makers' interest in any given research issue is an obvious threat to long range scientific efforts. Moreover, the usurpation of the scientific community's autonomy in setting research priorities undermines the scientific imagination's pursuit of research avenues whose promise is apparent only to the trained researcher.

To compound the difficulties, the emergence of research as 'big business' with effective lobbies has a serious, often deleterious, influence on the ordering of research priorities. The research establishment, thus, has been able to drown out the creative voices and ideas of female, minority, and younger investigators, who lack the political clout of more experienced research centers.

The imposition of politically-motivated constraints upon research constitutes an additional danger, according to Lipman-Blumen's analysis. The investigation of politically-sensitive issues may be hampered by interest groups who, fearing undesirable or embarrassing findings, mount intensive lobbying efforts to reduce research budgets and prevent such research initiatives.

The last abuse analyzed by Lipman-Blumen is the seduction of the research community through the creation of 'science advisors' to counsel policy makers. While such roles are potentially feasible for policy-minded researchers, the science advisor role contains an inherent risk: the use of the advisor to legitimate questionable policies that the policy maker wishes to pursue.

After analyzing this impressive catalogue of hazards confronting the policy-oriented researcher, Lipman-Blumen addresses the question of whether there is any hope for the dialectic between research and social policy. To answer this, Lipman-Blumen differentiates a wide range of research strategies, briefly linking them to specific policy needs and special research problems: basic research; applied research; descriptive research; analytical research; cross-sectional and longitudinal research; cohort and cross-cultural research; interdisciplinary research; policy and impact analysis.

In the final section of the chapter, the author suggests that we are in a transitional social period, one in which the traditional sex role definitions and institutional arrangements are undergoing serious change. Lipman-Blumen suggests that at sequential stages in the movement toward sex equality, different types of social policy and appropriately linked research strategies are required. She enlarges the dialectic between research and social policy to include implementation and warns that, without workable implementation plans, the dialectic between research and social policy becomes a Pyrrhic exercise.

INTRODUCTION

All the problems that activists and policy makers catalogue against researchers have their mirror images — in the complaints that researchers raise against policy advocates and developers. Researchers are quick to point out the manifold difficulties that they confront in their efforts to study policy relevant issues.

In this chapter, we shall present an overview of the problems that researchers face in their dealings with activists and policy makers. Then we shall attempt to delineate a set of research strategies that offer considerable potential for policy relevant research. And finally, we shall sketch briefly the special research and policy needs in the transition period from traditional and unequal to modern, equitable sex roles.

PROBLEMS RESEARCHERS EXPERIENCE WITH THE POLICY COMMUNITY

Researchers present their own brief against the policy community. Their arguments revolve around two gargantuan issues: 1) the policy people's overestimation of their understanding of social phenomena; and 2) their misuse of research.

A. The Overestimation of Understanding Social Phenomena

Because social science research takes as its focus problems that beset everyone in the course of everyday life, policy makers often overestimate their understanding of social phenomena. Researchers complain that policy people do not understand the difference between systematic analysis and experiential understanding of these events.

This problem stands out clearly when contrasted with the more 'invisible' scientific domain of the natural sciences. The nuclear physicist does not have his/her understanding of atomic structure challenged or lightly dismissed by the layperson, even though all of us live in an environment surrounded by atoms. The social scientist who deals with family behavior patterns finds him/herself challenged routinely by the nonscientist, since everyone has had some experience either growing up in or creating a family. That most families face serious problems at different points in time and that these problems tend to be exacerbated by changes in the social context in which they exist is testimony to the sensitive observer that family dynamics are *not* as transparent or amenable to diagnosis and treatment as the lay analyst may think.

Feminist researchers cite a variation on this complaint: the failure of activists and policy makers to recognize the relevance of new, feminist research on sex roles. Researchers, themselves aware of the limitations of even the latest research, face policy makers and activists who think all the results are in on sex differences and sex roles. 'We know everything we need to know' is the position they often take. Social policy on sex roles only recently has come to be viewed by policy makers as a domain in which they possibly might require expert advice. The value of indigenous — that is, female, particularly feminist —researchers is only recently being recognized by the male-dominated policy world.

Few women social scientists have been taken seriously by policy makers. The official role of science advisor commonly is a male preserve, a situation attributable in part to the relative paucity of women in the upper ranks of the scientific 'establishment'. Alva Myrdal and Rita Liljeström in Sweden and Evelyne Sullerot in France, plus a handful of women social scientists in other countries, stand out as relative exceptions.

As a result, social policies promulgated in legislative bodies and the courts around the world historically have been developed by male legislators and jurists who have demonstrated complete faith in their own understanding of women's nature and roles. So-called protective legislation for female workers, as well as marriage and divorce laws, serve as good examples of policies created by generations of male legislators and jurists, who relied on their own often misconceived and imprecise notions about differences between the sexes and the 'special' attributes of females. (See the role of US Supreme Court Justice Brandeis in 'protective' labor legislation for women workers described in Chapter 3.) More recently, the advent of International Women's Year marked a growing recognition of the need to include women in policy bodies considering sex roles.[1]

Still another aspect of the seemingly experiential nature of social science creates problems for researchers. The contradictory findings and recommendations of social scientists easily become part of the public debate. Mass media focus easily on the 'more understandable' social phenomena, in contrast to the 'more technical' fields of physical science. Mass media compound the problem by imprecise reporting and attempts to popularize the subject matter. This feeds the policy makers' argument, discussed earlier, that social science is merely the elaboration of the obvious.

While comparable debates and conflicting theories and research findings exist in the world of physical science, the more invisible and esoteric nature of the phenomena involved makes even those debates and contradictions that emerge into the public arena less comprehensible and, therefore, less reportable. As a result, scientific debates that rage within the physical and medical sciences are more hidden from general view, while the general public often takes a ringside seat at the controversies and contradictions within the world of social science. Only as the debates within the field of physical and medical science begin to impinge upon our daily existence (i.e., the dangers of recombinant genetic research, the safety of flu vaccines, the carcinogenic potential of saccharine), does the social policy relevance become clear. Only then does the public become more involved. Even so, the technical background necessary to evaluate physical and medical science research presents a more resistant filter to public participation and criticism.

The researcher thus deals with policy makers, who, like the larger public, tend to overestimate their experiential expertise in matters of social phenomena. Policy makers' misjudgment of their understanding of social problems inclines them to minimize the importance and **utility** of social science research. Where policy judgments are required in the face of conflicting physical science and medical results, policy makers tend to move cautiously; however, they are more likely to point to the existence of conflicting results in social science research as a rationale for discounting it altogether. Policy makers thus may fail to recognize the importance of the distinction between sophisticated experiential knowledge of the general, educated public and the systematic analysis of social science research.

Family policy repeatedly falls victim to this misunderstanding in the policy community. Research that calls for changes in family patterns of living and work comes very close to the core of our daily experience. The call for changes in living arrangements, financial responsibility, relationships between spouses, and between parents and children, as well as those between the family and the educational system, poses serious threats to established ways of life. The threat to the 'vested interests' of males within the home, the world of finance, the occupational, educational, and political spheres understandably provokes outraged cries from those who are being called upon to share their privileges.

Policy makers qua individuals, as well as representatives of vocal constituencies, respond to such fundamental issues with caution, some confusion, and possibly defensiveness. The political sensitivity of many of the issues surrounding day-care centers, abortion, female labor force participation, and affirmative action marks them as issues that legislators, particularly those looking to the next election, would prefer to avoid. But increasingly, women's groups are pressing their point and refusing to accept inaction on the part of legislators.

B. The Misuses of Research

The second comprehensive set of problems for researchers who feel responsible for the use made of their work stems from activists' and policy makers' misuse of research. As suggested in Chapter 1, policy makers, pressed for immediate response to urgent social problems, expect research to produce immediate results. And they rarely sympathize with the researcher who values the pro bono function of research. Policy people frequently demand results on a timeline that research cannot deliver. While some problems can be dealt with on the basis of 'quick turnaround' research, many serious social problems require more systematic and long-term research efforts. As we shall discuss later, different types of research are applicable to different social problems. Knowing *when* to use *which* research strategy is an important element in the research-social policy process. However, social policy people, impatient for immediate results, may decide to eliminate altogether the research component from the social policy process.

Researchers complain that policy people often do not understand the difference between fact finding and genuine systematic research. Fact finding, useful in its own right, is not a substitute for more sophisticated types of social science research. However, policy makers and activists, often unable to interpret research findings, flee from the shadow cast by a regression equation. Fact finding, including the culling of statistics from voluminous census reports, can tell the policy planner much about the past and present state of the world. But the kind of information the policy maker needs to understand the processes involved demands a more sophisticated level of analysis, a level which requires research training.

In addition, the policy maker fails to understand how fact finding is distinguished from both theory building and methodology. Fact finding, alone, cannot provide the predictive power that well conceptualized and tested theories offer. Blumberg's chapter is an example of a nascent theory which could offer policy makers a way of predicting women's needs in different cultural settings. Predictive power, based on refined theories, is necessary if policy makers are to design meaningful social policies to address these needs. The various methodologies of social science, from the simple to the complex, also represent a neglected area of potential social science contribution to policy formulation. Methodologies are, as we shall discuss below, the tools by which a wide array of knowledge, necessary to policy development, can be provided.

Policy makers have been known to use research in still other more negative ways: as a substitute for action. Policy makers who wish to create the illusion of taking action while actually delaying any programmatic steps may call for an unnecessary in-depth study. Research, in such cases, becomes an euphemism for non-action. This use of research is correctly diagnosed by impatient activists as a 'tabling effort', a stalling tactic on the part of policy makers. Such abuse of research may be difficult to eliminate, particularly in light of the cost and profits involved in research efforts. To make matters worse, activists ironically blame researchers for the policy makers' negative use of research as a delaying mechanism. Careful monitoring of demands for research by activist groups could go far in reducing such abuses.

Policy makers often perpetrate even greater abuses by harnessing selected research to support policy initiatives designed to manipulate women's roles. Scott's chapter provides an excellent example of how social policy may be conveniently promulgated to change women's roles to serve the currently perceived societal needs and then 'supported' with selected (or selectively interpreted) research findings. Thus, when labor shortages require the influx of women workers, fertility control measures, including abortion, are made readily available – in fact, encouraged – with research data proffered in justification. When the birth rate drops and labor surpluses exist, social policy is revised to curtail access to contraceptives. And, again, research is pressed into service to rationalize this turnabout.

Another misuse of research concerns the political determination of 'relevant' (and therefore fashionable) research topics. The designation of research 'priorities' becomes a political issue in its own right. Researchers complain that support for on-going research on critical problems may be curtailed as political winds shift. Examples of this abuse abound in the United States where mental health may be the 'in' topic for Congressional funding one year, and aging or desegregation may emerge as the politically 'hot' research issue the next year. A president's (or president's wife's) or cabinet member's particular interest may become the current research priority and drain research funding from other needed work.

As research enters the league of 'big business', still other political abuses occur. Research institutes recognize the 'coming trends' and often fashion their own priorities to dovetail with available funding patterns. Different segments of the research community may take a more aggressive political stance by lobbying policy makers to support research in their special areas of expertise or interest. Strong professional associations may have the resources and political 'clout' to convince their representatives that continued support is necessary in their special research area. In the United States, research on sex roles suffers noticeably, since it lacks any institutionalized lobbying strength to promote its cause.

The 'big business' aspect of the research enterprise has serious fall-out for those social scientists most likely to be engaged in sex role research – particularly female, younger and minority group investigators. In fact, many independent sex role researchers whose work may be somewhat less 'establishment' approved and potentially more creative and original may be totally squeezed out of the funding competition. Academically-based investigators may be hard pressed to compete with the 'professional' research companies which have considerable expertise in 'grantsmanship'. It is somewhat ironic that, after US women activists pressed for the creation of legislation to fund programs and research on sex roles issues, much of the actual funding went to male investigators and male-owned research and program development operations.

Earlier, we catalogued several shortcomings of research that are inherent in the research enterprise itself. Often, however, researchers accuse policy makers of creating additional problems by imposing politically-motivated constraints upon the research. Sometimes the political consequences are underscored so heavily by policy makers that researchers impose the constraints upon themselves. For example, there is increasing reluctance for policy makers (or funding sources) to encourage researchers to undertake research that may result in a politically sensitive group appearing in a negative light. Such considerations have stirred major controversy within research communities. Witness the debate over racial differences in intelligence studies and the recent call for a moratorium on studies of sex differences. When politically-sensitive issues become entwined with research considerations, the difficulties may begin to comprise a Gordian knot. Researchers, often anxious to accommodate the demands of funding sponsors (which, in turn, are attuned to policy makers' attitudes) may be reluctant to clarify the effects such political constraints may have upon the research results.

Researchers point to the separate, but related, abuse of research by policy makers in the occasionally deliberate seduction of the scientific community (or a relevant segment of it) to validate social policy that policy makers wish to pursue. Visible high status members of the scientific community may find themselves in the role of 'science advisor' to policy makers, when, in fact, the advisory role consists of little more than putting the stamp of scientific approval on predetermined political strategies. Seduction by the importance, glamour, or perquisites of the 'advisor' role may be more than the individual scientist can resist (or even distinguish) from the legitimate consultant role. Carefully maintained links to the larger scientific community represent one safeguard that advisors to policy makers may use in preserving their scientific perspective and integrity.

Having assessed the seemingly endless difficulties emanating from both sides of the research-policy maker collaboration, is there any utility to such efforts? Should the researcher give up any hope of contributing to the development of social policy? Should the policy maker abandon any expectation of help from research? How, if at all, can research be helpful in formulating social policy, particularly social policy related to sex roles?

C. Differentiation of Research Strategies and Uses

Policy makers tend to see research as an undifferentiated activity. The differences between advocacy research, propaganda and policy analysis, as well as between fact finding and social science research (discussed above), are not very well understood by policy makers and activists. Those closer to the research world recognize that the same problem may be studied from several vantage points, for different purposes, and with multiple research strategies. One primary service the research community can render in the name of social policy is the clear explanation of the different types and uses of research strategies.

1. The Misunderstanding of Basic Research

Policy makers and activists tend to group all research in one general category of basic research. They respond to 'basic research' as a negative shibboleth. Many policy makers fault basic research as too remote from the practical demands of daily problems, too time-consuming, and too costly.

To add to the problem, basic research, which starts from the premise that knowledge has intrinsic importance, is not geared to creating immediate solutions. Applied research, somewhat closer to the policy maker's approach, prizes knowledge about phenomena which can be changed, preferably instantly. While basic research may serve as the launching pad for applied research, policy makers rarely recognize that it need not always precede applied research. In fact, applied research can point the way for needed basic research. More importantly, they are not substitutes for one another.

The policy maker/activist needs the researcher's guidance in distinguishing when the problem requires basic vs. applied research, or other types of research strategies (which we shall discuss below). For example, basic research can develop models of the social phenomena producing and perpetuating sex role inequities. Applied research is necessary to test and refine the validity and utility of these models. Policy makers need the guidance of researchers in distinguishing where each is appropriate. Without this guidance, the policy maker can hardly be blamed for a generalized disdain for the research enterprise.

A few examples will suggest what we mean. Researchers interested in building our knowledge base can study female labor force attachment as a problem in basic research in order to describe its historical patterns, its current status, its component factors and their interaction, as well as those contextual factors that influence and impinge upon it. Alternatively, female labor force attachment may be approached from an applied research perspective that may seek to understand how changes in related factors, such as work schedules (including flexitime), day-care centers, apprenticeship and vocational educational programs can strengthen continuous participation in the work force.

While the purposes of basic and applied research may differ, the two research strategies should not be artificially separated. Basic research often produces the knowledge base which is essential to applied research. Applied research often produces findings which are essentially basic research. Frequently, basic and applied research merge into one process of investigation and are distinguishable only in the distinctive ways in which the research findings ultimately are used.

Both basic and applied research are tributaries for social action. They can be carried out in tandem or separately. Social action uninformed by appropriate research efforts may be a waste and a detriment to the cause of equalizing the status of women. Research, both basic and applied, can be a short-cut to the solutions of many serious problems women and the people close to them face.

2. *Descriptive and Analytical Research*

Descriptive and analytical research are two distinct research strategies useful in dealing with women's unequal status. While considerable rhetorical concern is voiced about sex discrimination in the educational and occupational systems (see Trotter, chapter 15), women continue to face tremendous barriers in their quest for equal opportunities to learn and to work. 'Sex discrimination', however, is a sponge-like concept, absorbing bits and pieces of definitions of inequality, stereotyping, social and economic disadvantages, to name a few. How can the social policy maker and the activist mount the attack on this seemingly amorphous and insurmountable problem?

In the United States, prohibitions against sex discrimination have been created both by legislation[2] passed by the Congress and Executive Orders of the President. Descriptive research laid the groundwork for these important legislative mandates. Statistical descriptions of the distribution of females in the educational and occupational worlds served as the basis for developing these legislative initiatives. In addition, several key court decisions have been influenced by descriptive studies that revealed the size of the female labor pool compared to the actual numbers of females in a given factory, organization, department or university. Statistical descriptions shed considerable light on the differential educational programs, including athletics, offered to female and male students.

These descriptive studies have been useful in demonstrating the epidemiology of the problems besetting us. Descriptive studies take the social temperature, describe the symptoms of our social ills. Analytical studies are equally necessary to understand the processes by which the disease occurs. One could argue that the time has come to move research on sex roles to the analytical level in order to fashion realistic solutions to the problems so well described.

Descriptive research can tell us how many women go to medical school and how many enter the various specialities within medicine. They can describe the segregation of women in various medical specialties. But, analytic studies are necessary to understand the underlying processes whereby women are safely tracked and sidetracked into traditional 'feminine' specialties within the larger male medical domain.

Social processes that involve sex roles are both subtle and blatant (Bernard, 1976), individual and institutional (or psychological and structural) (Safilios-Rothschild, Chapter 13); they are not revealed in purely descriptive studies. The dynamics of sex discrimination in the educational and occupational systems must be understood as a process, or a set of processes, in order to identify the critical intervention points.

Identification of potential intervention points is a necessary step before the activist and the policy maker can aim the artillery of social action and legislation. One example is analytical research that focuses on how sex roles are learned before children even enter school and what processes within the family and the educational system reinforce and sustain sex role stereotypes (National Institute of Education, Contract # NIE-C-74-0139, 1974). Such analytical research offers the sophisticated activist and policy formulator the necessary direction and knowledge for meaningful social intervention.

This is not to argue that there is no longer any need for descriptive research. Rather we are suggesting that analytic research can build on the base provided by descriptive work to offer understanding of the dynamics — rather than the parameters — of social phenomena.

3. Long-term and Short-term, Longitudinal and Cross-Sectional Research

Activists and policy planners often complain about the length of time research takes. They argue that social action cannot wait while researchers spend years investigating problems. Such an argument overlooks the many different types of research designed for different purposes, as well as the different timelines involved. As we have suggested earlier, some problems can be investigated in relatively short-term research; others may require longer-term efforts. Still others can be attacked simultaneously using both approaches.

Cross-sectional research, which compares different groups at a given moment in time, is often erroneously substituted for longitudinal studies. Longitudinal studies, which follow the same group over a sufficiently extended time period, record developmental changes and give us information that can be only imperfectly, if at all, inferred from cross-sectional studies. For example, developmental differences between adolescent and older females cannot be assessed by comparing one group of youngsters and a different group of mature women. Patient, long-term follow-up of the same subject population — unpopular with policy makers — serves a vital research purpose.

Cross-sectional, or one-time, research usually requires limited time investments. For example, studies that test new techniques for teaching spatial visualization skills to females may be conducted in a relatively short time, even a matter of weeks or months. However, studies that seek to understand if and how the maturational or developmental processes involved in spatial visualization are different for males and females may require a longitudinal design that studies the subjects repeatedly over a period of years.

4. Cohort Studies and Cross-Cultural Research

Research that attempts to disentangle the developmental, or ontological, effects from historical or social context effects must compare different age cohorts that arrive at a given life stage at different moments in social history. Cohort studies prevent our mistaking specific historical influences for universal developmental trends. For example, studies of American youth who reached adolescence during the Great Depression of the 1930s probably would reveal a strong work ethic, coupled with an emphasis upon individual economic security. A comparable study of individuals whose adolescence occurred during the affluent 1950s and 1960s would create a strikingly different portrait of American adolescent development and adult profiles.

Cross-cultural research provides still another research strategy that has particular relevance for social policy on sex roles. Cross-cultural studies offer a potent antidote to the 'genetic imperative' perspective that argues that basic and enduring genetic differences distinguish the sexes and account for their divergent life styles and histories. For example, cross-cultural comparisons of the distribution of women in the labor market around the world quickly make it apparent that cultural conditions have greater influence than genetic makeup on women's occupational choice. Thus, the 3-4 percent ceiling on female engineers that has held for many years in the American labor market can no longer be attributed to genetic inabilities of women, when we see that in the USSR 38 percent of the engineers are women.

Cross-cultural research faces many obstacles, including those of language and other cultural differences. The technical difficulties of organizing a cross-cultural research project often are compounded by policy makers who limit funding for such research on the grounds that cross-national studies are motivated more by the travel-lust of researchers than the need for purposeful, comparative work. This is a serious problem, particularly in the US, where currently proposed policy strategies could be improved or possibly eliminated by a careful study of the experience of other countries which have instituted similar policies.

Careful analysis of both successful and unsuccessful political solutions in other cultural contexts would conserve time, effort and expense in less experienced countries. The Swedish example (Baude, Chapter 6; Safilios-Rothschild, Chapter 13) deserves careful examination in terms of family and educational policies that impinge on sex roles. Not only is it necessary to understand which policies did and did not work in another culture; it is also imperative to identify critical cultural differences between countries that may make policy viable in one context and useless in another.

Many examples come to mind that demonstrate the importance of cross-national studies. Recently in the US, considerable pressure has developed for government-supported day-care centers. Much controversy exists about the effects of day care on children of different ages, for differing periods of time, by different types of caretakers (Woolsey, 1977). Before we engage in large-scale programs, it is important to examine, among others, the experience of Swedish day-care and leisure-time centers, Israeli kibbutzim, and the French L'École Maternale. Tempting as it may be, there are potential difficulties in translating other cultural experiments into new contexts. Cross-cultural studies are necessary to identify the adaptations that must be made as social programs migrate across cultural and national borders.

5. *Interdisciplinary Research*

Interdisciplinary studies are crucial among the various social and physical sciences in order to integrate our understanding of individuals in a social context. Too often research is focused only on the individual or only on the institutional level. Social and physical dimensions too frequently are studied separately. Far too little research integrates individual genetic, biological, and psychological factors with institutional, economic, sociological, legal and political variables.

Interdisciplinary research presents special difficulties to the researchers involved, but the long-term potential gains seem to warrant such efforts. Research strategies that seek to integrate the personal, interpersonal, and institutional levels will provide a more realistic, broad-scoped understanding of why females and males are involved in their current sex-linked patterns. Studies that link individual differences in attitudes, coping abilities, achievement styles, cognitive and affective skills with cultural conditions, legal, political, economic, educational and religious structures will go far toward laying the groundwork for intelligent and successful social policies and programs.

A related issue is the need to study male, as well as female, roles in order to understand the dialectic that is at the core of human interaction (Pleck, 1974). To be effective and meaningful, social policy, as well as research, must not be limited to the female terms of the discrimination problem. Both research and social policy must treat structural (i.e., legal, economic, political, occupational, religious, etc.) and individual factors that inhibit free and broad life options for males as well as females. The new options that social policy seeks to provide must go beyond the individual or group level; these options must encompass all aspects of our society including all of our social institutions that traditionally have created strong resistance to change.

The factors that inhibit or enhance the life opportunities of males must be included in whatever research and resultant programs we design. Any strategy to change or improve the female role, while ignoring the male role, is doomed to failure. This failure is inevitable, since changing one half of the social structure is bound to bring changes, intended or otherwise, to the other half of social roles. Interdisciplinary efforts are necessary to understand the dynamics of male and female roles.

6. Mapping Sex Roles Onto Sexual Behavior

A related problem is the artificial separation of the research on sex roles and sexual behavior. At the present time, sex roles tend to be studied by sociologists and sexual behavior by psychologists, psychiatrists and sex therapists. A clearer understanding of why males and females, at different ages and under different circumstances, make the life choices that they do will only emerge when we take the necessary step of mapping sex roles onto sexual behavior (Lipman-Blumen, 1975). Social policy that attempts to provide support for sex role options without taking into account the influence of sexual beahvior will fall short of the mark.

7. Policy and Impact Analysis

The recently ubiquitous demand for policy and impact analysis — a specific assessment of policy implications for specific targets — is partly an outgrowth of policy formulators' frustration and dissatisfaction with the current state of research. Policy and impact analysis are distinguishable from one another, as well as from other traditional forms of social science research.

Traditional social science attempts to relate two or more social factors to one another and to understand the nature of the relationship(s). Policy research, by contrast, attempts to assess the potential efficacy of policies that are proposed as solutions to social problems. Policy research attempts to examine a proposed piece of legislation to understand what it does and does not provide, what constraints are imposed by such legislation, whether the legislative language conveys the intent of the lawmakers, and how that legislation dovetails with or contradicts existing legislation. Policy research, imprecise as it is, has been around for a very long time. Impact research, a more recent development, grows out of the need to go beyond the rather narrow limits of policy analysis.

Recently, activists of many hues — from environmentalists to women activists — have urged legislators to demand impact statements. Impact analysis attempts to predict the possible effects of proposed social policy on a wide range of groups within the community, as well as upon resources, environmental conditions, and a host of other factors. It is an effort to forecast the long- as well as the short-range effects of legislation, both for specifically identified communities (such as women, Blacks, Hispanics, low-income groups, teenagers) and more broadly defined institutions (such as the family, the church, the neighborhood).

Earlier research aimed at reducing infant mortality failed to address the question of the impact such a reduction would have on other aspects of life. As a result, when the infant mortality rate began to fall in countries around the globe, researchers and policy makers alike were unprepared for the concomitant rise in population, abortions, maternal suicides, and projected food shortages (Berelson et al. 1966).

Any policy change has potential second- and third-order effects whose consequences cannot be ignored. A growing recognition of this fact has led to a reactive swing of the pendulum. It is becoming de rigueur among policy makers, as well as activists, to demand an 'impact statement' for each new piece of proposed legislation. At least one American policy maker has suggested that all legislation be examined in terms of its potential impact on the family.

The call for impact statements is essentially a call for responsibility. However, the question is more complicated because of the primitive state of 'impact analysis'. Although the building blocks for impact analysis — such as simulation and other techniques — are available, no standardized or validated methodology for impact analysis exists at the present time. As a result, many different techniques — most implicit and unscientific — are employed under the general rubric of 'impact analysis'.

While the motivation behind the call for impact statements is laudable, this demand is a two-edged sword. At present, as noted above, there is no standard recognized methodology, no required training, no accountability, no validity check to assure us that what is presented as an 'impact statement' is anything other than the prejudices and values of the individual analyst. As a result, the same program or policy might be viewed with alarm as a spur to divorce, a deterrent to marriage, an impetus to abortion, or welcomed as a protection against illness, a reduction in social security benefits, a decrease in maternal mortality — all depending upon the individual analyst's metric, values and perspective. The question of responsibility becomes increasingly complex.

Because no standardized method for developing impact statements exists, there is no reliable way to evaluate their validity. In addition, the lack of agreement that any special technique or expertise is needed for developing impact statements means that anyone — without concern for training, sophistication, and general background — is a likely candidate for developing impact statements. Thus, we see that impact statements can be a dangerous weapon, particularly in the hands of the naive or those who would use an impact statement for politically dubious purposes.

To add to the problem, impact analysis is in danger of becoming a fad, touted as a panacea for our long history of ignoring the future. Even in those cases where we have tried to predict future effects, long-term social and economic trends have been capricious and difficult to forecast. Nonetheless, a reasonable beginning can be made by applying available techniques, such as computer simulations.

Existing technology can be adapted to project future effects on different segments of the community. Currently, we see frantic attempts to develop impact research; however, much work in this area remains to be done. Systematic methodologies must be forged to forecast with greater accuracy the fallout from our present sex role patterns and proposed social solutions. Without it, we can continue to expect an 'oversell' by researchers, eager to meet a new 'overdemand' by activists and policy makers. Premature and feverish attempts to meet unrealistic demands can only be followed by disillusionment on the part of policy makers and the target constituencies.

TRANSITIONAL PERIOD

Different stages in the women's movement and general social changes require different types of social policy, as well as different research strategies. In the early stages of the movement, descriptive studies demonstrating the existence of sex discrimination served a crucial purpose in underscoring the need for legislative support of social change. Once certain landmark pieces of legislation provided the legal basis for social change, studies that monitor the adherence to the law became more relevant.

Long-range and comprehensive social changes will require continual, systematic tracking in order to ensure both adherence to the law and necessary adjustments to an emerging social reality. Analytical research must continue to provide a detailed understanding of the social processes we would try to alter. Longitudinal, as well as cross-cultural, studies must be conducted to prevent costly errors in social policy. Intervention-oriented research must follow on the heels of analytical studies that give us reliable leads to critical turning points in the differing life cycles of females and males.

In the transition period between a traditional sexist society and the more egalitarian society envisioned by the women's movement, traditional views must be subjected to hard questioning. Such questioning may expose the untenable and mythical bases of many assumptions regarding sex roles. We may expect the weakening of traditional roles, behavioral patterns, and institutional structures before new, more adaptive substitutes are developed. In the interim period, special social arrangements, buttressed by the support of social policy, are necessary.

Affirmative action plans, for example, with all their initial difficulties, are necessary transitional supports. Ultimately, more egalitarian social institutions will make such legislation obsolete; however, in the transition period, social policy planners will have to provide comparable support across a broad institutional spectrum. Special attention to failures and missteps in this transition period hopefully can lead us to develop more useful socialization practices for the coming generations.

Many questions remain to be answered. These questions range from the very specific to the more general. As new patterns of choice for females and males develop, we need to study their short- and long-range consequences. The relationship among socio-economic and political structures and sex role patterns remains to be documented (Scott, 1974). Relationships among ethnic background, social class and sexism represent another broad area calling for investigation. Social programs aimed at different ethnic and socio-economic groups must be tailored to fit with cultural constraints that set the parameters of social living within those groups.

During the transitional period, particularly, we need to understand how to move both traditional cultures and enclaves of traditionalism within more modern cultures toward a non-sexist society. This may involve understanding, possibly reinterpreting or modernizing religious doctrines, as well as political theories. Research has an important role to play in understanding when social policy and action require justification by traditional belief systems, and when social policy and action must be presented as a break with tradition.

Female achievement, leadership and group membership patterns represent other critical areas of research from which we can learn how best to encourage women to assume leadership roles. Such studies are valuable in preparing large cadres of women for leadership roles as legislative supports clear the way for their entry into such positions.

Studies of parent-child relationships are important to our understanding of the effects of family patterns not merely on children, but also on their parents, throughout the course of the life cycle. Family patterns in different cultural settings are critical sources of information for an informed family policy. New living arrangements among single parents must be studied, and alternative support systems tested, in order to develop programs that will benefit heterogeneous populations in changing societies.

The dialectic between research, social policy and implementation is crucial. Without it, we run the danger of creating legislation and action programs that are ineffective and wasteful, that fail to broaden the options for females and males, that are unable to motivate individuals to experiment with new options once they are available. Such failures are ammunition for those who would interpret them as evidence of the natural inabilities of women.

The present time is a crucial point in the movement toward a non-sexist society. It is a time when myths must be shattered — not by rhetoric, but by understanding based on knowledge. This does not mean all social action and policy must await research results.

We already have considerable knowledge on which to base reasonable social policy advances. Nonetheless, a continuing dialectic must be forged in which research feeds social action and policy, and policy formulation and implementation point to the remaining and emerging problematic areas for research. Only when this dialectic is ensured can we expect an egalitarian society in which females and males experience the full potential of their lives.

NOTES

1. It is symptomatic of the American male political establishment's sense of omniscience on 'women's issues' that the original US delegation to the Mexico City Conference was composed entirely of male State Department personnel. Only after vociferous protests by major women's organizations in the US was the delegation revised to include women.

2. The Equal Pay Act, Title IX of the Educational Amendments of 1972, Executive Orders 11246 and 11375 have all been put in place.

REFERENCES

BERELSON, Bernard, Richmond K. ANDERSON, Oscar HARKAVY, John MAIER, W. Parker MAULDIN, Sheldon J. SEGAL, *Family Planning and Population Programs: A Review of World Developments,* Chicago Ill.: Chicago University Press, 1966.

BERNARD, Jessie, 'Where Are We Now? Some Thoughts on the Current Scene,' *Psychology of Women Quarterly,* 1 (1) 1976, pp. 21-37.

LIPMAN-BLUMEN, Jean, "Changing Sex Roles in American Culture: Future Directions for Research," *Archives of Sexual Behavior,* Vol. 4, No. 4, 1975, pp. 433-446.

NATIONAL INSTITUTE OF EDUCATION, *Development of Models for Understanding the Processes Involved in Sex Discrimination in Educational Systems.* RFP No. NIE-C-74-0139, 1974.

PLECK, Joseph H. and Jack SAWYER, *Men and Masculinity,* Englewood, NJ: Prentice-Hall, 1974.

SCOTT, Hilda, *Does Socialism Liberate Women?* Boston: Beacon Press, 1974.
WOOLSEY, Suzanne H. 'Pied Piper Politics and the Child-Care Debate, *Daedalus,* 106 (2), Spring 1977, pp. 127-45.

3

WHERE RESEARCH AND POLICY CONNECT:
The American Scene
Sandra S. Tangri *and*
Georgia L. Strasburg
*US Commission on Civil Rights,
Washington DC*

Using the United States as their example, Tangri and Strasburg examine the relationship between policy-making and research. They lay out the political structure of the three branches of American government – executive, legislative, and judicial – to identify the potential impact points for science and suggest the ways in which social science research is relevant and possible within each of these contexts. They suggest the ways in which social policy, viewed as an 'informed choice of alternative options', can and should be supported by relevant research, as well as some of the hesitancies that policy makers in all branches of government have about social science.

In the second half of the paper, Tangri and Strasburg examine several criteria for 'usefulness' of research and suggest the strains and conflicts that researchers confront in their attempts to design and conduct 'policy-relevant' research. Taking research on the psychology of women as a case in point, the authors indicate the ways in which such research could be used for policy purposes. Their analysis underscores the professional risks that researchers must be willing to take vis à vis their own social science colleagues if they wish to engage in research that may influence policy decisions.

Work on this article was done by the authors in the course of their duties as employees of the Civil Rights Commission. However, the views contained herein are not to be attributed to the Commission on Civil Rights. Special thanks to Lenora McMillan for her expert assistance in our legal research.

INTRODUCTION

Social policy is supposed to be the informed choice of alternative options, based on comparisons in terms of costs and benefits, and effect on incentives (Rivlin, 1971). From our point of view, the costs and benefits are both psychological and economic, social and individual. We would like to know who will benefit, who will be harmed, and to what extent. We would like to know, in order to inform policy, what unintended as well as intended consequences can be foreseen, and if necessary, avoided or provided for. This is a taller order than most social science research is equipped to meet at present.

To have an impact on equity policy, it is not sufficient to conduct research on women or minorities, or any other disadvantaged group. Most academic research on these topics finds its way into dissertations, journals, professional meetings and, occasionally, books. It rarely contributes to the decision-making process on issues of importance to us: affirmative action, childcare, educational equity, job desegregation, etc. Yet many of us are interested in making social policy more responsive to women. It is easy to feel that the researcher's product is not a rational, scientific process for the most part. It is a political process, and we would like to suggest how research can play a role in it.

There are two parts to this paper. One has to do with the possible impact points for social science within the federal policy-making apparatus, the other with how to produce research which is more likely to have an impact on that process.

POTENTIAL IMPACT POINTS FOR SOCIAL SCIENCE RESEARCH

Policy-making takes place from the local school board to the Supreme Court. Although we will be discussing policy-making at the federal level, many of the recommendations we will make apply to any level. If one is interested in influencing the city council, the parole board, or the high school principal, one needs to identify the possible entry points at which one's research can make a contribution, to know when it is timely, and to adapt the research to its needs.

Our research on federal policy-making suggests a number of potential impact points, each with varying degrees of efficacy. A complete analysis of this process might provide an evaluation of the relative effectiveness of each. However, our purpose is more limited. That is, to introduce the reader to the possible users of policy-relevant research, and to delineate the characteristics of this research which make it useful. We have tried to flesh out this outline by using examples of issues relevant to women.

Our overview of the federal policy system can be divided by the traditional separation of powers in the US government: the executive, the legislative, and the judicial. They all use research of different kinds for various purposes and this use is, of necessity, increasing.

The Executive Branch

The executive branch is an apt starting place for our survey, both because it represents the pinnacle of political power in the US and because it has played a major role in initiating civil rights policy by means of the Executive Order privilege since 1941.

At least four distinct subsystems provide information and advice to the President. Probably the most visible is the Cabinet with its concomitant sub-cabinet committees and the corresponding executive departments, such as the Departments of Health, Education and Welfare, Justice, and Labor.

The executive departments and their corresponding agencies are major users of social science, through extramural and intramural research functions. Nearly two thirds of the nation's research and development is financed by the federal government and 55 percent of this work is through agency contracts and grants to the private sector (Cronin and Greenberg, 1969). Other avenues by which social science is filtered to top agency policy-makers are journals, newspapers, books, conferences and personal contacts (Caplan, 1975).

A good example of an executive agency's commitment to social science research is the Women's Bureau of the Department of Labor which, in its dual role as a user and producer of social science research, has contributed heavily to the formulation of policies affecting women. Established in June 1920, the Women's Bureau's concise, in-house descriptive research documenting the legal and economic status of women has been used consistently in Congressional hearings. In the published hearings preceding passage of Title IX,[1] research conducted by the Women's Bureau constituted the largest single source of data documenting the effects of discrimination against women, and certainly made a significant and powerful contribution to the hearings. Whereas this illustrates the use of agency research by Congress, what follows illustrates the use by an agency of non-government research.

When President Johnson signed Executive Order (EO) 11375 on 13 October 1968 he gave the responsibility for implementing affirmative action to the Secretary of Labor, who in turn delegated his authority to the Director of the Office of Contract Compliance. On 17 January 1969, the Office of Federal Contract Compliance published proposed guidelines and interested persons were given the opportunity to file written data, views or arguments concerning these proposals. Additional public hearings were held in August 1969 in which many social scientists and educators participated, augmenting their testimony with social science findings.

A second advisory subsystem in the executive branch consists of the White House personal staff (including policy and program advisers, legislative liaison staff, and political and appointed advisers), and special counsels and consultants to the President (Cronin and Greenberg, 1969). After the President signed Title IX into law in June 1972, the White House initiated the Office of Women's Programs in February 1973, the first direct advisory channel to the President for women's issues. The staff of this office resigned en masse in May 1974 in the face of Nixon's increasing preoccupation with the Watergate scandal (Freeman, 1975). At the present time, the Carter administration has established the Office of Public Liaison, one of whose units is an office for the special concerns of women. This office is now undertaking an in-house research effort to document discrimination against poor working women, as well as using outside research to document their position papers.

A third advisory subsystem in the executive department is the network of outside consultants tapped by the White House to serve on permanent and temporary advisory commissions. The exact extent of the influence of these commissions, ad hoc groups, and task forces is varied; however, selective interviewing of congressmen and senior members of the bureaucracy reveals that more and more policy emanates from these White House collectivities (Cronin and Greenberg, 1969). Five such groups are described below.

President Kennedy established the President's Commission on the Status of Women in 1961, at the behest of Esther Peterson, then Director of the Women's Bureau. Its 1963 report, *American Women*, documented how thoroughly women were denied equal opportunity. Although the report did not lead immediately to concrete legislation, state commissions on women were established in response to its recommendations. These commissions are still in existence and continue to utilize social scientists and social science in their in-house research efforts.

The Citizen's Advisory Council on the Status of Women (CACSW) grew out of a recommendation from the President's Commission in 1963. The Council and its reports have been able to function as a feminist voice within the government. Although effectively defunct since 1976, the CACSW drafted EO 11375 which was signed by President Johnson on 13 October 1967 to extend the President's affirmative action plan to include remedies for sex discrimination.

The Nixon administration's response to the concerns of women was initiated by Arthur Burns, then in charge of setting up White House task forces in the Fall of 1969. This led to the creation of the President's Task Force on Women's Rights and Responsibilities chaired by Virginia Allan. The Task Force's Report in April 1970, *A Matter of Simple Justice,* used descriptive research to document systematically sex discrimination in the political, economic, and social spheres. Its strong statement (p. 19) regarding the Office of Federal Contract Compliance's lack of responsibility in carrying out its implementation of EO 11375 resulted in the issuing of the long awaited guidelines. The President's Task Force on the Status of Women in 1970 made numerous administrative and legislative suggestions, many of which resulted in legislative enactment.

On 9 January 1975, President Ford created the National Commission on the Observance of International Women's Year (IWY). The Commission is limited to 42 members appointed by the President from private life, and two members each appointed by the President of the Senate and the Speaker of the House. The life of the Commission was extended in 1975 and in that same year the Congress allocated five million dollars to run state-wide conferences on women, which culminated in a national conference in Houston, Texas in November 1977. The Commission was slated to expire on 31 March 1978.[2] In preparation for the state and national conventions, the IWY has conducted large scale in-house research efforts as well as utilized the services of other government research bodies. In addition, extramural research has been contracted out extensively.[3]

The fourth advisory subsystem in the executive branch is the White

House support staff. This includes, for instance, the Bureau of the Budget, the Council of Economic Advisors, the Office of Science and Technology (OSTP), and the Civil Service Commission, among others. Each of these offices has research capabilities, including particularly the utilization of the social sciences, and social scientists are often used as part-time consultants. In recent years, over 200 scientists and engineers have served as part-time consultants to OSTP alone (Cronin and Greenberg, 1969).

Each of these persons, committees, institutions, and funding activities is a potential access point and potential user of our research. The relative accessibility and receptivity of each depends on a variety of factors, many of which cannot be foreseen, but includes: the composition of the group; the time frame in which it operates; the size of its budget; the political intent of its mandate; the particular personalities involved; and, last but not least, the nature of the research being presented. The task of predicting or measuring the extent of impact of a given piece of research is extremely difficult, and is not attempted here.

These factors, which influence the degree of receptivity to social science in the executive branch can equally be said to influence the receptivity in other branches of the federal policy-making apparatus. The next two sections of this paper will briefly delineate the possible access points in the legislative and judicial branches, and these will be followed by a discussion of the factors which influence the utility of the research to its potential users.

The Legislative Branch

The United States Congress makes the laws of the country and directs the oversight of federal law enforcement. It operates on a two-tenths of one percent of the annual national budget. If this seems small, think of it as the cost equivalent of operating the Pentagon for three days.

One of the major recommendations of the Commission on the Operation of the Senate (*Modern Senate*, 1976) was to strengthen the Senate's ability to achieve 'future-oriented and integrated examination of major policy alternatives' (p. 47) and to 'assess the effectiveness of past actions' (p. 43). To accomplish these ends, the Commission suggested: '1) Early identification of major problems. 2) stimulation of systematic analyses and research efforts; and 3) translation of the results into concise syntheses setting forth the pros and cons of major policy alternatives' (p. 44).

It should be evident that in these tasks there is a large role that could be played by social scientists, particularly those who want to influence the course of political events, utilizing both their professional skills and their political vision. To contribute toward this end, we have identified some of the major channels for the flow of information, both internal and external to the Congress.

Internal Research Support.

Of the internal sources of information and analyses available to Congress, the four congressional support agencies, the Congressional Resource Service (CRS), the Government Accounting Office (GAO), the Office of Technology Assessment (OTA), and the Congressional Budget Office (CBO) are the most answerable to the immediate needs of Congress, and the most flexible in responding to its changing needs (*Modern Senate*, 1976).

The CRS and the GAO are the primary research arms of Congress, and are funded by legislative appropriations. The Legislative Reorganization Act of 1970, in response to increased research needs, expanded the role and service capabilities of both the CRS and the GAO. They are not accountable to the executive branch, and they provide services for individual members of Congress and for their committees. Their services range from supplying specific information to an individual congressperson, to carrying out sustained analyses for oversight, appropriations or authorization programs. They have a combined annual budget of approximately $186 million and employ 6,000 persons. However, their ability to conduct long-range comprehensive policy analysis has been submerged in meeting short-term rush demands for factual materials (*Modern Senate*, 1976). Since January 1971, when the Legislative Reorganization Act became effective, the CRS has increased its staff of researchers and undertaken additional activities in order to implement the directives of the Act.

The ensuing staff capability of CRS has resulted in more in-depth research assistance to both committees and personal staff members. Congresspersons and their personal staffs rely heavily on the CRS for the traditional *Digest of Public Bills* and *Special Reports*. In conjunction with the research and information activities customarily performed by the CRS staff, the Service is attempting to identify emerging policy issues and establish continuous liaison with congressional committees.

The Government Accounting Office (GAO) has specific authority to review programs for Congress. As of 1971 it also has increased responsibilities to assist Congress in its oversight functions. Thus, although either house of Congress or any Committee may request a program analysis by GAO, the research conducted at GAO is more likely to be done for committees.

The Office of Technology Assessment's basic function is to provide congressional committees with assessments which identify a broad range of consequences, social as well as physical, which will accompany the uses of technology. Their budget provides for approximately 6.5 million dollars of intra- and extramural research of which half is allocated to research relating to the social aspects of technology.

The Congressional Budget Office gives Congress an overview of the federal budget and weighs the priorities for national resource allocation. According to Charles Mosher (1977), this office will play an increasingly important role in Congress. Its present Director is Alice Rivlin, an economist who has written insightfully about the role of social science in policy-making (Rivlin, 1971).

Staffs

Another internal source of information is the professional staffs of the members of the committees, of individual congresspersons and student interns and policy fellows. The staff have the capacity for great influence on congressional decision-making. They often control the flow of communication to the office and the congressperson, and staff expertise and judgment is expected on a wide range of activities and critical variables (Hammond, 1973).

As early as 1946 the Legislative Reorganization Act recognized the need for increased professionalization and specialization among committee and personal staffs, and a trend toward social science experts has been clearly expressed since that time.[4] For example, in 1972, Dr. Bernice Sandler, a psychologist, was hired as 'educational consultant' to Edith Green's staff, and her contacts with academic women and familiarity with social science findings contributed significantly to the passage of major legislation affecting women's education.

Intern and Fellows Programs

The Intern and Fellows programs offer opportunities for social scientists and additional congressional access to social science research. The summer intern program was set up formally in June 1965, and a student congressional intern was authorized for each member for several months. These interns range from secondary students to postdoctoral fellows.

The American Political Science Association's Congressional Fellows program was established in 1953. Fellows spend two months at the CRS, four months on a committee staff and four months in a House or Senate office. A similar program for other social scientists would be extrememely useful. Since 1953, more than 571 political scientists and journalists have participated in this policy experience. A feminist political science fellow on Senator William Brock's staff provided the inspiration for the equal credit opportunity title which was proposed by Brock as an amendment to the Fair Credit Billing Act and adopted into legislation (Freeman, 1975).

In addition to these formal internal structures there are several informal groups of members of Congress which meet regularly to discuss their common interests and new information bearing on these (e.g., the Democratic Study Group, Wednesday Night Group, and Women's Caucus).

Aside from the internal ability of Congress through structural and individual processes to obtain social science information, a number of significant external sources are utilized extensively, including assistance by the executive departments, private consultants and contracts, professionals who testify before legislative and oversight committee hearings, lobbyists and constituents. Assistance by executive departments has been very important to women's legislation. In Representative Edith Green's oversight committee (the Ad Hoc Subcommittee on Discrimination Against Women) hundreds of legitimate and leaked reports from the Office of Civil Rights (HEW) supplemented the committee's findings (Freeman, 1975).

Consultants

The 1970 Legislative Reorganization Act authorized committees to hire part-time or temporary consultants, a practice which has become increasingly popular. It is possible for these consultants to be social scientists. In addition, some offices have set up informal advisory committees on specific issue areas, often asking university professors in their districts to help congressional staff develop and conduct research on legislation.

Hearings

The role of social scientists in congressional hearings has been mentioned before.

The Judicial Branch

DeTocqueville, in one of his insightful remarks about the American system, concluded that 'scarcely any political question arises in the United States that is not resolved sooner or later into a judicial question.' (Bradley, 1961: 290). Still, the courts are not traditionally viewed as active policy-making bodies, but rather as 'interpreters of the law.' While it is true that the courts are essentially 'reactive' (in that an individual citizen must bring his/her complaint before the bench before the courts can act), 'reactive' is not to be construed as 'passive'. This distinction is most dramatically drawn by the alternative interpretations of the Constitution as a literal, inflexible document or as an adaptive and dynamic legal tool.

The shift of the Supreme Court in the twentieth century from its longstanding focus on property rights to civil rights under Chief Justice Earl Warren leaves no doubt that the meaning of the Constitution changes or is clarified to a large extent in accord with the value preferences of the justices as they respond to the varied political, economic, and social moods and problems of the times (Rosen, 1972).

These complex political, economic, and social problems have aroused debate within the judicial system as to whether the Constitution can be interpreted strictly by nomological means or whether, as Felix Frankfurter asserted, 'the types of cases now calling for decision to a considerable extent require investigation of voluminous literature, far beyond the law reports and other legal writings.' (Frankfurter, 1957).

The need for 'extralegal' information in the judicial process has come to be known as sociological jurisprudence. Proponents of this approach claim that the court's 'decisions cannot rest alone on syllogism, metaphysics, or some ill-defined notion of natural justice, although each will play its part' (White, 1972). They assert that law is ultimately concerned with social behavior, and research on the social implications of legal decisions could make an appropriate and necessary contribution. The Supreme Court has indicated in recent years that it considers social science an authoritative body of knowledge which can reflect empirical reality, and it is reasonable to expect that social science will play an increasing role in the future.

Although the future of sociological jurisprudence looks bright, the use of 'extralegal' facts in court decisions is a recent and disputed development in the jurisprudence process. The increased use of sociological information can be attributed primarily to Justice Louis Brandeis. The 'Brandeis brief' has come to mean a 'source of information or vehicle that has been used to bring social science findings to the attention of the Court' (Rosen, 1972: 201). The Supreme Court's formal recognition of the 'Brandeis Brief' came in 1908 in the Muller v. Oregon case. Many consider this to be the case that tilted the balance in the traditional tension between social science and the law. In fact, the recognition of this brief using social science data was perhaps only due to the 'great presence and persuasive pleading of Louis Brandeis himself' (Rosen, 1972). Because Muller v. Oregon is a landmark case, and because the social science findings represented 'research on women,' Muller v. Oregon is a classic case for feminist social scientists.

In 1905 Curt Muller, the proprietor of the Grand Laundry in Portland, Oregon was convicted of violating a state statute speficying that 'no female can be employed in a mechanical establishment, factory or laundry more than ten hours during any one day' (Rosen, 1972: 77). This case was popularly referred to as The Case of the Overworked Laundress. Muller brought the case to the Supreme Court and drew a formidable opponent: Louis D. Brandeis represented the state of Oregon.

Brandeis recognized that radical social welfare measures required an equally radical defense before the Court. Brandeis therefore asked his sister-in-law, Josephine Goldmark, to gather 'facts' published by experts in the field with respect to labor and women. A research staff of ten under the direction of Ms. Goldmark was formed, and a radical kind of brief was drawn up. Over one hundred reports by physicians, economists, factory inspectors, and sundry bureaus of statistics comprised the bulk of the brief. In fact 'only two of the brief's 113 pages resembled the traditional forms of advocacy' (Rosen, 1972: 78).

Brandeis' extralegal sources were used to substantiate four specific hypotheses: (1) that women are physiologically different from men and are more susceptible to injury resulting from unregulated industrial conditions; (2) that excessive hours of labor generally endanger the health, safety, and morals of women; (3) that shorter workdays for women produce economic benefits for the employer; and (4) that shorter workdays foster individual health and improve homelife. For these reasons, he argued, the court should uphold Oregon's limitation of working hours for women. Brandeis persuaded the court that his massive collection of facts was relevant to the process of judicial interpretation, and he received a decision in his favor.

While the Brandeis brief in Muller v. Oregon set an historically important precedent in jurisprudence, it also raises some of the problems and fears associated with the use of social science in the courts. The studies cited in the brief were used to argue for a policy which, though liberal for its time because it protected women from some harsh aspects of industrial employment, is considered by most feminists today to be conservative, discriminatory, and undesirable. Thus, because the value context has sufficiently changed, the studies might be interpreted today so as to support a quite different judicial decision, e.g., that if those hours of work are harmful to women they are probably also harmful to men, and everybody's hours should be shorter. Alternatively, the studies themselves might be challenged, as much on the basis of new values, as on methodological grounds.

A second concern has to do with the validity and reliability of the studies' findings and whether different findings would support different judicial decisions. Or, as others might say, whether the interpretation of the Constitution can rest on the shifting sands of social science. David Cohen and Janet Weiss (1977) have explicated how the inherently tentative nature of social science findings on school desegregation (as well as on other matters) has affected court decisions beginning with the role of Kenneth Clark's research on Black children in the Brown decision. The danger in this trend is that, as Morroe Berger has said, 'we may reach a point where we shall be entitled to equality under the law only when we can show that inequality has been or would be harmful.' (1957).

These issues, combined with the wide gaps in the literature, and the inappropriateness of the adversary system for discovery of truth (Wolfe, 1976) tend to make for some apprehension about the growing use of social research findings in the courts, particularly in the Supreme Court. As in other arenas of policy-making, social science cannot ultimately answer value questions. Essentially, the court is always faced with the task of weighing and choosing values. The courts cannot ask social science, for example, whether equal job opportunity is more valued than family stability. But social science can explain the etiology of social behavior, the effects of the law on social behavior, the probable consequences of legal decisions, and how values and goals can best be realized (Rosen, 1972).

With these tasks in mind, social research could make a contribution to the development of affirmative action policy in the courts and other pressing social issues. Most civil rights suits rest their positions on the 14th Amendment's guarantee to 'equal protection and due process under the law.' But, as Douglas (1966) conceded, 'the conditions of what constitutes equal treatment for the purpose of the Equal Protection Clause do change.' Justice Harlan called for social science's help in 'understanding fact situations that might suggest the need for new conceptions of what constitutes due process and equal protection' (Rosen, 1972: 223) under the law.

HOW TO MAKE RESEARCH ON THE PSYCHOLOGY OF WOMEN MORE USEFUL

The first part of this paper addressed the question, 'where and how is social science research used in policy-making at the federal level?' This was intended as information for you, the producers of the research, on an important set of potential users of your work. This part of the paper addresses the question of what kind of product should you have to offer. At this point many readers will automatically shut down at the thought of having their choice or method of research dictated by any considerations other than scientific merit and their own curiosity. Yet many researchers are also interested in seeing certain social changes take place and may even assume that their own research should play a role in such changes. The reasons for this not happening very often have been discussed by Crain (1976); Special Commission on the Social Sciences of the National Science Board (1969); Komarovsky (1975), especially the article by Merton; Cohen and Weiss (1977), and Caplan et al (1975). Lipman-Blumen (1974, and in Chapters 1 and 2) and Tangri (1976) discuss such issues specially in the context of sex role and sex difference research. Since there is ample discussion on why academic research is not useful to policy-makers, we will focus on how it can be.

Janet Weiss (1976) has usefully differentiated three kinds of 'usefulness' that research can have. One is the intrinsic usefulness of studies which are persuasive because they address policy-relevant questions and meet high standards of clarity, consistency, comprehensibility, technical quality, have findings which are statistically and socially significant and convergent with those of similar studies, and which suggest alternatives for action which are consistent with the data. Meeting these criteria, or as many as possible, would maximize the persuasiveness of the research. These standards or criteria are, of course, not new to us and we accept most of them as readily as we do the principles that we learned in our first statistics course. Note, however, two criteria which we do not usually accept or apply to our choice and conduct of research: that it address policy-relevant questions and that it suggest alternatives for action. Typically, our recommendation at the conclusion of a study is that more research is needed. Nonetheless we think most of us would not be adverse to addressing more deliberately policy-relevant questions and suggesting alternatives for action. This seems reasonably consonant with our intuitive sense that research on the psychology of women is — or should be — 'relevant.'

A second kind of 'usefulness' is what Weiss calls 'intellectual' usefulness, that is, research which affects the climate of belief by changing society's understanding of its own functioning. This occurs when research provides a new conceptual framework for looking at social phenomena. Her example is radical behaviorism; we would add psychoanalytic theory and the feminist critique. Another kind of intellectual usefulness creates a shift in focus by interpreting old information in a new light, e.g., by redefining problems as non-problems (e.g., working mothers and 'latchkey' children; homosexuality) or non-problems as problems (e.g., the standard work week; the old boy network). Or it is research which challenges a social myth about the dynamics of a problem by offering a more accurate understanding about how social institutions work. Good examples in our area of interest are Kate Millett's *Sexual Politics* (1969), Phyllis Chesler's *Women and Madness* (1972), and Adrienne Rich's *Of Woman Born* (1976).

Weiss argues that 'social science research which changes social beliefs can have dramatic, although indirect, effects on the policy process' (p. 237), and that 'since intellectual usefulness may be the most interesting and, in the long run, most productive way in which social research is useful to government' that we should not neglect it in favor of the other two. This is hard to argue with, and no doubt each of us would like at least once in our lifetime to make a contribution of new concepts, focus, or framework that makes that kind of difference.

But, if you like to take long shots, let us suggest here her third kind of 'useful' research, which is political usefulness. The factors which make research politically useful are: being available when needed (i.e., the timing is right); communicating what was done, what was found, and what it means in language policy-makers can understand; focusing on variables which policy-makers can do something about; producing findings which suggest action alternatives which are politically and financially feasible; the researcher being perceived as objective by the policy-maker; and the scope of the conclusions being appropriate to the scope of decisons which can be made about the subject (i.e., advocating sweeping social changes ignores the incrementalism of policy-making, just as it ignores the fact that most research is also incremental). In later writings, she includes the extent to which the findings conform to the policy-makers' own views as another important predictor of a study's usefulness (Weiss, 1977). Meeting such criteria will maximize the chances that some government policy-maker will introduce the research in some form into the political debate. Please note the modest objective. Even meeting all these criteria (which is seldom possible in any one piece of research), is not considered likely by itself to change the opinion of any policy-maker.

Also note that there are contradictions between some of the criteria for the three kinds of usefulness. To be persuasive, research should produce findings which are convergent with other similar research, whereas to be intellectually useful, research may well present conclusions quite divergent from accepted wisdom or the "state of the art". Politically useful research should produce conclusions whose scope is practicable, whereas intellectually useful research may produce quite radical and sweeping conclusions.

Two types of research are now in vogue and make fair bid to being the most important kinds of policy-relevant research around. Evaluation research, which tries to measure the extent to which an ongoing program is achieving its objectives, can be used for fiscal oversight purposes, or for analytical purposes to make corrections which will better achieve a program's objective. Thus one might want to evaluate Women's Studies Programs to determine to what extent they enhance women's motivation to stay in school, or to do well; whether they create an active, successful coterie of research scholars, whether they meet the intellectual and social support needs of women students, or reduce instances of sexist bias in classroom teaching — or whatever the original objectives were conceived to be, as well as others now deemed relevant. Evaluation has its own host of methodological and interpretive problems, and discussions of these can be found in Rivlin (1971), and Tavris (1976), etc.

The other is impact evaluation which is prospective rather than post-hoc: it is an attempt to anticipate the outcomes, both intended and unintended, of policy decisions or programs prior to enactment. Pilot testing may be one methodology for this purpose, other approaches are in the nature of forecasting from models or simpler regression equations. Thus one might do research on the probable impact of terminating Medicaid funding for abortions on: 1) illegitimate births; 2) teenage pregnancy; 3) births in different segments of the population; 4) illegal abortions; 5) maternal mortality rates; 6) child abuse, etc. Or one might do research on the impact of trends in workforce participation by mothers on: 1) need for child care; 2) maternal health and welfare; 3) child health and welfare; 4) divorce rates, etc.

Note that these examples begin with a 'problem' or program or anticipation of a problem. This is one basic difference between policy-oriented research and academically-oriented research. Most academic research begins with a theory, concepts or models and the quest is for theoretical progress, not solving social problems. However, it is possible to find policy implications in some of the typical academic research on psychology of women, although beginning with a conceptual variable tends to leave the applicability more problematic. A classic example, we feel, is the research on motive to avoid success.

The initial reception to this research was a terrific 'aha!' experience, a sense of subjective identification with a phenomenon which rang true. The policy implications, though never spelled out, seemed to suggest that recognition of this double-bind that potentially successful women confront would change the climate of opinion and make it more sympathetic to achieving women. Another implication (also not spelled out), was that sex roles and the socialization for them that created the motive were, after all, only human creations and could be changed.

However, the later reaction was more negative in terms of political and policy implications, suggesting that such research tended to place blame for women's non-achievement on themselves and therefore women had to change themselves. Much subsequent work with this variable tended to fuel the latter position because it used fear of success as an independent variable to predict various achievement-related or counter-achievement outcomes.

A different research strategy could have made fear of success (FOS) the dependent variable resulting from various social and institutional arrangements. The policy implications that could be drawn from this research might have dealt with ways to re-arrange such settings in order to minimize development of motive to avoid success and its effects. In the recent issue of *Psychology of Women Quarterly* devoted to achievement motivation, and of *Sex Roles* devoted to FOS research, together totaling 16 articles, not one mentions the possible significance of the research for any social policy. I believe a larger sample of issues would reveal the same thing. That, of course, is not unusual for an academic journal. Both of these issues are excellent examples of the incremental nature of social science. None of the articles attempt a fundamental redefinition or shift in how we think about our society. They are neither 'intellectually useful', as Weiss defines it, nor 'politically useful', nor even 'intrinsically useful', since they fail to meet two of those criteria: addressing policy relevant questions and suggesting alternatives for action.

This does not mean that they have no value. The term 'usefulness' is used in a context of policy-making only. Either the editorial policies screen these kind of articles out, or such articles are seldom submitted to these journals. Certainly 'applied research' does not enjoy the same status as unapplied research.

There are two issues in doing 'politically useful' research with which academic researchers need the most help. One is choosing the research questions, the other is disseminating the research findings. In the first case, although most researchers are resistant to advice on what their research agenda should be, it is very clear that the present collective agenda in academic research on women's issues is pretty removed from policy concerns. Yet, we do want to move beyond talking to ourselves in our own esoteric but comfortable world, and to use our research expertise to address the issues that concern women in a way that policy-makers will listen to but without binding ourselves to *their* research agenda.

Secondly, once a 'useful' piece of research is done, it must be disseminated beyond the academic journals and in a form that makes sense to this 'new' audience. This can be done by an individual researcher in the capacity of an informed citizen, as part of a professional organization with a lobbying arm, or as an expert providing testimony or consultation to policy makers. It can also be done by having the research appropriately targeted, published in periodicals more likely to be read by policy-makers. Some of these roles require very little time, e.g., a phone call to your representative. We often feel, however, that we cannot possibly take on one more role in our already crowded and overcommitted lives. For this reason, a model for an ongoing relationship between activists and researchers developed by the Federation of Organizations for Professional Women is very attractive as it addresses the question of bridging the gap between research and policy without converting researchers to activists (or vice-versa). In *Effecting Social Change for Women*, they write:

> We began...with the erroneous notion that improved dissemination of relevant research results was a key...to utilizing knowledge to effect desired change. We learned...that it is not sufficient to disseminate research findings. Dissemination and understanding do not necessarily result in action. What became apparent is that it is not just a matter of *translating* research into action, but rather it is essential to plan and design the research with specific goals of social change in mind (Brown, et. al., 1976: 27).

Recognizing that there are differences in 'concepts, priorities, timing, approach, assumptions, and starting points' between activists and researchers, they propose that an ongoing exchange between them is essential to 1) produce the needed research, and 2) keep up with the constantly changing 'goals, research, and action strategies required to reach the goals' (p. 31). The model consists of eight action stages beginning with identification of desired social change and call for collective action, through assignment of responsibilities, strategy development sessions, implementation of research and of action agendas, dissemination of results, and identification of new or modified goals. The term activist here refers to persons whose field of action is policy-making.

The role of the activists in this process is to contribute their knowledge of what needs to be done and their understanding of what has been attempted in the past. This perspective helps the researchers consider their research priorities and the possible policy implications of their research.

The role of the researchers is to contribute knowledge of completed and ongoing studies relevant to the targeted problem; their perspective helps the activists frame their questions in research terms; and they can develop research designs which incorporate mechanisms for ongoing evaluation by the activists (p. 18). New questions need to be asked, new paradigms are needed, and doing this may take the researcher outside her original field (p. 29).

The challenge to be useful is a different one from doing clever, careful, theory-derived research. Trying to answer it may even alienate you from your colleagues. It is less likely to have weight in a tenure decision. It is tainted by being timely (and therefore assumed to be 'quick and dirty'). And if your research is done in the capacity of a federal employee, as ours is, you are likely to be accused of having been co-opted. On the other hand, there is the possibility that it will be cited in Congress, presented in testimony, influence the shape of legal guidelines, or — as happened with some work we did not long ago — become part of the conversation between a commissioner and the President.

NOTES

1. Title IX of the Educational Amendments of 1972 prohibits sex discrimination in education institutions receiving federal money.

2. In March 1978, following the expiration of the IWY Commission, President Carter, by Executive Order, established a National Advisory Committee for Women and an Interdepartmental Task Force on Women to implement national policy initiations.

3. For example, Edith R. Conlin, *Legal Status of Homemakers* (n.d.).

4. Of all the administrative assistants listed in the 1972 Congressional Directory, less than 10 percent had never attended college, 13 percent had some college, 41 percent had a BA, 15 percent an MA, 18 percent a law degree, and 2 percent a PhD. The educational level of legislative assistants is even higher (Hammond, 1973: 246). Many of these degrees are in the social sciences.

REFERENCES

BERNARD, J. *Women and the Public Interest.* New York: Adline-Atherton, Inc., 1971.
BERGER, M., 'Desegregation, Law, and Social Science', *Commentary*, 1957, 23, 471-76.
BROWN, J. S., J. LEAR and D. L. SHAVLIK, Effecting Social Change for Women. Washington, DC, Federation of Organizations for Professional Women, October, 1976.
CAPLAN, N., A. MORRISON and R. STAMBAUGH, *The Use of Social Science in Policy Decisions at the National Level.* Ann Arbor, Mich.: Institute for Social Research, 1975.
CHESLER, P., *Women and Madness.* New York: Avon Books, 1969.
CITIZEN'S ADVISORY COUNCIL ON THE STATUS OF WOMEN, *Women in 1975.* **Washington, DC, 1976.**
COHEN, D. K. and L. A. WEISS, 'Social Science and Social Policy: Schools and Race', in C. H. Weiss (ed.), *Using Social Research in Public Policy Making.* Lexington, Mass., D. C. Heath and Co., 1977, pp. 67-83.
COMMISSION ON THE OPERATION OF THE SENATE, *Toward a Modern Senate.* Washington, DC, 1976. (*Modern Senate.*)
CONLIN, R., 'Legal Status of Homemakers Study'. (n.d.).
CRAIN, R. L., 'Why Academic Research Fails to be Useful', *School Review*, May 1976, 337-51.
CRONIN, T. E. and S. D. GREENBERG, *The Presidential Advisory System.* New York: Harper and Row, 1969.
DE TOCQUEVILLE, A., *Democracy in America*, P. Bradley (ed.), New York: Vintage Books, 1961.
DOUGLAS, W. O., 1966: Harper v Virginia State Board of Elections, 383 US 663, 667 (1966). A dissenting opinion.
FRANKFURTER, F., 1957: Ferguson v. Moore-McCormack Line, 352 US 521 (1957). A dissenting opinion.
FREEMAN, J., *The Politics of Women's Liberation.* New York: David McKay, Inc., 1975.
GREEN, M., *Who Runs Congress?* New York: Bantam Books, 1975.
HAMMOND, S., 'Personal Staff of Members of the US House of Representatives'. Unpublished dissertation, Johns Hopkins University, 1973.
HOROWITZ, D. L., *The Courts and Social Policy.* Washington, DC: The Brookings Institution, 1977.
KAHN, L., 'The Dynamics of Scapegoating: The Expulsion of Evil.' *Psychotherapy: Theory, Research and Practice,* in press 1977.
KANTER, R. M., *Social Science Frontiers.* New York: Russell Sage Foundation, 1977.
KOMAROVSKY, M., (ed.), *Sociology and Public Policy: The Case of Presidential Commissions.* New York: American Elsevier, 1975.
KONEFSKY, S. J., *The Legacy of Holmes and Brandeis.* New York: Collier Books, 1961.

LIPMAN-BLUMEN, J., 'The Dialectic Between Social Policy and Research'. Keynote Address, WEAL Conference, December 1974.
LONGAKER, R. P., *The Presidency and Individual Liberties.* Ithaca, N.Y.: Cornell University Press, 1961.
MILLET, K., *Sexual Politics.* New York: Avon Books, 1969.
MOSHER, C., Interview on 18 May 1977.
NATIONAL COMMISSION ON THE OBSERVANCE OF INTERNATIONAL WOMEN'S YEAR, *To Form a More Perfect Union.* Washington, DC, 1976.
ORENSTEIN, N., 'Information, Resources and Legislative Decision-Making: Some Comparative Perspectives On....' Unpublished dissertation, University of Michigan, 1972.
PRESIDENT'S TASK FORCE ON WOMEN'S RIGHTS AND RESPONSIBILITIES, *A Matter of Simple Justice.* Washington, DC, 1970.
REDMAN, E., *The Dance of Legislation.* New York: Simon and Schuster, 1973.
RICH, A., *Of Woman Born.* New York: W. W. Norton and Co., 1976.
RIVLIN, A., *Systematic Thinking for Social Action.* Washington, DC: The Brookings Institution, 1971.
ROSEN, P. L., *The Supreme Court and Social Science.* Chiacgo, Ill.: The University of Illinois Press, 1972.
SANDLER, B., Interview on 28 May 1977.
SPECIAL COMMISSION ON THE SOCIAL SCIENCES OF THE NATIONAL SCIENCE BOARD, NSF. *Knowledge Into Action: Improving the Nation's Use of the Social Sciences,* Washington, DC, 1969.
SPECIAL SUBCOMMITTEE ON EDUCATION OF THE COMMITTEE ON EDUCATION AND LABOUR OF THE HOUSE OF REPRESENTATIVES, *Discrimination Against Women,* Sec 805 of HR 16098, Washington, DC, 1971.
TANGRI, S., 'Using Sex Role Research to Guide Public Policy'. Paper presented at Russell Sage College Conference on Sex Roles in American Society, May 1976.
TAVRIS, C., 'Compensatory Education. The Glass is Half Full', *Psychology Today,* Sept. 1976, 63-74.
WEISS, C. (ed.), *Using Social Research in Public Policy Making.* Lexington, Mass.: D. C. Heath and Co., 1977.
WEISS, J., 'Using Social Science for Social Policy', *Policy Studies Journal,* Spring 1976, Vol. 4 (3), 234-38.
WHITE, B., 1972: Miranda v. Arizona 384 US 436 (1966) A dissenting opinion.
WOLFE, E., 'Classrooms and Courtrooms'. Paper presented at the National Institute of Education, Conference on Education, Social Science and the Judicial Process, Washington, DC, February 1976.

4

DEMOGRAPHIC INDICATORS OF THE STATUS OF WOMEN IN VARIOUS SOCIETIES

Nadia H. Youssef
University of Southern California, USA and
Shirley Foster Hartley
California State University, Hayward, USA

Youssef and Hartley examine the policy-relevant research on the reproductive and productive roles of women in eighty countries and, on the basis of a number of demographic indicators, make available to policy makers the relationship between the status of women and the economic level of the countries. They analyze literacy rates, enrollment trends, educational levels, marriage rates, age at marriage, and fertility behavior of women. In addition, Youssef and Hartley examine various aspects of women's labor force participation and spell out the policy implications of the relationships among all of these variables. Youssef and Hartley do not claim that all policy-makers everywhere are amenable to persuasion by such research, but they believe it is an obligation of researchers to clarify the implications of demographic trends for policies that influence the status of women.

In recent years there have been a variety of articles and research papers on the status of women and its implication for fertility levels, labor force participation and so on. Much of what has been presented, however, is fragmentary, either in terms of a few pertinent variables or in limited geographical or cultural segments: nations, states, cities or sub-groups within. Gradually over the last two decades, data for the less developed countries of the world have been added to that of the statistically advanced nations. This had made it possible to obtain and compare systematically quantitative statements which are indicative of the status and position occupied by women in almost all parts of the world.

We offer this work as an example of social research that is policy-relevant. We believe that at least some decision-makers are attentive to factual data as they relate to the various theoretical and rhetorical issues held by advocates of specific social legislation, implementation, or enforcement. Social scientists have a significant service to perform in the gathering, organizing and analysis of pertinent information. Those who create and carry out social policy need to understand, as the following will demonstrate, the interrelatedness of education, age at marriage, childbearing, and the labor force contributions of women.

In this chapter we shall (1) examine the range of variation in quantitative measures of the status of women available for 80 countries; (2) review the interrelationships among these indicators; and (3) examine social policy implications for some of these variables. Information for this research has been obtained primarily from United Nations publications, specifically the Demographic Yearbooks, the International Labor Office Statistical Yearbooks and the UNESCO Yearbooks, covering the mid-1960s to early 1970s. In certain instances we have had to resort to national censuses as well. Caution must be used in examining these data, since the information is subject to idiosyncracies in definition and in internal methods of collection. In most countries data gathering methods are still being perfected, and in none do we expect absolute accuracy. As with most sociological measurement, these are 'indicators' of underlying behavioral variety in human group life.

WOMEN'S STATUS: THE THEORETICAL ISSUES

Researchers face a particularly difficult problem in trying to define and measure the status of women on a cross-cultural basis. One reason for this is that the subject matter has been stripped of its theoretical guidelines. The ethnocentric evolutionary model which has associated the equalization of the sexes with industrial-economic development has been challenged by contradictions between the 'ideology' of egalitarianism and the empirical reality. In highly competitive industrial systems in which major sources of power and prestige are derived from achievement-based attributes, women have been denied equal access in the competition for highest educational, occupational and income opportunities (Knudsen, 1969; Van den Berghe, 1973; Wilber, 1975).

Working with a set of countries located at different developmental levels, Safilios-Rothschild has demonstrated an inverse relationship between industrialization and female emancipation. Specifically, she concluded that (a) it is in countries at *medium* levels of economic development where women are provided with the greatest opportunity to work, to work after marriage and to enroll in college; (b) it is in the *least* advanced economies where greatest opportunities are available for women to compete with men in professional employment and where women often comprise an impressive ratio of all professional workers (Safilios-Rothschild, 1971: 96). As to the role of modernization in the developing world, it recently has been argued that the flow of Western cultural values into parts of Africa often has negatively restructured sex roles. The influx of Western values actually has been shown to depress the status accorded to African women in the traditional setting, by pushing women toward greater dependency on men (Van Allen, 1974: 60-67).

Such conflicting findings have created a theoretical vacuum. The current search for a new orientation attempts to find a golden mean between evolutionary-economic determinism and cultural relativism. We believe that both theoretical and policy discussions require measurement and analysis of female status on a cross-cultural basis, recognizing that there is no current consensus on an operational definition to replace subjective definitions of 'high' or 'low' status. Our bias is in the direction of valuing human choice among recognized alternatives. The indicators available for 80 countries reflect the extent to which women continue to fulfill the traditional functions of marriage and childbearing and/or the degree to which they have gained access to educational and occupational resources that facilitate choices in other areas of their lives.

HISTORICAL PATTERNS

The low status of women and the scarcity of options available to them have been historically related to the very high death rates prevalent in the world until about 1800. The average ages at death then were nowhere much higher than 35 years, and it was only about 20 years of age in the most primitive societies. Even as late as 1920 in India the average age at death was only 20. This means that all surviving groups had to have high fertility ideals and performance in order to balance high mortality. Survival of human group life, therefore, depended upon the reproductive potential of women.

Today life expectancy has shown unprecedented improvement, doubling the average number of years lived in most parts of the world, with the result that most societies are now faced with dangers of overpopulation, rather than biological extinction. The issue now is whether or not the revolutionary change in death rates has been accompanied by corresponding modifications in women's traditionally ascribed roles. Given that it is no longer necessary (and is dysfunctional for the biosphere) for women to spend most of their adult years bearing and suckling their offspring (see figure 1), to what extent are they participating in institutional alternatives to their traditional functions?

Figure 1. Average Proportion of a Lifetime Devoted to Childbearing in the Life of a Woman.
Less Developed vs. More Developed Nations

Less Developed Countries, one-third to one-half average lifetime

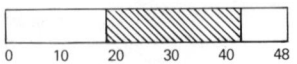

More Developed Countries, one-seventh average lifetime

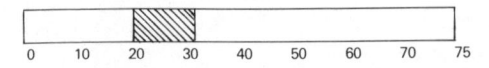

Adapted from Sullerot, 1971:75

THE TRADITIONAL ROLE: MARRIAGE AND CHILDBEARING

There are two basic cross-national indicators of female nuptiality patterns: (1) the proportion of women reported as 'currently' or ever-married by the end of the reproductive period (ages 45 to 49), and (2) the timing of marriage, reflected in approximate terms by the proportion of women aged 15 to 24 reporting themselves single or married at census time. (See Appendix, Table 1.)

The Universality of Marriage

Most of the countries of sub-Saharan Africa, Asia and the Islamic world show an amazing facility for marrying off their women: between 98 and 100 percent are married before age 49. A second group of countries report 90 to 97 percent of their women married; these include the United States, the Socialist bloc, Western Europe and Israel.

Singlehood becomes more frequent among women in Northwestern Europe and in the southern or Mediterranean countries. Paradoxically, nuptiality is at its lowest (70 to 85 percent wed) in ideologically conservative Latin America where the traditional, confined-woman culture is idealized. In Jamaica, an extreme case, only 60 percent of all women aged 45 to 49 report themselves ever-married at census time. It would appear from detailed national studies that women in countries at either extreme of marital patterns have little choice in their marital fate (see Hartley, 1975, 1978).

The Timing of Marriage

Statistics suggest that the more universal is marriage within a society the younger is the nuptiality age. This is true for the African, Asian and Muslim women among whom 75 to 90 percent of those between the ages 15 and 24 are already married.

For the majority of countries in the world, the percentage of women between the ages 15 and 24 reported married ranges between 25 and 50. This pattern is typical for women in most of Latin America, Northwest Europe, Western nations in general and the Socialist bloc. Women marry much later, however in Chile, Greece, France, West Germany,

Sweden, Italy, Portugal and Norway where only 20 to 25 percent of the 15 to 24 year olds are married. In Japan, Yugoslavia, Ireland, Switzerland and Spain, only about 10 percent of women of the early ages are married, suggesting an average nuptiality age in the late twenties.

Childbearing

The fertility of a woman is universally recognized as one of the most important determinants of her status. In many cultures of the world, motherhood has been the sine qua non of womanhood. The young girl validates her worth by producing children, preferably male children. The older wife has received praise and respect in the repeated process of childbearing and childrearing. Boserup (1970: 212) notes that propaganda for birth control often cancels the primary basis of prestige for women and requires, therefore, profound changes in educational and labor force opportunities for 'the second sex'. It should be evident from Figure 1 that in the less developed lands today (as historically in the world) from one-third to one-half of the entire lifetime and almost all of the adult years of women are spent in childbearing and rearing, while in the advanced countries less than one-seventh of the average lifetime of women is spent bearing children. Although all societies have had some primitive means of birth control, today there are the complete means of fertility control wherever knowledge, availability, and motivation are all present. The wide variation in actual use of fertility controls may be inferred from a variety of indices.

The crude birth rate is the most widely available indicator of fertility. It represents the number of births in a given year per thousand persons in the population. Contemporary crude birth rates range from a low of 13 or 14 in Sweden, Finland, Hungary and Belgium to a high of 50 and more in a number of African countries and Pakistan. The less developed nations tend, in fact, to maintain rates 2½ to 3½ times greater than the more developed nations. Yet, because the crude rate uses the total population as its denominator, odd age distributions may distort the comparisons we are interested in examining.

The general fertility rate is the number of births per thousand women aged 10 to 49. For the years 1960 to 1968, these ranged from 50.3 in Hungary to 263.1 in Tunisia. The proportion of women of appropriate ages actually giving birth was five times higher in Tunisia than in

Hungary, Czechoslovakia or Poland; that means that in a given year from one in twenty to one in every four women gave birth to a child.

Age-specific fertility rates show even greater variation from one nation to another. Women aged 25 to 29 are the most prolific childbearers world-wide. Contrasting the numbers of births per thousand women of specific age groups in Sweden and in Venezuela as in Figure 2 gives a visual image of the potential for variation. It should be noticed that even at the relatively late age of 35 to 39, the proportion of women in Venezuela giving birth is higher than at the peak ages in Sweden. Nor do these two countries represent the extremes. The 10 to 19 year old age group presents the greatest contrast, with a range from 2.6 births in Japan to 196.9 in Dahomey. Five countries reported fewer than 10 and five countries over 100 births per thousand young women aged 10 to 19. (See Appendix, Table 2.)

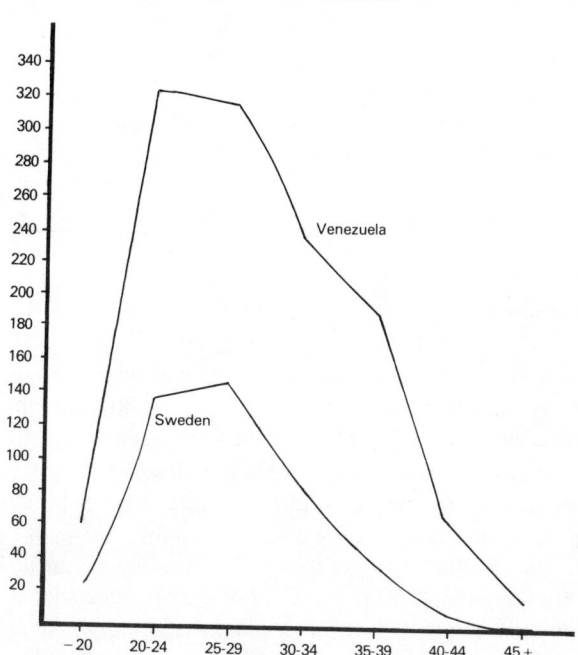

Figure 2. Age Specific Fertility Rates of Venezuela as Compared to those of Sweden.

Source: United Nations, *Demographic Yearbook, 1969* (New York: United Nations, 1970) Table 15

Nonmarital fertility serves as another indicator of the status of women. Births outside of socially and/or legally defined family units tend to imply that the father is unwilling to make a long-term commitment to the woman and his own offspring. (That poverty is not the cause is clear from the impoverished families of Asia, the Orient and the Middle East.) Childbearing out of wedlock is almost universally more limiting for the woman than for the man. Disadvantages for the child and the larger social group have led all societies to prefer the 'principle of legitimacy' — the designation of a sociological father for the long term care of children. Social groups have developed a myriad of means of discouraging births out of wedlock which nevertheless range from 0.0 to 74 percent of all births (Hartley, 1975).

RESOURCES THAT FACILITATE CHOICES: EDUCATION AND WORK

We have used or computed several different indicators of past and present educational attainment for women of the world: the female literacy rate in absolute and relative terms, the median years of schooling for women aged 25 and over, and the current female enrollment figures in secondary and higher educational programs as a proportion of the total student body. (See Appendix, Tables 3 and 4.)

Literacy Rates

Providing women with the minimum opportunity for enlightenment is reflected in the proportion of females in each society who can read and write. Unfortunately, such a 'skill' has been attained only by a limited segment of the world's women. Although almost all women as well as men in the highly industrialized nations are literate, in Latin America only 40 to 60 percent of the women claim to be able to read and write. The literacy rate of Asian women, in all but India, varies between 35 and 55 percent, while in Islamic societies and India the proportion of women who are said to read and write ranged from 6 to 15 percent. African countries report from two to ten women per hundred as literate. Even these low rates may overestimate functional literacy, since in many places the ability to write one's name qualifies for the literacy label. It may be supposed that these low levels merely reflect the educational deficiencies of the poorer nations. To what extent is discrimination against women implied?

The female/male ratio in literacy gives the number of women who are literate for every 100 literate males. Sex differentials in favor of the male are found to be most blatant in the Islamic nations and sub-Saharan Africa where there are two, three or four literate males to every female able to read and write. In Latin America the ratios, ranging from 80 to 99 per 100, run as high as those reported by the Socialist bloc and the Mediterranean countries.

Median Educational Attainment

The years of formal education reported for adult women aged 25 and over reflect the history of past educational priorities. The highest median of education recorded in the 1960s was 10.7 years for the United States, with England and Canada following with nine to ten years as the reported median. The European, including Socialist countries reported median years of female education at 3.1 to 4.7 years, with only a few higher reports.

Differences among Latin American women were striking. For example, in Uruguay, Argentina and Jamaica, the median education approximated 7 years, but in Nicaragua, Colombia, Ecuador and Paraguay the median of 1 to 2.6 years was only slightly higher than the corresponding median reported for African, Asian and Muslim women. Since a minimum of 5 years of schooling is judged necessary for long-term retention of literacy skills, most of the adult women of the world are condemned to functional illiteracy. Unless there is a dramatic turn to adult education programs (suggested by Myrdal, 1970), women in the less developed countries will continue to be excluded from the modern world.

Current Female Enrollment Trends

Current data on secondary school enrollments suggest that substantial improvements appear to have taken place. In all but the African-Asian context secondary education has become more equalitarian. In more than 40 of the 80 countries covered in this study, women comprise between 45 and 55 percent of the currently enrolled student body. In Africa, the Islamic countries and in Asia, there are two to three boys for every girl in second level schools. In India, Pakistan, Liberia and Syria, girls were only one in five students and in Mali, Nepal, and Libya, they comprised one in seven.

At university levels, the world-wide picture is not encouraging for women, although the situation certainly has improved in some areas over time. In the largest number of countries, from every continent, there are two or three males to each female registered. Women have the greatest opportunities for university education in the socialist nations, France, the United States, Israel, and most Latin American countries, while, in the Afro-Asian nations, only one in five to ten university students is a woman.

Employment Outside the Home or Farm

Throughout history women have worked; yet, unless they have the opportunity to work for pay, they remain as dependent as children on others for support. We will review several indicators of the position women occupy in the world of work. (See Appendix, Table 5.)

The activity rate is the percentage of all adult women who are working in the non-agricultural labor force. It is assumed to reflect at least minimal wage and salary earnings and the possibility of independence. In the 1960s, female employment was at its maximum in Jamaica, England, Scotland, and Finland, where approximately 40 to 42 percent of all women aged 15 and above were working in non-agricultural employment. Other Northern and Western European countries, Japan, and the United States follow. Female non-agricultural employment is considerably lower in Southern Europe and all of Latin America, typically between 15 and 25 percent of adult women. As for the African, Muslim, Indian and Nepali women, they are practically excluded from non-agricultural occupations, with only two to eight percent participating.

The female ratio is the percentage of workers who are women. It indicates that the relative contribution of women to economic production is greatest in Hungary, Finland, and El Salvador, where women comprise 42 to 44 percent of the entire work force. In the majority of industrialized nations and almost all of Latin America, the female ratio ranges between one-fourth and one-third of the total number of non-agricultural workers. Women's relative contribution declines in the

Mediterranean countries, in the Netherlands, and Venezuela, where the female ratio has been as low as in traditional India, Nepal, and Taiwan (between 20 and 25 percent). Women are virtually dispensable in African and Islamic non-agricultural productivity, comprising only six percent of the workers.

On the issue of whether women are distributed on a par with males in positions of power, authority and prestige in the occupational world, it is clear that equality is nowhere to be found. Although women often comprise 30 to 60 percent of the 'professional' category, they are consistently filling the teaching, nursing, social service functions, not the highest positions of power, prestige and pay.

The lowest level unskilled jobs in the world continue to be 'manned' by women. Of the 80 countries examined, 21 report the female ratio in lowest level occupations to be 75 percent, 17 others report it to be 66 percent and 10 more report that over 55 percent of the lowest jobs are filled by women who are a minority of the paid labor force. However, in the Islamic nations even low level domestic jobs are ceded to men, because of the strict seclusion and exclusion of women.

To summarize, these indicators imply:

1. Important similarities in female behavior in the United States, Canada, Australia and New Zealand and the Socialist bloc of countries.

2. Frequent dissimilarities in women's options between Southern and Northwest European countries. The former tend to be more traditionally oriented; the latter attempt to follow standard behavior patterns set by the United States, Canada, Australia, New Zealand and the Socialist bloc.

3. Dissimilarities among this very large number of countries are found to be greatest for different levels of industrialization, rather than by Western vs. Socialist bloc economic ideology.

4. Among non-Western women, uniformity in female behavior between Islamic, North African and Middle Eastern societies, India, Cambodia, and Nepal contrasts with the patterns displayed by women in other non-Islamic Asian societies.

5. Striking inconsistencies are apparent with respect to the options available to women in Latin American society, where female behavioral patterns coincide with both extremes of the highly industrialized Western nations in some aspects, and with non-Western traditional settings, in others.

CORRELATIONAL ANALYSIS

Having reviewed the incredibly wide range of variation in indicators of the status of women, it is important to observe the interrelationships among these measures. Most of the correlations reported in Table 1 had been hypothesized in detail in our initial formulations and many are extensions or confirmations of earlier research. In some cases, the correlations were not as high as had been anticipated, e.g., the relationship between age at marriage and the proportion of women aged 45 to 49 who were reported as ever-married. In other cases, the correlations were higher than anticipated (e.g., the series of correlates of female illiteracy). Some comparative r's were unanticipated (e.g., that the crude birth rate was more powerfully related than the general or age-specific fertility rates to female illiteracy and low Gross National Product was surprising). Finally, some correlations were of interest, because they were relatively new measures (e.g., the female to male ratio of illiteracy indicates that relative equality in proportion literate was strongly related to higher ages at marriage, less universal marriage for women, greater female participation in the paid labor force, per capita GNP, and, of course, negatively related to fertility). Current ratios of females in secondary and higher education were less powerfully correlated than this indication of prior imbalance in educational opportunities.

Because of the high intercorrelations and circularity involved in causal analysis, multiple regression analysis was not appropriate to these data. It may be of interest to note, however, that if we assume GNP to be the dependent variable, the proportion of women illiterate, the age of women at marriage, and crude birth rate explain 62 percent of the variation in the per capita productivity of nations.

THE USE OF DEMOGRAPHIC INDICATORS IN SOCIAL POLICY FORMULATION

Social research and analysis in the area of our discussion allow decision-makers a better grasp of what people actually do — in marriage, child-bearing and family planning, etc. — in comparison to what they say. Research permits an understanding of the disparity between actual behavior and what legislatures, law, and religious doctrine decree. The

TABLE 1
Correlational Matrix

	MARRIAGE		EDUCATION				FERTILITY						NON-AGRICULTURAL WORK PARTICIPATION			
	% Single 15-24	% Ever Married 45-49	Illiteracy Fem.Rate	F/M Ratio	Ratio Female/Enrollment Second.	Univ.	CBR	GFR	Age-Spec. Rate 10-19	35-39	Illegitimacy Rate	Ratio	Activity Rate	Ratio Fem/Labor Force	Ratio Fem/Professional	GNP per Capita
MARRIAGE																
% Women Single 15-24	1.0															
% Women Ever Married 45-49	−0.54	1.0														
EDUCATION																
Female Illiteracy Rate	−0.70	0.40	1.0													
Female/Male Illiteracy Ratio	0.74	−0.61	−0.86	1.0												
Ratio Female Second.Enrollment	0.73	−0.57	−0.81	0.87	1.0											
Ratio Female Univ. Enrollment	0.53	−0.27	−0.61	0.55	0.71	1.0										
FERTILITY																
Crude Birth Rate (CBR)	−0.62	0.12**	0.81	−0.73	−0.66	−0.55	1.0									
Gen. Fertility Rate (GFR)	−0.33	−0.22	0.74	−0.45	−0.43	−0.41	0.78	1.0								
Age-Specific Rate 10-19	−0.46	−0.11**	0.65	−0.36*	−0.34*	−0.30	0.59	0.74	1.0							
Age-Specific Rate 35-39	−0.22**	−0.21**	0.68	−0.45	−0.40	−0.38	0.78	0.89	0.49	1.0						
Child/Woman Ratio (Ch/W)	−0.52	0.02**	0.58	−0.58	−0.51	−0.44	0.85	0.76	0.49	0.78						
Gross Reproduction Rate (GRR)	−0.59	0.08**	0.79	−0.73	−0.64	−0.52	0.95	0.85	0.57	0.86						
Illegitimacy Rate	−0.17**	−0.66	0.58	−0.29**	−0.004**	−0.116**	0.81	0.81	0.86	0.69	1.0					
Illegitimacy Ratio	0.02**	−0.75	0.34	0.04**	0.17**	−0.02**	0.57	0.58	0.81	0.49	0.93	1.0				
NON-AGRIC. WORK PARTICIPATION																
Activity Rate	0.60	−0.35	−0.83	0.76	0.49	−0.76	−0.47	−0.28	−0.60	−0.44	−0.21**	1.0				
Ratio Female of Labor Force	0.55	−0.50	−0.68	0.73	0.40	−0.50	−0.21**	−0.083**	0.23**	−0.08**	0.16**	0.78	1.0			
Ratio Female of Professionals	0.60	−0.68	−0.63	0.81	0.64	−0.37	−0.32	.06**	0.2**	0.22**	0.42	0.57	0.72	1.0		
GROSS NATIONAL PRODUCT/CAPITA	0.47	−0.09**	−0.67	0.60	0.50	0.32	−0.78	−0.62	−0.42	−0.65	−0.53	−0.40	0.72	0.40	0.2**	1.0

+ unless noted by asterisks all correlations are significant at the .001 level.
* .001 < sig. < .051
** not statistically significant

use of these specific current data gives planners an idea of how their nation compares with others at similar or different levels of development. Indeed, the data allow a check on past progress toward national goals. Finally, these sorts of data allow policy makers to set realistic improvement goals and to check progress toward them.

Since we have been focusing on cross-national indicators of the status of women, questions of social policy formulation need to be approached in the same perspective. Although there may be vast and irreconcilable differences in the detailed and specific goals of social planners from one nation to another, particularly in terms of facilitating individual choice or requiring that individualism be subordinated to the 'general will', one of the most universally held values among national leaders is the improvement of the quality of life. The demographic indicators we have just examined have a massive contribution to make to our understanding of the possible mechanisms for improving human life on earth.

We have just seen that the higher the illiteracy of women, the higher is the birth rate, the lower the contribution of women to the labor force and the productivity of the nation, and the lower the per capita Gross National Product. One conclusion that may be reached is that the quality of life is enhanced for all persons in society when it is enhanced for women.

The impact of education may be seen most clearly, since it occurs prior to whatever else happens to adult women. The upgrading of education for women should be seen as a necessary means to an end — national growth and development — as well as en end in itself. More specifically, the following issues represent important policy considerations:

1. Whether the education of females is specifically directed toward domestic skills, child care and nutrition or is more general, the health and well-being of husbands, children and the nation are improved. Just recently, for instance, it has become obvious that among those countries at the lowest educational levels, mortality, especially infant mortality, has not continued its expected decline. Social research has shown that in many areas of Asia and Africa, poor, illiterate farm mothers have switched from breast feeding to bottle feeding in imitation of the more well-to-do in their own countries. Not only do they spend money they cannot afford for infant formula, but they do not understand the importance of or have the facilities to sterilize the mix. Often they suppose they will stretch the formula by adding more

water. Infants thus suffer from diluted nutrition and from disease organisms little understood by uneducated mothers. Husbands and remaining family members might have increased energy from a more balanced diet. Yet illiterate women can hardly be expected to maximize the nutritional value of food preparations.

2. Educational curricula should be revised in order to accelerate and diversify the educational and vocational training of women and girls in order to: (a) prepare women for full participation in the productive life of their countries, (b) eliminate sex labeling of occupational fields as exclusively appropriate for males or females, and (c) ensure that the content of the curricula is relevant to national production needs and priorities and to the realistic employability of women (Youssef, in Tinker and Bramsen, 1976).

3. As the education of women improves, fertility declines. Wife's education is far more important in this respect than husband's education. There are advantages to the smaller family and to the nation in limiting the rate of population growth. The family itself has fewer persons for the subdivision of food, income, land inheritance, etc. Women have more energy to devote to fewer persons and may find extra income for the family in freed time. Finally, policy planners have fewer children in the next generation to provide with education, health services, jobs, housing, etc.

4. Education directly facilitates the productive employment of women in the paid labor force. Their contribution is felt in a higher income and standard of living for the family, in higher national productivity reflected in an increase in GNP. The increase in tax revenue also allows an expansion of governmental services.

5. Not only is female literacy and educational level importantly related to the quality of life, but the ratio of female to male literacy indicates that the more *equal* the education (at low or high levels) of men and women, the higher the female participation in the paid labor force and the higher the GNP per capita. By itself this argues for a more equal distribution of whatever educational effort is being made.

With regard to marital status, age at marriage, and the interaction of these variables and variation in educational patterns, policy implications of these data again point to the importance of education for women:

1. The more equal the level of literacy and the male/female enrollment in secondary schools, the higher the age at marriage and the

more likely that some women may be allowed to choose not to marry.

2. Many national governments have tried to raise the legal minimum age at marriage with little real effect on village patterns. It may be that a new priority to equalize education could accomplish what legalistic pronouncements could not.

3. The effect of heavy rural to urban migrations has upset traditional marriage patterns and often has aggravated the exploitation of women. Single women or those deserted by migrant husbands often have found nothing but prostitution awaiting in the urban slum. Low levels of education and a lack of economic opportunities in rural or urban areas make them marginal persons. Women need possibilities for useful employment even if at a low wage, in both rural and urban settings.

Fertility and fertility control still may be among the most difficult areas for policy formulations. It is clear that people do not want to feel coerced into limiting the size of family. The recent election in India provided a message for those who would zealously limit the number of offspring per family. Yet again, education holds out some hope that people will see the long-run problems in each family trying to maximize its own advantage at the expense of the common good.

1. When women's participation in the process of development is seen as a means of increasing real per capita income over time, and when the struggle for development is a race between capital accumulation and population growth, high fertility becomes a major obstacle to the improvement of living standards.

2. It is likely that since most of the people of the world have been socialized to think in terms of women's reproductive role rather than in terms of their strictly productive contribution to the social group, these latent ideals will remain a powerful determinant of policy formation. Planners need to be reminded, therefore, that one-half of the productive talent of a nation is lost if women are not contributing directly to the welfare of the society.

3. Because of the lack of provisions for old age in many countries, the desire of women for several sons (so that at least one will provide security) is often even greater than the husbands' desire for male offspring (Williamson, 1976). With the several daughters born while trying to produce sons, the numbers of children actually wanted could double or triple the population of parents within one generation in some countries or rural communities. These numerous births sap the energy of women, restrict their future options, and deprive the society of their contribution to the whole.

With regard to women's participation in the paid labor force:

1. It should be recognized that freedom of choice in roles is possible for, at best, an elite and small minority of women from the upper socioeconomic brackets. The vast majority of women (like men) seek paid employment outside the home to economically support or improve the level of living for themselves and their families.

2. The employment of women on a wider scale would increase not only productivity but also purchasing power.

3. Planners need to be aware of the possibility that modernization may increase sex role stereotyping. It may mean that opportunities for male earnings outside of the home industry are increased while those for women are curtailed. Women, therefore, should be included in all training programs that take advantage of new machinery. Although it is often supposed that women are too delicate to run tractors, they are 'allowed' to do the more difficult stoop labor and hoeing. They are typically excluded from training programs in the building trades, yet they work in heavy construction throughout northern India.

4. Planners must consider that among employed persons, women have a more difficult time separating themselves from their other key roles of wife, mother, and homemaker than do men in separating themselves from the father role. Some policy considerations, therefore, need to be made for adjustment between women's family roles and the contribution they make to national goals. Some facilities for child care need to be included in overall planning.

5. A climate of social acceptance of the working wife-mother must also be fostered, if women are to be encouraged to make their contribution to the overall upgrading of the quality of life.

6. Part-time employment has both positive and negative aspects to be evaluated. Although it allows women to combine motherhood and work roles, it tends to keep wages low, lessens commitment among women to their occupational roles, fails to provide the same social security benefits as full-time employment, and fails to yield the desired lower fertility level among the married.

7. As societies mature, planners may find it as acceptable to grant maternity and childrearing leaves of absence with job security for women as they have given military leaves to men.

8. In all cases we have assumed that work for pay means equal pay for equal work, opportunities for women as for men to advance, and some control over the payment for work completed. Policy formulations will need to include legal guarantees in ownership and control of

property, inheritance, etc. for women as well as men.

9. Finally, it is hoped that social policy formulations will be examined and determined by groups that include women as policy-makers.

That social research in general and these types of data in particular are useful to policy formulations is evident from our review. We take it as self-evident that those who make social policy also attempt to educate the public about the issues under consideration. Social research data are again useful in the educational campaign to advance the position of women and men around the world in the quest for an improved quality of life for all.

REFERENCES

BLAKE, Judith and Kingsley DAVIS, 'Norms, Values and Sanctions', in E. Faris (ed.), *Handbook of Modern Sociology*. Chicago: Rand McNally, 1964.

BOSERUP, Esther, *Woman's Role in Economic Development*. New York: St Martin's Press, 1970.

GOLDBERG, Steven, *The Inevitability of Patriarchy*. New York: William Morrow, 1973.

HARTLEY, Shirley Foster, *Illegitimacy*. Berkeley: University of California Press, 1975.

HARTLEY, Shirley Foster, 'American Women as a "Minority"', *International Journal of Women's Studies*, 1, 2, 1978.

INTERNATIONAL LABOR OFFICE, *Yearbook of Labor Statistics*. Geneva: United Nations, annual editions.

KNUDSEN, Dean, 'The Declining Status of Women: Popular Myths and Failure of Functionalist Thought,' *Social Forces*, 48(2), 1969.

MYRDAL, Gunnar, *The Challenge of World Poverty*. New York: Random House, 1970.

REPUBLIC OF CHINA, *1972 Taiwan Demographic Fact Book*. Taiwan: Ministry of Interior.

SAFILIOS-ROTHSCHILD, Constantina, 'Toward a Cross-Cultural Conceptualization of Family Modernity,' *Journal of Comparative Family Studies*. Vol. I(1), 1970.

SAFILIOS-ROTHSCHILD, Constantina, 'A Cross-Cultural Examination of Woman's Marital, Educational and Occupational Options,' *Acta Sociologica*, 14 (1971): 96-113.

SULLEROT, Evelyne, *Women, Society and Change*. World University Library, 1971.

TINKER, Irene and M. B. BRAMSON (eds.), *Women and World Development.* Overseas Development Council, 1976.

UNITED NATIONS EDUCATIONAL, SOCIAL AND CULTURAL ORGANIZATION, *Statistical Yearbook.* Paris: United Nations, annual editions.

UNITED NATIONS ECONOMIC AND SOCIAL COUNCIL, *Commission on Status of Women* Addendum. Doc. 3/CN. 6/575/ Add. 3. New York: United Nations, 1973.

UNITED NATIONS, *Demographic Yearbook.* New York: United Nations, annual editions.

UNITED NATIONS, *Statistical Yearbook.* New York: United Nations, annual editions.

VAN ALLEN, Judith, 'Women in Africa: Modernization Means More Dependency,' *The Center Magazine* VII(3), 1974.

VAN DEN BERGHE, Pierre, *Age and Sex in Human Societies: A Bio-Social Perspective.* California: Wadsworth Publishing Company, 1973.

WILBER, George, 'Occupational Achievement.' Chapter 4 of a report for the Manpower Administration from the Public Use Sample of the 1970 Census. Lexington, Kentucky: Social Welfare Research Institute of the University, 1975.

WILLIAMSON, Nancy, *Sons or Daughters.* Beverly Hills: Sage Publications, 1976.

YOUSSEF, Nadia, 'Cultural Ideals, Feminine Behavior and Kinship Control,' *Comparative Studies in Society and History,* 15(3), 1973.

YOUSSEF, Nadia, *Women and Work in Developing Societies.* University of California, Berkeley: Institute of International Studies, 1974.

APPENDIX

TABLE 1

The quantity and timing of female nuptiality in the world

Country	Percent females 45-49 'ever married'	Percent females 15-24 'single'
Dahomey	99.6	16.5
Congo	99.5	25.7
Mali	99.5	11.6
India	99.5	17.1
Nepal	99.5	15.2
Libya	99.3	13.9
Iran	99.3	35.1
Pakistan	99.2	15.9
Taiwan	99.2	28.3
Algeria	98.9	34.8
Egypt	98.9	43.5
Turkey	98.6	46.8
Albania	98.5	51.9
Indonesia	98.5	37.2
Bulgaria	98.1	55.9
Liberia	98.0	26.8
Morocco	97.9	22.7
Tunisia	97.9	57.0
Burma	97.9	47.2
Japan	97.9	84.5
Kenya	97.8	34.1
Thailand	97.7	62.7
Syria	97.4	18.7
Mozambique	97.3	47.2
Israel	97.1	69.9
Jordan	97.1	52.1
Madagascar	97.0	44.9
Iraq	97.0	49.8
Rumania	96.1	54.2
Cambodia	95.9	59.5
Zambia	95.7	n.a.
Ceylon	95.6	n.a.
S. Africa (colored)	95.2	68.3
United States	94.6	67.5
Greece	94.4	78.5
Puerto Rico	94.2	64.3
Hungary	94.1	62.3
Yugoslavia	94.1	84.3

Table 1, *continued*

Country	Percent females 45-49 'ever married'	Percent females 15-24 'single'
Czechoslovakia	94.0	65.2
Angola	93.3	32.9
Australia	92.5	**68.7**
Mexico	91.4	60.7
Denmark	91.1	67.7
France	91.1	77.6
Canada	90.9	71.0
West Germany	90.9	74.8
Belgium	90.6	19.7
Poland	90.6	19.7
New Zealand	90.6	64.8
Netherlands	90.5	64.8
United Kingdom	90.2	65.6
Sweden	90.0	75.9
Bolivia	89.2	66.0
Austria	88.6	68.8
Luxembourg	88.0	70.0
Brazil	87.2	30.8
Italy	86.8	77.5
Scotland	86.4	68.3
Argentina	86.2	73.1
Finland	86.1	74.4
Spain	86.0	85.8
Peru	85.5	65.5
Uruguay	85.5	**42.5**
Ecuador	84.7	61.3
Portugal	84.6	77.1
Guatemala	84.1	52.7
Switzerland	84.0	82.2
Norway	83.0	75.1
Iceland	83.3	72.8
Costa Rica	82.6	66.5
Chile	81.3	76.9
Columbia	80.3	67.5
Ireland	79.4	82.4
Nicaragua	78.3	58.6
Honduras	71.7	59.2
El Salvador	71.1	62.1
Panama	71.1	61.8
Paraguay	70.9	72.8
Venezuela	70.2	59.4
Jamaica	59.5	93.7

Source: United Nations, *Demographic Yearbook 1968* (New York: United Nations, 1969), Table 7.

TABLE 2 Fertility Measures for Countries in the World (c 1960)

Countries	Crude Birth Rate	General Fert. rate	Age spec. rates 10-19	Age spec. rates 35-39	Gross Reproduction Rate	Child/Woman Ratio	Illegitimacy Rate	Illegitimacy Ratio
Low fertility								
W. Germany	12	—	—	—	—	327	13.0	4.8
Finland	13	56.5	18.4	47.4	1.1	382	8.5	5.1
Luxembourg	12	51.4	13.2	30.9	1.1	330	—	—
Sweden	14	58.3	25.2	35.4	1.1	303	19.7	16.3
Austria	14	64.7	31.3	45.8	1.3	348	28.1	12.0
Belgium	14	57.4	15.3	41.7	1.2	368	5.6	2.5
Hungary	15	50.3	25.7	19.7	1.0	332	12.4	5.0
Bulgaria	15	56.4	38.4	15.5	1.1	300	25.3	9.6
United Kingdom E & W	15	64.5	24.8	40.2	1.3	336	20.2	8.3
Netherlands	16	66.6	10.8	55.0	1.3	469	3.6	2.0
Denmark	16	67.3	27.0	36.3	1.3	350	17.1	10.2
Greece	16	62.7	15.6	45.1	1.2	362	2.2	1.1
United States	16	61.4	31.8	35.6	1.2	488	23.5	9.7
Canada	16	62.4	21.4	50.6	1.2	468	17.9	8.3
Czechoslovakia	17	52.8	22.7	21.6	1.0	359	—	5.4
Switzerland	17	63.3	11.7	46.1	1.1	332	7.1	3.8
Italy	17	62.2	21.6	57.6	1.2	331	4.2	2.0
Norway	17	67.0	21.0	52.1	1.3	378	9.2	5.6
Poland	17	52.6	14.8	38.9	1.1	477	15.3	4.9
France	17	61.9	13.1	50.0	1.3	298	14.5	6.1
Yugoslavia	18	63.3	26.5	40.2	1.3	415	26.0	8.3
Japan	19	58.5	2.6	19.6	1.1	291	1.6	0.9
Spain	19	72.3	4.5	79.7	1.4	382	4.9	1.4
Rumania	20	87.3	40.0	63.9	1.8	284	—	—

Table 2, *continued*

Med fertility							
Iceland	20	80.6	39.0	76.4	1.6	—	85.6	30.0
Portugal	21	73.3	14.5	86.2	1.4	398	22.0	7.4
Australia	21	68.9	24.1	50.5	1.4	423	17.8	7.7
New Zealand	22	82.1	31.3	49.6	1.5	677	24.1	13.0
Argentina	22	73.0	26.7	69.5	1.5	417	60.9	26.4
Ireland	22	81.0	6.7	133.9	1.9	521	3.5	2.6
Uruguay	23	—	—	—	—	405	—	20.0
Scotland	—	68.3	22.7	48.5	1.7	385	78.4	7.4
Puerto Rico	25	91.7	42.5	83.1	1.9	664	48.3	23.2
Chile	26	95.9	33.9	115.3	2.7	619	11.9	17.7
Taiwan	27	98.7	18.1	67.8	1.9	917	1.3	1.6
Israel	28	86.8	15.3	85.7	2.4	532	—	0.6
Ceylon	30	122.0	22.9	157.6	2.9	948	—	—
Costa Rica	34	173.0	52.9	225.8	3.4	875	—	25.8
Albania	35	163.1	30.0	245.1	2.7	830	3.6	1.4
Jamaica	35	189.5	69.2	137.2	2.5	693	189.5	74.1
Panama	37	134.7	64.8	118.3	3.2	748	170.4	70.0
Egypt	37	—	—	—	3.4	702	—	0.0
Tunisia	38	263.1	56.6	350.9	—	880	—	0.3
Brazil	38	—	—	—	2.6	667	—	12.9
Burma	40	—	—	—	2.9	—	—	—
Turkey	40	—	—	—	3.2	700	—	—
So. Africa (colored)	41	160.5	54.2	177.9	3.0	—	—	—
Venezuela	41	158.3	61.6	188.2	3.3	839	190.3	53.2
Madagascar	—	123.6	57.6	133.8	2.9	437	—	—
Cambodia	—	144.6	44.8	191.6		650	—	—

Table 2, continued

Countries	Crude Birth Rate	General Fert. rate	Age spec. rates 10-19	Age spec. rates 35-39	Gross Reproduction Rate	Child/Woman Ratio	Illegitimacy Rate	Illegitimacy Ratio
High fertility								
India	42	—	—	—	2.7	659	—	—
Peru	42	108.2	31.1	155.7	3.1	735	125.8	48.9
El Salvador	42	170.3	66.1	191.2	3.3	739	206.6	67.2
Guatemala	43	162.0	67.7	191.7	3.2	781	—	67.4
Mexico	43	153.4	—	—	3.2	726	112.6	22.5
Mozambique	43	—	—	—	—	652	—	34.3
Thailand	43	120.3	18.3	178.8	2.3	697	—	—
Bolivia	44	—	—	—	—	—	—	17.2
Congo (D.R.)	44	145.7	63.2	80.4	2.4	596	49.4	6.7
Nepal	45	—	—	—	—	570	—	—
Iran	45	—	—	—	3.1	851	—	—
Ecuador	45	145.0	38.5	218.7	3.2	752	136.3	32.2
Colombia	45	132.7	34.3	178.6	2.7	779	92.9	23.4
Paraguay	45	—	—	—	—	766	—	43.0
Nicaragua	46	150.9	62.2	184.6	2.9	824	—	53.4
Libya	46	—	—	—	3.3	857	—	—
Indonesia	47	104.5	45.5	159.0	2.8	714	—	—
Jordan	48	—	—	—	3.4	815	—	—
Syria	48	—	—	—	3.5	956	—	—
Kenya	48	—	—	—	—	728	—	—
Honduras	49	151.5	62.7	196.6	3.1	857	185.1	64.5
Iraq	49	—	—	—	3.5	—	—	—
Angola	50	—	—	—	—	702	209.4	32.6

Table 2, continued

Zambia	50	---	---	---	849	---
Morocco	50	---	---	3.4	845	3.8
Liberia	50	---	---	---	600	---
Algeria	50	65.8 (?)	7.9 (?)	64.9 (?)	3.4	940	---
Mali	50	---	---	---	757	---
Pakistan	51	---	---	3.7	832	---
Dahomey	51	226.9	196.6	166.4	3.3	837	---

Sources:

United Nations, *Demographic Yearbook 1965* (New York: United Nations, 1966), Table 20
United Nations, *Demographic Yearbook 1968* (New York: United Nations, 1969), Table 8
United Nations, *Demographic Yearbook 1969* (New York: United Nations, 1970), Tables 15, 18, 20, 21, 23
United Nations, *Demographic Yearbook 1972* (New York, United Nations, 1973), Table 5
1973 World Population Date Sheet.

Illegitimacy rates computed from births by legitimacy status (1959, 1965 Yearbooks) and numbers of unmarried women (aged 15-44) for each country (1962, 1963 Yearbooks).

* Caution must be used in examining these data, since in many cases there are inconsistencies in national reporting, e.g., the Crude Birth Rate for Tunisia appears too low in relation to other rates they report. In many countries the data gathering methods are still imperfect and in none do we expect absolute accuracy.

TABLE 3

Educational levels of women in the world

Country	Percent Illiterate Women Aged 15+	Ratio Female/Male Literacy Rates	Female Ratio/Current Enrollment Secondary Level	Higher Educational Level
Mali	99.5	46	19.1	10.9
Mozambique	98.9	46	45.3	38.6
Nepal	98.5	63	18.8	17.2
Angola	98.2	46	40.8	33.7
Dahomey	98.2	46	26.4	16.1
Libya	95.9	11	12.9	9.4
Liberia	95.8	30	21.0	19.3
Congo	95.1	46	29.2	1.0
Morocco	94.0	27	25.7	14.5
Pakistan	92.6	26	12.0	15.2
Algeria	92.0	26	29.2	22.4
Kenya	90.0	46	25.8	15.0
Iran	87.8	37	32.6	25.9
Egypt	87.6	31	31.3	23.1
Cambodia	87.3	63	22.9	9.8
Iraq	87.2	36	25.6	38.7
India	86.8	32	23.5	21.2
Jordan	84.8	30	30.2	25.6
Tunisia	82.4	28	28.0	21.0
Syria	83.2	31	24.2	16.9
Madagascar	73.0	46	38.5	35.9
Turkey	72.6	42	28.0	18.7
Indonesia	71.0	52	33.0	21.0
Guatemala	68.0	71	45.0	16.7
Burma	66.0	63	n.a.	37.0
Zambia	65.0	56	25.0	20.0
South Africa	60.2	–	48.1	26.0
Honduras	58.5	85	45.0	16.0
El Salvador	55.5	82	50.0	22.5
Peru	52.4	64	41.2	34.2
Nicaragua	50.8	98	45.8	25.5
Portugal	44.6	80	42.4	40.3
Thailand	43.9	71	40.7	39.0
Taiwan	42.0	63	40.2	34.8
Bolivia	39.3	65	37.2	17.3
Venezuela	38.0	88	49.4	34.5
Ecuador	37.3	88	44.7	24.5

Table 3, *continued*

Country	Percent Illiterate Women Aged 15+	Ratio Female/Male Literacy Rates	Female Ratio/Current Enrollment Secondary Level	Higher Educational Level
Albania	36.9	–	40.8	29.9
Ceylon	36.0	75	n.a.	29.0
Brazil	36.0	91	50.0	30.0
Paraguay	32.1	84	44.2	41.0
Greece	30.1	76	40.5	32.5
Mexico	29.8	90	39.4	20.0
Columbia	28.9	95	48.8	24.5
Yugoslavia	28.8	79	44.8	38.2
Panama	27.6	98	52.7	46.0
Israel	22.0	86	51.7	43.4
Puerto Rico	21.7	90	51.0	52.7
Chile	17.6	98	52.7	40.5
Spain	17.6	90	43.4	24.0
Costa Rica	16.4	99	48.3	41.8
Rumania	16.3	79	41.8	42.8
Jamaica	15.2	108	54.2	44.3
Bulgaria	14.7	90	47.7	48.8
Norway	12.0	100	47.4	29.2
Italy	11.2	90	43.9	38.4
Argentina	9.7	98	52.6	41.3
Uruguay	9.5	100	52.6	40.4
Poland	6.2	97	57.4	43.9
Finland	6.2	90	51.3	48.9
Hungary	3.1	100	57.9	44.7
Belgium	2.4	100	45.5	26.0
Czechoslovakia	2.4	99	55.5	37.6
New Zealand	2.0	100	48.0	28.0
Japan	2.0	–	48.3	28.7
West Germany	2.0	100	46.1	26.7
United States	1.8	100	50.0	40.0
Australia	1.8	100	48.0	29.0
Canada	1.8	100	45.6	38.0
England	1.0	100	48.5	37.8
Scotland	1.0	100	49.2	39.3
Switzerland	1.0	100	53.0	21.7
Sweden	–	100	50.5	36.7
Ireland	–	100	48.0	30.0
Iceland	–	100	48.0	24.8

Table 3, *continued*

Country	Percent Illiterate Women Aged 15+	Ratio Female/Male Literacy Rates	Female Ratio/Current Enrollment Secondary Level	Higher Educational Level
France	–	100	51.3	42.0
Denmark	–	100	51.2	36.2
Netherlands	–	100	45.1	26.8
Austria	–	100	40.9	26.9
Luxembourg	–	100	43.1	29.5

Sources:
United Nations, *Demographic Yearbook 1963* (New York: UN, 1964) Tables 12, 13; United Nations, *Demographic Yearbook 1964* (New York: UN, 1965) Table 33; United Nations, *Demographic Yearbook 1971* (New York: UN, 1972) Table 18; UNESCO, *Statistical Yearbook 1972* (Paris: UN, 1973) Tables 3.4 and 4.1; *UNESCO Statistical Yearbook 1973* (Paris: UN, 1974) Table 1.4; United Nations, *Commission on Status of Women* Economic and Social Council 25th Session. Doc 3/CN. 6/575/Add.3.

TABLE 4

Median years educational attainment for women 25+ in various societies

Median Years	Countries
9.3 to 10.7	Canada, Scotland, Northern Ireland, England, U.S.A.
5.1 to 7.9	Uruguay, Norway, Switzerland, Poland, Czechoslovakia, Japan, Argentina, Jamaica, Israel, Ireland, Hungary, Australia
3.1 to 4.7	Austria, Rumania, Italy, Spain, Costa Rica, Bulgaria, Panama, Yugoslavia, France, Finland, Netherlands, Iceland, Chile, Greece.
1.0 to 2.6	South Africa, Nicaragua, Dominican Republic, Colombia, Ceylon, Ecuador, Paraguay
Less than one year: .50 to .98	All Sub Saharan Africa; All Asia (except Japan); All Muslim countries; El Salvador, Guatemala, Honduras, Mexico, Bolivia, Peru, Venezuela, Portugal

Source: UNESCO Statistical Yearbook 1972. (Paris: United Nations, 1973), Table 1.5.

TABLE 5

Female labor force participation patterns in non-agricultural economic activities around the world: 1965-1970

Country	Work participation rate (females 15+)	Ratio female/total non-agricultural labor	Ratio female/total professional workers
Jamaica	42.0	29.7	62.7
Finland	41.0	44.4	52.0
England	40.4	36.3	38.3
Scotland	40.4	36.3	43.9
Denmark	38.2	36.7	50.9
Hungary	37.8	41.7	46.4
Japan	37.7	35.7	37.0
West Germany	35.1	34.3	33.1
Sweden	34.3	35.0	42.9
Czechoslovakia	32.3	38.2	34.6
United States	32.2	33.6	42.0
Belgium	32.0	33.1	42.2
Austria	31.2	36.6	40.3
New Zealand	29.3	29.8	44.4
France	29.3	32.9	43.0
Iceland	28.6	31.2	35.5
Canada	28.4	29.7	41.7
Australia	28.3	29.7	42.0
Bulgaria	26.7	35.5	42.2
Uruguay	25.9	29.6	57.4
Ireland	25.7	33.0	50.9
Israel	24.9	27.1	49.1
Nicaragua	24.5	37.6	42.9
Poland	24.1	34.7	49.4
Luxembourg	23.2	25.7	41.1
Norway	22.9	27.2	37.2
Argentina	22.1	25.2	58.7
Chile	22.1	29.6	48.4
Netherlands	21.9	23.8	39.1
Paraguay	20.0	39.4	61.4
Puerto Rico	19.6	31.0	50.2
Taiwan	19.4	24.7	32.5
Colombia	18.9	33.8	47.3
Ecuador	18.0	30.4	46.4
Italy	17.8	24.3	37.0
Rumania	17.7	29.2	44.4
Brazil	17.6	29.6	59.8
El Salvador	17.4	40.4	52.3
Costa Rica	17.2	30.3	56.0

Table 5, *continued*

Country	Work participation (females 15+)	Ratio female/total non-agricultural labor	Ratio female/total professional workers
Mexico	16.9	28.2	37.6
Panama	16.8	37.0	56.5
Bolivia	16.4	36.5	n.a.
Peru	16.2	29.6	46.0
Spain	15.7	22.5	33.3
Portugal	14.8	25.3	49.6
Switzerland	14.3	32.8	31.4
Yugoslavia	14.0	26.0	43.0
Honduras	13.8	36.9	57.1
Guatemala	12.7	32.0	38.9
Greece	12.5	21.9	34.3
Thailand	12.4	37.3	33.9
Iran	12.1	18.0	25.7
Indonesia	11.9	30.9	35.6
Cambodia	11.9	27.9	n.a.
Zambia	11.0	12.9	21.0
Venezuela	11.0	24.8	43.2
Ceylon	10.3	15.8	38.7
India	8.4	20.6	16.1
Morocco	6.1	14.3	15.0
Egypt	5.9	11.5	23.9
Syria	5.4	10.3	26.8
Tunisia	4.8	9.5	17.3
Mozambique	4.5	2.0	n.a.
Angola	4.2	13.4	14.3
Libya	4.1	6.7	11.5
Algeria	3.9	6.7	20.9
Turkey	3.3	7.9	20.8
Iraq	3.1	6.0	n.a.
Pakistan	2.3	7.2	9.6
Liberia	2.0	12.3	26.6
Nepal	1.9	20.8	6.4
Jordan	1.8	6.0	30.4

* Comparable labor force statistics are not available for the following countries: Dahomey, Congo, Mali, Albania, Burma, Kenya, Madagascar, South Africa (colored)
Sources: United Nations, *Demographic Yearbook 1964* (New York: United Nations, 1965), Tables 8, 9. United Nations *Demographic Yearbook 1972* (New York: United Nations, 1973), Tables 8, 10. International Labor Office, *Yearbook of Labor Statistics 1969* (Geneva, UN, 1970), Tables 2A, 2B. International Labor Office, *Yearbook of Labor Statistics 1972* (Geneva, UN, 1973), Tables 2A, 2B. Republic of China, *1972 Taiwan Demographic Fact Book* (Republic of China: Ministry of Interior, 1973), Tables 6, 28, 29.

5

A PARADIGM FOR PREDICTING THE POSITION OF WOMEN:
Policy Implications and Problems

Rae Lesser Blumberg
University of California, San Diego

In this chapter Blumberg attempts to provide a theory of sex stratification – i.e., a paradigm for predicting the position of women within and among different countries, classes and times. Such a formulation may be of use to policy makers because it delineates certain key factors that seem more influential in determining the degree of equality with which women will be treated in a society. Blumberg insists that the most relevant standard of comparison of women's degree of equality in a society is with the men of their group, not the level of female status in some other country or era. Thus, in conceptualizing the position of women, we should not compare the position of women in, let us say, Ruritania, with the position of women in Urbanalbia and measure development in terms of narrowing that gap. The gap that needs closing is the gap between the sexes within both societies, however much higher the level of women in Urbanalbia may be than that of women in Ruritania.

In Blumberg's paradigm, the central variable which appears to account for much of the difference in status between men and women is each sex's relative economic power. In this chapter, she analyzes the degree to which women's relative economic power, as well as other factors such as their political position, and the extent to which males use force against them, influence their control over key life options. These include relative freedom to initiate marriage, terminate a union, exercise household authority, move about spatially, and so forth. The policy implications of this research may be limited by the point made by Tangri and Strasburg that not all the forces that determine the gap between men and women are amenable to policy intervention.

I. INTRODUCTION

Within the last decade, under the impetus of a growing Women's Liberation Movement, more and more people around the world came to perceive that Rousseau's famed quote — 'man is born free, yet everywhere he is found in chains' — might more describe the current condition of women. In recognition of the increasing impact of the Women's Liberation Movement in many parts of the world, the United Nations declared 1975 to be International Women's Year. It is too soon to tell to what extent women's chains have been broken, i.e., to what extent this movement will succeed in advancing its goals, but it is not too soon to attempt an assessment. The increased light on the problem of sexual inequality has not always brought increased enlightenment for policy makers. Recent research has produced large amounts of contradictory data, so that it is hard to tell which have been more numerous and non-concordant: indicators of the position of women or remedies aimed at improving it.

How can policy makers then assess the relative gains and losses of women from different countries or from different classes and life conditions within any one country? How can they sort through the welter of well-intended plans and programs to see which are efficacious? How can they foretell the impact of particular programs? Policy makers cannot yet adequately answer these questions because two important prerequisites have been lacking, namely: (1) a way to measure female status which permits comparisons of the relative equality not only of women vs. men but also among women themselves in different times, places, classes, conditions, and countries, and (2) a testable theory that specifies the crucial factors affecting woman's relative position and thus permits us to predict her progress, given certain changes in these key variables. Ideally, such a theory would permit us to order these factors in both importance and sequence. If supported by the data, even a partial theory can be useful to policy makers by providing a framework for evaluating particular programs and policies.

A good illustration of the need for appropriate measures may be drawn from United States data. If, for example, we measure in terms of the opportunities and achievements of women today vis-à-vis those of women in 1900, we conclude that there has been considerable improvement.[1] But if we use income as our measure and compare the disparity in income between men and women today with the disparity in recent years, we find that it has increased.[2] If we use as our measure the greater equality in 'morals and manners', it is even more difficult to speak. Have casual sex and no-fault divorce, for example, brought greater relative benefits and status to women than to men? Or is this merely another illustration of the dictum: a rising tide floats all the boats? Women's apparently increased freedom or progress in some areas turns out, on closer analysis, to be matched by a comparable change among the men of their group, so that the total net change in the women's relative position is zero. Part of the difficulty in pinning down female status consists, then, in deciding how to sift through and weigh the multiplicity of measures.

Since there is so little agreement as to which are the most important determinants of less-than-equal female status, however measured, it is no surprise that the remedies proposed to raise it are confusingly numerous and inconsistent. Is the crucial determinant a climate of institutionalized sexism that must be attacked first? How? By educating people? Or subjecting them to good-will messages designed to change their attitudes? Do the negative images of women in the media and/or children's textbooks require correcting before large-sacle progress can be made? Or is it equal work at equal pay? Daycare? The Equal Rights Amendment? Or will a socialist revolution be necessary before any fundamental change will occur? And, given the less than total sexual equality manifested in contemporary socialist countries, what else might be required other than government ownership of the means of production? Or are the biological determinists correct in arguing that women are doomed to less than full equality by their reproductive and endocrine systems, so that even when given a chance at full equality, as in the pioneer-era kibbutz, they will soon end up in second place, minding the children and doing the laundry as before?

Which of these remedies treats root causes of sex inequality and which treats mere symptoms? So many proposals cannot be sorted out without a scorecard. And that is a synonym for theory. To move toward a general theory of sex stratification, I have formulated a paradigm for assessing and predicting relative female equality vis-à-vis men. It is hoped that this paradigm may provide a partial solution to policy makers' problems in measuring and fostering female progress. A summary of this paradigm and a synopsis of my attempts at a preliminary empirical test of it constitute Part II of this chapter. In Part III, some implications for policy are briefly explored.

II THE PARADIGM

One clear effect of the barrage of publicity surrounding the Women's Liberation Movement and the International Women's Year has been to heighten awareness of the diversity of women's position around the globe. The differences in relative sexual equality of Swedish women vs. their Saudi Arabian sisters are spectacularly evident. The differences in sexual position of Swedish women vs. their Soviet sisters are more subtle. But we must not forget that it is not enough to compare women's positions with each other. Rather, the principal comparison must be between the women vs. the men of their group.[3] That is the heart of sexual stratification. And that is the major burden of our discussion here.

Are women invariably the second sex? Among known societies of recent date, women seem to be completely equal with men only among the gentle, communal Tasaday of the Philippines.[4] When this group was discovered in 1971, hunting was not practised, but both sexes gathered and shared collectively in control of the means of production and decision-making (see, e.g., Fernandez and Lynch, 1972). Other groups with virtually complete sexual equality, such as Zaire's Mbuti Pygmies of the Ituri Forest and Namibia's !Kung Bushmen of the Kalahari Desert, also have shared communal control of the means of production and a foraging economy. But other paths to equality exist: among the Iroquois of the colonial-era United States, for example, the means and fruits of production were controlled almost wholly by the women, who owned the land, raised most of the food, allocated the surplus — and influenced the political and war decisions of the men as well (see, e.g., Brown, 1975). In comparison to the above groups, those Swedish and Soviet women seem second class citizens in many respects. How can we account for the great differences in relative sexual equality among the world's peoples?

Let me present a summary of my paradigm of sex stratification, in which I attempt to tackle this question (see also Blumberg, 1974; 1978 forthcoming). The paradigm is intended to apply cross-culturally, under diverse historical conditions, and although its basic focus is on how equal women are to the men of their group, it permits us to compare the position of various groups of women across time, classes and countries as well. It is conceived as a paradigm of sex stratification, and hence, although female reproductive functions are taken into account, its principal explanatory variables are those of theories of stratification, not those of biological sex differences. After all, women bear and nurse babies — and tend to be physically smaller than males — everywhere, but everywhere their degree of relative equality is not the same.

Theories of stratification are couched in terms of relative power and relative privilege (see, e.g., Lenski, 1966). Differential power begets differential privilege, i.e., possession of the former can be translated into the latter. Although there are a multiplicity of manifestations of privilege — involving differences in status, prestige and deference, as well as in possessions, prerequisites, prerogatives and freedom — there seem to be only a few sources of power relevant for a group's inequality systems. It is as though the sources of power were mighty rivers flowing into a swampy delta, whereupon they split into a labyrinth of channels of privilege, more of which are blind or meandering than direct.

So it is differential power which underlies inequality. Max Weber defines power as 'the probability of persons or groups carrying out their will even when opposed by others' (Gerth and Mills, 1946: 180). Concerning the 'rivers' of power, Lenski, for example, distinguishes only three: the power stemming from control over property, that derived from position in a society's politico-administrative hierarchies, and that based on force or coercion. In short, economic power, political power, and the power of force. How do women fit into all this?

In the Marxian view, economic power is the mainstream, with the other sources of power acting as tributaries. According to this view, a society's economic arrangements exert the most important influence on its other institutions, such as the political, legal, familial, and ideological systems. And people's degree of relative control over the society's means of production constitutes both their main power resource and the greatest shaper of their life chances and privileges. Whether economic power is this important for a society's inequality system is a subject of raging controversy in the social sciences. But, I propose, there seems to be less doubt with respect to its women.

A. Woman's Most Important Form of Power: Relative Economic Control

Consider the matter comparatively. There is no known society where women achieve even a fifty percent share of political power. With respect to the power of force, the situation is worse: women rarely exercise it and are frequently its victims, i.e., wifebeating is widely distributed around the world. Only for economic power does the empirical evidence run the gamut. Thus, there are societies where women have virtually no control over the means and fruits of production, relative to the men of their class or society (e.g., the Rwala Bedouin). Contrast this with the situation of the Iroquois, where women's relative economic power apparently approached totality. In fact, there are ethnographic accounts of a fair number of widely scattered pre-industrial societies (in most of which women are hoe horticulturalists and/or market traders) where women exercise more economic power than their menfolk. In short, the extant empirical evidence shows economic control to be the most achievable power source for women.

Theoretically, I also consider it the most important vis-à-vis female status. Let us hark back to the problem of measurement that I suggest has plagued efforts to assess the position of women. I already have outlined what I view as the central determinant of overall female position, namely the degree of female economic power relative to the males of her class or group. Let us now return to that 'swamp' of differential privilege, and choose the most relevant way of measuring the extent to which females approach equal treatment and opportunities vs. their menfolk.

B. Woman's Most Meaningful Privilege: Relative Control of One's Life

Two broad classes of privilege include status or prestige on the one hand, and autonomy in one's own life on the other. I argue that the latter involves a more direct translation of power and is more relevant as a measure of relative sexual equality. The former may lead one to quite misleading conclusions. Take, for example, one aspect of the status-prestige complex, deference. Victorian 'ladies' were placed on a pedestal and treated with ritualized deference. But how much of a life can one lead from a pedestal? And how high a pedestal is it if its occupant cannot vote, divorce without disgrace, or administer her own property after marriage? Similarly, are we to accept that US women are equal in status to US men just because their average 'occupational prestige' score is about the same as that of US men (Treiman and Terrell, 1975)? That result seems due to the fact that women are concentrated in a narrow range of clerical and sales jobs which are considered 'white collar' in terms of prestige. But women's equal 'occupational prestige' score does not translate into equal wages, let alone equal overall status (recall that the latest figures, cited in footnote 2, show women employed full-time year-round earning not much more than half their male counterparts).

The measurement approach I have chosen involves assessing females' relative freedom and control over their own lives. It consists of examining a series of life events and opportunities that occur in all known human societies, and then assessing the relative equality of women vs. the men of their class or group with respect to each of them. I term these events and opportunities 'life options', and find them useful not only as macro measures of women's position in a group, but also as indicators of equality at the micro level of a woman's interaction with her intimates.

Life Options. To emphasize, what is of interest here is not just the absolute level of female freedom with respect to these situations, but how that freedom compares to that accorded to the males of her class or group. An incomplete list of life options that potentially exist for both sexes in all societies includes relative freedom to: (a) decide whether, when, and whom to marry; (2) dissolve a marriage; (3) engage in premarital sex; (4) engage in extramarital sex; (5) regulate reproduction to the extent biologically feasible (including not just family size, but also timing of first birth, spacing, sex ratio, and the type of 'intervention' (see Davis and Blake schema, 1956) used to accomplish these, such as contraception, abstinence, abortion, infanticide, etc.); (6) move about spatially without restriction; (7) exercise household authority; and (8) take advantage of educational opportunities.[5]

Since I am proposing that the relative equality of a woman's life options is affected principally by her degree of power from all sources (which boils down to economically-derived power for the most part, I further argue), I do not wish to include any life options which relate directly to economics, politics or force. This is to avoid tautology (e.g., women's economic power gives her greater freedom to take advantage of occupational opportunities). Of course, such an approach does not preclude our examining, say, female occupational distributions, relative wages, unemployment, etc., in terms of the paradigm. Rather, it precludes including them in any index of life options that might be tested as a dependent variable of relative female economic power.

C. The Road to Female Economic Power

My definition of female economic power involves women's degree of control, relative to the males of their class or group, of the means of production and allocation of surplus. How do women gain such power? The means of production include, of course, land, capital, and labor. For women to gain control of a sizeable proportion of the first two, I suggest, they presumably must have begun with a strategic contribution to the third. I shall not propose that work alone normally leads to economic power; if that were the case, peasants, slaves and workers long ago would have inherited the earth. But women's role in economically productive activities, i.e., the extent to which they 'bring home the bacon,' does seem to be a first step down the road to economic power. In the jargon of the social sciences, it seems to be necessary but it is clearly insufficient. In other words, it seems to be a precondition to further progress down the road to economic power — rather like the toll at the first gate.

A long list of theorists have viewed female productive labor as a first stepping stone toward equality.[6] Is it? Sanday (1973) examined a small sample of 12 pre-industrial societies and found no case where women contributed little to production yet enjoyed a high position (by her criteria). Conversely, she found that high status could not be predicted from high productivity: in some groups where women played a major productive role, their overall status was low, whereas in others, it was high. Clearly, other factors intervene between women working and their acquiring a significant degree of relative economic power. But we cannot consider these until we have tackled the prior problem: under what circumstances do women participate in the main productive activities of their society?

1. Female Participation in Production

Actually, before turning to this problem, still another step backwards is necessary. This one takes us al¹ the way back through human evolutionary history, in fact. There is a common misconception that women in most times and places were little more than economic parasites. Their domestic and childcare activities were not seen as productive, and in this view women contributed little else but love (also nonproductive) to the household economy. (As Parsons and Bales (1955: 151) put it, men are the principal providers, 'whereas the wife is primarily the giver of love...') Historically, it's dead wrong.

The mainline of human evolutionary history is characterized by only a handful of techno-economic bases (see, e.g., Lenski and Lenski, 1974): foraging (hunting and gathering) which for several million years apparently characterized all human groups; horticultural (which first emerged in the Middle East some 10,000 or so years ago); agrarian (also of Middle Eastern origin perhaps 5,000-6,000 years ago); and industrial (dating to roughly 1800 AD in England and parts of Northwest Europe). Horticulture is done with digging stick or hoe on small, garden-size plots; agriculture, most typically, involves plow cultivation on large, cleared fields. These historical facts give us the background for the following information on contemporary pre-industrial societies.

Foraging societies: in virtually all but Arctic groups, the major part of the food supply (typically, 60-80 percent, per Lee and DeVore, 1968) is gathered, not hunted. And women are the principal gatherers in the overwhelming majority of such groups, according to my calculations with Murdock's *Ethnographic Atlas* (1967) computer tape (a collection of data on some 1,170 pre-industrial societies).[7] In short, women tend to be the primary providers of the food supply.

Horticultural societies: the *Ethnographic Atlas* contains sex division of labor data on 376 societies in which shifting hoe cultivation is the main economic activity. In only about one-fifth of these, my calculations show, is the labor force predominantly male. Moreover, the accepted archaeological view (see, e.g., Childe, 1964: 65-66) is that early horticultural cultivation and its development emerged as the work of women.[8]

Already we have accounted for all but the last fraction of one percent of some perhaps three to four million years of human habitation on earth, and find that women apparently were the primary producers in most of the societies involved.

Agrarian societies: here history makes a dramatic reversal. Women play only a minor productive role in the overwhelming majority of agrarian societies. (As it happens, most such groups use non-irrigated cultivation. In the minority where the main crop is irrigated paddy rice, women play a larger productive role.) Since female subjugation is nearly universal in such societies (see, e.g., Michaelson and Goldschmidt's comparative study of 46 peasant groups, 1971), it is interesting to note that every one of today's presently industrialized societies — both capitalist and socialist — sprang from an agrarian base. If that is one's recent past (and one hasn't studied anthropology), a 'woman as parasite' interpretation of history is not surprising.

Industrial societies: women are typically one-fourth to one-half the labor force in these societies, with the higher percentages found more frequently in the socialist ones. Historically, this seems the first time that female participation in production has taken place under conditions of almost total separation from children.

For a last death blow to the 'woman as parasite' myth, let us return to the *Ethnographic Atlas* (which also includes sex division of labor data on two other techno-economic bases, fishing and herding). Aronoff and Crano (1975) have used the *Atlas* to calculate that as a worldwide average, women contribute 44 percent of the food supply. Fine. Now back to the problem of the conditions under which women are economically productive. How can we account for the enormous cross-societal variation in female participation?[9]

Specifically, I suggest, two principal factors are involved: (a) the extent to which the economic activity in question is compatible with a woman's childcare responsibilities, especially breastfeeding; and (b) the state of the available labor supply relative to demand.

(a) *Compatibility with childcare, especially breastfeeding.* Considering that the baby bottle is a nineteenth century invention and that ethnographic data show that in the majority of human societies children are not weaned from the breast until at least two years of age, the paradigm must consider a *biological* constraint on a woman's labor. During many of her prime working years, she has to be in proximity to her youngest child several times a day. Brown (1970), Whiting (1972) and I all have proposed rather similar lists of the characteristics of tasks that are compatible with such childcare obligations. In general, those activities which are done close to home or do not require hard, fast travel; which are not dangerous to any small children in the vicinity; and which may be easily picked up, interrupted, and then restarted are less likely to inconvenience the mother and/or harm the child. Brown makes a persuasive case that physical strength seems much less involved as a factor. Interestingly enough, by these criteria, both gathering and hoe horticulture emerge as compatible activities par excellence. And, as we have seen, the empirical evidence shows them to have predominantly female labor forces. (Conversely, incompatible activities, such as hunting or herding large animals, have overwhelmingly male labor forces, according to additional calculations using the *Ethnographic Atlas.*)

(b) *The dynamics of labor demand vs. sex-specific supply.* But compatibility is not the whole story. Even in pre-industrial societies where women must breastfeed each child, there are cases of women in modally male activities and vice versa (Murdock and Provost, 1973). Moreover, if only compatibility were involved, we could not explain high female employment in industrial societies, both capitalist and socialist. For many of these women are working mothers, and there is no question that most of them experience considerable extra hassle arranging childcare while working in these 'incompatible' industrial-economy jobs. The presence of large numbers of mothers of young children working in an 'incompatible' activity is a good tip-off of high labor demand that cannot easily be filled by the available, less child-burdened supply (see, e.g., Oppenheimer, 1973). Perhaps non-child-burdened females are already in short supply — and males are not in sufficient surplus at the normally better-paying jobs open to them to be pushed into the activity. For even in socialist industrial societies, women fall far enough short of equality for their labor to be concentrated in lower-paid job categories.

To generalize, compatibility of an activity with child-care responsibilities may be a facilitating factor and its converse an inhibiting factor for female participation. But demand seems to outweigh 'compatibility' considerations. In societies of less than complete sexual equality, we may predict that when females in large numbers are pulled into modally male, and/or 'incompatible' activities, (1) the activity is important for group survival; and (2) there is a shortage of available males. Conversely, when males in large numbers enter modally female, and/or 'compatible' activities, we may predict that either (1) the activity is both crucial for group survival and plagued by a severe shortage of available females, or (2) there is a severe glut of available males relative to the demand for labor in modally male activities. This second situation — glut pushing the unemployed sex into the other's activities — does not occur under conditions of sexual inequality when it is females who are in oversupply, I suggest.

2. From Work to Economic Power

Economic productivity provides females with the entry fee, so to speak, to the yellow brick road leading to the Emerald City of economic power. What are the way stations along the road? My paradigm delineates three. First, women's work *may* be somewhat translatable to economic power, provided that both the work and the workers are of sufficient 'strategic indispensability.' Strategic indispensability factors bear strong relation to the variables labor economists might consider in weighing the bargaining power of a given labor force. Second, women may be speeded along the road if the kinship arrangements of their society favor residence and descent patterns that make it more probable for females to have strategic access to kin group property. Third, the social relations of production of the larger society may advance or retard women's progress toward economic power, with — all other things being equal — highly class-stratified societies providing an additional barrier to women's achieving relatively high economic power as compared to their menfolk.

(a) *Strategic indispensability factors.* What makes for strategic indispensability for a group which is working in production but initially has no separate claim on the means or fruits of that production? Let us consider the matter for women.

First, the women's economic activities should be important to the group — providing a significant proportion of total output (or diet), and/or having high 'short-run substitution costs.' This means that replacing the activity on short notice would be a difficult and costly process. For example, if females were to be barred from filling secretarial jobs starting tomorrow, one can imagine that the transition would be costly — and chaotic.

Second, the women producers themselves must be valuable to the group, once again because they produce an important proportion of total output, and/or could not be replaced quickly without tough and expensive hassle. It should be stressed that mere 'substitutability at the margin' is enough to weaken women's position. In general, it appears that if even 5-15 percent of a labor force can be easily substituted, then this is enough to undermine the group's bargaining position regardless of the importance to the society of its product.

However, it seems that women, like peasants, are frequently victims of a situation where they are substitutable at the margin: underutilized people like themselves are available locally, or can be brought in, to their detriment. Concerning peasants, I invoke Lenski's (1966: 281-84) assertion that in traditional agrarian (plow-agriculture based) societies, 5-15 percent of the population was composed of a class he terms the 'expendables'. These were the excess sons and daughters of the peasant population which the dominant classes were unwilling to support on the land, even at bare survival level. Frequently, they migrated to the cities where their life conditions as beggars, coolies, prostitutes, petty thieves, and the like, were generally so miserable that they rarely reproduced their numbers. But each generation their ranks were replenished by more migrants from the land.[10] I suggest that it is precisely the existence of this surplus labor population that is a principal cause of why peasants almost everywhere have so little economic power in comparison with their economic contribution. The existence of the expendables (let alone the additional landless peasants who attempt to survive on the margins of the village economy) guarantees 'substitutability at the margin' — i.e., any individual peasant is replaceable, and by people who had been trained as peasants prior to being pushed off the land.

So too for women, I suggest. In pre-industrial societies where women are important but powerless producers, I suggest that we will find substitutability at the margin built into the system, with the extra women coming from trading, slaving, raiding or polygyny. In industrial capitalist societies, the reserve army of housewives is eminently tappable. In short, if even a small reserve of potential replacements exists, women's chances for parlaying production into power are eclipsed, unless the women can come up with some other sources of strategic indispensability that will prevent these extra bodies from being used against them.

Clearly, the position of a work force is strengthened to the extent its members can gain control of the labor process. The next three strategic indispensability factors are relevant in this regard.

Third, then, is female control of the technical expertise involved in their production. Stinchcombe (1966) makes a parallel argument for peasants share-cropping for absentee landlords — and suggests that such peasants, recognizing the landlord's lack of contribution to production, may be able to take advantage of a period of political instability to gain control of their land.

Such a situation is more probable in the presence of the fourth variable, that women work autonomously of direct male supervision. Oboler (1973) emphasizes this factor in writing about African market women. Their menfolk cannot supervise their trading (and thence take the profits) because the men are not up on the latest price movements and trends of the market.

The fifth variable is that labor movement classic, 'Organize!' In other words, their position can be improved where women producers can organize in their own behalf. Here the characteristics of the work situation seem greatly to influence the possibilities of successfully banding together. For example, do the women work in or belong to units which can benefit from economies of scale and can be used as a base for collective organization? Historically, this seems to have been relatively infrequent.

There are also external factors which influence a producer group's strategic indispensability, and constrain or facilitate its potential for economic power. As a sixth factor, I propose the existence of groups competing for the women producers. Or, to phrase it negatively, a producer group is unlikely to advance if it is caught in the only game in town with no escape in sight. Let us speculate about an example from history — what happened following the Black Death in England vs. East Prussia (based on Reinhardt, 1974). In both places, heavy peasant deaths created a labor shortage, which one might presume should benefit the survivors. In England, this occurred; in fact, a free yeoman class arose that became the ancestors of today's 'county class' (Ziegler, 1969). But in the frontier zone of East Prussia, a previously free yeoman group became serfs tied to the land. The difference? In England, the crown already was in competition with the nobility for power, and the peasants benefited from the conflict and competition. Conversely, there was no crown-noble power struggle in East Prussia; the nobles were the only game in town, and operated as feudal warlords. Peasants don't often live, if I may offer a generalization, to see their harvest burned two years in a row. The nobility was able to secure its now-scarce labor supply by coercion. In short, the absence of countervailing power groups may reduce the advantages producers may otherwise derive from economic importance, even in the presence of severe labor shortage. And vice versa.

(b) *Kinship arrangements*. The next element to be considered above and beyond the strategic indispensability factors is the society's kinship system. Harking back to the discussion of countervailing groups, women producers' position clearly is not helped if all kinship institutions are lined up on one side: the males'. While it is possible for women to gain strategic indispensability points in a patrilineal-patrilocal group (one which reckons descent only through the male line, and in which the young couple live with the groom's paternal male kin), it would be like swimming upstream against the current. Similarly, even in a society whose kinship institutions are organized around maternal kin, it is possible for women to be under the thumb of males (most often, their brothers; see Schlegal, 1972). But it is less likely, and in general, the average position of women is better in matri-centered groups than in those emphasizing paternal kin (Leavitt, 1971; Gough, 1971). In particular, where the wife can continue to live with or near her female relatives while the husband is separated from his kin, women's degree of autonomous control over the family or group's productive resources is facilitated. Also, kinship systems emphasizing maternal kin are much more likely to permit women full inheritance rights than the patri-centered system. (And, as discussed below, females' relative inheritance rights turn out to be one of my operational measures of their economic power relative to their menfolk.) In fact, in their provision of a possible organized cohort of female kin, and in their link to control over property via inheritance, kinship institutions provide women with the potential to get a direct share in economic power without necessarily having to work for it. If the kinship institutions are sufficiently favorable to females, women could theoretically reap the benefits even without a significant contribution to production. But in practice, such a situation — where women are the idle 'coupon clippers' of kinship — seems empirically rare.

(c) *Social relations of production.* The third independent influence on women's relative economic power is the society's social relations of production, i.e., who controls its means of production, and allocates its surplus production. Simple foraging (hunting-gathering) societies that produce little or no surplus tend to have communal relations of production: the means of production are available to all members of the group, and any surplus windfall that may come along is shared widely. Those simple horticultural groups which seem deliberately to avoid producing and accumulating much surplus (e.g., the Kuikuru of the Amazon basin) also tend to follow this pattern. The Israeli kibbutz (collective settlement) does strive to produce surplus, but because it also is deliberately socialist by design, members own everything collectively. Does communal ownership always mean communal control in which females carry equal clout in economic decision-making? In a word, no. Resources 'owned' by the community may in fact be controlled by a subgroup not representative of the total community — especially with respect to sex composition. This has occurred in the kibbutz, where in the course of a generation, women gradually were edged out of the important agricultural production jobs and into the low-ranked kitchens and laundries from which they supposedly had been liberated (see, e.g.,

Spiro, 1963). As a result, they have retained very few representatives in the kibbutz' economic committees, the main locus of economic power and decision-making (see Blumberg, 1976a, 1976b).

But although sex differences in economic control occur more than occasionally in classless communal societies, they tend to be considerably more pronounced in societies with class stratification. These are groups where one class has disproportionate control over the means of production – and any surplus generated. In such societies, a woman's economic control is influenced by: (a) the nature of the larger stratification system and her class position within it; as well as (b) her contribution to production and its strategic indispensability vs. those of the men of her own class; and (c) the resources she derives from her kinship connections vs. those accruing to males of her class (de facto kinship rules and resource allocation patterns may vary by social class in complex societies; see, e.g., Stack, 1974). Suppose a society is set up in a very inegalitarian manner, and we are interested in the position of the women belonging to a class comprising, say, 50 percent of the population which controls only 5 percent of the wealth. This information does not tell us how that 5 percent is allocated between males and females of the class. Here, the relative economic position of a woman (vs. that of the men of her class) may be expected to vary according to the power points accruing to her from her productivity, strategic indispensability and kinship connections. To propose a broad generalization, it seems that in societies where the overall position of women is relatively unfavorable (e.g., agrarian ones), the lower down in the class system we go, the less of a gap we find between the relative economic position of men and women. Their lot may be misery, but it is shared in a sexually more egalitarian manner than among the affluent.

D. Woman's 'Poker Chips of Power'

To recapitulate, I first suggested that economic power is both the biggest and most achievable 'poker chip of power' women have been able to command in the high stakes game of sexual stratification, where the prize is greater control over one's life. Then I went on to delineate the road to economic power.[11]

But economic power is not the whole story. What else can be seen as poker chips of power affecting the outcome of sexual equality?

Force and political position, the other two dimensions mentioned by Lenski, clearly are of some importance. As noted, however, they are invariably male-dominated, and can be used to oppress and restrict women.

The situation is perhaps clearer with *force*, which Randall Collins (1971) invokes as the major explanation of sexual inequality in his theory: to him, males' greater size and sexual aggressiveness are what keep females down. But the empirical evidence to date makes this problematic. For example, among our nearest primate kin, the apes, male sexual dimorphism (their greater size and strength) is unrelated to male dominance (see, e.g., Leibowitz, 1975). And among the simplest foraging groups, the gentle, egalitarian Tasaday, Mbuti and !Kung, women apparently are rarely or never subject to male use of physical or sexual force.

Political power I view as a less important determinant of how much control women are able to achieve over their own lives. But I confess that I have not tackled the principal puzzle concerning political power: why, from its first emergence as a separate dimension among simple pre-industrial societies, women typically have such a small formal role. This is evident in a number of groups where women remain full economic partners and may have informal political influence, but take little if any official role in the emerging formal political structure (e.g., of headman and council).

Be that as it may, I propose that where women have economic clout, they can use it to win substantial physical and normative immunity from males' direct use of force against them (after all, the European feudal lords desisted from bullying the rising bourgeoisie after a certain point, lest they kill the goose that had begun to lay such nice gold eggs). And women's economic clout should win them some political influence, and ultimately, perhaps, some share in political power.

A variety of other factors have been mentioned in the sex stratification literature as influences on women's status but only two more will be mentioned here. These are (1) the ideology of general male superiority, and (2) men's participation in childrearing and domestic tasks. An ideology of male supremacy is alleged to have a negative influence on women's status. Conversely, male participation in the stereotypically female childcare and household activities is asserted as being conducive to sexual egalitarianism (see, e.g., Rosaldo and Lamphere, 1974). These factors may correlate with women's status, but I don't see them as substantially influencing it. At best, they may intervene between the main poker chips of power and my proposed main measure of female status, relative equality of life options. But the two factors themselves, I propose, are shaped by women's position with respect to the principal chips.

The last several paragraphs have presented, in an offhand manner, predictions about the relative strength of economic clout vs. other poker chips of power in influencing the favorableness of female life options as compared to those of their male counterparts. Let me now review and make explicit the major predictions of the theory.

E. Predictions from the Paradigm

I have proposed a paradigm to account for the position of women relative to the men of their group or class. Among the assertions this theory is intended to test are the following: (a) a woman's position is most affected by her relative degree of control over the means of production and the surplus generated by that production; (2) a precondition for such relative economic power is not just participation in production, but strategic indispensability as a producer; (3) women's relative economic power also may be facilitated by kinship arrangements (e.g., those governing marital residence and descent) that take females into account and thus help them to gain access to kin property; (4) women are more likely to be oppressed physically and politically where they do not have any appreciable economic power; and (5) women can translate power into greater control over their own lives, i.e., greater equality relative to the males of their group with respect to basic life options.

F. A Preliminary Test of the Paradigm: Synopsis of Results

I have begun to test parts of this theory with data from a pilot sample of 61 pre-industrial societies. Using the *Human Relations Area Files* (a collection of ethnographic information on several hundred largely pre-industrial societies), it was possible to code these 61 societies in terms of most of the variables mentioned above.[12] Among the variables that have not yet been coded are the 'strategic indispensability' factors. Thus I cannot ascertain whether there is empirical support for my speculations concerning how women get an observed degree of relative economic power in the first place.

But females' relative economic power is measured as discussed above: the proportion of the means of production controlled by women; the proportion of surplus (if any) allocated by them; and, in addition, the extent to which women could accumulate wealth without restriction, and the extent to which they share in inheritance.

Force was measured by the circumstances under which men beat their wives (ranging from apparently never to 'at will'). Political power was measured in terms of relative female clout in local level governance, i.e., their degree of representation in the council or equivalent as well as their relative political weight overall.

Life options, the dependent variable, was measured by an index combining four factors. They included women's relative freedom with respect to: (1) initiating a marriage; (2) ending a marriage; (3) premarital virginity, and (4) exercising household authority.

Among the other variables measured were: sexual division of labor in the main productive activities, system of marital residence, system of descent, ideology of male supremacy, and male participation in childcare and domestic tasks.

Some preliminary results. Most spectacular was the support for the hypothesis that women's relative degree of economic control over the group's productive resources and surplus would prove the strongest influence on relative female equality in life options. Also as predicted, mere participation in production made no difference on life options. There was no effect even when women were the main labor force in the society's most important productive activity (recall that slaves have often been in this position — and remained slaves). In the preliminary computer analysis, after a series of statistical operations which social scientists term 'multivariate analysis', three things came out clearly: (1) the independent variables (economic power, force, political power, marital residence, ideology of male supremacy, male domestic/childcare participation, etc.) were able to account for most of the variation in the index measuring the dependent variable, life options (R^2 = 0.56 in the preliminary runs); (2) women's degree of economic power proved by far the most important predictor of their life options (in the same runs, R^2 = 0.47 — well over 4/5 the explained variance); (3) of the remaining factors in the regressions, only force had any significant net impact on female life options over and above that produced by women's economic power — i.e., all the other variables 'washed out' when subjected to multivariate analysis. Yet force explained only some nine percent of the variance in life options. Moreover, other multivariate analyses showed that the higher women's relative economic power, the less likely they were to be beaten. In other words, force did show some independent explanatory power, but clearly took a back seat to the economic control variables in the present analysis. Since this analysis also shows that economic power tends to win the 'weaker sex' relative protection from male use of force against them, doubt is cast on Collins' postulation of male size and aggressive strength as the primary underlying cause of lower female status.

The results seem to cast even more doubt on explanations of female status that come closer to straight biological determinism than Collins' sophisticated arguments (e.g., that of Firestone, 1970). But the results do not support an equally monocausal explanation based on economic determinism either. The paradigm considers economic power as the most important factor affecting sex stratification, but not to the exclusion of other variables. And built into the paradigm is an appreciation of a biological difference that precludes sex stratification from being considered as just another illustration of some more general stratification theory: only females bear children and lactate. Sex division of labor and life options are correspondingly affected even though other non-biological factors may mediate how, as well as prove more important in determining women's overall status.

Yet despite the pattern of findings, it is impossible to say that this preliminary test 'proves' any of the hypotheses to be correct. After all, the results are preliminary, the pilot sample was fairly small and contained significant departures from randomness, and a number of variables from the paradigm remain unmeasured to date.[13] Still, clear empirical support for the paradigm has emerged — especially concerning the proposed importance of female economic power as a determinant of female life options. So even at this stage of the game, the paradigm may produce a partial answer to two questions I suggested had to be answered before policy makers would be able to formulate relevant and effective programs aimed at enhancing female status. These were the questions of how the position of women is to be measured most meaningfully, and what are the most important factors influencing that position. I suggested that these questions could best be answered in the context of a predictive theory of sex stratification. Strictly speaking, this paradigm is not yet a rigorous theory. But it's a start, and a seemingly promising one at that, if predictive power (i.e., 'explained variance') is used as the criterion.

III. IMPLICATIONS FOR POLICY

Does the preceding analysis imply that women cannot expect full equality in today's world from anything short of a complete, revolutionary reorganization of society? Is what is needed a total reorganization in which women would be equally represented among the leaders and cadres of the new system — and hence able to have equal voice from the very start in the designing of the new social structures intended to free them? Given the still incomplete state of knowledge about the factors that affect sex stratification, would women even know what kind of social-structural designs to insist upon, should the appropriate opportunity — revolutionary or otherwise — arise? Opportunities to start from scratch are relatively rare in human history. Yet enough projects, research, theory and statistics have been generated which, if properly codified, might even now provide a set of preliminary guidelines not only for the ultimate goal of sex equality, but also for improving the lives of the world's women now.

Is there anything in this chapter that might help policy makers toward that more limited goal? Perhaps the major message to be culled from my work on the paradigm to date is the seeming utility — for policy planners, social science research and the women themselves — of focusing on females' (vs. males') relative life opportunities for both the measures and the means to improve women's position.

Concerning the measures, the list of suggested life options could be extended and made more isomorphic with the types of indicators already being collected by many governments. The call for additional indicators to measure female status has been recurrent in recent years. I am suggesting that wherever possible, those indicators be assembled simultaneously for both males and females, so that ratios may be calculated. The ratio of something like, say, girls' vs. boys' primary school enrollments[14] could be used to measure progress over time, between countries, and across the major lines of cleavage within a society: social class, rural-urban, ethnic. And if the results of these comparisons were made known in non-technical terms to the women themselves, the dry statistics might even become a consciousness-raising tool. For they make salient how well different groups of women are doing against not only each other, but also the men in their lives. Valuable information, one might expect, for women with a new vision of expanding opportunities on their horizons.

Far more important than the measures, however, are the means to provide such expanding opportunities. And here, the paradigm has focused on economic opportunities. Given the increasing educational prerequisites for most paid employment, jobs cannot be separated from schooling. Both types of programs must be provided before females can be expected to gain the 'poker chips' to be cashed in for greater autonomy in their personal lifespace. But schools and job creation are expensive; they require commitment of scarce resources, and usually imply reallocation of existing revenues. Are there reasons other than justice or the good of the national soul (as if these should not be reason enough) for expanding educational and economic opportunities for a nation's females? Let us give merely one example. As it happens, in many of the countries where the dilemma of allocation of scarce resources is likely to be most cruel, the answer seems to be an emphatic 'yes'.

These are the countries suffering the consequences of rapid population growth. Most are poorer Third World nations where, often, each new mouth (as Enke, 1960, first discovered for India) means a net drain on national resources. In these countries, providing employment for males, let alone females, is often a losing race. New development is likely to be capital, not labor, intensive; typically, half the rapidly increasing population are dependents under age 15; and the migrants keep streaming to the cities at a rate ever faster than the jobs. In these countries also, female employment rates (especially in the modern sector) are often quite low.

Yet, as recent studies show, the weight of the evidence indicates a substantial and inverse correlation between female status factors and fertility (see, e.g., Birdsall, 1974; Sipes, forthcoming; Dixon, 1974; Germain, 1974; Ware, 1975 and Chaney, 1973). Female employment in modern sector jobs outside the household seems generally well associated with lower fertility — and female education even more so. Moreover, Boserup (1974) makes the argument that even in the high unemployment Third World countries under discussion, getting women into the economic mainstream should increase the pace of development. At the extreme, it might be that every dollar spent on education and employment for boys not matched by a dollar spent for girls may ultimately be lost to such nations in the subsequently higher fertility of those girls. At the very least, however, getting females into schools and employment would seem to have clear utility beyond altruism. At stake are not only economic goals, but also the commitment to relieve human suffering and make a more equitable life available to all.[15]

But even if the policy planners were to provide the schooling and the jobs, the weight of the paradigm makes it appear that strategic indispensability and power are not automatic fringe benefits of work. In the final analysis, it may well be the degree of organization and consciousness of the women themselves that will determine just how far along the road to equality the provision of economic opportunity will lead.

NOTES

1. A 'good news' approach to the position of US women tends to stress women who have become shining (but not necessarily numerous) exemplars of some achievement. For example, federal 'affirmative action' guidelines and changing economic conditions have led to a bevy of stories about 'female firsts' — the handful of Jackie Robinsons of our day who have integrated selected male bastions from the Little League to West Point — and their somewhat more numerous sisters who are taking up carpentry, computers, credit cards, politics, law, medicine, and other macho mainstays. Much of this seems similar to the spirit of the cigarette slogan that tells its intended female audience just how far they've come — while characterizing them as 'baby'. On closer examination, much of the 'good news' involves comparisons between the position of some group of women at two points in time or social space: e.g., in 1900, there were almost no women Xs; now look at Thelma Token and the hundreds of other tradition-breaking women who have become Xs since 1970 (substitute appropriate Xs and dates to suit).

2. In contrast to the 'good news' discussed above, much of the 'bad news' concerning the present status of United States females involves comparing the relative position of women vs. men over time. The example referred to in the text merits more detailed examination in this regard. It appears that there has been a steadily increasing economic disadvantage of US women vis-à-vis men going back nearly forty years. Knudsen (1969) documented the trend from 1940-64; more recent US Bureau of the Census figures show it is continuing. First, let us examine what has been happening with full-time year-round workers.

In 1955, women workers in this category earned $0.64 for every $1.00 made by their male counterparts (i.e., the wages of these females were more than one-third less what the men earned). By 1970 this was down to $0.59 for every $1.00. The latest government figures, for 1975, show that the ratio dipped again: full-time year-round women workers were down to $0.57 for every $1.00 earned by their masculine counterparts. When we compare total money income for all men and women over 14 years of age, we find that the erosion of women's position is even steeper: in 1947, women's income stood at $0.46 for every male $1.00. By 1970, Census figures show that it was down to a mere $0.34 (Ehrlich, 1974:1). Of course, this last set of figures includes many more women than men who work part-time, receive social security, welfare or other transfer payments, or just aren't in the labor force at all, so of course we should expect female income to be a smaller proportion of male than for the full-time year-round workers compared above. But for both groups, we are faced with an apparently paradoxical growing gap in income in a time of supposedly increasing sexual equality. This growing wage gap is analyzed in terms of the paradigm presented in this paper in Blumberg, forthcoming.

3. In simple, preclass societies, we can compare the women to the men of the total group, but for class societies we have to examine the position of women separately for each class, for it may vary greatly by stratum. To underscore this distinction, most subsequent references to male/female comparison are phrased something like this: the position of the women relative to the men of their class or group.

4. Among the Tasaday, the evidence is still incomplete. My paradigm of sex stratification examines the degree of relative inequality of the males and females in a specific group but makes no assumptions about any potential upper limits on sexual equality, including the controversial topic of whether hormonal differences militate against it, as alleged by Goldberg, 1973/74.

5. Two other approaches to female status involving the notion of life alternatives or options, and including some of the variables on my list, may be found in Safilios-Rothschild, 1971; Boulding, 1972.

6. A partial selection from the list includes: Martin and Voorhies, 1975; Oboler, 1973; Leacock, 1972; Engels (Leacock edition, 1972); Sacks, 1975; Benston, 1969; and Lenin (in Benston, 1969).

7. George Peter Murdock's *Ethnographic Atlas* has been frequently — and often justifiably — criticized for a wide variety of methodological problems. There are undoubted weaknesses in defining the sampling unit and in failing to pinpoint all variables to the same location and/or time, for example. The *Atlas* presents data on dozens of variables which Murdock and like-minded anthropological colleagues deemed most relevant for the study of the world's pre-industrial societies; other social scientists find the variables included wanting. It is certain that there are a number of errors scattered among its codes on some 1,200-odd societies. Nevertheless, over time, the *Atlas* has shown its worth in dozens of studies whose findings have stood up to other data sources. In general, its economically-linked variables have proved the most trustworthy — and seemingly the least likely to be affected by 'Galton's problem' (where two variables seem to covary not because of any functional link but rather due to the happen-

stance of joint diffusion). Yet overall, it remains the largely-unimpeached, largest-scale data source for macro-societal comparative research.

8. According to the archaeological record, horticultural cultivation apparently evolved slowly over millenia, rather than springing from some sudden discovery that seeds sprout into plants. All foragers ever studied already know this but rarely adopt the more arduous and regimented life of cultivation in the absence of strong pressure. Today the pressure is likely to come from governments eager to increase their control as well as 'modernity' among the few remaining foraging groups on earth. But historically, population pressure seems to have been the most frequent and plausible stimulus to the emergence of cultivation (see, e.g., Binford, 1971; Flannery, 1971; Meyers, 1971). After all, cultivation provides the possibility of increasing the total group food supply.

9. Actually, the spread is quite great. My calculations with the *Ethnographic Atlas* revealed that it ranged from about two percent of societies where women contributed virtually nothing to the food supply to roughly the same percentage where they contributed two-thirds or more.

10. Why this excess fertility? In contrast to the standard Malthusian explanation (that peasants breed, primarily out of animal-like ignorance, up to the limits of the food supply), I suggest that the peasants continued to produce those extra sons and daughters for basically rational reasons of utility. There has been a recent convergence of studies suggesting that births tend to be limited or spaced in accordance with life conditions, and evidence has been mounting to support the proposition that people in the pre-industrial societies exhibit high fertility under certain conditions that make large numbers of children economically useful (see, e.g., Polgar, 1972, 1975; Birdsell and related references in Lee and Devore, 1968; Faris, 1973; Mamdani, 1972; Schnaiberg and Reed, 1974; Blumberg, 1978). Returning to the problem of the 'expendables', I have suggested that just because these excess sons and daughters of the peasantry were barely even a surplus labor force as adults does not mean they were not useful to their parents as children. Often the only one of the three factors of production (land, capital, labor) the peasant producers can control is labor costs — by growing their own labor force (see Blumberg with Garcia, 1977). In agrarian societies, children may become economically useful as young as age six, returning more to the parents in labor, babysitting, etc. than the costs of feeding and maintaining them. In such societies, the extra children may be what is needed to keep ahead of the landlord — surplus extraction in the form of 'rent' always comes off the top of peasant output. Thus, peasants in societies where their surplus is skimmed off the top by the dominant classes are not (paraphrasing Mamdani, 1972) poor because they have many children; they have many children because they are poor, and the children represent a potential solution to the problem of their poverty. Hence the origin of the class of expendables seems to be found in the social relations of production.

11. It would appear that women may traverse the road to relatively equal (or better) economic power under a variety of circumstances, most of which seem to involve their capitalizing on their strategic importance in production in a period of larger economic flux. In most instances, this would probably involve an economy with sufficient sex division of labor in major economic activities to give

women a sphere in which they controlled technical expertise and day-in, day-out work flow. For example, in a previously communal economy moving toward surplus accumulation and ownership on a non-communal basis, the women might gain control of the means and surplus of production involved in their contribution to the economy. In a non-communal economy, an unimportant sphere always controlled by women might suddenly mushroom in importance and demand; or conditions of political instability and strife might facilitate women taking over control of the means and surplus of production involved in their work from those (men) who had previously held it. But the example of the communal Tasaday gatherers should alert us to the possibility of equal economic power being exercised by women in the absence of either or both sex division of labor in production and non-communal economic control.

12. The *HRAF* were initiated by Murdock almost a generation before the *Ethnographic Atlas*, and have been subject to at least as much criticism. The *HRAF* organize ethnographies under a complex system of 700 separate categories. The categories are basically a multiple-reference filing system for the actual pages of the ethnographies (vs. the alphameric codes of the *Atlas*). The *HRAF* and the *Atlas* share many of the same methodological pitfalls (see note 7), and both contain many, although apparently non-systematic, errors. But both have stood up fairly well to the tests of time and many studies. Overall, despite all the flaws, the *HRAF* remain the richest multi-society data source for comparative research. As with the *Atlas*, one seems on the most solid ground with the techno-economic data. And a substantial amount of the variables I coded from the *HRAF* fall into this category. When used with appropriate caution, I feel, the *HRAF* can generate reliable and valid results.

13. A more detailed treatment of the paradigm, the sample, the coding, and the results to date is in preparation (Blumberg, forthcoming).

14. See Youssef and Hartley, Chapter 4.

15. As Tinker (1976), Boserup (1970) and many others increasingly point out, development planning that does not take women explicitly into account may often leave them in a worse position than before. In a number of countries with a tradition of high female economic autonomy (via food crop cultivation and trading, or market trading in general), the independence and economic well-being of the women often are undermined by the economic changes and dislocations accompanying 'development', and the incorporation of previously less-affected areas into the world economy. Food crops are replaced by export crops — often to the disadvantage of the female cultivators of the former; handmade goods sold at local markets are replaced by cheap mass-production imports sold through foreign-originated new distribution networks — again, often to the disadvantage of the female petty traders and merchants. And development assistance provided to women has focused more around family planning, nutrition and childcare than restoring or enhancing their economic opportunities.

REFERENCES

ARONOFF, Joel and William D. CRANO, 'A Re-Examination of the Cross-Cultural Principles of Task Segregation and Sex-Role Differentiation in the Family.' *American Sociological Review,* 40 (1975): 12-20.

BENSTON, Margaret, 'The Political Economy of Women's Liberation.' *Monthly Review,* 21 (1969): 13-27.

BINFORD, Lewis R., 'Post-Pleistocene Adaptations', pp. 22-49 in Stuart Struever (ed.), *Prehistoric Agriculture.* Garden City, New York: The Natural History Press, 1971.

BIRDSALL, Nancy, 'An Introduction to the Social Science Literature on "Woman's Place" and Fertility in the Developing World.' Washington, D.C.: Interdisciplinary Communications Program, Smithsonian Institution, 1974.

BIRDSELL, Joseph B., 'Some Predictions for the Pleistocene Based on Equilibrium Systems Among Recent Hunter-Gatherers,' pp. 229-40 in Richard B. Lee and Irven DeVore (eds.), *Man the Hunter.* Chicago: Aldine, 1968.

BLUMBERG, Rae Lesser, 'Structural Factors Affecting Women's Status: A Cross-Societal Paradigm.' Paper read at the meetings of the International Sociological Association, Toronto, August 1974.

--'Kibbutz Women: From the Fields of Revolution to the Laundries of Discontent,' pp. 319-44 in Lynne Iglitzin and Ruth Ross (eds.), *Women in the World: A Comparative Study.* Santa Barbara and Oxford: ABC Clio, 1976a.

--'The Erosion of Sexual Equality in the Kibbutz: Structural Factors Affecting the Status of Women,' pp. 320-39 in Joan I. Roberts (ed.), *Beyond Intellectual Sexism: A New Woman, A New Reality.* New York: McKay, 1976b.

--*Stratification: Socioeconomic and Sexual Inequality.* Dubuque: Wm. C. Brown, 1978.

--*Woman's Fate: a Cross-Societal Paradigm and Studies of Sexual Stratification.* Manuscript in preparation.

BLUMBERG, Rae Lesser with Maria-Pilar GARCIA, 'The Political Economy of the Mother-Child Family: A Cross-Societal View,' pp. 99-163 in Luis Leñero-Otero (ed.), *Beyond the Nuclear Family Model.* London: Sage, 1977.

BOSERUP, Ester, *The Role of Women in Economic Development.* New York: St. Martin's, 1970.

--'Employment and Education: Keys to Smaller Families.' The Victor Bostrum Fund Report No. 18, spring 1974.

BOULDING, Elise. 'Women as Role Models in Industrializing Societies: A Macrosystem Model of Socialization for Civic Competence,' pp. 11-34 in Marvin B. Sussman and Betty E. Cogswell, *Cross-National Family Research.* E. J. Brill, 1972.

BROWN, Judith K., 'A Note on the Division of Labor by Sex.' *American Anthropologist,* 72 (1970): 1074-78.

--'Iroquois Women: An Ethnohistoric Note,' pp. 235-51 in Rayna R. Reiter (ed.), *Toward an Anthropology of Women.* New York: Monthly Review Press, 1975.

CHANEY, Elsa, 'Women and Population: Some Key Policy, Research and Action

Issues,' in Richard Clinton (Ed.), *Population and Politics: New Directions for Political Scientists.* Lexington, Mass.: Lexington Books, 1973.

CHILDE, V. Gordon, *What Happened in History,* rev. ed. Baltimore: Penguin Books, 1964.

COLLINS, Randall, 'A Conflict Theory of Sexual Stratification.' *Social Problems,* 19 (1971) : 3-21.

DAVIS, Kingsley and Judith BLAKE, 'Social Structure and Fertility: An Analytic Framework.' *Economic Development and Cultural Change,* 4 (1956): 211-35.

DIXON, Ruth, 'Women's rights and fertility.' The Population Council, Reports on Population/Family Planning, No. 17, January 1975.

EHRLICH, Howard J., 'Selected Differences in the Life Chances of Men and Women in the United States'. Baltimore, Md: Research Group One, Report No. 13, 1974.

ENGELS, Frederick, *The Origin of the Family, Private Property and the State.* New York: International Publishers, 1972.

ENKE, Stephen, 'The Gains to India from Population Control: Some Money Measures and Incentive Schemes.' *Review of Economics and Statistics* (1960), pp. 175-80.

FARIS, James C., 'Social Evolution, Population and Production.' Paper presented at the IX International Congress of Anthropological and Ethnological Sciences, Chicago, 1973.

FERNANDEZ, C. A. II and Frank LYNCH, 'The Tasaday: Cave-Dwelling Food Gatherers of South Cotabato, Mindanao.' *Philippine Sociological Review,* 20 (1972) (3) : 279-330.

FIRESTONE, Shulamith, *The Dialectic of Sex.* New York: William Morrow, 1970.

FLANNERY, Kent V., 'Archeological Systems Theory and Early Mesoamerica,' pp. 80-100 in Stuart Struever (ed.), *Prehistoric Agriculture.* Garden City, New York: The Natural History Press, 1971.

GERMAIN, Adrienne, *Some Aspects of the Roles of Women in Population and Development.* United Nations 1974.

GERTH, Hans and C. Wright MILLS, *From Max Weber: Essays in Sociology.* Fairlawn, N.Y.: Oxford University Press, 1946.

GOLDBERG, Steven, *The Inevitability of Patriarchy.* New York: William Morrow 1973/74.

GOUGH, Kathleen, 'The Origin of the Family.' *Journal of Marriage and the Family,* 33 (1971) (4): 750-71.

KNUDSEN, Dean D., 'The Declining Status of Women: Popular Myth and the Failure of Functionalist Thought.' *Social Forces,* 48 (1969): 183-93.

LEACOCK, Eleanor Burke, 'Introduction' to Engels, Frederick, *The Origin of the Family, Private Property and the State.* New York: International Publishers, 1972.

LEAVITT, Ruby R., 'Women in Other Cultures,' pp. 393-427 in Vivian Gornick and Barbara K. Moran, *Woman in Sexist Society.* New York: Basic Books, 1971.

LEE, Richard B. and Irven DE VORE, (eds.), *Man the Hunter.* Chicago: Aldine, 1968.

LEIBOWITZ, Lila, 'Perspectives on the Evolution of Sex Differences,' pp. 20-35 in Rayna R. Reiter (ed.), *Toward an Anthropology of Women.* New York:

Monthly Review Press, 1975.

LENIN, V. I., *Passages from On the Emancipation of Women*. Moscow: Progress Publishers, 1969. Appendix to Margaret Benston, 'The political economy of women's liberation,' *Monthly Review*, 21 (1969) : 13-27.

LENSKI, Gerhard E., *Power and Privilege: A Theory of Social Stratification*. New York: McGraw-Hill, 1966.

LENSKI, Gerhard E. and Jean LENSKI, *Human Societies*. New York: McGraw Hill. 2nd Edition, 1974.

MAMDANI, Mahmood, *The Myth of Population Control: Family, Caste, and Class in an Indian Village*. New York: Monthly Review Press, 1972.

MARTIN, M. Kay, and Barbara VOORHIES, *Female of the Species*. New York: Columbia University Press, 1975.

MEYERS, J. Thomas, 'The Origin of Agriculture: An Evaluation of Three Hypotheses,' pp. 101-21 in Stuart Struever (ed.) *Prehistoric Agriculture*. Garden City, New York: The Natural History Press, 1971.

MICHAELSON, Evalyn Jacobson and Walter GOLDSCHMIDT, 'Female Roles and Male Dominance Among Peasants.' *Southwestern Journal of Anthropology*, 27 (1971) : 330-52.

MURDOCK, George Peter, 'Ethnographic Atlas: A Summary.' *Ethnology*, 6 (1967): 109-236.

MURDOCK, George Peter and Douglas R. WHITE, 'Standard Cross-Cultural Sample.' *Ethnology*, 8 (1969): 329-69.

MURDOCK, George Peter and Caterina PROVOST, 'Factors in the Division of Labor by Sex: A Cross-Cultural Analysis.' *Ethnology*, 12, (1973): 203-35.

OBOLER, Regina E., 'Economics and the Status of Women.' Paper presented at the meetings of the American Anthropological Association, New Orleans, 1973.

OPPENHEIMER, Valerie Kincade, 'Demographic Influence on Female Employment and the Status of Women.' *American Journal of Sociology*, 78 (1973): 946-61.

PARSONS, Talcott and Robert BALES, *Family, Socialization and Interaction Process*. Glencoe, Ill: Free Press, 1955.

POLGAR, Steven, 'Population History and Population Policies from an Anthropological Perspective.' *Current Anthropology*, 13 (1972): 203-11.

--'Population, Evolution and Theoretical Paradigms,' pp. 1-25 in Steven Polgar (ed.), *Population, Ecology and Social Evolution*. Mouton: The Hague, 1975.

REINHARDT, Hazel H., Personal communications with author, Madison, Wisconsin, 1974.

ROSALDO, Michelle Zimbalist and Louise LAMPHERE, 'Introduction', pp. 1-15 in Michelle Zimbalist Rosaldo and Louise Lamphere (eds.) *Woman, Culture and Society*. Stanford: Stanford University Press, 1974.

SACKS, Karen, 'Engels Revisited: Women, the Organization of Production, and Private Property' pp. 211-34 in Rayna R. Reiter (ed.), *Toward an Anthropology of Women*. New York: Monthly Review Press, 1975.

SAFILIOS-ROTHSCHILD, Constantina, 'A Cross-Cultural Examination of Woman's Marital, Educational and Occupational Options.' *Acta Sociologica*, 14 (1971) : 96-113.

SANDAY, Peggy R., 'Toward a Theory of the Status of Women.' *American Anthropologist,* 75 (1973) : 1682-700.

SCHLEGEL, Alice, *Male Dominance and Female Autonomy: Domestic Authority in Matrilineal Societies.* New Haven: HRAF Press, 1972.

SCHNAIBERG, Allan and David REED, 'Risk, Uncertainty, and Family Formation: The Social Context of Poverty Groups.' *Population Studies* 28 (1974).

SIPES, Richard G., PhD dissertation (Suny-Buffalo) on inverse relation between fertility and female status in 17-society sample, forthcoming.

SPIRO, Melford E., *Kibbutz: Venture in Utopia.* New York: Schocken Books, 1963.

STACK, Carol B., *All Our Kin: Strategies for Survival in a Black Community.* New York: Harper and Row, 1974.

STINCHCOMBE, Arthur L., 'Agricultural Enterprise and Rural Class Relations.' pp. 485-97 in J. L. Finkle and R. W. Gable, *Political Development and Social Change.* New York: Wiley, 1966.

TINKER, Irene, 'The Adverse Impact of Development on Women,' pp. 22-35 in Irene Tinker and Michèle Bo Bramsen, (eds.), *Women in Development.* Washington D.C.: Overseas Development Council/American Association for the Advancement of Science, 1976.

TREIMAN, Donald J. and Kermit TERRELL, 'Sex and the Process of Status Attainment: A Comparison of Working Women and Men.' *American Sociological Review,* 40 (1975) (2) : 174-200.

WARE, Helen, 'The Relevance of Changes in Women's Roles to Fertility Behavior: The African Evidence.' Paper presented at the annual meeting of the Population Association of America, Seattle, April 1975.

WHITING, Beatrice, 'Work and the Family: Cross-Cultural Perspectives.' Paper read at the Conference on Women: Resource for a Changing World, Cambridge, Mass., 1972.

ZIEGLER, Philip, *The Black Death.* New York: Harper and Row, 1969.

II
THE DELIBERATE USE OF POLICY TO CHANGE SEX ROLES

6
PUBLIC POLICY AND CHANGING FAMILY PATTERNS IN SWEDEN 1930-1977

Annika Baude

National Board of Health and Welfare, Stockholm

For the last four decades, Sweden has engaged in a consistent effort to change family and sex role patterns through the deliberate use of public policy. The Swedish experience has commanded the attention of social scientists and policy makers who would use social policy to equalize the roles of women and men in the family, in the workplace, and in the society at large.

Ms. Baude's paper is almost a paradigm of the relationship among policy, research, and sex roles. A basic policy of full employment for a relatively small labor force has been the undergirding on which the new sex-role structure has been predicated. Ms. Baude makes crystal clear that it was the need to attract women into the labor force that informed policy vis-à-vis women. It was not, therefore, a matter of women having to influence policy makers, but rather policy makers having to influence women. The implementation of policy with respect to women rested on research. Ms. Baude gives great credit for the subsequent policy on sex-roles to the 1962 book edited by E. Dahlström — published by an independent research institute and financed by private industry — which incorporated research from sociology, psychology, social psychology, industrial economics, and economics and greatly stimulated thinking on sex roles.

Swedish policy has not feared to experiment. Baude refers to several such experimental programs. A number of the programs have succeeded admirably. Some have not as yet. The housing program, for example, suffered from lack of recognition of the changes taking place in the family. Whether more adequate research could have corrected this is an interesting question. Education has also proved to be slower than anticipated in changing sex roles. Just passing laws which erased sexism from the schools was not enough to overcome the weight of tradition emanating from the home and from the outside world. It was not lack of research knowledge of the socialization process (as the Dahlstrom book made clear), but lack of ways to influence it by the schools. Quite aside from the contribution to the topic which this book addresses, Ms. Baude's review of the Swedish experience in social legislation constitutes a major contribution in and of itself.

DEVELOPMENT OF THE SOCIAL WELFARE SYSTEM

From the 1930s until the fall of 1976, when a non-socialist coalition government took office, governmental power in Sweden remained in the hands of the same party, the Social Democrats. This 45-year period of political continuity is one important reason why Swedish social policy has been able to develop consistently along certain main lines. Goals have been set and then gradually, but steadily, implemented. To be sure, many of the reforms carried out by the Social Democrats have had the support of the other major political parties as well.

That equality between the sexes ought to prevail has always been a basic tenet of the Social Democratic Party. It was not until rather recently, however, that the real meaning of such equality and the substantial social changes necessary to achieve it have been discussed, either among the party's leaders or its members. At the same time, many of the programs undertaken as part of the Government's overall social policy have had an important impact on women and their status in society.

The predominant family pattern in Sweden up to the mid-1960s was the single wage-earner family, in which the man assumed economic responsibility for his wife and children. The State's contribution to family support mainly took the form of direct economic assistance of two types: a basic child allowance paid for every child regardless of the parents' income and an income-related housing allowance. Several important 'classless' public services were introduced early, including free maternity and child health care for all, as well as free lunches for all school children and free tuition through the university level. But

Translation: Jeanne Rosen.

provision of such an essential service as nursery schools in general and extended day care for those children whose parents both work did not begin in earnest until the 1960s, when child care finally came to be regarded as a public responsibility.

Within marriage, women have enjoyed legal and economic equality with men since passage of the 1920 Marriage Code. Moreover, no formal obstacles hindered women from being gainfully employed. Since 1925, women have had the right to hold government jobs on equal terms and since 1947 they have been entitled to the same salary for these jobs as men. In addition, since 1939 employers have been prohibited from firing a woman because of marriage or pregnancy. But other than these instances, there has been little labor legislation directed specifically toward women.

One other public action which was of great importance for the situation of working women came in 1955. In that year the State assumed responsibility for medical insurance for every inhabitant, and all working women became entitled to a six months' leave of absence with practically full pay in connection with childbirth. For home-working women similar benefits were instituted.

The major social welfare reforms carried out from the 1930s until the Second World War and then continuing during the 1950s and 1960s have, from the outset, been applied on an individual basis. This means that benefits are not tied to the family breadwinner, as is the case in the social insurance systems of many other countries. This principle of individually applicable benefits applies to the basic pension system (1935), the general health insurance system (1955) and the supplementary pension system (1960). On the other hand, the benefits paid out under the health insurance and supplementary pension systems are related to each person's income, which means that those with a low income, or none at all, during certain periods of their lives receive lower benefits. This puts women in particular at a disadvantage, in part because many women stay at home to care for children and so have no income, and in part because women who do work are generally paid less than men. Still, women have an advantage in another way, since both the general pension and the supplementary pension systems pay survivor's benefits to widows (and children), but not to widowers.

Single and divorced mothers have been entitled to cash advances on their child support payments since 1930 in those cases where a father does not pay adequate support, the rationale being that the State must step in and help support women and children when men do not meet their economic obligations. During the last several decades, the level of this support has been successively increased — as have the amounts paid out in general child allowances and housing allowances — so that a single mother need no longer give up her child for economic reasons, as could happen earlier. More and more emphasis, however, is now being put on providing vocational training and child-care services, so that single and divorced mothers can support themselves and their children by working.

The various social welfare programs briefly touched upon above constituted only a part of the State's welfare policy during this period of development. Measures involving employment and education were also vital, and these are discussed below. Passing mention should be made here, finally, of the Government's housing policy. To provide decent housing for everyone — and particularly for families with children — has been a major goal since the 1930s.

SOCIAL CHANGES DURING THE 1950s AND 1960s

The 1950s and 1960s were decades during which sweeping population shifts took place in Sweden. Changes in the structure of the economy implied a wholesale population move from rural to urban areas. The demand for labor was great. The public sector grew rapidly. As a result, women had a better chance to find work than at any time since industrialization began. Much new housing was produced, and more and more families lived in apartments that were modern and easy to care for. Household size decreased because of the splitting up of families and the decline in the number of children per family. The educational system expanded, brightening the prospects for young people to enter higher status occupations than their parents.

During the 1950s, the number of women in gainful employment increased, primarily because middle-aged women entered the labor market in greater and greater numbers. Women in their 40s, whose children were leaving home, were ready for a 'conditional release'. They had fulfilled their 'maternal responsibilities' and were now able to seek employment.

Throughout the 1960s, married women continued to seek employment in greater and greater numbers, now at all age levels. Even mothers with children of school and preschool age began to take jobs. By the beginning of the 1970s, about 50 percent of mothers with children under 7, and about 60 percent of mothers with children under 17, were gainfully employed. By 1977, these percentages had increased to 66 and 73 percent respectively.

Employed Women as a Percentage of All Women, 1963-1975 (part-time work included)

	1963	1967	1971	1975
Women 35-44 *without* children under 7 years*	63.4	70.2	71.5	82.6
Women of all ages *with* children under 7 years	38.0	37.6	45.8	60.7

* Children in Sweden begin school at the age of 7.

A common pattern until rather recently, however, was for mothers with small children to work only part-time, often in the evenings and on weekends. Gradually the number of hours that these mothers work has increased. In 1977 more than 80 percent of the working mothers with children under 7 years worked 20 hours per week or more.

LABOUR MARKET POLICY AND WOMEN

Ever since the Social Democratic Party first came to power, it has attached great importance to its labor market policy, which in turn reflects its commitment to a full employment society. In the 1930s, when unemployment was an acute problem, the goal of full employment applied first and foremost to men. Gradually, an effort was made to create employment opportunities for those formerly outside the labor force. Not until the last few years, however, has it become obvious that the goal of full employment must apply every bit as much to women as to men.

Labor market policy has aimed both at keeping unemployment at a low level and at stimulating new groups to enter the labor force. One important aspect of this policy since the 1960s has been retraining courses for men and women who are or risk becoming unemployed.

This retraining effort, which has become more and more extensive, is directed toward women as much as toward men. Courses are largely full-time, and participants receive a subsistence allowance. Women at home, despite the fact that they are not considered unemployed in the usual sense, are eligible for such retraining courses and allowances.

The 1960s also saw the beginning of special courses and other measures designed to stimulate women to enter the labor market. In particular, much effort has gone into encouraging employers, through information programs and even incentive payments, to recruit more women for traditionally male jobs. Thus it can be said that at the central level, the Government's labor market policy has unquestionably been concerned with helping women achieve a position in working life equivalent to that of men, primarily by encouraging and easing their entry into the labor market. On the local level, however, the implementation of these goals has unfortunately been very slow.

When it comes to questions involving level of pay and working conditions for women, the Government has had little influence, since such questions do not lie within the official 'sphere of influence'. Such matters are regulated by agreement among the parties directly involved. Indeed, it was not until 1962 after an equal-pay agreement had been established between the Swedish Confederation of Trade Unions (LO) and the Swedish Employer's Confederation (SAF) that Parliament finally ratified ILO Convention No 100 of 1951 demanding equal pay for equal work regardless of sex in all spheres of activity including private enterprise (as had earlier been legally established for the public sector).

The State in its role of employer, of course, has responsibility for the work conditions existing within the civil service. In 1925, women were granted the right to hold all government jobs exclusive of the clergy and military, and, since 1947, female civil service employees have been guaranteed the same pay and terms as men with similar jobs. In the public sector, just as in the labor market in general, however, men and women have very often held different kinds of jobs, so that equal pay legislation has not had a decisive influence. In those professions such as teaching and medical care where men and women have held equivalent jobs, equal pay legislation has made an important contribution to the equality of women.

In keeping with its desire to improve the opportunities available to women in government service, Parliament since 1976 has required State authorities, when they submit their annual funding applications, to describe the measures being taken in their departments to promote women to higher positions. Since promotion often involves additional training, child supervision costs incurred by women participating in a training course are reimbursed. An effort is even underway to provide child supervision right on the site of such courses.

The State as employer has taken the lead in trying to adapt work conditions to employees' needs. Shorter work hours have been possible for some State-employed parents of small children since the 1950s. In 1970, instructions were issued which emphasized even more strongly that an employee's need for a reduced workday is to be met, and that this is to apply to employees on all levels and of both sexes. According to the State's directive, 'part-time work ought to be a possibility for those who perform routine as well as more highly qualified work. Special regard should be given to the difficulty of employees to arrange for child supervision'.

In 1972, the Government appointed an Advisory Council on Equality between Men and Women, responsible directly to the Prime Minister's office. In the instructions to this Council, the Prime Minister explained that 'the distribution of work between men and women which now characterizes our society....locks men and women into separate roles and obstructs free personal development. The demand for equality...involves changes not only in the conditions of women but also in the conditions of men. One purpose of such changes is to give women an increased opportunity for gainful employment and to give men an increased responsibility for care of the children'.

The Advisory Council has engaged in various efforts, which in turn are expected to function as models for the labor market in general. Examples of these activities include:

(1) an experiment in fifteen counties to place women in traditionally male jobs in industry: over 2,000 women have found jobs through this program.

(2) an experiment within one industry to institute a 6-hour workday with two shifts.

(3) a special 'equality grant' to employers who train men and women for jobs now dominated by the opposite sex.

After making an extensive analysis of part-time work, the Advisory Council concluded that such work does not promote equality between men and women. In the long run, it felt, reduction of the working hours in one's ordinary job for certain periods of one's life ought to be a practical and economic possibility for both men and women.

At the Advisory Council's instigation, the State has made additional efforts on behalf of job equality between men and women. One hundred public employment offices across the country have been authorized to hire new staff members whose special task is to seek out opportunities for women to enter the labor market, and to ensure that women are encouraged to make a free choice of job or training program without regard to traditional models. Furthermore, Parliament has decided that companies which receive financial assistance under the Regional Development Program — which seeks to stimulate location of industries in certain economically depressed areas of the country — must employ at least 40 percent of each sex in the newly-created jobs.

The goal is not only to open up traditionally male jobs to women, but also to do the opposite. There is, for example, an experiment now underway giving male applicants preferential consideration for admission to preschool teacher training programs. The number of male preschool teachers has, as a result, increased substantially in recent years.

Legislation prohibiting sex discrimination has been considered, but the position of the former Social Democratic Government was that such legislation would not be an effective means of achieving equality. The matter is much discussed, however, and the present coalition Government is currently preparing such legislation for consideration.

SEX ROLES AND EDUCATION

During the late 1950s and throughout the 1960s, an enormous expansion of the entire educational system took place in Sweden. Compulsory education was extended from six or seven to nine years with the introduction of the 9-year comprehensive school. The capacity of the gymnasiums (secondary schools) was increased until facilities were adequate to admit 80-90 percent of each age group. Even university-level programs expanded greatly to meet the increased demand for higher education from those graduating from the gymnasium.

A new program for financing higher studies through a combination of grants and loans, begun in 1964, made it economically feasible for all who could meet the admission requirements to attend a university or professional school. For young women, who to a greater extent than young men had been impeded from pursuing their educational ambitions because of economic dependence on their parents, these reforms have meant greatly improved educational opportunities. All these reforms are part of the continuing struggle for equality. The goal is that all young people are to have the same educational opportunities regardless of their parents' economic and social status, regardless of where in Sweden they live, and regardless of sex.

Boys and girls in the Swedish comprehensive school system receive the same instruction in all subjects, with the exception of gymnastics above a certain age level. Sewing and woodwork, as well as home economics and child care, are obligatory for both sexes. Sex education is part of the curriculum at all levels. Text-books are submitted to a text-book committee, and one important criterion for book selection is that the text and pictures avoid portraying men and women in traditional roles only, but, instead, present an egalitarian distribution of roles between men and women both at home and at work.

In the statement of goals and purposes which Parliament set forth at the time of the basic school reform of 1962, the question of equality between the sexes was discussed only in general terms:

> [The school is supposed to meet] the needs and requirements of society for such qualities in men and women as will inspire and promote the democratic principles of cooperation and tolerance between the sexes and between people of different races and national origin.

However, when the basic school curriculum was revised in 1969, it was stressed that the question of sex roles should be *explicitly* dealt with as part of the instruction in various subjects. The view of the school's responsibility in this area had, in other words, changed considerably in seven years.

The revised view is that the school must

> promote equality between the sexes — in the family, in the labor market and in the community at large. This should be achieved partly by treating boys and girls the same at school, partly by working to counteract the traditional attitudes to sex roles and stimulating pupils to question the differences between men and women with respect to influence, work assignments and wages that exist in many sectors of society...The schools should assume that men and women will play the same role in the future, that preparation for the parental role is just as important for boys as for girls, and that girls have reason to be just as interested in their careers as boys.

A number of studies and experiments were undertaken during the early 1970s to determine how to increase both teachers' and pupils' awareness of how they are influenced by entrenched sex role attitudes. These studies resulted in a number of suggestions which are now in the process of being implemented. Among other things, Parliament has approved an experimental program, to be carried out over the next five years, for giving special training to five people from each school — a total of 1,200 basic school and 300 gymnasium participants. Teachers, other school personnel, and students are to be included. These people, in turn, are to take the initiative in their schools for implementing the curriculum plan's intentions of giving students a broader view of men's and women's roles, both at home and on the job.

Great effort is made in the schools to stimulate both boys and girls to choose a career without regard to traditional sex roles. Extensive vocational guidance is provided at all levels by counsellors who are trained to guard against the impact of sex role stereotypes on vocational choices.

The whole field of adult education, both through the classical means (of voluntary organizations, e.g., in evening classes) and through municipally-provided courses, has undergone a tremendous expansion in recent years. One goal has been to enable those with only six or seven years of schooling to advance to the same educational level as today's youth. Many women at home have taken advantage of this opportunity; indeed, women now comprise a majority of such students. In addition, access to higher education has been made less restrictive. Now, even those who have never attended a gymnasium can be admitted if they have at least five years' work experience, which can include work in the home. Furthermore, care of one's own children can now be counted as part of the practical experience required for entry into certain educational professions.

INCOME TAX AND WOMEN'S GAINFUL EMPLOYMENT

The income tax system is not, strictly speaking, a part of the social welfare policy. Still, it must be considered in this context, since its influence on a family's choice of life style has proved to be considerable.

The federal income tax system in Sweden is progressive, i.e. higher incomes are taxed at a higher rate than lower incomes. Until 1970, married couples and couples living together had both their federal and local taxes calculated on the basis of their combined income. This joint taxation was based on the premise that a marriage is an economic unit, and that the taxable capacity of one spouse could not be assessed without regard to the income and resources of the other spouse.

Since 1971, however, each partner in a marriage or joint living arrangement has been taxed on his or her own income, without regard to the other partner's income. Families in which both husband and wife work are consequently no longer taxed at as high a rate as before, since both can now take advantage of the lower tax rate on lower incomes. Thus, it is no longer a tax disadvantage for a wife to change from homemaking to gainful employment. To ease the pain of this tax reform for families where only the husband works, the new system includes, as a temporary provision, a modest tax credit for women who stay at home.

DEBATE OVER SEX ROLES

It was in 1962 that the concept of sex roles was emphatically introduced into the on-going Swedish debate over social issues. In that year, a comprehensive interdisciplinary study entitled *The Life and Work of Women*[1] was published. The book quickly came to be regarded as an important document. Its findings provided a scientific basis for a widespread discussion during the 1960s on men's and women's roles in society.

The concept of 'women's liberation' as something relevant only to women fell into disgrace, to be replaced by the view that the problems of women were inseparable from the problems of men and of society in general. It was argued that a change in the position of women, both at home and in working life, could never be accomplished without a simultaneous change in men's lives as well.

By describing men's and women's roles from the perspectives of psychology, socio-psychology, sociology and economics, the book set out to prove that sex roles determine the choices and opportunities of both men and women in most areas of life. Much of what had long been regarded as typically male or female due to 'the nature of things' was shown to have much less to do with nature than with tradition and custom, the appropriateness of which was now called into serious question. Nor was the earlier ideal of sex equality, based on the equal worth of men and women despite their differing roles, considered valid, since it led in reality to oppression and restriction of the 'weaker' sex, women.

The principle of free choice that was much discussed in the 1950s and early 1960s also fell into disrepute. It became clear that it was not politically possible to give support to women in their role as housewives and at the same time promote equality for women in the labor market.

Another important message of *The Life and Work of Women* is that it is of vital importance for the younger generation to have contact with adults of both sexes. It was pointed out, for example, that boys who grow up without any meaningful contact with their fathers face an identity crisis and at the same time unconsciously acquire a negative attitude toward those aspects of their personality that they consider feminine. The term 'compensatory masculinity' was coined to describe how boys lacking close-up models of male behavior find their ideal of masculinity among the heroes that populate the fantasy world of the mass media.

It was also pointed out that there is little to be envied in the man's role, given all the demands put on males, beginning in childhood. Men have a higher predisposition to accidents than women; it is harder for them to stay in touch with their feelings; they run a greater risk of becoming alcoholics and criminals and of committing suicide, and they have a shorter life expectancy. All these facts aroused great interest when they were published, not least among men themselves. Indeed, the sex role debate conducted in Sweden during the 1960s was never directed *against* men; in fact, it was often directed *toward* men and their problems. It became more and more obvious that the role of women, both at home and at work, was closely bound up with the role played by men and that to improve the situation for women was to improve it at the same time for men.

SEX AND MARRIAGE

Two new birth control methods, the pill and the IUD, were introduced in Sweden in the early 1960s. The chances for women to regulate childbearing were further increased during the 1960s by a more and more liberal application of the law on abortion. When a new abortion law was finally passed in 1976, giving women the right to an abortion on request up to the eighteenth week of pregnancy, it was largely an acknowledgement and ratification of the situation already existing in practice.

The new abortion law also included a provision to expand the distribution of birth control information in order to meet the widespread need that existed. Advice on birth control is provided free of charge to all, regardless of marital status, as are certain birth control devices, such as the diaphragm and IUD. An extensive information program, supported by State funds, is conducted through youth groups and women's organizations. At the same time that the new abortion law was adopted, a second law was passed granting all men and women over 25 the right to be sterilized.

FAMILY LAW

The formal ties of marriage have come to be regarded as less and less significant in recent years. Many unmarried couples expecting a child choose to remain unmarried. In 1965, 14 percent of all babies were born out of wedlock. The figure climbed to 18 percent in 1970 and to 32 percent in 1975. In the majority of these cases, the parents continue to live together without marrying, so the child grows up with both parents present.

The attitude toward unwed mothers has changed considerably during this period. There is no longer any social stigma attached to being a single mother, and it is seldom that a single mother gives up her child.

In 1969, a Commission on Family Law was formed. Among other things this Commission worked on the issue of the rights of parents with respect to a child born 'out of wedlock'. Under earlier legislation, if an unmarried couple with a child separated, only the mother had a right to the child. The father lacked all custody and visitation rights. The law now has been reformed, so that the relationship of the father to his child is considerably strengthened. The decision as to which parent will have custody of a child is made with regard only to the child's best interests. The mother is no longer automatically given preference. Furthermore, a law passed in 1977 gives to both married and unmarried parents the right to decide on joint custody of a child in the case of divorce or separation. This is one more indication of the increased importance attached to a child's contact with his father, and of greater respect for the child as an individual.

The rules governing divorce also have been reformed. A 1973 law greatly simplified the process of divorce. The courts no longer have any interest in the question of guilt for the dissolution of a marriage, nor does infidelity have legal significance any longer. The number of divorces, which already had increased sharply during the 1960s doubled during the first two years after the new law went into effect.

PARENTAL INSURANCE

The economic support that goes directly to families with children in the form of general children's allowances and income-related housing allowances continues to be a basic element in Swedish family policy. Increases to compensate for inflation and also to raise the level of support occur from time to time.

However since early on, the economic support to families with children has been complemented to a greater and greater extent by the provision of services including free tuition, free maternity and child care, and free medical services, etc. The economic burden of providing for children is greatly eased. But the remaining issue is how to alleviate the burden on young parents of looking after their children. The solution calls above all for the expansion of child-care facilities. For the care of the very youngest children, however, it has been thought better to assist the families by increasing the level of cash support and by involving fathers more in such care.

In 1974, the parental insurance law passed, giving fathers as well as mothers the right to a paid leave of absence following the birth or adoption of a child. A parenthood benefit is paid for seven months to whichever parent stays home to care for the new-born child. The amount of compensation is roughly equivalent to 90 percent of one's lost income. Parents can each work part-time and share the care of the child, or they can take turns staying at home for several months each. The insurance system also compensates parents of young children for up to ten days of 'time off' a year to look after a sick child or to visit the baby clinic or the child's day nursery. A father may use this benefit to look after older children when a new child is born. In the spring of 1977, Parliament decided to extend this period to 12-18 days, depending on the number of children in a family.

A Commission on Family Assistance, charged with looking into these same issues, was appointed by the Social Democratic Government in 1974. In its instructions to the Commission, the Government took a clear stand on the question of men's and women's roles. 'The goal is that both parents be given the chance, on equal terms, to combine a job and good childcare in a satisfactory way.'

This Commission proposed that the period of full-time paid leave of absence for parents with a new-born child be extended from seven to eight months, with the proviso that neither parent be allowed to stay home more than seven months. In this way it was hoped that more fathers would be encouraged to take advantage of a paid parental leave of absence. It was further suggested that the eighth month could instead be exchanged for a shortening of a parent's workday from eight to six hours over a period of 20 months, so as to reduce the time that a very young child must spend at a day-care center.

This proposal was greeted by considerable opposition. The Swedish Confederation of Trade Unions (LO) expressed concern that it would be difficult for many workers to take advantage of a six-hour workday. There was also concern that it would be primarily women who would utilize this opportunity, thus increasing inequality between the sexes. The strongest opposition to the proposal, however, came from the Social Democratic Party's own women's organization, which felt that, by giving priority to a shorter workday for parents of small children, the goal of a six-hour workday for all would be undermined.

A new proposal was formulated during the spring of 1976 by the Ministry of Social Affairs. This time it was suggested that the existing seven-month period of parenthood benefits be extended one month, and this period be followed by leave-with-pay for work time equivalent to five additional months. This extra time could be used either in the form of a reduced workday any time until the child reaches school age, or in full-time leave of absence following, for example, upon the first eight months at home. A condition for getting this extended parenthood benefit, however, would be that it must be shared equally by the mother and the father. This proposal was vigorously espoused during the 1976 election campaign by the Social Democratic Party, which pointed out that it was the first family policy reform actively encouraging fathers to share responsibility for childcare.

The ideas from the Social Democratic proposal of 1976 have to a certain extent been carried out by the Coalition Government. On 1 January 1978, the parents' leave was extended to nine months after the birth of the child, the last month at reduced pay. The last three months can be used in the form of a reduced workday anytime until the child has completed his or her first school year. Contrary to the 1976 proposal, the benefits can be fully used by either of the parents, thus eliminating the requirement that some part of it be shared.

A law was adopted in 1978 aimed at supporting employees in their parental role by the possibility of reducing their work hours. According to this new law, the employer will not be able to deny an employee a leave of absence until the child is year and a half old. The employee cannot be refused the choice of reducing the normal daily workday by a quarter, i.e., to six hours, while the child is between a year and a half and eight years of age. The pay will be reduced in accordance with the reduction in working hours.

A Commission on Parent Education during various periods of the child's life is also currently at work. The goal is to reach all parents, beginning with their first visits to the maternity clinic. It is hoped that this contact can be maintained and further developed during the ensuing years through group activities affiliated with the child-care clinic, day-care center, school, etc.

CHILD CARE

Although State support of day care centers began as early as the 1940s, the level of such support remained at a very low level up to the mid-1960s. Priority was given to the building of housing instead, regardless of the services provided. The State encouraged local governments to invest in family day care, but communities were slow to respond.

The shortage of public-supported day care for the children of working parents was especially hard on low-income wage-earners, who did not have the money to hire someone to care for a child at home. The Swedish Confederation of Trade Unions (LO) has long been interested in the day-care issue and has pushed hard in Parliament for expansion of day-care facilities. During the 1960s, the level of State support was raised considerably. The number of day-care places increased, but still this increase did not begin to keep up with the increase in the number of gainfully-employed mothers of small children.

At present, close to 40 percent of the 380,000 children aged one to seven years, whose mothers are gainfully employed, have a place in a public day-care center or community-supported family day-care home. In 1975, a decisive step was taken to expand the number of places available; the State and local governments reached an agreement to provide 100,000 more day-care places and 50,000 more after-school places by 1980. This is to be the first step in a continuing program, which during the 1980s is to reach the goal of fully satisfying the demand for public-supported day care for the children of all parents who work or study.

Public child care, it must be emphasized, has not been promoted first and foremost for the parents' sake, but for the child's, as an important means of stimulating his or her personal growth. Three main goals may be distinguished. First, child care — particularly in the form of preschooling — aims at providing the child with the best possible conditions for all-round emotional and intellectual development. A second goal is to help children learn how to solve problems both on their own and in cooperation with others. Finally, children are encouraged to seek the knowledge needed so that when they grow up they can do their share to improve living conditions for themselves and others.

A considerable reorganization has occurred in the way day care and after-school centers are run, in keeping with the recommendations of a parliamentary Commission on Child-Care Centers which worked from 1968 to 1975. This Commission's efforts stimulated a broad and intense discussion which in turn led to an increased awareness of the needs of children on the part of politicians and the public in general. In recent years the attitude toward placing preschool children in day care institutions has grown more and more positive, and this has further increased the pressure for the expansion of such facilities.

DISCUSSION

The situation of the family in Sweden has changed dramatically during the last few decades. Fewer children per family, the flight to the cities, access to jobs for both husband and wife, and a rise in the standard of living have all contributed importantly to this change.

As late as the 1950s, it was still generally accepted that a mother's natural place was at home with her children as long as they required care and supervision. This was possible, of course, only if the husband's income was adequate to support the family. Those mothers who worked were forced to do so by economic necessity. Only well-educated women constituted an exception to the rule.

A wife who works or studies is today the normal pattern for the majority of Swedish families. The issue of whether or not it is desirable for a mother with preschool children to work, assuming that child care can be arranged, is no longer debated. The very fact that most women now work or study, with only relatively short interruptions for childbirth, has had a distinctly equalizing effect on men's and women's roles. Another equalizing development is that men have begun to be more openly interested in their children and to participate more in their care. In short, women have enhanced their identity as wage-earners at the same time that men have more fully assumed their identity as fathers.

Another current trend in Swedish society is toward greater democratization, especially as regards working life. This has resulted in an important reform concerning workers' rights which came into effect on 1 January 1977 and which affects the entire labor force, including those employed in both the private and public sectors. The purpose of this law is to give employees greater influence on decisions affecting them, through their labor unions. It thus affords greater opportunities to both men and women to help shape their working situation. In the long run, this law should lead to increased equality between the sexes in working life.

Just how far-reaching such changes are is difficult to judge. Traditional sex patterns still prevail in most areas of society, even though one can at the same time point to examples of the emergence of changing patterns.

There is no question at all, however, that a not insignificant liberation of women has occurred in recent years. New birth control methods have given women the chance to control their fertility, plan their lives and develop their potential without being forced to depend on men and marriage. At the same time, an ever wider range of educational and job opportunities has become available to women.

The intensive debate over sex roles that has been going on since the 1960s has made women very conscious of the new possibilities inherent in becoming independent. At the same time, women have been confronted by new expectations from society. They have been needed as human resources, and they have become the focus of increasing interest from politicians. Those women who have remained at home, either because they could not or would not fulfil these new expectations of gainful employment and self-sufficiency, have often viewed the debate over sex roles as a disparagement of their choice of a life style.

Earlier in this chapter, I referred to various laws and programs which I consider to have an important influence, both in the short and long run, on how men and women in Sweden shape their lives. I have taken a broad view of this subject, rather than confining myself to a discussion of those measures specifically related to family matters. (I have for this reason refrained from trying to define the concept of family policy.) I would now like to turn to an analysis of the way in which the various measures already discussed have contributed to changes in family patterns and norms. One interesting question to ask at the outset is: what is the ideological view of men's and women's roles in society that has explicitly or implicitly served as a foundation for the various government actions taken? Have the developments of recent years reflected a consistent or a contradictory view of sex roles?

Before taking up these questions, I wish to emphasize that an essential pre-condition for the emergence of new sex role patterns in Sweden was the rapid economic development that has taken place since the Second World War. The State's economic policy has resulted in a great increase in the human resources needed in both industry and the service sector, among other things as a result of the expansion of the public sector. This has played a decisive role, for it has provided the stimulus and the opportunity for new groups to enter the labor market. The policy of full employment, which has been given the highest priority in the economic policy throughout this period, has also had an extremely significant impact on providing job opportunities for women. Without sufficient jobs available for both men and women, equalization of sex roles would never have been achieved.

Democracy and equality have been leading principles in the ideology of the Social Democratic Party during the period we have been discussing and have provided much of the impetus in the struggle for reform. The precise meaning of these concepts, as they have been translated into concrete proposals and programs, has shifted with time. Demands and ambitions have been adjusted to the developments taking place in society. As I have already noted, there was at the beginning of the reform period in the 1930s no real understanding of what equality between the sexes meant or what changes were necessary to achieve such equality. This was true despite much invigorating debate about the changing role of the family and many reforms tending towards an equalization of at least the burden of family support. Women only recently had won their civil and political rights and established their legal and economic equality within marriage. That formal equality would not automatically lead to real equality appears not to have been discussed at all except within feminist circles. Alva Myrdal, among others, already was demanding at the beginning of the 1930s that women have the right to both motherhood and work, that child-care facilities be expanded, and that the workday be shortened. Fathers could then devote more time to their children.

Gradually the concept that both working women and working men should be covered by equivalent social benefit came to prevail. Such ideas no doubt lay behind the decision to design the social insurance programs so that support was granted to all citizens as individuals. Limiting such insurance to certain groups such as wage-earners or breadwinners would not have been consistent with the underlying political beliefs of the party then in power. The security of married women who were sick or elderly was not to be dependent on whether their marriage lasted or not. The victory of such an ideological outlook was reflected in the decision to require each individual to file his or her own income tax declaration.

On the other hand most social insurance programs were and still are designed to benefit those employed full-time, namely men. The amount of insurance paid out is based on the principle of lost income. The factors that often characterize a woman's working life — long periods of interruption, a late start, shorter hours, lower salaries — all mean that women receive lower benefits than men and, in certain cases, even fall outside the insurance system entirely.

When the important education reforms were planned during the 1940s and again in the early 1960s, the concept of equality was central. All young people were to have the same educational opportunities regardless of their parents' education or social position, regardless of where they lived, and regardless of sex. However, when these reforms were drawn up no one knew how a nine-year compulsory school system would function in practice. Few anticipated that a system designed to be fair and impartial and based only on ability would in fact be partly undermined by the various outside circumstances that had influenced and would continue to influence students while they were growing up. Few anticipated, for example, that students would be so strongly affected by their early childhood environment and by the attitudes which prevailed in the working world. The choice of a course of study and of a career continued to follow completely traditional lines even if the educational level attained was now higher than before.

The percentage of girls continuing on from basic school to the gymnasium is now as high as for boys, and the percentage of girls at the universities also has gradually increased, but at these levels too, when it comes to study and career choices, old patterns have for the most part persisted. Women are concentrated in a few lines of study which tend to lead to jobs in sectors of the labor market which are relatively constrained and regulated, with low salaries and without career advancement opportunities.

I believe that one of the reasons why the various school reforms have not yet had a greater impact on study and career choices among girls is the fact that girls receive a two-sided message during their school years. On the one hand, they experience equality in school. Boys and girls study the same subjects. The same expectations for continuing on to the gymnasium and after that perhaps even to the university apply to girls as to boys. The whole school environment is informed by an attitude of equality between the sexes. But the reality outside the school is something quite different. And this must make a satisfactory adjustment to that reality very difficult, particularly since there is little discussion in the school about how to combine work with child care.

Undoubtedly, those who implemented the school reforms believed that, regardless of what happened in later years, education was important for girls, since they were responsible for bringing up the next generation. The expression 'the long road to the sink' was typical of the critical remarks at that time. When the school reforms were first implemented in the 1950s it was still relatively uncommon for mothers to work. Child-care facilities had not expanded by a single place during the 1950s; there were only 10,000 places available. Part-time jobs were still scarce. Women's salaries were unreasonably low; the equal pay agreement was not adopted until 1962, the same year as the comprehensive school reform was finalized. The joint taxation system which persisted until the early 1970s adversely affected working women who were married or living with a man, even if they had a relatively low income. In other words, there existed at that time no expectation either on the part of general public opinion or on the official level that a woman should commit herself to a career with the same seriousness as a man should.

The situation has been gradually changing, however, through public opinion. Labor market policy from the 1960s on has put men and women on a more equal footing. Despite this, the two-bread-winner family has not been considered the norm until the 1970s.

Sweden has in the past had an urgent need for more workers. The labor unions were interested in keeping the level of immigration low. (It has nevertheless been considerable during recent decades.) Moreover, bringing in new families meant an expensive investment for communities in new housing, schools, and other services. Women at home, therefore, came to be regarded as an untapped labor supply. When the Labor Market Board in the early 1960s flooded much of the country with advertisements, conferences, and other efforts aimed at stimulating women at home to seek employment, many regarded the entrance of more women into the labor market as a temporary expedient. Women were considered a marginal labor supply to be drawn on during periods of prosperity. Few at that time gave any thought to what would happen if the economy took a downward turn. Nor was attention paid to the problem of the underemployment of women, which could be deduced from the employment figures. Finally, the authorities did not take seriously the obstacles confronted by women who wanted to work, such as the lack of adequate part-time jobs and child care. The expansion policy of encouraging immigration from foreign countries was an indication that problems of women in the labor market had not been properly analyzed.

Housing policy has been one area where the traditional view of men's and women's roles in society has clearly prevailed. The priority given to the expansion of the supply of decent housing since the 1930s became an even more serious commitment during the 1950s and 1960s. One million new dwelling units were built, which meant that a majority of families with children could live in modern, comfortable housing. This made housework much easier and so was a step forward in making it possible for both husband and wife to combine a job with care of the home.

But the family pattern which had been assumed when planning these new housing areas was the one characteristic of an earlier economic period, with a mother at home in each apartment. Collective arrangements for services and especially for child care were lacking, as were free-time activities for school children and other community services. Housing was located far from jobs, and the provision of public transportation was inadequate. The private automobile was given priority.

Thus, these new housing areas were already out-dated before they were even completed. They were inhabited particularly by young families who had to pay high rents. There was thus a great demand for jobs from young mothers living in such areas.

It was the women and children who suffered most from living in an environment not suited to the needs of the family. Many mothers were forced, for the sake of their children, to work shorter hours. This meant having to be satisfied with those types of jobs that were located close to home or that were available part-time. Single mothers, in particular, often confronted with a harsh economic situation and, therefore, forced to work full-time, were not at all well served by a housing environment in no way suited to the needs of working mothers and their children.

It was effectively argued during the debate over sex roles and equality during the late 1960s that the traditional family pattern was an obstacle to equality of the sexes in all areas of life.

In recent years the new family pattern, in which both parents work, has come to be accepted as the norm when State programs directed toward helping the family are developed.

There was still considerable labor shortage in many sectors of the economy in the early 1970s. If the Government's economic policies were to be implemented, and if such public services as health care were to be maintained at a satisfactory level, it was necessary that even more women should begin to work. It is against this economic background that one must view the revisions in the tax system adopted in 1971 and the accelerated expansion of day-care facilities during the 1970s. The ruling Social Democratic Party could no longer avoid taking a position on which family pattern to support if it wanted to be regarded as committed to equality. The Government's instructions to the Commission on a New Marriage Law in 1969 had represented a first concrete step toward the evolution of a new attitude toward family policy that would come to characterize the 1970s.

> There is no reason to refrain from using legislation on marriage and the family as one of the instruments in the struggle to shape a society in which every

adult takes responsibility for himself without being economically dependent on another and where equality between the sexes is a reality.

The impact of the revisions in the tax system has been great. This is one case in which there is good reason to credit State policy with causing a significant change in public opinion. Married men started to look with much more favour than before on the idea of their wives taking jobs. There was a large economic benefit to be gained from a wife's salary under the new tax laws, as long as that salary was above a very low level. While no careful study of the matter has been made, it is generally believed by those engaged in the sex role discussion that the introduction of individual taxation has been a turning point in the struggle for the liberation of women in Sweden.

The decision taken in 1975 to expand public day-care facilities until they fully met the demand for such a service meant that society had finally taken a definitive position in favour of a family life style in which both parents worked, even if they had preschool children.

How can one explain why adequate day care has *still* not been provided for all the children needing it? From an educational point of view it has been agreed since the 1930s that all children, at least above 2½-3 years, benefit from some contacts with their peers. Also, for the past 30 to 40 years, a by no means insignificant number of mothers of young children have been gainfully employed. Why was it not politically feasible at a much earlier time to commit the necessary resources to satisfying the need for public day care? Was it only when society required the labor power that young mothers could supply that the political conditions finally existed for supporting a program of day care expansion? The decision making lay within the communities and they were largely male-dominated. Furthermore, there were many who argued at the time that it was not good for children to be placed in day-care centers. Even as late as the early 1960s, the prevalent public opinion was that it was not in a child's best interests to spend most of the waking hours of the day in an institution.

Politicians' personal views on the proper role of women in society undoubtedly played a part in how they interpreted the developments going on in society and how they set priorities for government programs directed at the family. Many politicians looked with disapproval on women seeking gainful employment. They believed that they were helping women by supporting their role in the home. Their own wives were often at home; indeed, this made it possible for them to devote themselves completely to a political career. The experience of politicians regarding what was good for them unquestionably influenced their attitudes toward family policy issues in general. It seems as if many male politicians first began to change their views when their own daughters demanded day-care places for their children.

To construct and operate day-care centers and after-school centers involves a large expenditure of public funds. It remained a politically sensitive matter to advocate programs favoring the two-bread-winner family as long as such families were in the minority. Politicians were fearful lest any position in support of the gainful employment of young mothers would be interpreted as a disparagement of those mothers who chose to remain at home.

Nevertheless, the economic situation and the resulting labor shortage that prevailed during the 1960s did gradually lead to a new attitude toward the employment of women. When this happened, the question of how to solve the child-care problem could no longer be avoided, so various commissions were set up and charged with looking into the situation of families and children. The Commission on Child Care Centers, among others, did much to increase the public's understanding of how children develop, and of their need for more social contacts and a more stimulating environment than the nuclear family alone can provide. Some form of preschool came to be regarded as an important complement to family life.

At the same time that this discussion was going on, the first results of the comprehensive school reform were being reported. The school, it became clear, was not suceeeding in compensating children for an unsatisfactory environment during their pre-school years. It was hoped, therefore, that by expanding preschool programs there would be a better chance to achieve the goal of equality to which politicians were committed.

Day-care centers — the name of which was changed to preschools — came to be sanctioned by public opinion as providing a wholesome atmosphere for children. As more places became available, even highly educated parents were able to place their children in day care, and this further raised its prestige. Claims for the advantages of day care began to be put forward by new groups that could more easily capture the attention of politicians.

The laws passed in the 1970s regarding parental insurance and changes in the rules governing marriage and parenthood constituted an adaptation of public policy to the new living patterns. Joint custody of children after divorce was introduced, the father's rights in the case of a child born out of wedlock were strengthened, and divorce was made easier. Parental insurance was a recognition that the mother is not the only person important to a new-born child. It was pointed out during the debate over sex roles that both parents were important to a child's healthy development, and that men needed to spend time with their children for their own sake as well as the children's. The State, however, was rather ahead of public opinion when parental insurance was first introduced, even though the father's right to remain at home with a new-born child was advocated by the labor unions as early as the late 1960s. In 1974, the first year that the new parental insurance system was in effect, only 2 percent of eligible fathers exercised their right to stay home. In 1975, the figure rose to 6 percent and, in 1976, to 10 per cent.

I think it is fair to say that most fathers today feel the need to take a larger part in the care and raising of their children. A further broadening of the parental insurance program will undoubtedly mean that more and more fathers will begin to participate more fully in caring for their children.

We have seen in the course of this discussion how one public measure has been intertwined with another until, together, they have formed a network for the solution of those problems which have arisen as a result of technical and economic changes in Swedish society. Obvious improvements in the direction of greater equality among social groups in general, as well as between the sexes, have surely taken place in recent years. But new problems have arisen also, and much effort is now being directed at searching for solutions to these.

Those issues which, from the viewpoint of equality, are the most pressing today concern the expansion of public responsibility for child care and the organization of working life, in order to assure more participation and improvement of the work environment. Expansion of public child care must occur at an even more rapid pace, at the same time that serious attention is paid to the quality of such care. Working life must be organized to suit the needs of the total human being. It is not enough to compensate for poor working conditions by improving the quality of leisure time. The working situation itself must be improved so that it fosters self-development and self-fulfillment for all. This means, among other things, that men and women must work at the same places and be given similar tasks and responsibilities. The workday must be made shorter for all to allow people more time to enjoy family and communal life. Finally, a more flexible policy regarding the location of jobs is probably necessary. The ultimate goal must be to make working life less burdensome so that all individuals, in addition to having a decent job, have the chance to satisfy their private, cultural and political interests and to care for their families as well.

SUMMARY

I have attempted, in the foregoing discussion, to describe and explain the impact which government policies have had on the struggle to alter sex role attitudes, especially as they affect women. Obviously one cannot credit a single reform or one particular piece of legislation with the changes that have taken place. One can surely conclude, however, that the trend of public policy in general has been an important prerequisite for stimulating and facilitating such change.

Only a few of the reforms mentioned have been aimed primarily at increasing equality between the sexes. The school reform is one such example. But, as we have seen, this has not had the hoped-for effect regarding distribution of sex roles, because traditional attitudes have stubbornly continued to prevail in society at large.

Other reforms, which have not been aimed primarily at equality between the sexes, but, rather, have sought to promote social equality in the broadest sense, have nevertheless played a vital part in the development of a new role identity for women. Labor market policy is the most striking example of this phenomenon. The policy of full employment, which has been given the highest priority in economic policy throughout this period, has had an extremely significant impact on providing job opportunities for women. Without sufficient jobs available for both men and women, equalization of sex roles would never have been achieved.

If I were to choose one reform which has perhaps done the most to promote equality between the sexes, I would point to the introduction of individual income taxation. This reform brought with it a new chance to measure directly the value of the gainful employment of married women.

Finally, one should not underestimate the importance of the ongoing debate regarding sex roles. Such discussions have been widespread and have engaged many people on an emotional level, thereby influencing opinions and altering attitudes. Gradually a new consciousness of men's and women's roles in society, and of the need and opportunity for change, has been evolving.

This increased level of awareness can surely be expected to continue to influence public policy in the future and to lead to further reforms intended to achieve a more equitable distribution of roles among men and women. Those areas which at present appear in the most urgent need of action involve the expansion of day care, the shortening of the working day and the location of jobs. Not until these issues are also resolved can we look forward to the day when both men and women can function in accordance with their full potential in every area of their lives — on the job, in society, and within the family.

APPENDIX

Over-View of social issues and public actions affecting woman's equality during the 1950s, 1960s and 1970s.

Topic	Issues concerning equality	Public measures
Labor market policy	*1960s* How to expand employment opportunities for women? How to get men into traditionally women's jobs?	*1960s and 1970s* General and specific measures within labor market policy.
	1970s How to assure jobs for all?	*1970s* Setting of quotas for under-represented sex when Government assistance involved. Special service at employment offices to deal with issues affecting women.
Work environment	*1960s* How to improve working conditions for women?	Improvements for low income groups in the official sector.

Topic	Issues concerning equality	Public measures
	1970s How to improve the working environment for everyone?	Government's delegation on equality.
	Chance through Law on Joint Participation to liberate employees' resources.	Law on Joint Participation in working life.
Work hours	*1950s and 1960s* Need for more part-time jobs	*1970s* Time off to look after sick child, visit baby clinic or day care center or for fathers to look after older children when a new child is born.
	1970s No to 4-day work week. Reduced hours for parents. 6-hour work day for everybody.	Right to reduced hours for parents (1978).
Housing and living environment	*1960s* Housing environment inadequately adapted to new family patterns.	*1950s, 1960s, 1970s* Improved housing standards.
	1970s Need for co-ordinated planning of housing and work areas.	
Transportation	*1960s and 1970s* The importance of a well developed public transportation system.	*1970s* Some shift in emphasis from automobile to public transportation.
Services to familes	*1950s, 1960s, 1970s* Demand for more full-time preschool daycare centers.	**1960s** Successively increased State grants.
	1970s Demand from workers for night-time child care.	*1970s* Agreement (1975) to double the number of child care places by 1980.

Topic	Issues concerning equality	Public measures
	Demand for day-care for all children who need it.	Program for the 1980s with the goal of satisfying the demand for daycare.
Economic support to families with children	*1960s and 1970s* Participation of father in child care and significance of this for both father and child. How to stimulate fathers to share responsibility for children?	*1970s* Parental insurance (1975, 1976, 1977), 9 months paid leave per family per newborn child.
Income tax	*1960s* Demand for an income tax system in which marital status irrelevant	*1970s* Introduction of individual income taxation
Education	*1960s and 1970s* How to counteract the traditional attitudes toward sex roles? How to stimulate students to make career choices without regard to sex?	*1960s* Greatly increased access to and economic possibilities for education for all young people. *1970s* School curriculum based on the principle of equality between the sexes. Special activities in order to promote awareness of negative effects of present sex role pattern.
Sex and living together	*1960s and 1970s* New birth control methods. Woman's right to decide on termination of pregnancy.	*1970s* Woman's right to abortion.

Topic	Issues concerning equality	Public measures
		Increased access to birth control devices – sometimes provided free.
	1970s Father's importance to the child's development. Father's responsibility to share in raising the child.	Legal right of father strengthened regarding a child born out of wedlock or in the case of divorce or separation of the parents.

NOTES

1. Dalhström, E. (ed.), *Kvinnors liv och arbete,* Stockholm: Studieförbundet Näringsliv och Samhälle (SNS), 1962. English editions: *The Changing Roles of Men and Women,* London: Duckworth & Co., 1967; Boston, Mass.: Beacon Press, 1971.

7

WOMEN IN EASTERN EUROPE

Hilda Scott
Vienna, Austria

Ms. Scott's chapter shows in stark relief how policy in Eastern Europe has used the levers of power to achieve its goals even at the expense of women. When there was a crippling shortage in the labor force and women were needed to fill in the gaps, policy was used to entice women into the labor force and equality, as predicted by the socialist ideology, seemed within reach. But when 'equality' turned out to mean that women were being called on to perform two roles — in the home and in the work place — while men were called on to perform only one, the women began to respond to the increased costs of such one-sided 'equality' by greatly reduced fertility.

Now policy turned to ways to encourage increased fertility. And equality came to mean, especially in the USSR and Japan, not the sharing of role responsibilities by both sexes, but 'making it possible for women to synthesize their two responsibilities successfully.' And, in Bulgaria, more children. Only, apparently, in East Germany has the shared-role solution been encouraged. Not even here, however, by policy but by the media and in the schools.

It appears from this account that research was used, not to show how to counter the excessive costs to women of the two-role pattern, but how to shift more of the costs to their shoulders. As Scott points out, a profound sexism underlies all policy decisions in Eastern European countries. The contrast between East Europe and Sweden in this respect is thought-provoking. Sweden, too, had a severe labor shortage and it, too, sought to encourage women to enter the work force. But it has recognized the unfairness of the two-role pattern, which puts such a heavy load on women, and has sought to shift some of the cost to men. Sweden's success is slow, but perceptible.

Study of the position of women in the countries of Eastern Europe which have followed the Soviet lead provides a unique opportunity to observe the impact of similar goals and similar programs, motivated by a single ideology, in six very different settings. This article will examine the effect of some aspects of social policy on the status of women in these countries, with special attention to Czechoslovakia.[1]

Women's status has changed markedly in the area since the Second World War as far as legal rights, education and employment are concerned. Closer analysis of the course of this change reveals that it has not been one of undifferentiated continuity, however. A period of apparently dramatic progress can be identified, lasting roughly until the beginning of the 1960s, succeeded by a decade in which the benefits of 'emancipation,' as it is still called, underwent reevaluation. In the present period, a model of emancipation has been accepted which bears close resemblance to the 'two roles' concept of women's equality, until recently widely regarded in Western society as the logical outcome of the battle for women's rights.

Although in theory there can be no real conflict of interest between men and women in a socialist society, in practice in these countries the socioeconomic goals set by men and the interests of women do not always coincide. It can be demonstrated that social policy, also designed by men, is directed primarily at advancing these goals, thus creating an imbalance between women's rights and their possibilities of using them. Where conflict has arisen between the aims of the national economy and the requirements of women's equality, social policy has been used to redefine women's interests and the content of liberation.

THE FUNCTIONS OF SOCIAL POLICY

Socialists view social policy as one instrument for the distribution of the wealth that has been created by society. Since all wealth is the product of labor, it must be returned in one form or another to those who labored to create it.[2] Everyone is entitled to certain rights, guaranteed in the constitutions of the socialist states: to work, to leisure after work, to health, to security in old age and disability, and to education. Socialist social policy directs the way these rights are implemented through 'payment in kind' in the form of health care, free education, subsidized recreation and cultural opportunities, and an elaborate pension scheme. Family allowances are not viewed as hand-outs to the needy by the tax-payer; aid to families fulfils the socialist states' 'obligation toward its youngest citizens, set forth in the constitution.'[3]

Social policy has other functions, however. Since the planned development of all aspects of social existence is a basic tenet of East European socialism, social policy must obviously be part of that plan, and as such it is not neutral. It is a powerful tool for reshaping society. Social policy is given life through the national five-year and one-year economic plans into which its goals are incorporated, and these goals must, of course, be at one with the aim of the plan. Thus, social policy may be used in a frankly discriminatory way, in favor of the working class and against remnants of the bourgeoisie, to encourage the collectivization of agriculture, or internal population migration, or to influence the use and distribution of the workforce, by granting special benefits to a particular group. With respect to women, social policy is understood to help implement socialism's historic ideological commitment to full equality between the sexes. Obviously, with such a full agenda, the danger that social policy will sometimes work at cross purposes is considerable.

The countries of Eastern Europe interpret strictly Marx' and Engels' thesis that 'the oppression of women originated as an historical manifestation and was called forth not by biological but by social causes,' concretely by the origin of private property. Once private property has been abolished, 'the objective real conditions have been created for the reestablishment of equal relations between the two sexes.'[4] Although there are remnants of bourgeois mentality which must still be combatted, there can no longer be any basic antagonism between men and women; moreover, the fact that women play a very small role in planning and policy making should not per se result in decisions prejudicial to them. There is no room for the idea that socialist planning might have a built-in sex bias because it incorporates primarily male values and priorities.

STAGE I: THE ECONOMY'S GOALS AND THOSE OF EMANCIPATION COINCIDE

The period immediately following the communist assumption of power in Eastern Europe following the Second World War, that is approximately from 1948 to the end of the 1950s, was characterized by an upheaval in women's position which seemed to provide impressive proof of the correctness of socialist reasoning. Ancient legal codes were swept away, new constitutions and new laws were written. Overnight, in this relatively backward part of Europe, woman was given guarantees of her equality in the home, in education, in employment and in public life. Special measures protecting her in childbirth and motherhood were adopted, including paid maternity leave with job rights assured. Divorce was made easy; abortion was legalized. Most of Western Europe, not to speak of the United States, has still to match this record. At the same time, the goal of economic independence, declared by Marx and Engels to be the first condition for women's emancipation, following the establishment of socialism and the granting of legal equality, was wholly in harmony with the need of the economies of all the socialist states for human resourses.

Following the policy established by the Soviet Union, all the Eastern European socialist countries advanced the goal of creating highly industrialized states whose economies would be free from the influence of Western price fluctuations and trade boycotts. All had been characterized before the war by peasant agriculture and, except for Czechoslovakia and the Soviet zone of Germany (which in 1949 became the German Democratic Republic), very limited manufacturing experience. Moreover, most of these countries had suffered wartime population losses, and in some cases these were aggravated by postwar population transfers.

Soviet war dead are put at 25 million; in 1946 women accounted for 60 percent of the working age population. Poland lost seven million people through war deaths and population transfers, a decrease of 22 percent. Czechoslovakia's population was diminished by 2.1 million (15 percent) through the expulsion of ethnic Germans from its border regions. Romania transferred 75,000 ethnic Germans to the Soviet Union as laborers as part of its war reparations. The German Democratic Republic gained by transfers from other countries, but by the end of the 1950s had lost an equal number of people through emigration; and since more men than women chose to leave, the already existing sex imbalance was exacerbated.[5]

Women were actively recruited for jobs of all kinds. They were soon found doing heavy work on building sites, in foundries, in the power industry, and in many other unfamiliar jobs, as well as in the traditional female occupations. If, as Lipman-Blumen argues persuasively, role-change occurs in response to crisis, the labor shortage in postwar Eastern Europe offered a crisis par excellence.[6] By 1960, in all the countries considered here except Hungary, women made up at least 42 percent of the workforce, a figure not yet reached in any Western country in spite of the rapid expansion of women's employment in the years since then. Furthermore, in contrast to the West, where women's part-time work is common[7], the overwhelming majority of Eastern European women work at least a 40-hour week. Between 1950 and 1965, total employment outside agriculture rose some 70-100 percent in all the countries of the area except Czechoslovakia and the German Democratic Republic, which had no such reserves on which to draw. In these two countries and in Bulgaria, almost the entire increase in workers was accounted for by women, while in Hungary, women made up 70 percent of the increment.[8]

As men took over the multiplying responsibilities and prestigious jobs in industry, scientific research and government, women moved into positions which no longer represented peak careers for men. They poured into the fields of health, education, banking and insurance, public catering and communications until the whole 'non-productive' service sector was female-dominated.

Declining Birth-Rates Threaten Future Labor Reserves

The price to be paid for this success in drawing women into productive work outside the home became apparent in the early 1960s. The priorities assigned to heavy industry caused the indefinite postponement of the services which, according to Marxist theory and the governments' early promises, were to take over women's household tasks. The lag in the consumer goods' industries, mistakes in planning, and failures in distribution made shopping for essentials a chore consuming several hours daily. The housing shortage meant that few young couples had immediate prospects for a place of their own.

The clearest evidence that women found it impossible to combine full-time paid employment with motherhood under these conditions was the precipitate decline in the birth-rate which began in Eastern Europe immediately after the passage of liberal abortion legislation. The new laws which were adopted between 1955 and 1957 in the

Soviet Union and all the other countries, except the German Democratic Republic, were by no means uniform, although they all permitted induced abortions for a wide variety of social, as well as medical, indications. They ranged from extreme permissiveness in Romania, with pregnancies usually terminated in out-patient clinics, to cautious examination of each individual case by a special commission in Poland and Czechoslovakia. Even in the latter countries, however, abortion applications were rarely refused.

In 1966, Czechoslovakia was recording two abortions for every five live births, Hungary four for every three, and Romania (1965) four legal induced abortions for each live birth. Between 1955 and 1966 live birth rates dropped between 25 (Bulgaria) and 45 (Romania) percent.[9] The reasons women used to uphold their applications for abortion were largely social, with inadequate housing high on the list. In Czechoslovakia during that decade the percentage of abortion requests granted for medical indications never exceeded 22 percent of the total.[10]

STAGE 2: SOCIAL POLICY IS REAPPRAISED

Conventional socialist wisdom held that the new social system would remove obstacles to having children and that the birth rate would rise.[11] When this proved not to be the case, it was at first argued that young people were succumbing to bourgeois consumer society values. The rehabilitation of the social sciences in Eastern Europe in the 1960s encouraged numerous sociological investigations of the position of women, however, and initiated a period of reappraisal of family policy and, inevitably, of women's place in society.

Women's 'second shift' was discovered, and women were found to be neuroticized by the multiple pressures on them and their lack of free time. In 1960-61, Czechoslovak women spent four to six times as many hours on housework as men, their work-week was 25 percent longer.[12] Physicians declared children to be overtired from too long hours in day-care centers and from being returned too soon after illness. Employers complained that women were unreliable.

Nonetheless, the gainful employment of young mothers was and remains a necessity for the economy and for most families. This can be judged from the rate of employment by age group (Table 1). The employment rate of women most likely to have small children at home is very high, hardly less than that of older women. In Czechoslovakia in 1963, a per capita income of 600 crowns monthly or less meant that the family diet fell below recommended minimums.[13] But as late as 1968, 77 percent of all men employed outside agriculture had a gross monthly income of 2,400 crowns or less — too little to feed adequately a family of four.[14]

TABLE 1

Female labor force participation rates as percent of age cohort

Country	Year	age 25-29	age 30-34	age 45-49
Bulgaria	1965	83.8	87.1	81.1
Czechoslovakia	1970	78.8	80.0	77.3
German Democratic Republic	1971		79.0	
Hungary	1970	65.3	69.7	64
Poland	1970	75.1	79.2	79.2
Romania	1966	78.5	78.4	75.2
USSR	1970	86.3	92.7	90.6

Sources: Year Book of Labour Statistics, ILO, Geneva 1975; Jaroslava Bauerová, *The Status of Women in the Czechoslovak Socialist Republic* (Prague, 1975), mimeographed, distributed by the Czechoslovak Ministry of Foreign Affairs, p. 8.

Measures to encourage fertility

There could be no question of women returning permanently to the home. At the same time, economic goals did not permit a massive reallocation of resources to child-care facilities and household services. Yet an increase in the birth rate was judged essential to ensure an expanding, rather than a shrinking, labor reserve. All the East European countries began to take steps in the mid-sixties to encourage births by prolonging paid maternity leaves or raising family allowances or both; however, it was evident to some of the governments that more radical measures were necessary if their population policies were to be realized.[15]

Romania faced the problem head-on in 1966 by prohibiting abortion entirely for women under 40 with fewer than four children (except for medical indications and in cases of rape). At that time they banned the import of contraceptives. This measure was followed by 'a wave of suicides, particularly of young women.'[16] A spectacular leap in the birth rate the next year was followed by a decline and a levelling off, which demographers assume to be due to an increase in illegal abortions.[17] Romania also introduced a tax on childless persons, whether married or single, and tightened its divorce law.

Hungary and Czechoslovakia attempted to resolve the problem with a complex of measures, removing some of the economic and social pressures that caused women to restrict the size of their families before limiting their access to abortion. Hungary was the first (1967) to introduce a child-care allowance which pays a mother a monthly sum to stay home after the expiration of her 20-week paid maternity leave, until the child is three years old. As this did not attract as many women as expected, and as the number of legal abortions continued to exceed the number of live births, new measures were necessary. The Hungarian Council of Ministers passed a comprehensive resolution on demographic policy in October 1973, which increased the monthly family allowance and the child-care allowance, and at the same time made it difficult for a married woman who had not yet had three children to obtain an abortion except for medical reasons or in cases of rape.[18]

Czechoslovakia introduced sharply increased family allowances for the second, third and fourth child and low-interest loans for young couples with a partial write-off for each child born. The government prolonged paid maternity leave to 26 weeks and in 1971 announced a child-care allowance which permits a mother to stay home with her second and any subsequent child until it is two years old. Czechoslovakia also amended its abortion law in 1973 to rule out interruption of pregnancy for non-medical reasons in married women who do not have at least one child, except in special circumstances. One rationale for the changes in the abortion law in both countries was concern for women's health, because of a reported increase in pregnancies not carried to term and other late side effects in women who had had previous abortions. At the same time it was made clear that the purpose of this step was to increase fertility. 'The new regulations contribute to the further protection of the health of women and are part of the system of pro-population measures which have been adopted in recent years,' said the Czech Ministry of Health in explaining the new restrictions on abortion.[19]

Doubts cast on the value of day care

Woman's right to control over her own body thus became a casualty in the drive to meet economic targets. Another fundamental condition for women's equality, the provision of day-care facilities, began to undergo reconsideration, particularly with regard to the value of day-care for children under three. All the Eastern European countries had created a system of child-care institutions which, although far from meeting demand, gave rise to the expectation that another Marxist prophecy would be fulfilled, and child care would become a public responsibility. Exaggeration of the advantages collective care could offer, coupled with inadequacies in the facilities themselves, had, however, led to a degree of disenchantment.

In the early 1960s, because of the more liberal attitude toward Western research, some of the vast literature on 'maternal deprivation' began to reach the Eastern countries. In these countries, at least as far as institutionalized children were concerned, the possibility of emotional damage was reported confirmed by socialist experience.[20] The dangers of 'micro-deprivation', as well as the apparent increase in physical illness in infants who were sent to day nurseries too young and spent too much time there, were seized upon by many pediatricians, psychologists, and conservative policy makers, as well as by economists who found day care a drain on the budget, to justify suggesting that mothers stay home for several years. Poland made its negative attitude toward day care clear at the first international symposium held in Prague in 1966. Today it provides coverage for less than 25 percent of all its children under seven, the poorest record of all the countries in the area. Instead it offers mothers a three-year unpaid leave, at the end of the 16-18 week paid maternity leave, with job rights protected.

Professional opinion was by no means unanimous, either within or among these countries. Nevertheless, except in the German Democratic Republic, specific criticisms soon became broad generalizations. 'Medical research has shown that up to the age of three a child benefits most from direct maternal care,' a Czech handbook on legislation protecting pregnant women and mothers declared unequivocally.[21]

With equal assurance, one of the Soviet Union's most authoritative writers on demographic questions reported that the majority of sociologists believe women should be allowed to stay home with their children for from one to three years. In his opinion no more day nurseries for this age group should be established: 'Children in day nurseries are ill more often and lag behind children brought up at home in their physical, emotional and mental development.' He is, of course, concerned with the Soviet Union's birth rate and forecasts that if the trend does not change there will be no increase at all in the labor reserve by 1995.[22]

The inducements offered women to take prolonged child-care leaves have not eliminated the need for more day-care places, but the increase is very slow and there are waiting lists. In Czechoslovakia, the goal of 100,000 places originally set for 1970 had not been reached at the end of 1976. Ironically, a parallel shift of opinion, only moving in the opposite directions, has taken place in the West, so that several Western countries are now challenging the record in a field once monopolized by states with socialist programs (see Table 2).

TABLE 2

Labor force participation of women and child care in selected countries

Country	Year	Women as percent of labor force	Percent of children under 3 in care	Percent of children aged 3-6 in care
Czechoslovakia	1975	48.0	8.3	66.0
German Democratic Republic	1975	49.6	44.7	82.4
Hungary	1975	44.0	10.4	67.7
Poland	1974	46.0	6.7	40.0a)
USSR	1974	50.5	10.4	59.0a)
France	1975	37.0	15.0	90.0
Federal Republic of Germany	1974	37.0	15.0	90.0
Israel	1974	32.0	12.0	90.0
Sweden	1974	41.0	5-10	50.0a)
USA	1974	38.0		50.0

a) children aged 3-7

Sources: Computed from data in national statistical yearbooks, *Soviet Economy in a New Perspective* (Washington: Government Printing Office, 1976) p. 132; Alfred J. Kahn and Sheila B. Kamerman, 'European Family Policy Currents: The Question of Families with Very Young Children' (Columbia University School of Social Work: preliminary draft working paper, Oct. 1976, mimeographed).

Protective legislation rediscovered

With women's fertility a subject of so much economic and therefore political concern, the idea that women would soon take their place beside men at the same jobs was also exposed to second thoughts. Protective legislation already on the books had not been enforced, because it was believed that under socialism the interests of management and labor were synonymous, and that favorable working conditions would be created as a matter of course.

In the reform spirit of the 1960s, it came to light that rules governing safety and hygiene were being widely violated. The extensive protective legislation introduced in Czechoslovakia as part of the Labor Law of 1965 attempted to protect women preferentially, in view of their maternal function and their extra burden as homemakers.

This protective legislation naturally had the effect of legalizing the already existing division in the labor market. Once women were to be protected against extremes of temperature, vibration, harmful substances and many other things, and prohibited from lifting heavy weights and from working at night, their usefulness to industrial employers was limited.[23] Thus, while women's share in industrial employment increased, the types of jobs open to them decreased, and their concentration in the traditional consumer goods industries and in the service sector became more marked. This shift inconvenienced some employers and some industries; however, the movement of women toward 'suitable' employment was generally viewed favorably, because it freed the male population for skilled jobs in construction and heavy industry, which is where the labor shortage is really felt.

The effect on women's education

The consequences for women's education and training follow naturally, as a result both of girls' choices and of the quotas set by schools for female enrollment. There is a considerably higher participation by girls in technical courses in Eastern Europe than in Western countries, but a major reason for this is that places in all educational institutions are determined by the needs of the economy. Applicants who cannot enter the school of their choice must select another field.

Women are no longer being encouraged to set their sights at unconventional jobs demanding the mobilization of hitherto untapped qualities. In 1973, Czechoslovak girls expressed interest in only 10 to 15 percent of the places reserved for them as apprentice lathe and milling machine operators, only one-third of the openings offered them to become skilled textile workers. The majority of female apprentices in these technical branches had originally applied to learn the art of jewellery making or shop window arrangement, or pastry baking, photography or hairdressing — branches for which applications exceeded places by several hundred percent.[24] Girls are only 6 percent of the trainees for the engineering industry, which alone accepts 28 percent of all apprentices, while they make up 95 percent of all youngsters receiving training to become textile workers.

In the past decade, the number of girls attending secondary vocational schools has increased absolutely and as a percentage of the total student body. Only 22 percent of them now study in industrial lines, however, as opposed to 28 percent a decade ago, while they represent 90 percent of students in nursing, teaching, library and secretarial work. At the university level, the proportion of women in technical courses has remained stable for a decade at 15 percent, but women's opportunities for work in this field and at the level for which they are trained are considerably poorer than men's.[25]

In agriculture, the physically arduous hand cultivation of crops traditionally has been done by women. Now it is gradually being taken over by tractor drivers and combine operators, jobs not considered appropriate for women. The earnings of the men who replace them are twice the pay the women received. Young women are trained chiefly for livestock, dairy and poultry production. In Czechoslovakia, women make up less than 20 percent of apprentices in agriculture, so that the realtive earnings and division of labor between men and women in future cooperative farm families are not difficult to forecast.

At the same time, it is not feasible to implement protective legislation in many jobs where women may work. In retail trade, it has proved impossible to enforce the ban on weight lifting imposed a decade ago. Night work must be permitted women in the health services, in communications, and in other branches which otherwise could not operate without interruption. In some textile plants, women work night shifts because the plan could not otherwise be fulfilled.

Consequences of the child-care allowance

The actual effects of the child-care allowance and other pro-natal measures on women's fertility are difficult, if not impossible, to judge. Both Hungary and Czechoslovakia recently have experienced a sharp rise in the birth rate which cannot be explained entirely by the increase in the age group most likely to bear children. This apparent success may influence social policy in other Eastern European countries. In the opinion of some experts, however, in the long run such measures 'may have an adverse effect on fertility by rendering women's professional autonomy even more precarious and exposing it to greater opposition.' Even the declared preferences of women who give priority to motherhood over employment are not to be trusted, since they are 'subject in the medium term to social, economic and cultural pressures of uncertain outcome.'[26]

Developments in Czechoslovakia and Hungary offer some support for this prediction. When a young mother goes back to work after her child-care allowance expires, she finds that there has been no appreciable improvement in services, and her husband spends no more time on housework than he did before. A Czechoslovak woman today devotes four to five hours daily on housework because of the stagnation of services, the inadequacy of shopping facilities, and the inefficiency of household appliances. Gainfully employed women spend more time on domestic work than they did in 1968, before the introduction of the five-day week, because they can devote Saturday mornings to chores.[27]

The new mother who does not want to lose her qualifications by staying away from work for a long period finds it difficult to secure day care for her child. Employers, on the other hand, are reluctant to consider qualified young women for responsible jobs, because they can be expected to have children and disappear into the home for several years. The difficulties of finding temporary replacements adds to employers' reluctance. It is economically more effective to hire a man from the outset.

Márkus in Hungary, basing her judgment on life histories written by 1,000 women for a competition in 1972, finds that most women do not consider that housekeeping for a small family supplies sufficiently satisfying content to the day. She found that this is particularly true of women who were employed and then stayed at home for three years drawing the child-care allowance. The attitude of previously employed women to the seclusion of the home is in most cases definitely *negative*, almost regardless of the place their gainful employment had occupied in their lives.

Confirming my own observations in Czechoslovakia, Márkus notes a loss of popularity, among the youngest group of women, by the 'emancipated' model of the family. The 'emancipated' family was favored by many of their mothers' generation, for whom work outside the home gave meaning to life. Márkus finds these young women favoring the 'bourgeois' model, in which family effort is devoted to the organization of consumption, and she attributes this to the lack of objective social conditions for the practical realization of emancipation.[28]

STAGE 3: EQUALITY IS REDEFINED

Together with these developments, the Eastern European definition of equality has undergone a transformation. 'Bourgeois ideology makes a cult of the mother-housewife,' and therefore considers women's two roles to be mutually exclusive. Socialism is now credited not with freeing woman from her home-making responsibilities, but with making it possible for her to synthesize her two responsibilities successfully.[29]

The Soviet Union attempted to incorporate this view in the plan of action put before the UN International Women's Year Conference in Mexico City in 1975. The Soviet Union proposed an amendment to follow the first sentence of paragraph 16, which declares that women and men should have equal rights, opportunities and responsibilities. The Soviet Union proposed that this should be followed by the words: 'The State and society must create conditions enabling women successfully to combine their duties as mothers, workers and citizens.'[30] This attempt to institutionalize 'women's two roles' did not meet with the approval of the conference, nor did a similar amendment offered by Japan.

Bulgaria has improved upon this definition by increasing the dose of motherhood in the mix. According to the decision of the Politburo of the Central Committee of the Communist Party of Bulgaria for 6 March 1973:

It is the task of our Party and State policy to facilitate women in combining their chief functions and obligations in such a way as to *particularly stimulate and enhance their role as mothers*...Motherhood is a social and biological function of women which in its vital importance for society ranks first in the complex of all her functions. It is an essential condition for her own self-confidence and happiness...Our device is therefore: *'More children in every Bulgarian family...'* (Italics in the original).[31]

THE EXPERIENCE OF THE GERMAN DEMOCRATIC REPUBLIC

Alone among the Eastern European countries, the GDR offers an alternative response to the problems created by a labor shortage and a falling birth rate. It has what must be one of the most difficult demographic situations in the world, the product of two world wars and heavy emigration of trained personnel to the West. It has suffered a 15 percent decrease in its population of working age from 11.7 million in 1950 to 9.9 million in 1973. The GDR shares with the German Federal Republic the lowest birth rate in the world and has recorded a world record zero population growth or less since 1969. Faced with a choice between the future labor force and current economic growth, it has chosen the latter.

The GDR does not distract its employable women (84 percent of whom now are studying or are economically active) with inducements to produce a larger generation of future workers. On the contrary, since 1972 it has offered abortion on demand, and it provides the most complete day-care coverage of any country in the world (see Table 2). (It should be pointed out that this is facilitated by the low birth rate and the low rate of housing construction).

The critical lack of technically trained experts has prompted legislation and government directives requiring individual enterprises to train women for jobs in technology and management. Work driving trucks, tractors and combine harvesters, which is out of bounds for Czechoslovak women, is not considered harmful for German girls. The GDR apparently believes (along with a good many demographers in Western European countries, where the possibility of the fertility rate settling permanently short of the replacement level is a real possibility) that it makes more sense to deal with the consequences of this trend than to invest in trying to reverse it.

TABLE 3

Distribution of female labor force by economic sector in Czechoslovakia and the German Democratic Republic, 1965 and 1975

Sector	Czechoslovakia 1965[a]	1975[a]	Ratio[b]	German Democratic Republic 1965[a]	1975[a]	Ratio[b]
Women as percent of total labor force	44.8	48.0		46.7	49.6	
Industry	41.1	44.7	0.93	39.9	43.7	0.88
of which						
textile[c]		69.6	1.55 ⎱		70.0	1.60
clothing[c]		84.2	1.88 ⎰			
Construction	14.0	16.9	0.35	9.7	14.9	0.30
Agriculture	51.2	47.2	0.98	47.8	42.9	0.86
Transport	19.4	24.2	0.50 ⎱	33.9	37.3	0.75
Communications	58.1	66.0	1.37 ⎰			
Trade & public catering	71.6	75.7	1.58	67.2	71.4	1.44
Non-productive branches [d]	53.5	59.6	1.24	68.0	72.3	1.46

a) women as percent of labor force in sector
b) ratio of percent women in sector to percent women in total labor force in 1975
c) ratio of percent women in textile and clothing to percent women in industry
d) health, education, culture, municipal services, public administration, banking and insurance
Note: These figures do not differentiate between blue and white collar workers; thus, the segregation is more pronounced than appears here.
Sources: Statisticka rocenká CSSR 1975, p. 138; 1976, p. 113; *Statistisches Jahrbuch der DDR* 1976, pp. 55, 128; Jaroslav Martilík, 'Spotrební průmysl a pracovní síly,' *Svet hospodarství*, 23 January 1976.

Although comparable figures are difficult to obtain, it seems evident that a larger proportion of girls now are receiving training for skilled and supervisory jobs in industry in the GDR than in Czechoslovakia, two countries which are on approximately the same economic level. It will be interesting to follow the long-term results of this policy. At present, the same pattern of occupational segregation exists in both countries, and, if anything, it is more marked in the GDR (see Table 3).

The traditionally female, lower-paid branches of industry and the 'non-productive' sector (health, education, culture, banking and insurance, services) employ a disproportionate percent of women. This pattern suggests that the same basic obstacle to equality operates in the GDR as in the other Eastern European countries; insistence that the abolition of capitalism balances the scales, and that no further analysis of the relationship between the sexes, nor of the structure of society and its goals from this perspective, is necessary.

Conflicts arise in 'the new socialist family.' since the equality of women creates new expectations. But under socialism these contradictions undergo a fundamental change by becoming non-antagonistic in nature. While family policy 'focuses on the strengthening of relations of equality between married partners' under socialism, and in the GDR education and the media are said to encourage participation by men in homemaking and the care of children, this kind of equality is not facilitated by the actual policies chosen. In the GDR, as elsewhere, women carry the main burden at home, a fact which is freely admitted. Measures are intended 'to harmonize the various aspects of a woman's life, that is, her work, her studies, her political activities and her family responsibilities...The development of women to socialist personalities is impossible unless the two factors of employment and family can be brought into ever-closer harmony.'[32]

Men have no difficulty harmonizing work and family responsibilities, and, therefore, nurseries and improvements in supplies and services are regarded as special benefits for women. For this reason, too, the monthly 'housework day', a GDR specialty, is granted to women only, and the reduction in the workweek from 43¾ to 40 hours without a reduction in pay applies to mothers of three children, but not fathers. These privileges are granted to women only because in fact they are the ones who do the work, the editors of *Für Dich*, a popular weekly, replied to a reader who wrote to inquire what had happened to the idea of real partnership. 'The strict demand for total sharing of the responsibility has legitimate material disadvantages, as often men still have a higher income or a more responsible job than their wives.'[33] This argument runs in the by-now-well-worn groove. Men are able to have better paying jobs, because their wives keep the house going. Women have poorer paying jobs, and, therefore, it is natural or at least practical for them also to do the work at home, which is worth less than work in the 'outside world' (in fact, in Marxist terms is nonproductive). Women's two jobs are not brought into ever-closer harmony, because this is not one of men's priorities; there is other more pressing business which demands attention.

CONCLUSION

Social policy in Eastern Europe has supported a high degree of female participation in the labor force and has offered women job protection as well as financial security in motherhood. Inevitably, in view of their numbers, women occupy many jobs which are not held by members of their sex in other parts of the world. However, social policy is still based on time-honored male-centered concepts of society and the family, and, however generous and democratic the subjective intentions of the men who formulated it, it is essentially aimed at making a male oriented society function better. While apparently leaning over backwards to create conditions more favorable for women, it tends to solve problems at women's expense, and in the long run to create obstacles to the equality it purports to advance.

NOTES

1. The six countries are Czechoslovakia, Bulgaria, the German Democratic Republic (generally acknowledged to have the highest living standard in the area), Hungary, Poland, and Romania (the most backward, with 40 percent of its workforce still engaged in agriculture). The total population of the area is 105.5 million.

2. As stated by Engels: 'Labour is, besides the earth, the only source of wealth; capital itself is nothing but the stored up produce of labour...According to what we may call common fairness, the wages of the labourer ought to consist in the produce of his labour' (Frederick Engels, 'A Fair Day's Wage for a Fair Day's Work', in *A Handbook of Marxism* [New York: International Publishers, 1935] p. 200).

3. Senta Radvanová et al., *Žena a právo* (Prague: Orbis, 1971). p. 213.

4. The argument is, of course, from Engels's *The Origin of the Family, Private Property and the State*; the formulation here is from Jaroslava Bauerová, *Zaměstnaná Žena a rodina* (Prague: Práce, 1974), p. 32. She speaks of 'reestablishment'

because she accepts as fact 'a long period of matriarchy' as the first form of human society, in which woman 'was not only free but held a highly honored position' (ibid, p. 31).

5. Norton T. Dodge, *Women in the Soviet Economy* (Baltimore: The Johns Hopkins Press, 1966), p. 15; Henry P. David, *Family Planning and Abortion in the Socialist Countries of Central and Eastern Europe* (New York: The Population Council: 1970), p. 10; Marilyn McArthur, 'The Saxon Germans: Political Fate of an Ethnic Identity,' *Dialectical Anthropology* 1, no. 4 (September 1976), p. 355.

6. Jean Lipman-Blumen, 'Role De-differentiation as a System Response to Crisis: Occupational and Political Roles of Women,' *Sociological Inquiry*, Vol. (2), 1973, pp. 105-29.

7. In Sweden, for example, women made up 41 percent of the workforce in 1974, but 37 percent worked part-time (Elisabet Sandberg, *Equality is the Goal* [Stockholm: The Swedish Institute, 1975], pp. 17, 21).

8. Jerzy Berent, 'Some Demographic Aspects of Female Employment in Eastern Europe and the USSR,' *International Labour Review*, 1010 (January-June 1970), pp. 175-91.

9. David, op. cit., gives details of abortion legislation and abortion statistics through 1969. In spite of the difficulties of estimating the impact of legal abortion on the birth rate, he concludes that the declining birth rates were accelerated by the legalization of abortion (p. 19). The data were certainly interpreted this way in Eastern Europe.

10. Karel Vácha, 'Důsledky zákona o umělém přerušení těhotenství,' *Demografie* 12, no. 1 (1970), pp. 49-50.

11. During the Stalinist period it was felt necessary to discover a 'law' governing population under socialism to match Marx's capitalist population law (see Hilda Scott, *Does Socialism Liberate Women?* [Boston: Beacon Press, 1974], p. 160).

12. Blanka Filipcová, 'Některé vyśledky a metodologické problémy výzkumů mimopracovní doby a volného času,' *Sociologický časopis* 2, no. 5 (1966), p. 654.

13. Václav Zápotocký, 'Výživa v domácnostech podle počtu dětí,' *Demografie* 8, no. 2 (1966), pp. 107-16.

14. Calculated from figures given in *Statistická ročenka ČSSR* (1969), p. 131.

15. 'The socialist states have a very active population policy, in which social aid to families with children creates a complex of measures. The basic trends of population development are a direct part of the program of communist parties, and are planned and conceived in connection with the development of the national economy' (O. Schmidt, 'Populační vlna neopadá,' *Hospodarské noviny*, 29 August, 1975, p. 11.

16. Jiří Prokopec, 'O potratech 1966,' *Zprávy státní populační komise* no. 3 (1967), p. 31.

17. David, op. cit., pp. 129-30.

18. The decision of the Hungarian Council of Ministers is printed in full in French in 'Aspects Sociopolitiques et Démographies de la Planification Familiale en France, en Hongrie et en Roumanie,' *Dossiers et Recherches* No. 2 (February 1977), Institut National D'Études Démographiques, Paris, pp. 117-27.

19. 'K novelizaci předpisů o interrupci,' *Zdravotnické noviny*, 7 July 1973. Evidence by Western and East European gynaecologists in support for the argument

that legal induced abortions lead to serious late complications was presented by Prof. Alfred Kotásek, Chairman of the Czech Gynaecological Society, in a paper read to the Fourth European Congress of Perinatal Medicine in Prague, August 1974. US experts do not consider such findings conclusive, because the various foreign studies are not comparable and do not allow for all possible variables. The first comprehensive US study is now under way at Boston Hospital for Women. The introduction of improved methods of abortion, such as the use of prostoglandins, changes the whole picture in any case.

20. See Josef Langmeier and Zdeněk Matějček, *Psychická deprivace v dětství* (Prague: Statní zdravotnické nakladatelství, 1963).

21. Vladimír Vitásek, *Pracovní podmínky těhotných žen a matek* (Prague: Orbis, 1973), p. 107.

22. V. Perevedentsev, 'Familienpolitik in der Sowjetunion,' *Wiener Tagebuch* no. 12 (December 1975), pp. 12-15 (translated from *Nash Sovremmenik* no. 6 [June 1975]). The Soviet labor shortage is estimated at 800,000 a year for the next five years, increasing to 1,300,000 thereafter (Murray Feshbach and Stephen Rapaway, 'Soviet Population and Manpower Trends and Policies,' in *Soviet Economy in a New Perspective* [Washington: US Government Printing Office, 1976] p. 151).

23. In the East Slovak Iron Works, one of Czechoslovakia's most important plants, the number of women employed doubled between 1963 and 1964, and increased by 72 percent between 1965 and 1969. There was only a 5.2 percent increase between 1970 and 1973 'as a result of very strict measures regulating women's employment' adopted by management, 'although women are the most obvious source of labor' (Michal Haňdiak, 'Postavenie a Možnosti uplatnenia sa žien v priemyselnom podniku,' *Sociologia* 6, no. 5 (1974), pp. 434-37. In 1973, women made up 22 percent of the plant's personnel, and, according to a survey made by management, the majority were satisfied with their work.

24. Bauerová, op. cit., p. 105.

25. Calculated from figures given in *Statistická ročenka CSSR* for 1968 and 1975. From time to time the press published criticism of failure to use women's qualifications. It is reported, for example, that almost half the students specializing in textile technology at the Liberec College for Engineering and Textiles are women, but most of them receive jobs after graduation in the personnel departments of textile plants or in other positions where their training is wasted (Ivan Soukup, 'Jak připravujeme budoucí generace techniků,' *Rudé právo*, 21 October 1976). A woman writer complains: 'We have a high percent of qualified women – but how do we treat their qualifications?...Why are qualified women often shifted to sectors where their qualifications are not fully used? Is it given by their natural mentality, their maternal function, their household duties and their position in the family? These are, I think, questions to which we are not yet able to give a satisfactory and unequivocal answer; but from the point of view of the aims of socialist society we must seek this answer...' (Štěpánka Kudělková, 'Využít kvalifikace žen,' *Rudé Právo*, 23 July 1976).

26. Paolo de Sandre, 'Critical Study of Population Policies in Europe' (paper presented at the Council of Europe Seminar on the Implications of a Stationary or Declining Population in Europe, Strasbourg, September 1976).

27. Bauerová, 'Druhá směna' zaměstnaných žen,' *Práce*, 11 June 1975. A

Czechoslovak government spokesman announced that expansion of services to 'housewives' in the 1971-75 economic plan had fallen far short of targets. Volume handled by public laundries had increased 6.4 percent instead of the 25-30 percent planned; by dry cleaners by one percent instead of 20 percent. Services to motorists, however, had expanded considerably more than expected, by 87 percent (Václav Blecha, 'Služby stále na pořadu,' *Hospodarské noviny*, 7 May, 1976).

28. Mária Márkus, 'Changes in the Function of Socialization and Models of the Family,' *Revue Internationale de Sociologie* 11, no. 3 (December 1975), pp. 204-23.

29. Bauerová, 'Socialismus a osvobození ženy,' *Rudé právo*, 24 June 1975. Note that this article and the one referred to in Note 27 above by the same author appeared in different newspapers within a few days of each other. She is a sociologist specializing in problems of women.

30. 'Draft World Plan of Action to be Submitted to the World Conference of the International Women's Year in Mexico City 19 June – 25 July 1975,' UN Economic and Social Council document E/CONF. 66/5 (mimeographed).

31. The decision of the Politburo is given in full in English as Appendix 2 to the 'Note verbale date 16 April 1975 from the Permanent Mission of Bulgaria to the United Nations addressed to the Secretary-General,' UN General Assembly document A/10088 June 5, 1975.

32. Herta Kuhrig, *Equal Rights for Women in the German Democratic Republic* (Berlin: GDR Committee for Human Rights, 1973) pp. 15-28. The author is the 'Deputy chairman of the scientific advisory council "Women in Socialist Society" at the Academy of Sciences of the GDR.'

33. *Für Dich*, no. 30 (1976). I am indebted to Irene Fick for this reference.

8

SOCIAL POLICY AND THE FAMILY IN NORWAY

Harriet Holter
University of Oslo, Norway and
Hildur Ve Henriksen
University of Bergen, Norway

Holter and Ve Henriksen present a comprehensive overview of Norwegian social policy from the post-second world war period through the present day. They examine the Folk Pension and Insurance System as the early core of Norwegian social policy, whose goal was full employment and economic growth. The period following the second world war saw an increased GNP and elevated standard of living in Norway. Since the mid-1960s, however, new problems, such as increased incidence of mental illness, crime, alcoholism, drug addiction and hidden unemployment, have arisen from the post-war conditions of urbanization, industrialization and labor mobility.

The authors suggest that social policy more recently has been used to 'repair damages' in the 'sphere of reproduction' emanating from the system of production. Holter and Ve Henriksen suggest that social policy aimed at the system of production has failed to alter the 'core structure' of the economic system. They argue that the compensatory social policy targeted at the family and related institutions is not adequate to deal with the resulting socio-political problems. The analysis of social policy and the family focusses on social problems as indices of the 'malfunctioning' of traditional institutions.

The authors call attention to the use of 'family policy' to solve problems beyond the parameters of the family, such as the society's general standard of living and employment needs. And ironically, non-family social policy aimed at special populations, such as the sick and the elderly, has had profound influence on the institution of the family by draining it of previous traditional functions.

The development of state-supported child care is seen as the State's recognition of its responsibility to the welfare of children. Other aspects of family life, including relationships among family members, remained the private responsibility of individuals.

Until the early 1970s, Norwegian social policy was not explicitly concerned with the position of women, despite some earlier legal protections with regard to marriage. Holter and Ve Henriksen contend that the changing economy of the late 1960s and early 1970s was the main factor in drawing mothers of young children into the labor force, and that the question of working mothers was not, until then, part of the official debate on the family. As a result, Grønseth's sociological analysis of the family only recently is being taken somewhat more seriously by politicians, trade unionists, and industrialists, who previously dismissed it as impractical.

The period from 1945 to 1970 focussed its rhetoric and policies primarily on one aspect of the family: the welfare of children. The 1970s has witnessed an expanded debate that now includes other aspects of family policy. Demographic trends have revealed changing family patterns, and the growing demand for counseling services for family units, rather than individuals, signals a new challenge to policy makers.

Public debate about the most desirable form of family structure is marked by contradictions. But an emerging theme is the relationship between the family and the State, as well as the State's responsibility to individuals qua individuals within society. Within this debate, issues of public vs. private functions of the family are salient. Child-care institutions, health clinics for mothers and pre-school children, the integration of children's and parents' milieux, the increasing importance of the father's role, pregnancy rights and parental leave, as well as the position of women and other questions remain at the heart of the social policy debate in Norway.

Holter and Ve Henriksen present a cogent analysis of the role of social policy in responding to and creating social change within the family. The role of social policy in the 'functional drainage and functional renewal' of the family institution is suggested and issues of individuation, privatization, and intimazation are explored.

I. NORWEGIAN SOCIAL POLICY: A SOCIAL-DEMOCRATIC SOLUTION TO PROBLEMS OF A CAPITALIST ECONOMY

A. Social problems and social policy

During the post-war period in Norway the term 'social policy' has become increasingly all-embracing and diffuse. In the 1920s and almost until the second world war, social policy mainly connoted government measures that eliminated the more pronounced results of poverty and illness. The legislation and the aid systems were seen mostly in a narrow financial frame of reference. Public support of an individual was a benevolent help, not the right of every citizen as it is today. Moreover, social policy had strong overtones of moralism and educational purposes. In the mid-1930s when the Labor Party came to political power in Norway, social policy rapidly developed into one of the instruments whereby a Social Democratic labor movement hoped to reach some of its goals: equality among the classes and security for large groups of the population.

Within approximately 30 years, a social security system – a Folk Pension and Insurance system – was established, embracing old people, the disabled of all types, unwed mothers, orphans, the unemployed and the sick. The Folk Pension is – together with a child allowance for all children, a free, extensive, modern health service, and housing subsidies – in a sense, the core of Norwegian social policy. This policy has been developed in a rather pragmatic way, with due consideration to goals of even higher priority than equality: full employment and economic growth. During the post-war period, a moralistic view of social problems lost ground and was replaced by considerations of justice and rationality.

A steady increase in the GNP and in the general standard of living characterizes the whole post-war period in Norway. By and large, full employment has been the rule, and lately the production of oil promises new possibilities for a welfare society. Some of the social problems inherent in poverty and open unemployment have disappeared. Since about the mid 1960s, however, following in the wake of the concentration of industry, urbanization and labor mobility, social problems such as the incidence of mental illness, drug addiction, alcoholism, crime, and violence have increased rapidly. Tuberculosis has vanished; cardiovascular diseases and cancer are becoming more frequent. An open unemployment has replaced a hidden one: unemployment of the young, the old and some kinds of disabled who are superfluous in a modern system of production, but nevertheless are useful for many jobs in a more human and varied economic and ecological system.

Changes in the sphere of production, like increased concentration of capital, larger production units, pursuit of new markets, greater time pressure in work life, demands for mobility of labor and changes in job requirements, all have caused social and cultural changes which are easily termed 'social problems'. In public opinion, the very term 'social problem' at times seems to indicate something unpleasant that 'society' or the government should remedy. A diffusion of 'social' and 'political' problems is taking place.

The increases in social or social-political problems are met by the government with a fairly active social policy and an expanding budget of expenditures for social benefits. About 20 percent of the GNP is used for social and health purposes, and from 1961 to 1973 public expenditures for social welfare and health services increased on the average of 16 percent a year. The personnel in public social and health care institutions and agencies have increased almost accordingly. No other public sector has expanded as much in the last decade.

B. The production system and the sphere of reproduction

The above assessments of Norwegian social problems and social policy may be summarized in the following way: The government tries to repair damages caused by the system of production, in the sphere of reproduction — by giving support and aid in the sphere of reproduction.[1] These attempts at reparation are ex-post-facto attempts, as is illustrated below in an analysis of government family policy. Such a broad generalization is a controversial one, but seems to cover some of the main problems facing Norwegian social policy today. It does not imply that the Social Democratic Government is completely passive in the sphere of production; the opposite is true.

Government intervention in the system of private enterprise is, for various reasons, much more foresighted than interventions in the system of reproduction. Production intervention usually takes the form of support to industry or activities needed either to keep up employment or to vitalize districts in danger of economic and social decay; in addition, financial and budgetary policy favors the same purposes. At the same time, new legislation concerning the conditions of work in a broad sense is being enforced this year.

The core structure of the economic system is, however, untouched by these measures. To the authors, this implies that those social problems which the government tries to solve by social policy mainly in the sphere of reproduction may remain largely unsolved or become replaced by other equally difficult social-political problems.

A further discussion of Norwegian social problems and social policy in general is not intended here. To put the main theme – social policy and the family – in a proper frame of reference, however, four different perspectives on the phenomena called social problems may be called to attention:

Social problems may be seen as (1) individual symptoms, (mental illness, alcoholism, criminality, disability, etc. of individual persons); (2) characteristics of certain groups, (the old, the disabled, unwed mothers); (3) the malfunctioning of institutions or social organizations (lack of discipline in the schools, deficiencies of hospitals or prisons, the dissolution of the family, of the social networks, etc.); or, finally, (4) tendencies inherent in the basic organization or structure of society itself (the division between production and reproduction of labor, the contradiction between labor and capital or between the private property of capital and the collective character of production, the mechanisms of rejection of individuals in work life and the educational system). It is on the fourth level that 'social problems' may be seen as expressing an increasing social disintegration and isolation of the individual, and at the same time an increasing bureaucratic encircling of and dependence on the market. These are, however, not our main themes here. It is on the third level – social problems as expression of the malfunctioning of traditional institutions – that an analysis of social policy and the family should be undertaken.

II. SOCIAL POLICY AS FAMILY POLICY: 1945-1970

A. Family Policy 1945-1970

In one sense, all social policy is family policy. The family is an institution that is maintained or changed by forces 'outside' itself, and government intervention, for instance in the economy, in the educational system or in the health services, has implications for family life in general. Perhaps the most important element in Norwegian family policy in the broadest sense since the second world war has been the effort on the part of the Government to maintain employment and encourage economic growth. The first probably has contributed to the maintenance of stable family relations, whereas certain features of the growth-policy — resulting in concentration of industry and higher rates of mobility — may have fostered changes in family life.

In Norway, as in other Western countries, the post-war period has seen considerable changes in the reproduction sphere, and in family life in particular. This development did not accelerate, however, before the middle of the 1960s; until then, the Norwegian family institution remained fairly stable. Compared to the neighboring Scandinavian countries, for example, divorce rates were extremely low; the same was true of the number of married women in the work force.

As long as Norwegian family life appeared stable and traditional, social policy measures were governed by other considerations than those connected with the family institution as such. As a matter of fact, it may be maintained that before the 1970s those government measures that went under the heading of 'family policy' were intended to solve other problems than those connected with the family. The introduction of a child allowance for all children in 1945 was, first of all, part of a policy towards equalization of the standard of living; to some extent, the same is true of the system of housing subsidies. Even some recent proposals about family policy should be seen more in the light of employment policy than family policy, in spite of the terms used by the Government.

Social policy used for such broader goals frequently takes the form of support to special categories of the population. Thus, in the period 1945-70, those features of Norwegian social policy which were declared 'family policy' were above all policies for the children. The most profound influence on family life was nevertheless probably gained by the social policy concerning age and illness, even if these measures were not called family policy. As will be discussed below, until recently Norwegian social policy was not governed by any ideas about the suppression of women.

B. Family policy as a policy for the children

Since equality in the standard of living was one of the main goals of Norwegian post-war social policy, the question of redistribution of income among those with and without children was raised as early as 1945. The problem of cash grants versus support in naturalia to families with children — subsidizing housing, school meals, and children's clothing, for example — was given some attention. Those who preferred cash grants were of the opinion that giving support in the form of naturalia was equivalent to taking away the parents' responsibility for the care of their children and they maintained that parents know best what their children need. Those who wanted support in the form of naturalia stated that this was the best way to make certain that the support benefited the children; furthermore, by making use of this measure, the Government would be better able to integrate family policy with general economic and social planning.

In 1946, a Law on Children's Allowance was introduced in Norway as part of the first political program after the war. This program was the result of joint efforts of politicians from all parties, an indication of the care with which ideas related to the welfare of children were easily introduced in our country.

In the years after 1946, other measures were added to the system of children's allowance, such as social insurance for family supporters, the Government's promotion of the child-rearing payment in cases when the parents were not married, housing subsidies and health centers for mother and children. In the 1950s the taxation and housing policies developed a quality of 'family-centeredness' to such a degree that large groups of unmarried persons, both male and female, felt that they were given too small a share of the public benefits and consequently formed an organization to serve as a political pressure group.

In general, the type of family policy that appeared in Norway toward the end of the 1940s and in the 1950s had as its main goal the strengthening of the economic situation of the family with special reference to children. As family policy in this way became, basically, a policy for the redistribution of income, the authorities contributed to a definition of family problems of consumption. The debate was partly about the children's standard of living and partly about the levelling of income differences between families with children and other types of households. The question of how the family as an institution ought to function was only peripherally a matter of discussion in the years immediately following the second world war.

In family policy, as in other parts of the Norwegian Labor Party policy, scant attention was given to the views or principles of the party's left wing. It is symptomatic that although Norway had experts on the topic of sex education as early as in the 1930s, the politics on birth control and advice on the use of contraceptives were very slow to develop compared to elsewhere in Scandinavia. The typical labor politician was a supporter of the traditional view that the family institution should be preserved, and the question of methods of contraception was considered a private, individual matter. In one respect, however, the official family policy constituted a break with earlier views and policy: the acceptance in wide circles of a certain public responsibility for the economic welfare of the children. One might say that the children were viewed separately from the family, in the sense that economically child care became part of the public sphere, while other elements of family life, such as the marriage relationship and the relationship between parents and children, still belonged to the private sphere.

C. Family policy as a policy concerning old age and illness

Although social policy concerning old age and illness has not been considered family policy by the Norwegian Government, its implications for the family today seem so obvious that an omission on this point would be meaningless. Throughout the 1960s the Labor Party introduced, not without a considerable political fight, the above-mentioned Folk Pensions system through which all persons above the age of 67, whether they have had a job or not, get a pension. This system has also incorporated other types of social security measures for different groups: unmarried mothers, the handicapped and disabled of many types, widows and orphans. Consequently, in the beginning of the 1970s a clause in the family legislation stating children's economic responsibility for their old or ill parents was abolished. Along with the Folk Pension system certain other types of public aid to the old and the disabled have been introduced. Welfare centers, subsidized train and bus fares, old age homes and institutions, support for improvement of housing conditions of old people and special services in the homes of old people are among these. The almost complete shift of responsibility for the old and ill from the family to the public sphere, is, perhaps, the most complete and radical 'functional drainage' of the family in our time.

D. Family Policy as a Policy for Women

Government intervention to support women or to eliminate suppression of women for many years has been excluded explicitly from social policy in Norway. However, since large groups of women belong to those who are in special need of the contributions offered by the social insurance and other service systems, social policy measures in some respects favor women. The provisions for 'lonely providers' are among these. In other ways, as with certain types of pensions, there is still discrimination against women as wives.

Until the 1970s, government support of women as a group was most pronounced in the educational sphere and in certain attempts to secure equal wages in business and industry. In 1949 a tripartite Council for equal wages was established in Norway; this proved to be a constant and useful reminder to the Government and the public of the economic discrimination against women in their work lives.

In the period 1945 to 1970, Norwegian family policy focussed only in a very limited way on improving the position of women. The main legal protection of woman in marriage was established in the 1920s. Some improvements in the situation of unmarried mothers were made during this part of the post-war period. Furthermore, the public health insurance system which covers the whole population was improved in 1956 with respect to delivery services: cash contributions to the mother and free care in hospitals. In addition, a system of child allowances paid to the mothers was developed.

During many years of the post-war period, the number of married women in the work force, and especially mothers with small children, was much lower in Norway than in other industrialized countries. Only toward the end of the 1960s did this situation change, and the proportion of married women in the labor force increased from 11 to 23 percent during that decade. It is the contention of the present authors that there is a close connection between this increase in married women's employment and the decrease in that part of the male jobholders' salaries which is 'the family support' amount. In the 1950s and especially the 1960s, a tight labor market and expansion tendencies in the economy in general called for a greater part of the female population to enter the work force. Consequently, the 'family support' part of men's wages was reduced (or rather not increased as much as cost of living), and families with children could not manage economically unless the mother went to work.

The explanation that has been most widely accepted regarding the difficult economic situation of families with children is that of inflation. Inflation, however, can be seen as functional for creating a maximum labor supply. Other explanations of the increase in women's employment have been social-psychological taking into account women's isolated situation and their need to use their abilities. We do not contest these views, but think that they explain mainly the middle-class woman's situation. It is impossible to go further into this matter here. The fact is that the tendency for a large number of mothers with small children to enter the work force was not apparent in Norway until the middle of the 1960s, and the problems of working mothers were not an important issue in the official debate on the family before the end of the decade. The view that children need their mothers at home was strongly advocated in most political parties, including the Labor Party.

To the extent that it is possible to say that family policy in Norway was influenced by the ideology and theoretical discussion on the position of women, it was characterized by contradictions. On the one hand, attempts were made to strengthen the mother-child relationship, for example by establishing health centers for mothers and children. On the other hand, the government expressed faintly positive views on the participation of married women in the labor force. The conflicting attitudes are reflected in the rather weak interest in the building, and the very slow increase in the number, of day care institutions for children before the 1970s.

The interest on the part of government in a systematic analysis of the family institution as such was limited until recently in Norway. From the mid-1950s, the ideas of the sociologist Eric Grønseth on the relationship between the father's provider role, the authoritarian structure of the family, and the suppression of women, represent theoretical and practical suggestions for family reforms: equality between the sexes regarding the responsibility for work both inside and outside the family, combined with a child-care salary to be paid to that parent who chooses to take care of the child. Grønseth's suggestions presuppose considerable changes in the economy, changes which politicians, administrators, and representatives of private enterprise found incompatible with a rational and effective use of the labor force. Grønseth's ideas are taken far more seriously at present.[2]

The question of a child care salary (or as it has also been called, a 'housewives' wage') has been discussed off and on during most of the post-war period. But the cost of introducing a child-care salary seems almost prohibitive, and there continue to be doubts about the possibilities of financing such a salary. Questions about the method of financing arise. Should it be part of the general tax budget or should it come from the profit of private enterprise, etc.? Other negative views of the child-care salary have been presented: a child-care salary may tie the married women even more strongly to the home in that it may never be high enough to represent a free choice to most fathers. At the same time, a child-care salary may hinder married women from seeking employment outside the home.

It behooves an account of the Norwegian Social Democratic policy on the position of women to mention a certain reluctance to go as far as Sweden and Denmark in the liberalization of divorce and marriage laws. The changes that took place in the marriage legislation in Norway in the 1940s and 1950s must be viewed more as an expression of a desire to strengthen the position of the wife inside the family than of an attempt to liberalize the divorce rules themselves. The private sphere of Norwegian society has not been influenced to the same extent as the neighbouring countries by a liberal-bourgeois attitude toward sexuality, and today Norway is not following the same course as Denmark and Sweden in the liberalization of marriage and divorce legislation. Furthermore, this fact does not seem to create any serious protests in our country.

In one important respect, the position of mothers was strengthened during the years under discussion; in case of divorce, the mother is, in more than 90 percent of the cases, granted the right to keep the children. Also, on behalf of the children's welfare, she gets the family home. It may be a matter for discussion, however, whether the strengthening of women's position as mothers in the long run strengthens their position as women. A policy stimulating fathers to take care of their children over time may be more liberating to women.

Summing up, one might say that the welfare of the children became the focus of explicit family policy in the period from 1945 to 1970. The public authorities took charge of part of the economic responsibility, and also of the health of children, but did not in other ways interfere in the relationship between parents and children.

III. SOCIAL POLICY AND THE FAMILY IN THE 1970s

A. A Changing Family Institution

In contrast to the period 1945-70, the Norwegian family in the 1970s has become a focus of direct government concern and intervention. It is now possible, more than in the previous period, to distinguish a family policy as part of the total social policy. Obviously, this has to do with recent developments in the family institution itself and in the sphere of reproduction generally.

The period since the mid-1960s has seen a rapid change in Norwegian family life and an increase in problems apparently questioning the traditional family's possibilities for survival. Family size is decreasing, the fertility rate has been diminishing over the last 10 years, the number of children born out of wedlock is increasing. The relative number of marriages is, however, larger than ever before. At the same time, the age of first marriage is lower than ever, and couples are cohabiting more frequently without having confirmed their marriage legally (uncertified marriages). The number of spouses seeking guidance and treatment is apparently increasing and, according to investigations, the number of children and adolescents in need of psychiatric help is alarmingly high. These are phenomena which may be attributed to conditions in work life as well as in family and kinship relations. It may be a matter for discussion whether the family as an institution is tending toward dissolution or toward considerable change. Of equal importance is the apparent tendency to disintegration of the traditional, stable social networks that have been an informal support of an older family type. The development seems to be one of (possibly transitory) breakdown of the more traditional structure of the reproductive sphere.

As mentioned above, one of the events originating in the production sphere that has affected the family institution in Norway very strongly in recent years is the change from one-earner to two-earner families. This seems to have influenced considerably the Labor Party's attitude to bringing family policy into focus. Other trends in the production sphere also have been of consequence for the family institution and the development of family policy. One of these is a strong tendency toward concentration of production which has resulted in many types of problems: difficult situations for families that have to move to high pressure areas, and, correspondingly, problems for families that stay in local areas, losing many of their vital services like schools, places of work, health services, etc.

It has become apparent that limited possibilities for family members to share their daily lives has not been defined as a public issue nor granted status as an important problem in the same way as the economic problems of the family. The development within the economy in the 1960s and the beginning of the 1970s had as its consequence a crisis in family relationships, both qualitatively and quantitatively. Institutions rendering psychiatric services to families are growing in number and the established institutions increasingly are trying to support and treat the entire family unit instead of individual family members. This development is characterized by two trends: First, new institutions such as family counseling centers are created, and second, already existing institutions are changing their types of service from primarily individual medical care to treatment of whole families. The change in health centers for mothers and children is an example of the latter trend.

In the beginning of the 1970s, this situation gave new impetus to the principal debate on the family as a social institution. This debate, in which politicians also take part, is influenced from three different quarters: in psychiatric-psychological circles, the phenomenon of mental health is viewed in relation to the interaction patterns of family members; in the various groups that are influenced by Marxist ideas,, the focus is on the relationship between family and society; in the feminist movement, the interest is in women's position in the family and how this position influences their total life situation. Nevertheless, the ends and means of an official family policy are still quite vaguely formulated in Norway.

B. Increasing Focus on Family Policy: Recent Norwegian Trends

As mentioned in the introduction to this chapter, another difficulty in discussing family policy as a clearly defined topic is the understandable fact that government intervention itself is not guided by any clear conception of the family or the forces governing the family. Nor are policy makers very interested or willing to formulate goals or ideas as to what kind of family institution they want to support *and* why. Norwegian family policy then, above all, is characterized by a pragmatism that sometimes is reflected in conflicting measures and diffuse ideas about the family. This is fairly evident in the Norwegian official documents on family policy, of which the first and most important appeared quite recently.

In 1974 the Minsitry of Consumer and Administration Affairs presented a paper to parliament containing an analysis of the situation of families with children.[3] In the introduction to the paper the Ministry questions whether in Norway today a clear definition of the official goals of family policy is to be found anywhere. In this situation, the Ministry declares, a resolution agreed upon by the European Council may serve as a basis for the Ministry's own definition of such goals. In this resolution the European Council states that:

> the goal of the unity of the member nations in the Common Market is to facilitate the social development of the different members. Such a 'social development' is dependent on the formulation of an adequate family policy which meets the needs of the family both through economic and financial measures that may compensate for the burdens placed on the family; and through an adequate organizing of other services in order that the family, as a unit, and its individual members may have an opportunity to fully develop their capacities within society.

Toward this 'goal for family policy' the Ministry attempts to shape a new way of thinking about the relationship between the family and the state. The principles of cash payments and subsidies to families with children are replaced by the idea that an increase in the employment of married women in the labor force will be more effective than an increase in the children's allowance as a means of strengthening the economy of families. In this connection, the Ministry emphasizes the desirability of increasing the possibilities of each individual family member's free choice of occupation. It also stresses the importance of enabling each individual member to realize his or her abilities and interests, and states that the meeting of such individual needs will strengthen the family institution.

Furthermore, the 1974 parliamentary paper suggests that to enable a greater number of married women to enter the labor force, society must build more child-care institutions of different types — day-care institutions, leisure-time institutions, playgrounds, youth centers, etc. This also may serve the needs of children, because the general economic development has led to an impoverishment of the types of milieux in which children may play and have fun together. The Ministry contends that the home is no longer able to meet the needs of children and teenagers for social contact and creative play.

With regard to previous principles of Norwegian family policy, the parliamentary paper proposes certain changes in the definition of what are public vs. private functions in the care and socialization of children. The State should assume greater responsibility for the social welfare of the younger generations. On the other hand, the economic situation of the family is to a greater extent defined as a private responsibility for parents.

In parts of the paper, the Ministry attributes very important functions to the family. The family is presented as the institution which shall 'fulfill the family member's basic need for love, emotional health and material care and security'. The Ministry goes on to state: 'the family... is the institution that is chiefly responsible for the child's development into a member of society'. On the other hand, according to the same paper, families meet with considerable difficulties in fulfilling these functions and government institutions and agencies should establish other opportunities.

The 1974 parliamentary paper on the family has been met with considerable criticism. One major objection is that the paper indirectly serves the purposes of the expanding oil business and the tight Norwegian labor market in general. The conceptual framework of the paper is poor: it still relies heavily on the categories of family members – children, mothers, fathers – and does not develop concepts and ideas pertaining to the functioning of families and to family culture.

In many respects, however, the paper represents an advance beyond the treatment of family policy by previous governments. By presenting this paper, the Government for the first time makes itself available as a partner in a discussion on the functions of the family institution and the goals of family policy. Furthermore, some of the problems which the modern family has to cope with are very clearly described by the Ministry. One may agree or disagree with the evaluations and conclusions that are drawn by the Ministry, but it is appreciated that the Government presents its views on such a controversial subject.

There thus can be no doubt about the tendencies for government administration and public agencies to accept more responsibility for the reproductive functions in general. This is seen most clearly in the recent 'policy for the children'. As mentioned above, the public coverage of day-care institutions has, until recently, been rather incomplete. In 1975, however, the Government put into effect a new law on day-care institutions which explicitly stated that the municipalities were responsible for securing for children a good life situation by building and running day-care institutions or by economically supporting the building and running of such institutions. All municipalities were required to develop programs for the establishment of child-care institutions according to research on the need for them. The State will subsidize the cost of running the day-care institutions, and the municipalities may get inexpensive building loans from a State bank. The Government plans to increase the number of places in day-care institutions from about 40,000 in 1975 to 50,000 by the end of 1977. This represents coverage of 11 percent of the estimated need. By the end of 1981, the number of places in day-care institutions will be 100,000 — a coverage of 25 percent. The municipalities are to decide the rate of payment in the public day-care institutions according to the economic ability of the parents. The cost of family day care is paid partly by the parents, partly by the municipalities.

The Government recently has introduced a new law on health clinics for mothers and children which should increase considerably the number of such clinics which offer a series of free services to the pregnant woman, as well as to the mother and child from the child's birth until it reaches school age. Free medical and dental care for children in school (to 18 years) has been in effect for several years. The present trend in health service is toward paying greater attention to the child's emotional development and family situation. The father also is invited to attend these clinics.

The most recent development in policy on children appears in a 'paper on the situation of children' which will be presented to parliament by the Ministry of Administration and Consumer Affairs later this year (1977). The chief message of this paper is that children as a group must not be isolated from the world of adults. This has two practical implications. The paper states that the physical planning authorities must take children's needs into account to a much greater extent than before. Children must have sheltered playgrounds, and all building of living quarters must be planned so that a good 'neighborhood milieu' can develop, especially with regard to the children's needs. Furthermore, the parents must be integrated into the milieu of day-care institutions, and also into the different leisure-time activities that are being arranged by the authorities. The municipalities shall receive larger grants in order to develop better surroundings for children. New jobs will be created in the 'milieu-creating' field with special responsibility for the life of young children up to the age of 12 years. The paper explicitly states that the parents must be integrated into these activities. It is obvious that the Government has become aware of the increasing trend in our society to segregate children from adults and parents from children, and that there is a political desire to stop this development. To a certain extent, the paper also takes into account the further need for reduced working hours for parents with small children. Among the issues in the current debate on the situation of children is the possibility of instituting a 'parent's certificate' and a 'children's ombudsman' in order to secure more efficiently the rights of children.

Not only child care, but also other family matters lately have been subject to government intervention in Norway. One of the most important political initiatives of the Labor Government in the 1970s has been a proposal before parliament to establish free abortion, and furthermore to propose a law on the equality of men and women. Both proposals failed in parliament, but only by a narrow margin, and the present cabinet seems determined to renew these proposals if Labor is in power after the coming election.

The Government got more support in 1977 when introducing a new law on work environment, in which the rights of women during pregnancy and the post parturition period are extended in important ways. The law also introduces new ways of thinking about the father's role. All employed women have the right to an 18-week maternity leave. If the woman is married (or cohabiting), the couple may decide to divide some of these weeks between them. This is a completely new feature in Norwegian legal rules on maternity leave. The law states however, that the mother must remain at home for the first six weeks after childbirth, so that the choice between husband and wife only involves the remaining 12 weeks. Also, the mother may decide to use part of the maternity leave before delivery, whereas the father is granted no comparable liberty. During the 18-week maternity leave, the one who stays at home is granted 90 percent of his/her wage. (At the moment, the payment is calculated somewhat differently, but it is expected that the rule of 90 percent of the wage will be introduced in the near future.) Besides the right to 18 weeks of paid maternity leave, the mother or father has a right to further maternity leave up to one year (i.e., 18 weeks plus 34 weeks) without pay, but with full job protection. If the wife is not employed, the husband has no right to maternity leave with pay (or without pay). But all husbands, whether the wife is employed or not, may take two weeks off without pay, but with job protection. This leave is called 'welfare' or 'care' leave. In families where the mother is working, the father has a right to this 'care' leave, in addition to the above-mentioned right to share some of the 18 weeks with the mother.

In the arguments for fathers' rights to maternity leave, the main point has been the welfare of the baby, but argument that has been advanced suggests the importance of establishing close contact with their newborn children. But the furthering of equality between the sexes has also been given much weight.

In the same vein, another law was enacted in 1977, entitling both working mothers and fathers, to 10 days of leave annually for taking care of sick children under the age of 10 years. It should be noted that the new laws on maternity leaves and other facilities for parents cover couples who are not legally married as well.

The current debate in government circles, within the political parties as well as in the labor unions, concerns whether to give priority either to an increase in the number of weeks of maternity leave with pay, or to a general reduction in work hours (the 6 hour day) for parents with small children. It seems rather unlikely, if the latter alternative is chosen, that the reduction in payment which automatically follows a reduction in work hours can be compensated for. The discussion, however, focuses on the possibility of granting some kind of compensation to low wage earners.

In Norway, the 1970s have seen more activity in the field of family policy in a narrow sense than any earlier period. The children are — as in the earlier post-war period — still the main target of intervention, although now more clearly in a way that moves responsibility from the family to the State. Measures intended to influence the division of labor between the spouses and to make care of small children easier for parents, attempts to strengthen the position of women within the family, as well as developments of services aimed at solving internal marriage and family problems, are the main items in a variegated picture of government family policy at present. How these possibly contradictory measures are going to affect family life is an open question. Equally unanswered is the question of how to analyze the ends and means of such a policy, as far as the family institution is concerned.

C. Towards an Analysis of Family Policy

Government intervention in family affairs is seen by the authors as lagging behind the changes in family life itself. For example, only when circumstances other than public policy weaken the family's ability to solve the problems of the old or the incapacitated is government intervention established. The considerable shifts in the patterns of marriage and family that have characterized Western societies since the beginning of industrialization are mainly the results of changes in the production system. It may be true that the family is a strong institution as far as its very existence is concerned — few, if any, societies are without some kind of officially recognized family institution. Nevertheless, this institution is highly vulnerable to changes initiated in other spheres of society. The strict institutional division between production on one hand and reproduction of labor on the other that is found in capitalist societies is in one sense only apparent. The production system — work life, technology, economic development, the markets — more or less determines the patterns of the personal or private sphere. The social division between the production sphere and 'private' life serves several functions, one of which is to leave the owners and decision makers in the sphere of production free to pursue their goals without great regard for the conditions of the reproduction of labor.

Government social policy is of moderate consequence for the family institution compared to increased concentration of industry, the request for labor mobility, urbanization and the pursuit of new markets to maintain profit — trends which all deeply affect family life. It probably is not possible for government policy in a capitalist society to *initiate* such changes in family patterns as seen in Western societies in recent years. It seems feasible however, that government measures may counteract or stimulate somewhat the trends that are already present. Such measures may enlarge or diminish the effects of developments in the sphere of production on the family. As will be discussed briefly below, this should be the main frame of reference for evaluating a social policy as family policy. The complications, however, are obvious, first because the changes in family life are difficult to assess in a precise way, and, second, because these changes are the result of many (often socially invisible) circumstances in the economy and technology of capitalist society. Nevertheless, a few suggestions about the relationship between a government social policy and the development of the family institution may be briefly outlined, mainly by way of some examples.

The general social policy in Norway since the mid 1930s has aimed above all at support and aid to the individual, thereby (perhaps as an unintended consequence) making the individual less dependent on family and kin relations, and more dependent on public agencies and government bureaucracies. One of the implications probably is a functional drainage of the family institution, at least over time. The extensive social insurance system and health services in a country like Norway give considerable support to the individual with no conditions of family status attached; proportionately fewer services are rendered to the family as such. In the long run this may be an important contribution of government policy to the changes of the family institution: to stimulate and support the tendencies toward an individuation of the family members and functional drainage of the family. Inherent in such a development is a feedback process. Individual government support frees the individual from family ties and kinship. When this becomes a cultural pattern, family and kinship, in due course, is weakened and becomes less important to the individual, thus rendering the individual even more dependent on other social units which again may increase the need for government intervention, and so on.

The recent government activities in establishing day-care institutions and other facilities for children is another case in point. Such institutions, like schools, relieve families of part of their socializing functions and represent in the long run, again, a functional drainage of the family institution. In the same vein, social workers, psychologists and various types of government social services and clinics may replace kinship, neighbours and friends in their traditional tasks of giving advice and relieving tension within the family. Again, when this pattern becomes the dominant one, the older institutions and ways of problem solving lose their meaning and legitimation, thereby increasing the individual's need for alternative means of social support.

The public centers and agencies for family guidance and treatment obviously are intended to give support to the maintenance of individual families, and they may function as such to a large degree. A closer inspection shows, however, some of the complications of such supportive measures. One of the lessons of family therapy as it has developed throughout the last two decades is that stability and functioning of a family is not necessarily the same as stability and functioning of single family members. There are frequently conflicting interests among the family as a unit and one or more of its members. A collectivity is not upheld without costs — at least in the short run — to individual members.

Such contradictions may be inherent in other features of government intervention in family life. Considering one of the cornerstones of Norwegian family policy — the child allowance instituted in 1945 — this may solve many problems for the individual family. It is difficult, however, to know whether it strengthens the institution of the family in the long run.

A final example of the kind of analysis that may be undertaken concerns the popular or common image of what a family is and should be. Norwegian post-war family policy may be seen as a contribution to the ongoing change in the image of what a family is. Since public services and allowances cover unwed mothers and cohabiting couples as well as ordinary families, this may have expanded the concept of 'a family' and legitimized otherwise deviant ways of establishing families. A tendency towards a pluralistic marriage and family culture seems stimulated by the official policy. Furthermore, the Government's initiatives and distribution of contraceptive information, and its recent activities in favor of women's unqualified right to abortion are additional contributions to the establishment of a new marriage and family culture. Without unduly elaborating this theme, it seems reasonable to suggest that these elements of family policy support women's independence as partners, wives and mothers, and that the image of marriage as an intimate and mainly emotional bond is underlined.

These examples of possible relations between social policy and the changes in family patterns may be summarized as follows: in addition to studying policy measures influenced by the conception of 'a family', and the variations in composition and size of families, family policy may be analyzed in terms of its effects on the functional drainage and functional renewal of the family institution. Furthermore, such policy may be evaluated in relation to the family institution's tendencies towards individuation, privatization and intimazation. These last concepts, developed elsewhere by the authors[4], are in some respects specifications of the processes involved in the changing functions of the family. 'Individuation of the family' denotes the process whereby the individual family member to an increasing degree is integrated in other institutions than the family, and as an individual. Intimazation of the family points to the development of the family institution as a setting for close, intimate, personal relations, whereas privatization is a movement (quasimovement) toward a type of social closure of the family which makes public insight into a family inappropriate. Also, the influence of government policy on the internal role and power relations in the family may be assessed.

In relation to these family patterns, the social policy may be a substitution policy (substituting new for old ways of problem solving), a support policy or a policy of direct maintenance of families.

A policy of substitution consists of the establishment of public services that substitute experts, public agencies, courses, and publicly-organized care units for traditional family solutions to given problems. Day-care institutions and schools belong to a substitution policy which usually supports the tendency to functional drainage of the family. In evaluating this policy, it should be born in mind: (a) that the developments that make day-care institutions a reasonable solution to socialization problems do not originate in government policy: (b) that elements of a more collective socialization of children may be highly preferable to a totally privatized socialization in today's families and (c) that the independence of women may be increased by the present Norwegian child-care policy.

The supportive parts of family policy consist mainly of financial aids, like child allowances and housing subsidies. Economic family support of the type favored by the Norwegian government may be seen as a transfer of means to concrete families so that they are able to fulfil certain functions. In the long run, however, this may not stimulate the family as an institution since no self-supporting or problem solving device within the family is stimulated. On the other hand, money allowances and supportive services also tend to give families new tasks, namely to act as integrating units for the receipt of aid and services to the individual and the family as such. This may be seen as functional renewal.

As may be evident from the above section on Norwegian family policy in the 1970s, direct maintenance measures to an increasing extent are the focus of government interventions. The establishment of public family guidance and therapy agencies, the attempts toward involving the father in child care by providing leave from work in connection with the birth of a child or children's illness, the attempts — so far mostly on paper — to integrate the parents in the public activities and care of children, should be seen as a policy aimed directly at maintaining families as social units. This shift towards direct maintenance is a reflection of the severity of the pressures and problems which during the last decade have hit the whole sphere of reproduction and caretaking. Nevertheless, a maintenance policy is to some degree a contradiction of other features of government intervention in the reproductive sphere, especially the substitution policy that probably stimulates the tendencies to functional drainage of the family.

Some of the examples outlined above suggesting relations between government policy and family patterns indicate that inquiries about contradictions and dilemmas should be part of an analysis of family policy. One of the dilemmas concerns the relation between an institution and those individual units which at any given time constitute its 'members'. Support and aid to individual families may be all to the good for these families, but the same measures may not favor the family institution as such. As an established cultural pattern, some forms of public aid may not stimulate the family's ability to maintain problem-solving devices. Other types of public support may, however, institute self-carrying processes whereby a given social arrangement, like the family, may be maintained more effectively.

Another type of dilemma is illustrated above by reference to the possibly conflicting interest between individual family members and the whole family. This point of view may be extended to suggest the possibility of contradictory interests between categories of family members and the family as an institution. As is well known, the family institution of the Western world has for many hundreds of years remained strong, while at the same time the position of women and children within the family was weak. Moreover, the decreasing sociopolitical power of the family institution has been parallelled by a decrease in the powerlessness within family life of women and children. These historical facts point to a dilemma for Norwegian family policy that has become more visible in recent years.

IV SOCIAL POLICY, WOMEN AND THE FAMILY

A number of arguments could be advanced to show that the family institution, as it has been and still is structured in Western societies, contributes greatly to the oppression of women. The traditional family socializes children to the patriarchical sex roles; it stimulates private, individualistic patterns of identification, keeps women in unpaid work and in economic dependence on a husband, upholds the sex-typed division of labor and represses sexual drives. A family policy in support of the prevailing family institution accordingly runs the risk of keeping women oppressed. And precisely because a government family policy — for reasons mentioned repeatedly in this article — usually consists of weak measures, the possibilities of initiating new practices may be small[5]. It may be easier to support a 'going concern' — that is to support a modern version of the patriarchical family in which invisible patterns of male dominance prevail — than to initiate new family relations. Strong groups of feminists and left wing socialists generally — in Norway as in other Western countries — maintain the incompatibility of marriage, family life and women's independence, at least in any foreseeable future.

The main question for government policy seems to be, however, whether the present family institution may be supported in such a way as to develop into a family with equality between the spouses and with a fair amount of independence for each partner. The senior author of this paper has voiced the thesis elsewhere that the less important — socially and politically — the family institution becomes, the more are women permitted to share in family power[6]. Without going further into this question here, several conditions for the development of a family policy that is both supportive of women's independence and also of a family institution with some important functions may be pointed out.

When the Ministry and more recently Norwegian politicians in general talk about 'a family- and-equality policy', as if the interests of 'the family' and those of 'women in general' are inevitably in harmony, this is begging important policy questions about priority of interests[7]. It would, for instance, not be unreasonable to maintain that children's interests or well being are best provided for in a stable, high-functional type of family, whereas women's interests (as well as men's) under the present economic order are in a low-functional type. The present government activity in building and running public child-care institutions meets a long-standing demand from women's organizations in Norway. Most active feminists consider free public child care a necessary condition for the development of equality between men and women. In a competitive economy, the responsibility for children is a burden; only another type of production system can change this fact. If children remain the main responsibility of women, then children will be a burden to women, and a hindrance to equality and to that amount of liberation which may be developed within the limits of a capitalist society. As shown before, public child care does not necessarily constitute support of the family institution. In this situation, the a priori assumption that a policy in support of women's independence is also in support of the family hides the real problem. The first condition of a policy that aspires to combine incompatible interests is to acknowledge the dilemma and to analyze the incompatibilities. In this case, an analysis may show that public child-care institutions must be established and structured in certain ways to fulfill both the interests of women *and* those of the family institution.

The second condition for a clear family policy is inevitably the ability to choose between interests and to make this clear. In the present situation, the Social Democratic family policy gives priority to a low-functional family, at least in some important ways, without giving the reasons for this choice — which obviously rests on the tacit assumption that a lack of support for the traditional family does not necessarily imply lack of support for *a* family institution. The diffuseness about what kind of family institution is furthered, is, however, obvious.

The contradictions and dilemmas in Norwegian social policy show some of the difficulties in a Social Democratic administration of capitalist society. The Government cannot, for instance, prevent the family from changing into that type and form of social unit which best serves the production system of private enterprise, as long as this system is kept under minimal public control. It does seem feasible, however, to soften the transition from a traditional family system to a 'modern' family type and to gain some advantages for suppressed groups along the way.

NOTES

1. The term 'sphere of production' is here used to connote those activities or institutions that function to produce and market goods and services. The sphere of production is characterized by the necessity of producing for profit and by a property system which implies a contradiction between labor and capital. The sphere of reproduction comprises those activities and institutions

whose purpose is to reproduce labor — the family, the educational system, health services, social policy agencies and social policy apparatus, for example. This sphere is characterized especially by caretaking and socialization.

2. Erik Grønseth, 'Economic Family Policy and its Guiding Images in Norway' in de Bie and Presvebou (ed.), *National Family Guiding Images and Policies.* Louvain, 1967. — 'The Familial Institution: Alienated Labor-Producing Appendage to Market Society', in Reynolds & Henslin (ed.), *American Society: A Critical Analysis.* New York, 1973.

3. Stortingsmelding (Parliamentary paper) no. 51, 1973-74.

4. Harriet Holter, Hildur Ve Henriksen, Arild Gjertsen and Haldis Hjort: *Familien i klassesamfunnet* (The Family in Class Society). Oslo, 1975.

5. 'Strong' government intervention indicates in this paper those measures which are brought to bear in the sphere of production. 'Weak' measures are those applied to the conditions of reproduction.

6. Harriet Holter, 'Sex Roles and Social Change', *Acta Sociologica* 14 (1971).

7. The problem of women's different class interests is excluded in the present discussion, although it may be highly relevant to the implications of a family policy.

9

THE CHANGING ROLE OF WOMEN IN JORDAN:
'A Threat or an Asset?'

Nimra Tannous Es-Said
Supreme Ministerial Committee for the Relief of Displaced Persons in Jordan, Amman

In Jordan, as in other societies faced with transition, social policy often drives the reevaluation of women's status and role. A national policy focussed on economic and social development (i.e., the recent Five Year Plan) provided the impetus for encouraging women to work outside the home. Improved educational programs, initially aimed at educating men for the labor force and women for the domestic sphere, provided the basis for a more highly skilled work force. Urbanization and economic development, along with the talent drain created by substantial emigration, conjoined to create conditions conducive to women's labor force participation. The demand for female workers to fill clerical roles in urban areas spread to include a broad range of paid occupational roles.

Ms. Es-Said's analysis of the condition of Jordanian women suggests the strains inherent in periods of social change. Although economic demand is drawing workers from rural to urban areas, increasing the ratio of family members dependent upon a single wage earner, and encouraging women to enter the labor market, traditional attitudes and values tend to act as a brake on this trend. These traditional values sustain pockets of strong social taboos against women working outside the home.

Despite these contradictory forces, social policy planners explicitly are seeking ways to involve women in the social and economic development of Jordan. This demand of policy makers has provided a strong impetus to study factors that encourage or inhibit women's participation in the worlds of work and public life. International Women's Year, an example of the international agreements suggested by the Marchand chapter, has spawned numerous activities highlighting women's changing roles. Emanating from the expectations of IWY, seminars and research activities have focussed on the status of women in Jordan. The seminar chaired by Crown Prince Hassan is an example of a research activity promoted indirectly by international agreements and reverberating in still other advances in domestic social policy. Es-Said's work describes changes in income tax regulations that were a direct outgrowth of that one highly visible research activity.

I. INTRODUCTION

Although, according to the Koran (30:al), 'the most perfect among the believers are the kindest to their womenfolk', the actual role of Jordanian women in their society has rarely conformed to the teaching of Islam. Discrimination begins in infancy and continues into adulthood. Thus 'when the midwife announces the birth of a boy there is joy and firing of rifles, dancing and celebrations,' but if it is a girl, 'quietness befalls on the mother and the expectant crowd awaiting the birth of the child'. Interestingly, this discriminatory attitude is not confined to Moslem Arabs; it extends to the Christian communities as well.

The logic behind discrimination against females in Jordan stems from the fact that the female is lost to her family upon marriage. Thereafter, since the patriarchal structure of the family reckons descent through the male, the female's loyalties and obligations are transferred to her husband's family. Understandably, therefore, sons are more desirable, and bearing them confers more status upon the mother. This situation motivates women to have as many sons as possible in order to raise their own status and esteem in the family.

The role of women in Jordan is now undergoing great change. Recent re-examination of the existing division of labor and sex roles in society in light of Jordan's emerging economic and social needs has focussed much current research on the role of the Jordanian woman. Her significant participation in accelerating her nation's development cannot be underestimated. The recent Five-Year Plan for economic and social development (1976-80), for example, took into consideration the shortage of manpower as a result of the 'talent drain' emigration from Jordan. Thus, the search for human resources to implement the Plan became imperative. It was thought that womanpower represented a source that could and should be tapped. This hypothesis was based on the fact that out of the total population, estimated at 2,669,000, women constituted 49.2 percent of whom 57 percent live in the urban areas and 35 percent live in rural and Bedouin areas. Greater emphasis now is being laid on studying additional means of inducing women to work in paid employment, studying their problems as a working group, and creating incentives and rewards for their fuller participation in the nation's development plans.

Since the policy planners have openly demanded more effective participation by women in economic areas, the 'working woman' has become an interesting topic of research. Sociologists, psychologists, anthropologists, and others are studying the attitudes of working women, their basic motives for working, goal attainments, and the influence of education on women's occupational choice. Some researchers have gone beyond this approach to study the attitudes of a selected group within society, 'the elites', who are expected to become future planners, reformers and decision makers on matters relating to social change. Future elites, that is, future university graduates, presumably will promote forcefully progressive tendencies in the country.

II. HISTORICAL AND POLITICAL BACKGROUND

A. The history

Jordanian society in its present size and composition is very young. It came into being as recently as 1950 when part of what was formerly Palestine under the British Mandatory Rule was annexed. The influx of Palestinian Arab refugees in 1948 trebled the population with only a very small territorial increase. These events caused a profound disturbance in the old social equilibrium and introduced a drastic change in both the social structure and the political life of Jordan. This social upheaval was further intensified after the 1967 'June War', when over 250,000 displaced persons sought refuge on the East Bank of the Jordan. This situation added to the existing problem of population growth and uneven distribution of natural and human resources. The annexation of the two Banks brought together two population elements which differed greatly from each other in many ways.

B. The politics

Jordanian society has been faced during the last two decades with several waves of refugees flowing into the country. The influx of refugees kept Jordanian women preoccupied with providing relief services and establishing voluntary societies. Little time was left to exert pressure on the authorities and on society to organize women in political activities. In the absence of the Jordanian Woman's Alliance, which existed but was disbanded during the 1950s, any form of organized action for women's political rights was considered illegal and punishable.

The Arab National Union, a government union formed in 1971, was the first sanctioned party which allowed political participation by women. For most of the people, however, it was regarded as an imposed form of political organization. Perhaps the challenge which this party stimulated encouraged one woman to run for elections. She won and became a member of the executive body.

The Arab National Union is now disbanded. Women frequently complain about the lack of opportunities to exercise their full rights on an equal footing with men. The vigorous and relentless efforts of social reformers and pioneer women have been recognized by King Hussein, under whose reign Jordanian society has witnessed tremendous progress for women. Highlighting this progress was the amendment of the Election Bill which became effective in 1974, allowing women full political rights. These rights have not yet been exercised, however.

III. THE TRADITIONAL ROLE OF WOMEN

In order to fully understand the significance of the changing status of women in Jordanian society, it is important to examine the three traditional roles that Jordanian women have played as they relate to their families and to society. Generally, as in most Arab countries, rural women in Jordan have enjoyed a higher degree of freedom and participated as family workers in the predominantly agricultural economic activities, while urban women were secluded and segregated.

Village women. In village culture, the woman has had a unique position and dual role because of her economic contributions to her family. She not only performs tasks traditional to women the world over — child-rearing and home-making — but she also participates with her husband and family (before marriage) in all the economic functions of an agrarian society. The burdens of the peasant girl are heavy and start at an early age. At her parents' home, she is trained for her future duties as a mother and housewife by attending to her younger brothers and sisters, as well as helping her father or brothers in the field. The girl's freedom in the rural society is restricted at an early age (at about 10 years), after which negotiations for her marriage begin (if we consider the early marriage phenomenon as observed until the present day). Thus, the shift from childhood into adulthood in the socialization of the female Arab child is very sharp compared to the gradual transformation into youth and adulthood of her Western sister.

Bedouin women. In the open life of the desert, comradeship has developed between man and woman unknown in the congested, hemmed-in existence of town life. In addition to their domestic duties — childrearing and homemaking — Bedouin women assist in everyday life, tending to flocks, fetching water, and occasionally helping in agricultural activities. Furthermore, these women participate in the traditional form of hospitality in tent and house alike. This has resulted in a considerable amount of traditionally-sanctioned social contact between non-related men and women among the nomads and the villagers. Nevertheless, men and women form distinct and separate societies, with the family circle as the only locus for meeting on a daily basis.

Urban women. Among the working classes which constitute the majority of the urban population, the position of urban women is similar to that of rural women in many respects. Although the urban woman participates less in economic affairs than does her Village or Bedouin sister, we must not underestimate the advantage that she holds over them.

The urban woman finds herself in a dynamic world where the forces of change penetrate through different channels, mainly education and communication. Although seclusion and veiling remain phenomena of urban society in Jordan and the Arab world, it is, nonetheless, urban society which has been, and continues to be, the 'lever for change' through the Arab world as a whole, and Jordanian society in particular.

IV. TRADITIONAL SOCIETY IN TRANSITION

The influence of the family on the life of the individual in Jordan is much greater than in the Western world. While in the West the individual is the product of socializing factors, in Arab society he or she is much more the product of his or her family, which is best characterized as extended − patrilineal − patriarchal and endogamous.

There is ample evidence to indicate that the traditional family in Jordan is undergoing profound change − primarily in its function, and secondly as a social unit in the lives of its members. Among the social forces causing the change in the family structure is 'urbanization' where the centralized form of government has been adopted as an expression of Westernization. This has led to a rural-urban migration in search of new employment and adventurous ways of living which the villages do not provide. The concentration of wealth, industry, political power, economic opportunities and cultural activities in the cities has contributed to the attraction from rural to urban areas. As a result, the extended family that used to characterize Jordanian society is gradually giving way to a new form of conjugal family.

Marriage as a social institution in the structural pattern of Jordanian society has been exposed to considerable transformation, largely through the spread of education and the discarding of the veil. Consequently, the age at marriage has risen, and there has been a drain on the number of females who traditionally would have been dependent on marriage as an ultimate goal. It is significant to note that the Law of Family Rights of 1951 has recently been amended. The new law, the Personal Status Law (No. 61), the draft of which has been the subject of debate since 1974, became effective on 12 January 1976. It nullified all previous legislation, and is in conformity with Abu Hanifeh theological order. There is no doubt that the new legislation, though it did not introduce significant changes advantageous to women as a whole, is considered a more liberal law than the previous one. Of particular importance is the reduction in the legal marriage age from 18 to 16 years for men and 17 to 15 years for women (Article 5). Article 7 prohibits marriage between a woman younger than 18 years age to a man who is her elder by 20 years, unless she personally agrees and the Qadi is fully satisfied to that effect.

Guardianship over children by women after their divorce has been the concern of many reformers, secular and clerical alike. Article 154 of the new law provides that the mother has priority as custodian or guardian of her children. Article 162 holds that the mother's guardianship extends until the children reach puberty (provided she does not remarry). This article has brought much relief to anguished mothers who were living in fear that their children would be taken away from them by their fathers. (The old law provided mothers could keep male children until they reached seven years and female children until nine years.) Article 167 of the Personal Status Law pertains to the maintenance of relatives and affects the position and status of wives. It clearly provides that 'the maintenance of each person is from his own money except the wife whose maintenance is the responsibility of her husband.'

That the attitude toward marriage in Jordan has undergone considerable transformation is evident from the following statistics from the 'Multipurpose Household Survey for 1972'.[1] Comparative figures have been obtained for the years 1961 and 1972 respectively as shown below:

Age Group	Married Population (percent)	
	1961	1972
15-19 years	27.6	14.4
20-24 years	71.9	54.6
35-39 years	90.8	91.2

These figures show a marked decline in married population among the 15 to 19 age group between the years 1961 and 1972, in contrast to a slight rise in the ratio of married population among the 35 to 39 age group during the same time. These changes could be attributed largely to the expansion of education and the school years, matched with the thirst for knowledge among the younger generation who were pursuing higher education.

A. Indicators of Social Change

Education continues to be the strongest factor contributing to and affecting the rapid social change within the conservative Jordanian Society. It is considered the milestone for the progress witnessed today. Pioneers in social reform have often cried out that if you educate a woman, you educate a whole nation.

Comparative figures for women's enrollment in schools since the country attained independence in 1945/46 show that the proportion of female pupils rose from 28 percent during 1945/46 to 42.2 percent in 1971/72. Recent statistics for 1975/76 show that the proportion has reached 44.5 percent of the total student population in the country.[2]

It is noteworthy that the spread of education was not confined to the urban areas, but extended to the rural regions where the share in the Education Expansion Policy is enormously high. The Ministry of Education statistics for 1971/72 show that out of the total number of girls' schools (584), 56.8 percent are in the rural areas. The number of female teachers assigned to these schools constituted 33.7 percent of the total number of female teachers (5,751). Correspondingly, the female pupils in rural areas constituted 31 percent of the total female student population (55,020). (These figures are only for the East Bank of Jordan, since the West Bank has been under Israeli occupation since June 1967). Recent statistics published by the Ministry of Education for the 1975/76 academic year show that girls' schools number 845, constituting 35.9 percent of the total schools (2,356) in the East Bank.

Some adverse effects of expanded school enrollment among both men and women have been noted, such as increasing the ratio of dependency. The Multi-Purpose Household Survey of 1972 revealed that the size of the urban household is higher than the rural one. Among the surveyed households, 59.4 percent showed that they have six or more persons, compared to 57.2 percent in the rural areas. Households with ten or more persons constituted 15.2 percent, while the lowest ratio was among households with only four persons which showed 10.3 percent. The dependency rate, therefore, is calculated as high as 6.3 persons to 1 supporter in the urban areas. Thus, the social consequences of the spread of education have resulted in:

1) increasing the rate of dependency to 6.3 persons to one supporter or wage-earner;

2) limiting the full participation of the economically active and able population in the labor force to 38.9 percent; and

3) indirectly raising the ratio of single population to 67.5 percent for 1972 (during the first four months of 1972), compared to 60.9 percent for 1961.

B. Education and Employment for Women

Although female education is gaining increasing support, the initial motives were not to facilitate women's entry into the labor force, or to encourage their employment outside the home. Rather the motives were directed more towards preparing women to improve their traditional roles by becoming better mothers, more competent housekeepers, and more understanding wives. These assumptions are clearly confirmed by the Vocational Training Programs for women, which are domestic science, home economics, child care, sewing and handicrafts.

With the expansion of economic activities in the urban areas and the capital, Amman, commercial enterprises emerged, particularly banking establishments. The consequence was a strong demand for new types of commercial training courses for women: secretarial skills, shorthand/ typing, bookkeeping, filing and other related clerical duties. Private institutes, in which training courses were organized, were established from the early 1950s (after the influx of the Palestinian Refugees). Their graduates were in demand and placed in business establishments in both government and private sectors. Realizing the need for such training, educational authorities embarked on new training programs. Commercial training for women was begun as early as 1966. These programs are increasing to meet the high demand for female workers in the rapidly growing business centers.

V. THE BIG CHALLENGE

Women's work outside the home is relatively new in Jordan, dating from the early 1950s. Unique problems have arisen from this dynamic situation, particularly adjustments in family lives such as the changing relationships between husbands and wives, and daughters-in-law and parents-in-law. Most important, however, is the integration of the conflicting multiple roles of the working woman herself, who must simultaneously be wife-mother, housekeeper, and wage-earner.

The increasing number of educated women in Jordan, coupled with the expansion of education and the subsequent growth in economic activities and opportunities, presents the society with a challenge which directly affects the traditional roles and authority previously exercised by the family and its male members, as well as the sex roles in the larger society. The debate in the Arab world today, with Jordan no exception, is mainly concerned with the emerging role of women as wage-earners: how far should women be allowed freedom of choice in their professional and personal lives? Should women be encouraged to work outside the home? If so, should they be confined to certain professions or employments? What will the consequences be on the children and family? How much equality should women be allowed to exercise?

While modern reformers and open-minded parents, husbands and employers accept the complex social needs of their rapidly changing society, conservative quarters view this new role for women with caution and resentment. They stand behind tradition and argue that:

1) working women will be exposed to moral danger and temptation as their contact with men eventually may lead to infatuation;

2) working women will increase and diversify their expectations of men and become very selective about marriage choices;

3) employment outside the home leads married women away from traditional housewife and housekeeper duties;

4) by becoming wage earners, working women will create a threat to the male ego and ultimately the masculine authority within the family;

5) married women, especially working mothers with small children, who have no adults at home to care for the children during their absence, will neglect their children and deprive them of constant maternal care and surveillance. (This represents the strongest opposition to women in the work force); and,

6) because women's work implies the satisfaction of financial need, working women suggest dishonor upon the male kin of the family.

Those who support expanded roles for women recognize the advantages of a joint contribution and partnership of men and women within the family, in particular, and in the society at large. This group maintains that:

1) the increasingly complex exigencies of life cannot possibly be met by one wage-earner (usually the male within the family), while the female remains dependent on the male's earnings;

2) single women are concerned about the financial burden they impose upon their father and brothers, preventing the brothers from saving for their own marriage expenses;

3) a woman's education should be viewed as a 'capital investment in human resources' which could contribute to the national income of the country. By becoming self-supporting and/or supplementing the family budget, women in the labor force will be able to offer direct relief to the other wage-earners, thereby helping brothers and

sisters to pursue higher education;

4) social change and the introduction of modern household technology increasingly relieves women of drudgery and domestic chores and leaves them ample time for gainful employment outside the home;

5) societal norms do not allow married women, particularly working mothers, to place greater importance on their work than on their family; and,

6) wage-earning women tend to become conservative spenders and more particular with the family budget than those who are not working. On the whole, working women tend to become more practical in their everyday needs.

VI. EXISTING TRENDS OF EMPLOYMENT FOR WOMEN

The working woman in Jordan is an interesting phenomenon and is gaining increasing attention. She is challenging accepted values and is showing an awareness and readiness to meet the changing needs within society. The traditional non-material values are becoming weaker, making way for new material goals.

The Jordanian Constitution itself provides for equal employment opportunities for women. It maintains that, 'All Jordanians are equal before the law and duties regardless of creed, language or religion. The state secures the work and education within its capabilities and secures security and equal opportunities for all Jordanians' (Articles 1 and 2). The Constitution later states that 'Work is the right of all citizens and the state is required to provide it for all Jordanians through direction of the national economy and promotion measures and policies' (Article 23).

Although the Jordanian woman has access to most fields of work, such as medical and related services, social services, diplomatic service, police work, military service, journalism, engineering and law, her work at present is primarily confined to three fields:

a) White-collar jobs, most important of which are school teaching, nursing, secretarial and typing jobs, and social work;

b) Paid labor in factories; and,

c) Self-employment, which goes beyond sewing and hairdressing to ownership and management of retail outlets.

Most recent statistics on women's employment, drawn from the comparative figures for the years 1970 and 1975 respectively, show the evolution of women's employment trends (see Table 1). The largest percentage of the female labor force is in the service and public administration sectors, with the industrial sector second. The high participation of women in these fields is attributed to the large number of women workers in the Government, particularly in the fields of education and health, and in administration and the trades. By contrast, the low participation of women in the other sectors is attributed to social, educational and physiological factors (i.e., in the mining sector, for example, women workers constituted only 0.1 percent in the 1970 and 1975 Surveys).

Professional women in Jordan can be classified into three groups: specialized, technical and skilled (see Table 2). At the specialized level, which requires university education, women's participation is highest in library, script and museum warden jobs, followed by dentistry, economics and pharmacy. It is low in engineering and administrative work. At the technical level, which requires technical education after secondary education, the level of women's participation is highest in medical and chemical jobs and lowest in semi-engineering posts such as graphics and surveying. At the skilled level, which requires secondary education, whether academic or vocational, the ratio reaches a maximum in clerical jobs, while it drops to a minimum in private business.

Although the majority of the female labor force continues to be the wage-earners, the percentage has dropped (see Table 3). This drop could be explained by the rise of self-employed women concentrated in the industrial sector, where the participation of self-employed women now exceeds that of men. The percentage of women working for the family without wages has dropped, largely due to the access of women to the labor market at a mature age.

The total labor force in Jordan is still characteristically young, but has become, on the average, slightly older than it was (see Table 4). In addition, more married women are entering the labor force. For this trend to continue, support services such as nurseries and day-care centers are essential.

Geographically, the labor force as a whole, and the female work force in particular, are on the move in Jordan. The Amman Governorate, which comprised approximately 85 percent of the total labor force, contained 97 percent of all female workers in 1970 (see Table 5). In 1975, Amman claimed only 70.9 percent of the labor force and 70.8

percent of the female work force, while other areas, such as Irbid and Balqa, saw an increase in the female work force. These changes may be attributed to the spread of education, the expansion of industrial establishments in these areas absorbing the female labor force, and the steady change in attitudes towards the woman working outside the home. This general trend was most clearly observed in the Kerak and Ma'an Governorates, both of which fall in the southern region of the country where traditional conservative attitudes prevail and rule the individual's behavior and mode of living.

The preceding analyses should not imply that the road is paved for a woman to work wherever or whenever she wants. Alongside the above progressive picture, there still exist strong social and traditional taboos which limit female participation in the work force. Coupled with these taboos is the lack of motivation and incentives on the part of women, as well as an absence of familial encouragement. These factors impede a woman's more positive and progressive contribution, simultaneously paralyzing the national economy as a whole and creating conflicting values. The woman is left at the crossroads, where she fears to take a decisive step without sufficient support from her family or the immediate kinship network around her.

VII. LABOR LEGISLATION

Jordanian labor legislation maintains protective clauses for women (Labor Law No. 21 of 1960), and its amendments provide equalization in rights and responsibilities (Article 2, para. 10). One significant clause in the legislation pertains to public morale (Article 14) and prohibits the training of young women under employers who are unmarried. The most abused clause in the labor legislation provides that a single woman leaving her work for marriage is entitled to indemnity (Article 19a and e). This is not being implemented, as many establishments hold that women requiring resignation for marriage may not be given compensation or indemnity. The situation is particularly true and injurious in some banking establishments which prohibit the employment of married women, leaving them with two undesirable alternatives — either lose a good prospective job or relinquish the idea of marriage.

Jordanian labor legislation contains certain prohibitive clauses including prohibitions against women working with dangerous equipment and machines (Article 46), and restricting women from night work (Article 47).

A significant clause endorsed in the labor law requires employers to provide nurseries and day-care centers for working mothers. Maternity leave and benefits also have been provided by Articles 50, 51 and 52. Civil Service Regulations have provided for maternity leave and benefits. Benefits for female government employees also have been included in the Social Security Regulation (No. 6 for 1976), which requires that employees contribute monthly toward this fund.

VIII. RECENT PROGRESS

Like other countries, Jordan has joined forces with women throughout the world before, during and after the International Women's Year (IWY) 1975. Significant events relative to IWY have included the IWY Joint Committee, composed of representatives from government and private sectors, and various campaigns, and seminars. These and other activities have focussed attention on the important role of women and the necessity of supporting increased contributions by women in public and state affairs.

The most recent activity in the IWY program was the convening of a seminar on 'The Role of Women in Jordan', chaired by Crown Prince Hassan, who has been the catalyst for progress and development plans in Jordan. The seminar provided a forum within which to study the condition of women, their problems and aspirations. It focussed on ways to eliminate these problems and encourage fuller participation in the production process in order to raise the standard of the national economy. An immediate result of this seminar was the amendment of the income tax regulations to provide working women with separate deductions from their income, rather than figures against the income of their spouses. This amendment is but a first step in allowing the working woman to be considered a separate individual and not appended to her spouse in matters pertaining to income tax deductions.

IX. CONCLUSION

There is no doubt that the wheel of progress is turning in Jordan, but how fast will it proceed and what will tomorrow bring for the women of Jordan? How much more responsibility, in addition to their traditional roles, will Jordanian women be willing to shoulder?

Jordan is presently at a stage in its development in which long-range government economic and social planning is being used to improve utilization of resources and to assist the population as a whole in attaining a higher standard of living. The human factor is being taken into account in this process, both as a driving force behind production, and as an axis around which the nation's social and economic action must revolve. This presents a comprehensive national challenge, whose requirements can be met through continuous participation of citizens in the political, economic and social fields. Women's contribution to this development is a goal the people of Jordan must seek.

NOTES

1. The 'Multi-Purpose Household Survey 1972', Dept. of Statistics, Amman, 1974.
2. Education in Jordan in Figures 1975/76. Ministry of Education Booklet, 1976.

REFERENCES

DEPT. OF STATISTICS, Amman, *Man-Power Study (Amendment 1970)*.
-- *Man-Power Survey, 1970*.
-- *The Multi-Purpose Household Survey for 1972*. Amman, 1974.
-- *Labour Force Survey for 1975 (Preliminary Results)*.
-- *Labour Force Survey for February 1975*.

DURKHEIM, Emile, *The Division of Labour in Society*. Glencoe: Free Press, 1947.
ES-SAID, Nimraa, 'Part-Time Work for Women in Jordan'. Presented to the seminar on 'Development of Human Resources – the Role of the Jordanian Woman in Development (1976).
— — 'Women and Development in Near Eastern Countries.' MSS thesis, 1964.
FAKHOURY, Haifa, 'Attitudes of the Working Woman in Amman.' Unpublished MA thesis, 1972.
FREUD, Sigmund, *Das Unbehagen in der Kultur*. Vienna, 1929. English translation: Joan Riviere, *Civilization and its Discontents*. London: Hogarth Press, 1930.
IZZEDDIN, Najla, *The Arab World: Past, Present and Future*. Chicago: Chicago Regnery, 1953.
KHAYRI, M.O., 'Attitudes Toward the Changing Role of Women.' Unpublished MA thesis, 1974.
KILDANI, Violet, 'Female Teachers Survey.' Amman: Institute of Social Work, 1972.
MINISTRY OF EDUCATION, *Education in Jordan in Figures – 1975/76*. Amman: Ministry of Education, 1976.
— — *Report for 1975/76*. Amman.
NASIR, Sari, 'Working Women in the Changing Society of Jordan – A Sociological Survey.' *The Faculty of Arts Journal*, Amman University of Jordan, Vol. 1 (2), 1969.
PATAI, Raphael, 'Golden River to Golden Road' in *Society, Culture and Change in the Middle East*. London: Oxford University Press, 1962, p. 93.
WEBER, Max, *The Protestant Ethic and the Spirit of Capitalism*. New York: Scribner, 1958.

APPENDIX 1

TABLE 1

Distribution of female labor force according to economic activities 1970 and 1975.

Type of activity	1970 No	%	1975 No	%
Industrial sector	1,208	5.8	3,605	18.4
Services sector (public administration)	7,234	19.4	12,123	23.5
Financial and real estate sector	412	12.3	549	16.5

Source: Manpower Study 1970, Dept. of Statistics, Amman, Jordan

TABLE 2

Distribution of female labor force in selected professions according to academic qualifications (for February 1975).

	Type of Profession	No.	Percentage
A. Professions			
(Requires	Medical practitioners	25	5.00
University	Dentists	16	17.20
degree in	Pharmacists	23	10.90
sciences)	Veterinarians	1	2.20
	Engineers		
	Civil	7	3.40
	Chemical	1	2.00
	Agricultural	17	2.00
(Requires	Librarians, script and museum		
University	wardens	286	33.50
degree in	Economists	8	15.10
arts)	Production managers	3	4.30
	Accountants	72	3.40
	General managers	18	2.50
B. Technicians			
(Requires	Laboratory and X-ray technicians	8	10.00
2 years'	Chemists	33	9.10
additional	Opticians and optical technicians	1	7.70
education	Statisticians	3	6.50
after secondary	Surveyors	4	1.10
C. Skilled			
(Requires	Typists and stenographers	854	67.20
secondary	Registry and correspondence clerks	494	41.40
education)	Sales assistants	86	2.80
(Clerical)	Bookkeeping	23	0.20
(Self-	Wholesale and retail	112	0.80
employed)			
(Manual)	Tailors	2843	61.50
	Tricot and knitting	268	45.00
	Posts, telegraph and telephone		
	workers	166	12.80
	Bakers and pastry workers	52	3.40

TABLE 2 continued

Type of Profession	No.	Percentage
D. Semi-skilled		
Paper and cardboard factory workers	65	59.60
Cigarette factory workers	23	15.23
Farming specialists	10	15.23
Cargo laborers	183	12.57
Postmen	6	5.30
Crop and vegetable workers	17	2.35

Source: Labor Force Survey for 1975 — (Preliminary Results) Dept. of Statistics, Amman, Jordan.

TABLE 3

Distribution of female labor force according to employment for selected years (1970 and 1975).

Type of employment	1970 Ratio of females (Percentage)	1975 Ratio of females (Percentage)
Wage-earners	93.80	86.3
Self-employed	4.80	13.3
Family-workers	1.40	0.5

Sources: (1) *Manpower Study* (Amendment July 1970) — Dept. of Statistics, Amman, Jordan; (2) *Labour Force Survey* for February 1975 — Dept. of Statistics, Amman, Jordan.

TABLE 4

Distribution of female labor force according to selected age-groups 1970 and 1975 (in percentages)

Age-group	1970	1975
15-19 years	9.30	7.6
20-24	37.90	30.3
25-29	24.70	28.3
30-34	10.90	14.0
35-39	4.50	8.2
40-44	3.50	4.6
45-49	2.60	3.0
50-54	2.10	2.1

Sources: (1) *Man-Power Study* (Amendment July 1970) Dept. of Statistics, Amman, Jordan; (2) *Labour Force Survey* for February 1975 — Dept. of Statistics, Amman, Jordan.

TABLE 5

Distribution of labour force according to main centers of economic activity 1970 and 1975 (in percentages)

Governorate	1970 Total	1970 Female	1975 Total	1975 Female
Amman	84.90	97.1	70.9	70.8
Irbid	9.30	1.5	15.8	18.0
Balqa	2.10	0.9	4.6	5.2
Kerak	1.70	0.5	4.6	4.0
Ma'an	2.00	---	4.1	2.0

Sources: (1) *Manpower Study* (Amendment July 1970) Dept. of Statistics, Amman, Jordan; (2) *Labor Force Survey* for February 1975 — Dept. of Statistics, Amman, Jordan.

APPENDIX 2

SOCIAL SURVEY OF THE WORKING WOMAN IN JORDAN

The survey, conducted in 1965, included 220 respondents from different economic fields. About 58 percent of the respondents cited economic factors as employment motivators, while 72.5 percent cited social status and prestige. Sixty percent of the respondents cited economic and personal independence, while woman's feeling of usefulness was listed by 25 percent. Difficulties facing the respondents ranged from long hours (48.7 percent) to dual responsibilities (35.7 percent) which are the result of the conflicting dual roles the working woman is expected to play in modern times. Anxiety over children was expressed by 28.4 percent, consistent with other studies. Frustration due to absence of responsible jobs was reported by 25.6 percent, which equals the problem of authoritarian bosses. Ninety-six percent of the respondents described their relationship with their husbands as comradeships.

APPENDIX 3

FEMALE TEACHER'S SURVEY – 1972

This study, conducted in 1972, covered 1,550 female teachers from the Amman Governate. Financial reasons were most cited by both single and married teachers with dependent children in their families as basic motives for work (62.7 percent and 50.2 percent respectively). Developing society rated second (26.2 percent and 25.2 percent respectively). Goal attainment was stronger than economic independence (27.3 percent and 15.9 percent respectively), while social status rated second (14 percent and 15.9 percent respectively). The findings on the impact of education on attitudes were clear: among university graduates 64 percent stated natural right, while 53 percent of secondary graduates gave this response, and only 38.8 percent of those who attained less than secondary education chose it.

APPENDIX 4

POSITION AND ROLE OF WORKING WOMEN IN AMMAN – 1972

The study, conducted in 1972, sampled 120 women, including married women (35.5 percent), single women (61.7 percent), and divorced and widowed women (3.3 percent). Educational level of the respondents were as follows: 48.6 percent had university degrees, and 18.3 had secondary and vocational training. Respondents with primary education and less constituted only 15.8 percent of the total.

The findings of the study revealed that 51 percent of the college graduates preferred working with men and under male supervision, while only 8.6 percent of college graduates preferred to work with women. About 20 percent responded that their husbands objected to their employment, while 12 percent stated that they faced no objection. Almost 76 percent of the respondents stated that they did not meet objections from other members of their family (father, brother, uncle, etc.), while 24.1 percent stated that their family members did object.

Consistent with Dr Nasir's study was the type of jobs the respondents held: 21.1% were employed in teaching, 12.5 percent in nursing, and 10 percent in secretarial work. The only new employment observed in this study was telephone operator which rated 8.3 percent of the total respondents. Five percent of the respondents worked in social work.

Almost 90 percent of married respondents favored woman's work after marriage, while 16.6 percent did not. Of the single respondents, 68.9 percent agreed that women should work after marriage, while 25.6 percent disagreed. Widowed and divorced women within the sample disagreed or didn't know (50 percent and 50 percent respectively). As explained in the study, 'The attitude of married working women towards employment after marriage, especially in the case of children, is objective. ... Married working women look at the employment of all women, regardless of marital status, as a natural activity which is (part of) the process in any human's activities'. Single working women seemed to share these views. Thus, work is regarded by many women as both a choice and a right.

APPENDIX 5

ATTITUDE TOWARD THE CHANGING ROLE OF WOMEN – 1975

This study was submitted as an MA Thesis by Mr M. O. Khayri to the American University of Beirut. It covered 222 respondents, of whom 143 were males and 79 were females.

Mr Khayri confined his investigation to attitudes toward education and employment for women outside the home, attitudes toward decision-making by spouses regarding financial matters, and family planning, and attitudes of respondents toward conflict-solving within the family.

On the question of 'woman's right to work after marriage or before': 65 percent stated that they agree that women should work before and after marriage; 55 percent of the male respondents stated that they support their sisters' work, while 23 percent left the choice of work to their sisters. 'Equal pay for equal work' was supported by 73 percent of respondents, while 15 percent felt men should have more pay.

The choice for selection of profession and employment for sisters and daughters was as follows: 86 percent preferred teaching; 64 percent radio announcing; 65 percent TV; and 62 percent nursing. Secretarial work and air hostesses received moderate responses.

Regarding decision-making of spouses, 86 percent stated that both spouses should decide financial matters. On more personal matters affecting family size, family-planning methods and contraceptives, 91 percent agreed that spouses should decide jointly. On the question of conflict-resolution, 74 percent stated that both spouses should cooperate to solve their conflicts without outside interference.

APPENDIX 6

PART TIME WORK FOR WOMEN OUTSIDE THE HOME – 1976

This survey was conducted by the author in co-operation with a group of researchers during February 1976. The findings were submitted in a working paper for the seminar on 'Development of Human Resources – The Role of Jordanian Women', held in Amman in April 1976. The Survey covered 150 respondents distributed throughout the country, and 50 employers and institutions employing women in part-time paid or voluntary work. The purposes were 1) to encourage the utilization of women's presently unused energies in the comprehensive national development process through identification of work and activities which could provide part-time employment outside the house; 2) to remove obstacles which hinder female participation in the work force; and 3) to provide women with tangible and intangible incentives.

Since Amman, the seat of government, is the most important center for economic activities and power, and provides ample social, educational and recreational facilities, 70 percent of respondents worked in Amman. About 47 percent of the respondents were single and 36.1 were married. Basic motives for work: 58.1 percent cited economic reasons, 15.1 percent worked in order to improve their social and cultural status, and 16.6 percent worked to spend their leisure time gainfully. In addition, 82.6 percent replied that they supported their families either wholly or partially.

Types of employment: 66 percent of the respondents were wage-earners; 23.3 percent were self-employed; 8 percent worked only for their family; and 2.6 percent worked as part-time, unpaid workers in voluntary activities with welfare organizations. Typing, stenography and secretarial work seemed to be the dominant occupational group, indicated by 61.4 percent of the respondents, while sewing and tricot absorbed 17.5 percent and embroidery rated third. Hairdressers constituted 7.2 percent of total working women surveyed.

Families' attitude toward woman's work were positive: 53 percent stated their families did not object. Consistent with other studies were the ages of the working women: 25-29 seemed the most productive age-group for women, constituting 31.5 percent of the total respondents. Second was the 20-24 age-group (24.2 percent), while third was the 30-34 group (13.1 percent).

Problems facing part-time women workers ranged from inadequate pay (48.2 percent), transportation difficulties (36.6 percent), treatment of superiors (12.5 percent), and treatment by colleagues (2.2 percent). This reflects the changing attitude of male workers who are becoming increasingly more accustomed to women working alongside them, without posing a threat.

Regarding the problem of child care, 34 percent of the respondents suggested establishment of nurseries, 29 percent proposed training local baby-sitters at the family's residence, while 26 percent stressed the importance of transportation provision. (This is an important public service for encouraging women to do part-time work, since their work might take them out at different hours of day or night — i.e., radio, TV, telephone operators, and, frequently, secretaries.)

Of the employers surveyed, 30 percent were private, 15.1 percent were government, 12.3 percent were private welfare institutions, and 38 percent were 'others'. Reasons for employing women as part-time workers ranged from lack of full-timers, 24.3 percent; lack of qualified persons, 14.4 percent; and lower cost of part-time workers, 26.2 percent. Benefits derived from part-time workers included material benefits, 32.1 percent; less expense, 13.1 percent; helping working mothers who are handicapped, 13.1 percent; and benefiting from workers' previous experience, 8.4 percent. Better work results were cited by only 5.1 percent of the respondent employers.

10

FERTILITY POLICY IN INDIA

Vina Mazumdar
*Director, Women's Studies,
Indian Council of Social Science Research*

Ms. Mazumdar's chapter is an almost textbook example of the complexities of the relationships among research, social policy, and action. It illustrates the seriously dysfunctional consequences for women that may ensue when policies based on class biases and inadequate data lead to ineffectual or positively harmful programs. The initiators, supporters, and implementers of policy – the bureaucracies, learned professions, political parties, social workers, the media, designers, builders, and evaluators of programs – have all been victims of class bias, ignorance, and 'hidden assumptions'. Wrong diagnoses of the basic problems of Indian women – traditional attitudes, purdah, polygamy, child marriage, denial of right to marry, divorce, property rights – led to decisions which affected only a small segment of the female population, but left the masses of women untouched. These issues were irrelevant to them.

Thus, despite the apparent successes of women, as the result of policies and programs based on inadequate research, researchers in the 1970s found that the status of women had actually deteriorated alarmingly. The differentials between women and men in mortality, health care, medical services, literacy, education, vocational training, and unemployment had actually accelerated. Although research has documented these trends, it has not yet provided empirical evidence to validate explanations for them. That remains to be done. In the area of family planning, there has been a great proliferation of research, but it has been flawed by lack of understanding of class differences in the roles and statuses of women. The logic of reduced family size applies only to the middle classes, not to the subsistence economy in which most women live, or to the upwardly mobile who see children as an investment. The situation described by Ms. Mazumdar is an illuminating counterfoil to the situation in countries like Sweden or Norway, where policies and action are more closely monitored by social research.

I

Social policy in modern India has been influenced by many visible and invisible, internal and external, complementary and contradictory ideas and forces. Two typical representatives of the last type are policies for women's development and policies for population control or population change.

It is easy to find reasons for such contradictions in the heterogeneous character of Indian society, with its multiplicity of linguistic, regional and religious cultures, social inequalities, and wide range of peoples in different stages of historical and economic development. These differences and disparities have often been hidden by assumptions and images of traditional society which were generally the result of inadequate knowledge and reflected certain class biases. The problem becomes even more complex with the influence of differing (sometimes warring) ideologies of social and economic development, the constraints provided by a democratic federal polity, and the compulsions and dependence that result from poverty and underdevelopment in a world economy characterized by gross inequalities. To add to this, there are many institutional biases — some traditional, some carried over from the days of colonial dependency and some originating from contemporary forces outside the country — that influence attitudes within organized establishments which determine social policies. The bureaucracy, the learned professions, political parties, social workers, the media, the designers, builders and evaluators of development in its multiple forms, all are prisoners, to a certain extent, of institutional structures that were fairly effective for a society which changed very little for centuries, but which have become dysfunctional in times of rapid socio-economic and political transformation.

II

The policies for women's welfare and development, and the constitutional pledge of 'equality of status and opportunities' and non-discrimination on grounds of sex in law and public office were direct outcomes of the socio-political movements that convulsed Indian society during the hundred years before independence. They also represent a consensus among the elite, of non-opposition to women playing increasing, if not equal, roles in the process of national development.[1] Differences have, however, been sharp in the understanding of these roles or their implications, or the rationale for supportive measures to enable women to perform them adequately and effectively. Conservatives argue that children need healthier, better equipped, more conscious mothers to enable them to develop into conscientious, patriotic, constructive persons, and, hence, women need greater attention from nation builders than they have received before. Progressives adopt a more direct position; they argue for equality of opportunity, dignity and social justice for women as well as men on grounds of human rights. Radicals go a step further, and demand removal of all discrimination against women and equal rights and obligations, irrespective of sex, in social economic and political spheres. All groups agree on the basic instruments for development of the human resources of any modern society — education, protection of individual rights by law, and support of essential social services, namely, health, education and welfare, by the State. Women as the 'weaker sex' are generally regarded as standing in greater need of such services, not only for themselves, but also to ensure health and minimum living conditions for the future population. Even policies of population control have been justified as necessary to ensure better health, longer life, and better care for mothers and their children. This agreement between otherwise conflicting groups is a legacy of the movements that preceded independence.

The process of modernization begun during the colonial period developed both an inward and an outward thrust. The questioning of weaknesses within Indian society resulted in a movement for social reform in the Indian sub-continent, preceding the political movement for freedom from colonial rule. Improving the status of women was, from the beginning, a major objective of this movement. Historians generally have seen its origin in the influence of Western education and liberal ideas, the pressure of Christian missionary influence and the demonstration effect of the women's movement in Western countries. It is now possible to trace its indigenous roots also — in the pressure of urbanization on social institutions like the family, in the increasing communication gap between men and women in urban families, in the slackening hold of traditional familial authority on the younger generation, and in the increasing threat of urban prostitution and criminal activities which represented threats to the traditional social structure.

The urban bias of the social reform movement has been evident to scholars for some time. What was not understood for a long time were the middle class bias and wrong assumptions about traditional roles of women latent in the movement to improve their status in society. This becomes clear if we analyse the reform movement by its perception of women's problems and the instruments chosen for intervention. The main enemy was identified as obscurantist customs and traditional attitudes. Women were seen mainly as victims of 'purdah' or seclusion within the home, ignorance and oppressive marriage and property laws. Polygamy, child marriage, the oppressed condition of widows, denial of the right of re-marriage and divorce, and inadequate rights to property were particularly singled out for attack.[2] The instruments for change were education, reform of marriage and property laws, elimination of purdah and, above all, the combating of traditional attitudes which regarded women as inferior beings.

The reformers believed that education and the removal of these oppressive customs would enable women to develop into better wives and mothers. They did not question the validity of women's traditional role as the homemaker with tasks confined to the care of the family. On the other hand, reform was defended as necessary to strengthen the hold of traditional values in society. Since women were the custodians of traditional culture, greater efficiency on their part would strengthen the family as the basic unit of social organization and insulate the younger generation from the destructive influences let loose by westernization.[3]

Even a cursory knowledge of the lives of the masses of women, particularly in rural areas, would have demonstrated that these problems were unreal and irrelevant in their lives. A computation based on the 1931 Census reveals that less than 10 percent of the population of the Indian sub-continent at that time were affected by these oppressive marriage laws. The rest had always been permitted considerable freedom and flexibility in marriage, divorce and remarriage by the customs of their communities. Denial of education could hardly be regarded as sex discriminatory among the vast masses of illiterates. The same could be said about property laws for the vast millions who could claim little outside their name as property. Purdah was practised only in upper and middle class society, cutting across all communities. Among the working population, social norms were dictated by the necessities of economic survival. Women were men's partners as producers and sellers in agriculture, industry and traditional service. There was division of labour between the sexes, but the line of differentiation was not between work and home, between bread-winning and home-management, between harder and lighter tasks. The unit of labour was not the individual, but the family, or the household, with men, women and children sharing most tasks. This pattern continues wherever traditional forms of economic organization still prevail.

> Regional differences in the type and quantum of work expected of women expose the hollowness of the myths attached to these sex-linked roles. In the North-Eastern region, weaving is the monopoly of women but there are parts of India where a woman may not touch the loom. Embroidery work is a male activity in Kashmir and a female one in the Punjab and elsewhere. In agriculture the variations in women's tasks in different regions prove the invalidity of the assumption that men are supposed to do the heavier work. In the Northern hill regions, women carry heavy logs weighing 200 to 300 lbs., slice the timber and help in wood chopping. What is important is that the tasks assigned to men are considered more prestigious in most communities and regions. Women are generally the unpaid family workers.[4]

The major role of women in certain types of economic activity can be realized from the fact that, until 1921, women outnumbered men in agricultural labour and formed about one third of the labour force in mining, quarrying, livestock, fishing and other occupations in the primary sector, in manufacturing industry, construction and trade and commerce.[5]

These traditional economic roles certainly did not relieve women from their housekeeping or child-nurturing roles, nor did they guarantee for them equal status with men. There was not much option in the choice of occupation or life-styles, as the majority were expected to follow family trades. At the most, a woman could migrate, along with the family, from starvation in village agriculture or industry, to tea, coffee, rubber or indigo plantations, coal or mica mines, or the new jute and textile industries in the town. But the substantial value of their contribution to the family economy enabled them to enjoy, relatively, a far higher degree of freedom in social relations, particularly vis-à-vis men, than their counterparts in upper and middle class society. Their basic problems lay in poverty, excessive workload, insecurity and exploitation by their wealthy employers, and not in oppressive customs. Except for child marriage (which was prevalent among the majority of the population, except the tribal groups), the social reformers failed to perceive the needs of this majority.

The second factor that affected policies for women was their spontaneous and massive participation in the struggle for freedom from colonial rule. When women joined the political struggle in large numbers, the quality of their participation surprised even progressive leaders.[6] Equality between the sexes — at least in civil and political life — emerged as one of the goals of the freedom movement. The demand for equal franchise, which had been voiced by the nascent women's movement only in 1917 came to be accepted as a national objective by the majority of leaders by the 1930s and was incorporated in the political system after independence.

There is ample evidence that the movement for women's rights, particularly for the vote, in its earlier years was considerably influenced by its counterpart in Britain. The intial leadership of the women's organizations invariably came from upper class, educated families, and had extensive contacts with suffragist groups in the West. Their male supporters were close to the progressive liberal groups in Western countries and saw the women's desire to play some role in public life as a logical extension of the modernization process, and of education for women which was being advocated by all 'modernizers'.

The discordant, and perhaps unexpected, element in this picture of a gradual, smooth process — of improving women's position by some concessions to their aspirations, provided they qualified for the privilege by birth, education and social status[7] — was introduced by Mahatma Gandhi, who brought a completely new dimension to the debate on the women's question. Beginning from the basic premise that the subjugation and exploitation of women were the product of 'man's interested teachings, and women's acceptance of them', he broke away from the reform tradition. He preached a different philosophy — not only of absolute equality of rights between the sexes, but of the pragmatic necessity of enrolling women's support — to transform the nationalist struggle for the transfer of political power from British to Indian hands into a social revolution. This revolution would abolish social inequality of all kinds — between rich and poor, educated and illiterate, high castes and the untouchables, workers and non-workers, the industrial capitalist and the rural peasant, an authoritarian, oppressive alien government and the masses of the people of the country.

The non-exploitative social order that Gandhi visualized had to be achieved by the participation of the mass of the people and the resolution of social conflicts by non-violent protests. Women, he claimed, were better than men in waging non-violent protests because they had greater capacity for sacrifice and endurance, were less self-seeking, and had more moral courage. They must, therefore, become conscious of their historic role, reject the disgraceful role of being 'man's plaything', and extend their capacity for love and sacrifice beyond their families to 'embrace the whole of humanity'. Equality of legal and political rights, freedom from any coercion from the family or the society, and autonomy to choose their own way of moral and self-development were only basic conditions to enable women to play their destined role.[8]

One of the justifications for Gandhi's economic policy of reviving the village economy and cottage industry was to restore to women their lost economic strength. The decline of village industry because of increasing competition from mass-produced goods of modern technology and capitalist modes of production had eroded considerably women's productive roles and increased their burden and problems. This process had to be arrested through the revival of village industries and the restoration of women's economic base. Excessive burden of labour for no return and discrimination in wages demonstrated their exploited position.

> Today the sole occupation of a woman amongst us is supposed to be to bear children, to look after her husband and otherwise to drudge for the household...not only is the woman condemned to domestic slavery, but when she goes out as a labourer to earn wages, though she works harder than man, she is paid less.[9]

The radical note struck by Gandhi found a close parallel in the ideas of Karl Marx which influenced socialists of different shades in India:

> The emancipation of women and their equality with men are impossible and must remain so as long as women are excluded from socially productive work and restricted to housework, which is private.[10]

These two strains of social ideas, from different sources, were fused in the mind of Jawaharlal Nehru, who played a dominant role in the shaping of social policy in the first decade after independence. As President of the Indian National Congress in 1931, he steered the resolution that pledged the nation to a policy of sex-equality in law, and political and economic life after independence. As a leading member of the Constituent Assembly, he incorporated the pledge into specific articles in the Constitution of the Indian Republic. As Prime Minister, he steered the laws improving the rights of Hindu women in marriage, guardianship and inheritance, and special labour laws for the protection of women workers in factories, mines and plantations, making the passage of these laws a prestige issue for his government.

A new agency, the Central Social Welfare Board, was created to organize special measures to assist women, particularly in the rural areas, in their problems:

> We talk about a welfare state and direct our energies towards its realization. That welfare must be the common property of everyone in India and not the monopoly of the privileged groups as it is today. If I may be allowed to lay greater stress on some, they would be the welfare of children, the status of women and the welfare of the tribal and hilly people in our country. Women in India have a background of history and tradition behind them, which is inspiring. It is true, however, that they have suffered much from various kinds of suppression and all these have to go so that they can play their full part in the life of the nation.[11]

The First Five Year Plan admitted the significance of the new rights conferred on women, and held that they called for adequate provision of education and health services, including family planning. The implications of equality were clearly stated in the objectives for women's education:

> The general purpose and objectives of women's education cannot, of course, be different from the purpose and objectives of men's education. At the secondary and even at the university stage women's education should have a vocational or occupational bias.[12]

The early fifties thus came to be regarded as the period of women's triumph, with middle class women — from a background of restricted lives, confined to the roles of wives and mothers — entering administrative, professional and political employment as the equals of men. Institutions of professional education in law and technology which had until then barred women's entry, were compelled to admit them. Women entered new occupations in the modern sector in increasing numbers. Women from aristocratic families, both Hindu and Muslim, began to abandon purdah and sought public offices. Women were elected to Parliament and the State Legislatures, became Cabinet ministers, governors of States, ambassadors, vice-chancellors of universities and judges, and exercised their vote in increasing numbers in successive general elections. Local self-governing bodies, both in urban and rural areas, were asked to include a few women on their panels by nomination, if they did not come through election channels.

All these could suggest, as they did to most people concerned with social policy in India, that 'the revolution in the status of women', and the extension of their roles in society were well on the way. But the review undertaken in the early seventies by the Committee on the Status of Women in India reached a very different conclusion: 'Though women do not constitute a minority numerically, they are acquiring the features of one by the inequality of class, status and political power'.[13]

Three years after the Committee's Report, a group of social scientists have drawn attention in an even sharper manner to what they call 'the national neglect of women'.[14] The alarming deterioration in women's status, their research proves, began several decades ago, but has accelerated in the last three decades. Demographic trends, with growing differentials between men and women in mortality, access to health care and medical services, literacy, education and vocational training, and accelerated decline in employment provide, in their view, 'indisputable evidence of steady decline in the value of women in society.' The best indicator of this trend is the persistent decline in the sex-ratio in the population:

> Unless the economic and social utility of women is enhanced in the eyes of their families and the nation by opportunities to take part in socially and economically productive roles, the national neglect of women will continue. Erosion of productive roles emphasizes women's position as consumers and bearers of children, makes their lives cheap and easily expendable through increasing malnutrition and mortality, reduces employability through inadequate training opportunities and increases economic discrimination and exploitation.[15]

Development plans and supportive services have tended to view women only as target groups for social services, ignoring their productive roles. In consequence, development itself has contributed to the massive displacement of women from agricultural, industrial and trading occupations. The marginal increase in the number of women in the service sector cannot offset this trend, but the visibility of middle-class women in white-collar occupations has helped to build an illusion of progress, hiding the stark reality of the shrinking roles of the majority. Even in the service sector, much of the increased employment is in poverty-oriented occupations, i.e. personal and domestic services generated by population increase, especially in urban areas. Prostitution and traffic in women, the commercial use of females for career and business promotion, and illegal activities all point to growing use of women as commodities. The sex-specific roles prescribed by traditional society, even though limited, guaranteed greater dignity to the majority than its modern counterpart.

One traditional role that has expanded is the use of women as vehicles for display of wealth and status. Previously restricted to the feudal aristocracy, whose status required keeping their women idle and bejewelled, this practice is now imitated by new or aspiring entrants to the middle class. The payment of dowry to obtain a husband for a young woman, which had become difficult during the thirties because of opposition from the Gandhian women's movement, has, in spite of a prohibitory law, increased in volume and incidence, affecting even communities which had followed the opposite practice of paying brideprice until a few years ago.[16] There are many such examples of 'regression from the norms developed during the freedom struggle.' In politics, the emergence and fall of a woman Prime Minister has not succeeded in arresting the steady decline in the number of women in the legislative bodies, and in the parties' sponsorship of women for such positions. Gandhi's dream seems indeed to have receded very far from the social horizon of contemporary India.

III

The only explanations now available for these developments are still hypothetical, lacking empirical evidence. The patriarchal ideology inherent in the capitalist path of development; the choice of technology and forms of economic organization imposed by international capital; blind imitation of Western materialist values, life and consumption styles to the detriment of indigenous cultural values; urban middle-class and westernized bias in planning; over-concentration on economic growth and neglect of social development; increasing population and income disparity; or differential spread of the fruits of development among different classes of the population — one may select one or more of these explanations according to one's own ideological inclinations. Whether a substantial link exists between population growth, policies for its control, andthe trends in roles and status of women remains to be investigated.

Looking at the evolution of the population question in India, one can note certain significant trends. At a time when apprehensive and critical views of India's population growth were limited to members of the British administration, and sparked off indignant protests from nationalist leaders who regarded it as an imperialist conspiracy to explain away the failure to solve India economic problems, the women's organizations were the first to demand the provision of birth control services. When questioned about this 'dangerous trend' by some orthodox persons, Gandhi replied that women should have the right not to have children or to limit the number of children, though he would prefer sexual abstinence to contraceptive methods for this purpose. In his appeals to young people of both sexes to contribute a part, if not all, of their lives to the cause of national freedom and reconstruction, he exhorted them to forego or postpone having children, as this would interfere with their commitment to the national cause. Family planning services were developed only by some voluntary women's organizations in some of the metropolitan cities and were used only by educated families.

In the post-independence period, with a government committed to rapid economic development, the population question gradually emerged as a critical issue. During the First and Second Five-Year Plans, the problem of population growth and the need for family planning were viewed as a long term objective, depending essentially on 'improvement in living standards and more widespread education, especially among women.' The Planning Commission, however, admitted the need for positive measures to spread family planning education and techniques among the people. Efforts to restrain population growth were seen only as a complement to a massive development effort.

From the Third Plan, however, the control of population growth, with time-bound targets for reducing the birth rate, heavy investment in the administrative network to mount the family planning programmes on the lines of a military operation, and the adoption of financial incentives to make sterilization acceptable to the poor, emerged as crucial features of government policy. Abortion in cases of contraceptive failure was legalized and some State Governments began to initiate systems of disincentives, such as denial of maternity benefits to women after the birth of a third child. This change in emphasis relied heavily on the clinical, rather than the welfare, approach to family planning. The general health and welfare services suffered relatively as resources were diverted for family planning services. The administration of this programme became a parallel empire within the Ministry of Health in all the States, competing successfully for allocation of both funds and personnel.

In the case of women, maternity and child health services, adult education and family welfare — all of which had been identified as essential to improve their status in the earlier plans — suffered from lack of resources, and family planning began to be propagated as the most important developmental programme for women. Research sponsored both by government and external agencies which offered aid to India to control her population growth sought to emphasize improvement in the status of women as a *direct* consequence of acceptance of family planning. Unfortunately for such propagandists, most quality research in this field invariably indicated that the relationship was far more complex, viz., that improved status of women, with rise in the age of marriage, education, employment, better living conditions and general awareness in concert have a direct impact on the adoption of family planning methods. Evaluating the role of family planning in changing women's status in India, the Committee on the Status of Women observed:

> If the sexual role were the main determinant of male dominance and authority in a society, there would have been no communities in the world where the women are dominant, or equal, members. The status of women in any society depends on a complex set of social, economic, demographic and political variables, among which the woman's ability to control the size of her family could be a contributory factor. But in our view, emphasizing it as a direct cause of improvement of women's status is somewhat exaggerated, and ignores the evolution of women's status in different societies. The matriarch of many ancient civilizations and primitive communities certainly enjoyed a much higher status than the women with complete control on the size of their families in the developed, modern societies of the West today. Knowledge of family planning techniques may have liberated Western women from excessive pregnancies, but it has not basically changed their status in these societies either economically or politically. Even in the sphere of social attitudes, with all the progress in education, and different types of social freedoms and changing roles, their image as sex-symbols has been intensified, not eliminated.[17]

The draft Fifth Plan sought to correct the perspective, in view of the growing realization of the unpopularity and failure of the programme among many sections, and evaluation reports that coercive methods could not overcome the socio-economic and psychological resistance to population control. Official statements in 1973-74 indicated the Government of India's return to the original philosophy — that 'development was the best contraceptive.' The draft Fifth Five-Year Plan called for a minimum needs programme for the poverty-stricken masses. Extension of health services, integrated with family planning, particularly for the vulnerable groups — children, pregnant women and nursing mothers — was an important feature of the proposed programme.

Unfortunately this wisdom was abandoned during the recent period of national emergency, when the draconian powers assumed by the Government were used to revive the policy of reducing the birth-rate rapidly by all kinds of questionable methods. 'Sterilization became the symbol of tyrannical denial of all that one was entitled to expect from one's government'.[18]

The minimum needs and employment programmes which were the central theme of the draft Fifth Plan were whittled down to unimportant adjuncts in the final Plan, with no integral relationship to the design of long-term economic growth. The national population policy announced in April 1976 stated clearly that it was 'not a practical solution' to wait for education and economic development to bring about a drop in fertility. The results of the national elections of February 1977 have demonstrated clearly that population control divested of other developmental measures can bring about the fall of even the most powerful government.

IV

One consequence of the heavy investment in family planning was the proliferation of research. This is the one sector of social research which has received maximum encouragement, from both government and other funding agencies, national, international and foreign (i.e., donor agencies from rich countries). Such research has progressively revealed that fertility is influenced by a complex of many factors, social, economic, cultural and political[19], in which the individual's choice may play a minor role. 'Birth control and the small family norm have to find social acceptance before finding individual acceptance'.[20]

While many of these studies admit that the status of women plays a critical role in acceptance of family planning, they do not display any clear understanding of variations in women's roles and statuses in different classes and fail to see their influence on fertility choices. In assuming traditional values to be the source of resistance, and depending on propaganda regarding the advantages of the small family for the future, the propagators of this policy display biases similar to those that have influenced policies for women.

The logic and the rationale for the small family rest on the experience of the established middle class, which seeks to ensure its future by investment in income-generating property, and the education of children. Since the majority of this class comes from high caste Hindus or the aristocracy of other communities, their current aspiration harmonizes with their traditional cultural values, which attach higher status to non-manual occupations and emphasize careful nurturing of children. As the extended family begins to crack under the pressure of new socio-economic demands, and occupations shift outside the home, the emphasis on the nurturing[21] of children, and 'extended infantilism' puts increasing pressure on women, particularly in nuclear families. The breakdown of the extended family reduced the family pressure on young women to have more children. Since young women in this class also enjoy relatively easy access to education, better nutrition and modern health services, they are able to ensure far better chances of survival for their children. The care of children is socially accepted as a full-time occupation despite the inroads made on the mother's role by the educational system, peer-groups and other extra-familial institutions.

At the other end of the social structure, the family's subsistence depends on the household economy,

> Where little — be it agriculture, household industry, fishing, lumbering, forest-produce gathering, livestock and poultry keeping, the informal sector in urban livelihoods, construction, petty trade or commerce, or non-powered transportation, or the whole range of unorganized services — is possible without substantial contribution of unpaid family work, mainly for keeps, by all members of the household...This is necessary to enable the head of the household to extract the economic surplus from the pool of unrecompensed family labour. Such a process of extraction of surplus is made possible by the semblance of democratic sharing of whatever is available — food or starvation — within the household...So long as unpaid family labour remains the mainstay of the great bulk of economic activity in the country, the one-or-two child family will remain a far cry...[22]

Future is a meaningless concept when your entire effort is concentrated on daily survival. Malnutrition and high infant mortality, lack of access to education and health services, and the low cost of child-rearing when the children join the labour force from the age of five or six, make a large family a rational choice. At least that way one can ensure that one or two may survive to maturity.

Between these two comes a third group — the new entrants to, or the aspirants to the middle class, risen through education or some increase in prosperity or security from a job of supposedly higher status than traditionally enjoyed by the group. For this group, too, the small family appears unnatural. The slight improvement in economic or social prospects 'expands the horizon of expectations — children are seen as investments, who can receive these benefits and yield 'highest over-life-time' returns. 'Enterprise being seen by an Indian as centred on the household, anything that goes to enhance the wealth of the household is well worth investing in'.[23]

A typical characteristic of these mobile groups from the bottom of the pyramid is the sharp change in women's roles. The prosperous farmer, the industrial worker receiving higher wages or a first generation white-collar worker react uniformly in this matter. Their women are withdrawn from economic activity outside the home as this is believed essential to improving the family's social status.[24]

High fertility among these women is certainly not only from economic considerations, nor is it due to high infant mortality, because the access of this class to modern health services is far better now than that previously enjoyed. The explanation, it appears to me, has to be sought in other factors. If women cease to be economic assets to the family and become liabilities instead (as manifested in the increasing incidence and volume of dowry), and at the same time are not social assets through education and adaptive ability to their new social circumstances, the only way to maintain their value within the family would appear to be through bearing more children. This problem seems to call for much greater investigation than it has so far received.

The class variable in fertility research has tended to be over-simplified, using income as the indicator of class status. In societies like India's, however, the generational position is often a more important indicator of acceptance in a new class, rather than income or even education. The *Bhadralog*[25] find it much harder to assimilate the lower orders, whatever their income position. Their attitude to new entrants retains a social distance at least for one generation. Education is regarded as the great leveller of such class distinctions, but since education is not widespread among adult women of this class, its effect remains limited.

In regarding fertility as the result of individual choice by couples, the authors of the policy of population control ignore all these variables, as well as the inter-relationship among the class-structure, the roles of women and children and the manner in which these are being affected by the process of economic change. Increasing disparity in income and growing unemployment and underemployment among both men and women indicate a failure to develop a substitute for the household economy, or to improve the demographic quality of the population. In the Indian context, the latter depends on reduction of infant mortality and malnutrition, elimination of illiteracy, and minimum health services. These, in turn, depend on universal employment and raising the economic value of women 'by cutting down on unpaid family labour and introducing a system of social accounting where appropriate money-value is imputed to the work of women'.[26]

Such a change would threaten the present power-structure, which rests on inequalities and links among property, political power, ownership of land, and lineage systems — all of which seem to have an indirect influence on fertility, and on women's status and roles. The evidence of an inter-relationship between the pattern of development and these aspects of population change can be inferred from a simple periodization of development and population trends. The Indian economy experienced its first major growth during the first world war, slumped during the depression, but started growing again during the thirties. The second world war provided a further spurt, which continued well into the fifties, after which it began to slow down, except for a short period of buoyancy during 1973-74. The decline in women's work participation began around 1920, and accelerated after 1951. The sex-ratio in the population remained constant between 1921 and 1931, but dropped sharply after that. Regions which had a high sex-ratio and considerably higher work-participation of women changed character during the twenties, and began a declining trend in both the sex-ratio and the work-participation of women. The Scheduled Castes and tribal communities, which traditionally have maintained very high work-participation of women, and a relatively higher sex-ratio (particularly among the tribes), appear now to be joining the mainstream trend. Some ongoing studies indicate that in many of these areas, large-scale development and commercialization precipitate these changes even if they do not initiate them. The first sharp increase in the Indian population also took place in the twenties, and was accelerated during the fifties. Hitherto this increase has been attributed only to control of epidemics. While it is not suggested that public health measures played no role in this growth, recent investigations indicate sharp differentials in access to health services, between urban and rural areas, between rich and the poor, between men and women. It is necessary to investigate now whether other factors, like the changing roles and status of women and the nature of the development process itself also contributed to this growth.

A population policy, to be effective, will have to take this range of factors and variations into consideration. Just as compulsory schooling, or restrictions on the age of marriage become impossible to enforce where economic and social necessities go against them, the small family can only be acceptable when the family's situation makes it appear reasonable and attractive. The critical issues in bringing about this transformation lie in the family's economic position, the value of the woman, which depends on the roles that she performs for the family and the community, and the structure of social inequalities.

The unconscious middle-class bias in the population control policy has failed to understand the basic contradiction between the household economy of the poor and the individualist economy of the capitalist modern sector. The percolation of middle-class norms of behaviour to lower levels of society may create greater demand for social services, but they also increase the proportion of dependents in the population. The impact of this on sex-roles is disastrous — both for women's status and the population growth.

NOTES

1. The terms of reference of the Committee on the Status of Women in India appointed by the Union Government in 1971 included a review of legal and administrative provisions which sought to improve women's status, and suggestion of measures 'which would enable women to play their full and proper role in building up the nation'.

2. While these problems were more acute for Hindu women, it was admitted by Muslim, Parsee and other reformers that similar evils had also crept into their communities under Hindu influence.

3. For a more elaborate discussion of these ideas see Vina Mazumdar, 'The Social Reform Movement from Ranade to Nehru' in B. R. Nanda (ed.), *Indian Women from Purdah to Modernity*, Delhi: Vikas, 1976. Also *Towards Equality* — Report of the Committee on the Status of Women in India, Government of India, 1974, chapter 3.

4. *Status of Women in India:* synopsis of the Report of the National Committee, Indian Council of Social Science Research & Allied Publishers, 1975 pp. 28-29.

5. Advisory Committee on Women's Studies, Indian Council of Social Science Research, *Critical Issues on the Status of Women: Employment, Health, Education: Suggested Priorities for Action* 1977, p. 25.

6. Jawaharlal Nehru, *Discovery of India*, Bombay: Asia, 1972, p. 27.

7. The Constitutional Reforms of 1919 authorized the elected legislatures in the provinces to concede votes to women if they so desired. The Reforms Act of 1921 enfranchised a very small fraction of the Indian population, including women, if they possessed qualifications of wifehood, property and education. The Government of India Act of 1935 increased the number of enfranchised Indians and relaxed some of the previous qualifications. Women over 21 could vote provided they fulfilled the conditions of property and education.

8. M. K. Gandhi, *Young India*, 15 December 1921, 8 October 1921, 21 March 1927, *Harijan* 4 August 1940. See also Vina Mazumdar, op. cit.

9. M. K. Gandhi, *Young India*, 26 February 1918; quoted in *Towards Equality*, op. cit., p. 148.

10. Karl Marx and Friedrich Engels, *Selected Works*, Vol. 2, Moscow: Progress, 1972. p. 310.

11. Jawaharlal Nehru: foreword to *Social Welfare in India*, The Planning Commission, 1955.

12. Government of India, *First Five-Year Plan*, New Delhi, 1952, , chapter 33.

13. *Towards Equality*, op. cit., p. 372.

14. Indian Council of Social Science Research: Advisory Committee on Women's Studies, op. cit., p. 1.

15. Ibid, p. 2.

16. T. Scarlett Epstein: *South India Yesterday, Today & Tomorrow*. London: Macmillan, 1973; also M. N. Srinivas: *Changing Position of Indian Women:* Thomas Huxley Memorial Lecture: Royal Anthropological Society, London: 1976. Published in *Man* (new series), **12**, 12, August 1977.

17. *Towards Equality*, op. cit., p. 232.

18. Asok Mitra: 'National Population Policy in Relation to National Planning', *Population and Development Review,* New York, **3**, 3, September 1977.

19. For a brief review of sociological studies on Indian fertility behaviour, see M. N. Srinivas and E. A. Ramaswamy: *Culture and Human Fertility in India*, New Delhi: Oxford University Press, 1977.

20. Ibid, p. 29.

21. J. Bernard, *The Future of Motherhood*, New York: Dial, 1974.

22. Asok Mitra, op. cit., pp. 18-19.

23. Ibid, p. 12.

24. T. Scarlett Epstein, op. cit.; M. N. Srinivas *Changing Position of Indian Women, Man* (new series), Vol. 12 (2), August 1977 also D. R. Gadgil: *Women in the Working Force in India,* Bombay: Asia, 1965.

25. Literally meaning the 'respectable classes' or the gentry, distinguished from *Chotolog,* meaning 'small people' or the unrefined masses.

26. Asok Mitra, op. cit., p. 33.

III
WOMEN AS POLICY MAKERS

11

WOMEN AS POLICY MAKERS:
The Case of France

Claude du Granrut
Deputy Director,
Labor Department, Paris

Ms. du Granrut traces the uneven political fortunes of French women from post-second world war to the present time. She lays the blame for women's minimal role in French political life at the feet of the 'Government's economic policy, the presidential regime, party pluralism, negative attitudes, and cultural prejudices.' Ms. du Granrut notes the vast disparity between women's role in the French economy and the political world. She draws a picture of French political life in which women have been ignored, cast aside, and only recently noticed as a potential political force.

Ms. du Granrut sees the different priorities of French men and women as one source of their differing political orientations, a subject that she suggests requires understanding based upon research. Feminine values, which comprise a major portion of the differences in political orientation between French women and men, are suggested by du Granrut as the means for modifying the nature and exercise of French political power.

The most striking characteristic one observes about women in French society is the wide gap between the place women hold in the economy and their role in politics. While the position of women in the labor force has been steadily improving since the end of the second world war, their place in politics has remained virtually unchanged, if not worse.

Thus, the latest 1978 figures show that although French women make up 53 percent of the voting population, they represent: 3.7 percent of the deputies, or 19 out of 491; 1.3 percent of the senators, or 5 out of 295; 8.1 percent of the city council members, or 38,000 out of 470,000; and 1.6 percent of the mayors, or about 600 out of 38,000.

In contrast, the figures available on French working women show that they represent: 38.6 percent of the labor force; 22.9 percent of industrial workers; 66.1 percent of clerical workers; 44 percent of qualified workers; 22 percent of executives and liberal professions; and 4 percent of management (evaluation). Although women's salaries are lower than those of men holding similar positions (33.4 percent), their earnings represent 40 percent of family incomes.

French girls comprise 57 percent of the French 'bacheliers' (high school graduates). In higher education they account for half of the student body and obtain 48.8 percent of the diplomas, which in years to come should help to improve the overall position of women in the economy.

I. HISTORICAL EVOLUTION OF THE POSITION OF WOMEN IN FRENCH POLITICS

In 1945, when French women were given the right to vote, their participation in parliamentary elections resulted in the election of women as 8.1 percent of deputies, or 39 out of 480; 7.3 percent of senators, or 22 out of 300; and 1 Member of the Cabinet. For the first time, a woman was elected to serve as vice-president of the senate and several chaired important commissions in the National Assembly.

There are a number of explanations for this. First, French political leaders realized that women's right to vote had been postponed too long and that the political situation was ripe for a change. Second, many women had taken an active part in the Resistance Movement. Suffrage was, in a way, an official recognition of their participation and courage. Furthermore, to include women's names on the ballot was a good electoral asset, as leaders on the Left came to realize that giving women the right to vote would not necessarily mean a more conservative electorate. Third, the electoral system during this period included the division of France into large constituencies where parties could present as many persons as could be elected. After the election, each party received the number of seats proportional to the number of votes it gained. In a constituency represented by half a dozen seats in the National Assembly, it was easy to slip in the name of a woman. Fourth, at this time, two political parties were running the political scene, the Communist Party and the Popular Republican Movement. Both parties had developed new attitudes towards women in recognition of their sense of collective responsibility and of their interest in public life. It was felt that some efforts had to be made to integrate women and women's ideas into the political tickets. For this reason they encouraged a strange alliance between two powerful associations, one Catholic, the other Marxist. Working from different ends of the political spectrum, but along similar lines, both did much to train women for public life and public responsibilities, particularly in the city councils.

This period in which the political role of women improved did not last for a number of reasons. Two emerge as most important: a) a lack of real political work on the part of those women who had been 'accepted' in politics, and b) the structural changes taking place in French political life after the second world war.

The first backlash against women occurred in 1951. The Communist Party and the Popular Republican Movement were losing their impact, and their female representatives were the first to be put aside. Meanwhile, de Gaulle's party was gaining more and more influence, without including women in its ranks.

Important structural changes occurred in 1958, when the Constitution of the Fifth Republic established a new electoral system for the legislature: a uninominal constituency election with two ballots. France was divided into 487 constituencies. In each of these political parties would present only one candidate. Traditionally, parties chose the candidate they thought would get the most votes, and thus the candidate was rarely a woman. The fight was usually long and bitter, grounded in both ideology and personal characteristics, and it was thought that a female candidate would be unable to get as many votes as a man because of traditional sex prejudice.

The female representatives both in the National Assembly and in the Senate never recovered from this sharp drop. The few women who survived were those who had strong personal positions or strong financial backgrounds and were lost among the men. None of them became a member of the Cabinet; a few became Under Secretaries of State; only one chaired the Social Commission in the National Assembly.

At the same time, those parties which had helped the position of women were facing difficulties. The Popular Republican Movement had completely vanished, the Communist Party was at its lowest point, and the Socialist Party had not yet resolved its inner contradictions. Since the establishment of the Fifth Republic, none of the parties has produced a recognized female politician. Talented women have not been given a chance, while a great deal has been done for many young men. De Gaulle's party, in particular, in the 1967 elections sent quite a few young men called the 'young wolves' into difficult constituencies. These young male candidates were well-chosen and knew how to take advantage of their opportunities.

For most of the political leaders, among them de Gaulle, women's votes were gained without much effort. For Georges Pompidou, his successor, their votes were not ignored, but they were not particularly sought or regarded as a political force. French party officials are not solely to blame for women's lack of political clout. Unfortunately, their opinion mirrored public opinion, including that of most women. It is usually assumed that this is due to French Latin culture, which imposes on each sex a specific role: for men, an outside role and the right to represent the family interests in public; for women, an inside role — the care of the home and of the family. This analysis is superficial, however, and to it should be added the economic and political structure of the Fifth Republic, which had considerable ramifications for the political role women could play in society.

II. THE POLITICAL AND ECONOMIC STRUCTURES OF THE FIFTH REPUBLIC

A. The Government Structures

The new constitution established the current regime known as the Fifth Republic, which is based on the principle that the President and the Government chosen by the President have primary authority. Parliament's role was reduced to approval of the budget and government-proposed bills. The result was that French political life lay in the hands of a few, and decision-making for both political and economic issues was concentrated in Paris.

In the meantime, what is known as the 'technocratie' became increasingly important. Membership of this new type of power elite required qualities different from those traditionally attributed to women: abstract reasoning, instant opinions on everything, Grandes Écoles Diplomas, availability to serve Cabinet staff and, sometimes, devotion to one political leader or party. Also, being a true political leader meant having a history of holding a large number of posts: mayor, district local counsel, deputy or senator, party official and, if possible, member of government.

How could a woman enter such a political arena without the training and contacts traditionally reserved for men? How could a party take a chance on appointing or electing a woman?

B. The Government's objectives

The Government's objective of economic expansion did not really provide an opportunity for women to be heard. Besides the changes taking place in the organization of French political life, it should be added that de Gaulle and, after him, Georges Pompidou directed a policy which did not take into account women's normal daily problems and views. The first objective was to make France a strong economic industrial power, focusing on increased production, increased salaries, and more consumption. French Government economic policy had adopted the credo that better earnings made better living, and that economic expansion was the only way to social progress. The second objective was to maintain France's position in the world as strongly as possible, so that French people would feel that they were still considered a prestigious world power.

These statements are oversimplifications, but these objectives meant that women did not have the opportunity to draw the attention of the Government to such areas of concern as education, housing, conditions of work, public transportation and social services.

C. The French Government's disregard of pressure groups

To prevent a recurrence of the instability of the Fourth Republic, the

Fifth Republic made a point of disregarding the pressure groups that had disturbed it's predecessor and in general ignored any associations, local institutions or professional groups which were not officially recognized. Consequently, French women had no channel for real participation. They could not participate in collective responsibility, they had no opportunity to express their own ideas on housing, consumerism, family policy, education, working conditions or health facilities. How could they fight for their ideas when they were given no recognition? How could they know that the defence of these ideas lay in the hands of women candidates? Political scientists could state that women preferred to vote for men rather than for women, but perhaps with reason. It made sense not to vote for women, as women had neither the chance to be elected nor an opportunity to be heard.

Furthermore, party pluralism in French political life is somewhat absurd. Differences among parties are so small that they have to be exaggerated and then overcome when negotiation, that is election time, arrives. As spectators to this strange abstract game, French women, as a group, did not feel concerned. In summary then, the Government's economic policy, the presidential regime, party pluralism, negative attitudes, and cultural prejudices all worked to reject women as contenders in the political world and reduced almost to nothing their early first post-war attempts. Today, these obstacles still need to be overcome.

The events of 1968 and the rise of the leftist parties, especially the Socialist Party, could have meant the beginning of a change. Actually, it served to put the conservative parties on the defensive and reinforced the political status quo. Although women were beginning to enjoy improved economic and legal status, their political status remained low, as the parties still did not dare to send women into the political arena.

Thus, when President Giscard d'Estaing was elected, the overall picture of the French political scene, as far as women were concerned, was a disappointing one. Women who were getting more and more education were enjoying better positions and more autonomy in their professional lives; however, they were increasingly dissatisfied. It was clear that they could shift their so-called traditional conservative votes toward the parties on the left which were recognizing their demands.

This is certainly one of the reasons which made President Giscard d'Estaing recognize the potential danger of the situation. He therefore selected a truly remarkable woman, Simone Veil, as Minister of Health and three other women as Under Secretaries of State, one of whom dealt with women's affairs. Then two moved and François Giroud was discharged from women's affairs. While she was, however, Mme. Giroud prepared a project entitled, 'A Hundred Points for Women,' which laid out a program for reform. While these may only be small first steps, they have raised the hopes of many women who were distressed over their lack of representation in French political life. In 1978 Monique Pelletier was appointed Minister for Women's Affairs.

III. THE SITUATION TODAY

There has been a series of laws passed for women over the past four years. Most of the laws were passed to protect women in particular situations: widows, divorcees, unmarried mothers, pregnant workers. Some laws were aimed at opening the labor market more widely to women and, thus, to affect the public services, technical schools, and university level institutes.

One may ask if these measures have brought any improvement to the situation of women as a whole. Although they were well-intended measures, some of them may indirectly discriminate against women and also create unintended consequences for the specific problems of women workers. An example of this is the 2-year leave for young working mothers.

When we examine the current French political structure, we note still other changes. The number of women in party ranks has increased so that now from 10 to 30 percent of their members are women. Less than 10 percent are involved in party decision making, however. In the trade-unions, the situation is essentially the same.

As far as elections go, the number of women candidates for the March 1977 municipal elections was higher than in 1971, but the 25 percent rule which had been proposed by some has not been adopted by the Government. The result was that 8.5 percent were women. The number of women candidates chosen by major political parties for the general election in 1978 was not significantly higher than in 1973 and French political life did not show fundamental changes for women or for the society as a whole.

IV. CHANGES WHICH SHOULD LEAD WOMEN TO ENTER POLITICS

A. The changing image of French women through their economic role and financial autonomy

The number of economically active women has increased by 1.5 million within eight years. Over 25 percent of these women are now between the ages of 20-34 years. French women now represent 39 percent of the active working population, and this should increase to 40-42 percent, even 45 percent, by the turn of the century.

There are more young girls than boys finishing their 'baccalaureate'. Fifty percent of students in higher education are girls. They represent 35 percent of medical students, 25 percent of Grandes Écoles preparatory classes, and about 10 percent of Grandes Écoles students. These facts make it increasingly difficult for government policy to avoid helping women to acquire decision-making positions either in public service or in private business.

B. The growing demand of adult women for responsibilities 'outside the home'

The notion of 'motherhood', which centered around the home and confined women to the role of care and nurture of children and husband, is vanishing. Women are no longer so hesitant to enter into public life. Their work at home is being replaced or supplemented by their participation in paid work or volunteer work aimed at improving daily living conditions. Through these experiences, French women will soon be able to recognize that they also have what I call a 'personnalité sociale' — a social stature — and that they have a right, even a duty, to express their own ideas, to demand changes in housing projects, local economic planning, the administration of schools and so on, with an emphasis on priorities that often differ from those traditionally pursued by men.

The differences in priorities of males and females are also reflected in the language women use. This has emerged from their roles and relationships and places different interpretations and values on the world around them. While language differences between males and females are subtle and may be difficult assert scientifically, it is an area which merits serious attention. In politics, for example, the difference is more marked. Women's political talk is different from men's talk both in terms of the themes and words used. The sense of humor is different, and so is the level and tone of aggressiveness. Once again, this is an observation, rather than a scientific finding, but it is an area worthy of scientific research.

C. Changes in the structure of French society

A slow but real transfer of the power centered in Paris toward regional assemblies, local governments, and municipal councils could produce a new equilibrium between the Paris 'Rastignac' and the Provinces' new 'notables.' A remodeling of political parties might take into account the actions and motivations of those people whose priorities are not to produce and to consume more and more. The growing participation of men and women in local groups for sports, leisure, and cultural activities, a desire to revitalize and invest urban life with new collective services for young and old people, as well as for families should influence the emergence of new criteria for economic and social progress.

The urgent demand for an end to social inequalities, the need for improved quality of daily life, better housing conditions, the provision of recurrent training for new and more responsible working conditions, and the demand for democratic participation in local institutions, all lead towards new roots of power and a new setting for power. Although French women have a long way to go, this is a growing force. It is not yet an overwhelming force when compared to the many problems France has to face. It could become so, however, if women organized to promote it.

Women need a political strategy, however, if they are to improve materially their position and exercise political power. First, they should realize that the nature and exercise of power must be modified. The nature of power until now has been defined and represented by men's values. Women have to insert feminine values and action-oriented reevaluations. Second, the exercise of power has meant party politics only. Women have to organize their own pressure groups inside and outside the political parties through associations and through efficient participation in media and public opinion.[1]

Today many French women are politically-minded. Some are

preparing themselves in small groups dealing with everything from day-care facilities to courses on running for political office. These young women will transform the potential power of women into real power and will become tomorrow's politicians and economic executives of a new kind. They will set political life and economy on a larger scale, because they will bring back to our society what men have put aside — which is that 'privilege is a duty until it fades into equality' and that 'a reversal in value systems is as necessary for social progress as it is for better daily life.' French women will then have access to a new, enlarged political power which will secure their own way in politics. They will be in a true situation of becoming policymakers.

NOTES

1. For instance, one of the first changes to ask for is a change in the electoral system and a return to the one which was favorable to women.

12
WOMEN AS VOTERS:
From Redemptive to Futurist Role

Jessie Bernard
Pennsylvania State University, USA

Ms. Bernard's paper looks briefly at changing conceptions of the feminine role in policy making. She notes that in the past it was believed that policy making was not a suitable role for women, that the interests of women were well protected by fathers and husbands. When women did come to seek a part in policy making, one argument used was that policy making did, in fact, need the contribution only women could make in their feminine role. They could perform a redemptive function, countering many of the ills resulting from the exercise of male power. More recently, women have sought access to policy positions as a right and not as a gift to be bestowed upon them, nor have they accepted the idea that they had to 'deserve' or 'earn' policy positions. Actually, women do tend to vote on the humanistic side of most issues.

In the past, a considerable amount of the discussion, pro and con, dealing with female participation in the polity in the United States has rested on a certain conception of the roles of women as wives and especially as mothers. Opponents argued that in their role as wives, women did not have to participate; their interests were adequately protected by their husbands; and even if they did vote, since they were essentially minors, they would only vote as their husbands told them to (Duverger, 1955: 129). There would be no improvement or change in the polity. Or, if they voted independently, since they were not as intelligent as men, they would be unduly swayed and they would therefore have a disastrous effect on policy, voting for the wrong things for the wrong reasons. And anyway, in their role as mothers women already had all the power they needed: the hand that rocked the cradle ruled the world (Hess and Torney, 1967). Participation in the polity would coarsen and degrade women and unfit them for the gentler roles of wife and mother. In attenuated form, these arguments still echo down to the present.[1]

The proponents as well as the opponents of female participation in the polity also rested their case on the nature of women and their roles. They saw women performing a redemptive function since, as mothers, women were morally superior to men, purer, more altruistic. Julia Ward Howe had promulgated this principle: 'The very intensity of our feeling for home, husband, and children,' she had declared, 'gives us a power of loving and working outside of our homes, to redeem the world as love and work only can' (1888: 9). A considerable number of the early feminists accepted this concept of the redemptive function of women in the polity:

> The reformist women sought the vote not to free themselves but to reform society. They thought that with it working people could clean up their sweatshops, the traffic in liquor could be stopped, child labor eliminated, and society generally bettered. They were so concerned with fighting other people's battles that they could not conceive of themselves fighting solely their own (Freeman, 1975: 18).[2]

Others turned to the redemptive argument only when the grounds of justice got them nowhere (Kraditor, 1968). 'It was only when women argued that they needed it [the suffrage] as a social good, to help 'clean up' society, that the idea of suffrage became widely acceptable' (Freeman, 1975: 19n).

Some politicians themselves also believed this argument. They fought the movement for female suffrage on the bare chance that women just might succeed in cleaning up the political system.[3] There was, therefore, a sigh of relief when they noted that for many years not only were women not voting in large numbers but also that even when they did, nothing much changed. The amount of violence at polling places did decline and minor changes in other aspects of the system did occur. But nothing spectacular as the politicians had feared.

It is true that for some time after women were granted the vote the rate of participation in the polity was low.[4] Summarizing eleven studies, all before 1969, Costantini and Craik tell us that:

> The political behavior literature is replete with evidence that at all levels of political action from discussing politics to voting, to political letter-writing, to holding party or public office, women participate less than men. They appear to be less informed politically, and to display a lower sense of political involvement and political efficacy (1972: 218).

Still on the basis of this research, the authors add that 'women have tended to defer to the political judgment of men, in this country and elsewhere; sex roles have been so defined that politics is primarily the business of men.' Since these studies were made, the proportion of women who at least vote has now increased markedly and in the case of at least some of them, especially the young, has overtaken the proportion of men who do so (Bernard, 1975, Table 8:6).

But even though there was no articulated theory or actual attempt to 'redeem' the social world, neither was there a strong female lobby to press for their own interests. Even ostensible self-oriented arguments were cast in an other-oriented frame: 'political equality could only help women better perform their domestic functions' (Freeman, 1975: 19). There was not a 'woman's vote,' that is a self-interested vote, even on behalf of their own interests.[5] True, after the passage of the 19th Amendment, the leaders of the suffrage movement formed a League of Women Voters. But it was not designed for lobbying or exerting pressure on behalf of women's issues. It was, on the contrary, strictly, even blatantly, non-partisan, an educational organization for voters in general on behalf of issues of general, not necessarily women's, concerns.[6]

Only in the 1970s, with the resuscitation of interest in the equal rights amendment, did women on a large scale begin again seriously to learn the skills of political participation, of lobbying, of letter-writing, of assembling to petition redress of wrongs, of exerting pressure on their own behalf, rather than on behalf of others.[7] They did not see that it was women's peculiar obligation to clean up the ills of government or of society (Carden, 1974: 169). They based their case on the grounds, not of having to earn or deserve or justify a say in the running of the polity, but of having a right to it, a right as legitimate as men's. It was not something men had a legal right to bestow or withhold. Their case rested, in brief, not on greater moral qualifications or promises to be or do good, but on simple justice. They did not have to prove themselves morally superior or even equal to men in order to warrant more say in policy formulation. They did not have to promise to redeem society. And, most revolutionary of all, they began to see and seriously formulate their own issues rather than accepting the formulation of issues by men.[8]

As a matter of fact, whether women promised it or not, the contribution of women to general policy has actually tended to be altruistic, on the humane side, and their contribution to political life benign. A brief overview of the records of the 95 women who have served in the US Congress, for example, shows that many 'stood out for their strong identification with humanist issues: peace, child care, health and welfare . . . ' (Susan J. Tolchin, 1976). A Harris poll in 1972 reported that women were 'significantly more compassionate' than men about social issues such as hunger, poverty, problems of the aged, and racial discrimination. 'Women...are much more inclined...to vote and to become active not only for their own self-interest, but for the interests of society, the world, and, most of all, out of compassion for humanity' (Harris Poll, 1972: 75). And, despite Lipset's finding reported in 1960 and Costantini and Craik's report in 1972 that women tended to be more conservative than men, an analysis in 1976 of the voting record of the 19 women members of Congress showed them to be more liberal than their party leaders (Fritchey, 1976[9]). This was also the case among women Democrats in a California study made in 1964-65 (Costantini and Craik, 1972: 234). Their participation in party politics, similarly, as shown in this California study, has been more public-service than self-oriented. They have followed the 'vicarious-achievement' pattern which Lipman-Blumen and Leavitt (1977) have shown to be characteristic of women. Costantini and Craik report, for example:

> Politics for the male leader is evidently more likely to be a vehicle for personal enhancement and career advancement. But for the woman leader it is more likely to be a 'labor of love,' one where a concern for the party, its candidates, and its programs assumes relatively greater importance. If the male leader appears to be motivated by self-serving considerations, the female leader appears to be motivated by public-service considerations (pp. 234-35).

As Fritchey notes, 'women are seldom afflicted with machismo, the most dangerous vice of male presidents' and, perhaps, of most male political leaders.

Many men now agree that women should be fully represented in 'every area of decision making, problem solving, or institution building

— if for nothing else, just to make sure that their interests...are not being neglected or overridden' (Platt, 1975). And in some areas they should be more than equally represented 'to correct the distortions that men throughout history have imposed on our attitudes and our institutions' (Platt, 1976).[10]

The upsurge in recent years of the new orientation among women which justifies struggling for their own issues does not mean, in brief, that the old 'redemptive' or at least other-oriented stance has disappeared. Although many women simply want more of what they have been deprived of under the status quo, the fundamental argument for more input into policy by women is still for many in terms of a better world for everyone. As Elise Boulding reminds us, just 'giving women equal opportunity with men to do all the things that men now do' would not make the world more peaceful and just' (1977). Individuals of whichever sex who were in positions to dominate or exploit others would still be able to do so. What needs change is the structure of power positions, not merely the sex of its occupants.

Although Elise Boulding does not attribute innate[11] or intrinsic moral superiority to women, she does recognize that the millennial period of time in the past during which women have lived on the underside of history has equipped them well for the task of restructuring the future. John Platt makes the same point:

> ...there are certainly some areas where the current roles, or the current rejections, of women — no matter how these roles or rejections may change in the liberated future — give them a better understanding of the problems than most men have. This may be true in such areas as the rights of minorities, distributive justice, the rights of patients and the dying, child-care centres, consumerism and product safety, ecology and pollution control, new family and neighbourhood structures, the rights concerning privacy, advertising, television and the media, health insurance, the rights of the old, part-time and flexible working hours, the use of leisure, religious reform, education throughout life, world famine, and food and its distribution, population, health care and development in the poorer countries, and peace keeping (1975).

Life on the underside, Elise Boulding reminds us, may have inhibited women from innovation in the past (1976: 790), but it has not damaged their human potential (782). She, therefore, looks to women for innovation and creativity for the future:

Here the underside becomes a special resource. It is society's free fantasy space, its visioning space, its bonding space. It is a space in which minds can learn to grapple with complexities that are destroying the overside... (789).

Women, she argues, must be trained to use this free-fantasy, this visioning, not for redeeming the errors of the past but for creating better futures on the overside.

NOTES

1. For example: 'Given cross-cultural data about the political role of females,' Lionel Tiger tells us, 'it may constitute a revolutionary and perhaps hazardous social change with numerous latent consequences should women ever enter politics in great numbers. Even a but partly female-dominated polity may go beyond the parameters of "healthy" possibility, given the basic conservatism of species...' (1970: 259). It is interesting that he can conceptualize only in male terms; he speaks of a 'female-dominated polity' as though domination of one sex by the other were the only possible model for a polity.

2. For a somewhat fuller discussion of the redemptive function of the motherhood role, see Jessie Bernard, 1974, Chapter 18.

3. Credit was, in fact, given to the women's vote for the passage of the so-called Prohibition amendment.

4. A Chicago study in 1923 showed why. In the mayorality election in that city three-fourths of those who had not even registered were women. Illness, either of themselves or others they had to care for, was the commonest reason given. Disbelief in women's voting was given by about 9 percent, including 1 percent who gave husband's objection as the reason (Merriam and Gosnell, 1924).

5. For some of the obstacles in the way of female solidarity, see Jessie Bernard, forthcoming, 1979.

6. In some cities, the women in the League of Women Voters were so high-powered that they intimidated less well-educated women. The Women's Party exerted but minor influence.

7. Jean Baker Miller, a revisionary psychoanalyst, has given thoughtful attention to the theory of self-interest as applied to women. She argues that the cripplingly poor self-image women suffer from is not justified, that what have been defined by male standards as weaknesses in them — their greater need for bonding, their emotional expressiveness, their empathy, for example — can actually be their basic strengths. She reassures women that it is legitimate to

recognize their own needs and to work to see that they are met (1976).

8. They wanted protection for themselves against rape; they wanted better health services for themselves, including contraception and abortion; they wanted an end to discrimination against them in education, vocational training, job opportunities. They wanted protection against 'displacement' as housewives in middle life. They wanted recompense for their work in the home. They wanted credit on the same terms as men. They wanted into the social security system in their own names. They wanted a better public image in the media. An end to putdowns; changes in language, in forms of address...They found issues that stunned the world, so long had they been swept under the carpet.

9. It has to be recognized that constituencies that sent women to Congress were themselves undoubtedly more liberal than party leaders.

10. These distortions that have to be corrected — as contrasted with evils that have to be redeemed — were of this nature: 'There is a general feeling now that the contribution of Western men has tended to be objective, technological, manipulative, concerned with things not people, with death rather than life, with thought rather than feeling, with punishment rather than positive reinforcement, with decision rather than ongoing assessment, with intervention rather than nurturance, and with closed control rather than with the natural and ecological rhythms of birth and death and open-ended growth. Men should correct such distortion in themselves, of course, but it would seem to be an area of world outlook where women at least may be less blinded by the past, and where they could be of enormous help' (Platt, 1975). Compare with Jean Baker Miller's argument, footnote 7 above.

11. Sociobiology has recently introduced the concept of 'altruistic genes' and a considerable amount of evidence has been adduced to support it from the behavior especially of genetic females — worker bees and mother birds, for example (Wilson, 1975; 121 ff.) But we need not go that far to explain the humane and compassionate attitudes of women. In another place I have suggested that it was possible for women to be more compassionate because they have been more protected; they have not had to enter the fray (1974: 357 ff.; see also Harriet Holter, 1970: 231).

REFERENCES

BERNARD, Jessie, *The Future of Motherhood*. New York: Penguin, 1974.
—— *Women, Wives, Mothers*. Chicago: Aldine, 1975.
—— 'Models for the Relationship between the Worlds of Women and of Men,' in Louis Kriesberg, ed., *Social Conflict, Social Movements, Social Change*, 1978.

BOULDING, Elise, *The Underside of History: A View of Women through Time.* Boulder, Colo.: Westview Press, 1976.
— — 'Women and Social Violence,' in *Violence and Its Causes: Theoretical and Aspects of Recent Research on Violence.* Paris: Unesco, 1977.
CARDEN, Maren Lockwood, *The New Feminist Movement.* New York: Russell Sage, 1974.
CRAIK, Kenneth H., see Edmond Costantini.
COSTANTINI, Edmond and Kenneth H. Craik, 'Women as Politicans: The Social Background, Personality, and Political Careers of Female Party Leaders,' *Journal of Social Issues,* 1972, 28, 217-36.
DUVERGER, M., *Political Role of Women.* Paris: UNESCO, 1955.
FREEMAN, Jo, *The Politics of Women's Liberation.* New York: McKay, 1975.
FRITCHEY, Clayton, 'The Women's Caucus,' *Washington Post,* April 24, 1976.
GOSNELL, Harold Foote, see Charles E. Merriam.
HARRIS, Louis and Associates, *The 1972 Virginia Slims American Women's Opinion Poll.* New York: Published by the Authors.
HARRIS, Reuben, see Harold Leavitt.
HESS, R. D. and J. V. Torney, *The Development of Political Attitudes in Children.* New York: Doubleday, 1967.
HOLTER, Harriet, *Sex Roles and Social Structure.* Oslo, Norway: Universitetforlaget, 1970.
HOWE, Julia Ward, 'Opening Address,' *14th Annual Report of the Association for the Advancement of Women,* Woman's Congress, Detroit, 1888, p. 9.
KRADITOR, Aileen S., ed., *Up from the Pedestal.* Chicago: Quadrangle, 1968.
LEAVITT, Harold, Jean Lipman-Blumen, Susan Schaefer, and Reuben Harris, 'Vicarious Achievement Orientation'. Paper prepared for annual meetings of the American Psychological Association, 1977.
LIPMAN-BLUMEN, Jean, see Harold Leavitt.
LIPSET, Martin Seymour, *Political Man.* New York: Doubleday, 1960.
MERRIAM, Charles E. and Harold Foote Gosnell, *Non-Voting: Causes and Methods of Control.* Chicago: University of Chicago Press, 1924.
MILLER, Jean Baker, *Toward a New Psychology of Women.* Boston: Beacon Press, 1976.
PLATT, John, 'Women's Roles and the Great World Transformation' in Guy Streatfield, ed., *Women and the Future.* Guildford, Surrey: IFC Science and Technology Press, 1976; Binghamton, N.Y.; Center for Integration Studies, 1976.
SCHAEFER, Susan, see Harold Leavitt.
TIGER, Lionel, *Men in Groups.* New York: Vintage, 1970.
TOLCHIN, Susan J., *Women in Congress 1917 through 1976,* Joint Committee on Arrangements for the Commemoration of the Bicentennial. Washington: Government Printing Office, 1976.
TORNEY, J. V., see R. D. Hess.
WILSON, E. O., *Socio-Biology, The New Synthesis.* Cambridge: Belknap-Harvard, 1975.

13

WOMEN AS CHANGE AGENTS:
Toward a Conflict Theoretical Model of Sex Role Change

Constantina Safilios-Rothschild
Wayne State University, USA

Social policy writ large commonly is defined as those practices embodied in formal legislation, procedures, and programs. But social policy writ small is developed and implemented in a less formal manner at the microlevel of everyday social existence. In a sense, this is the practice of social policy. Ms. Safilios-Rothschild writes about women – as change agents creating and implementing social policy at the microlevel – of social life. She examines the question of how change can be created, both at the societal and the individual levels.

Safilios-Rothschild presents a set of theoretical perspectives that revolve around the use of 'confrontational conflict'. Her chapter stands in contrast to Es-Said's paper which discusses non-confrontational changes. These hypotheses and the strategies for change that flow from them arise from several theoretical domains within social science: conflict theory, small group research, crisis theory, achievement research, and leadership theory. Ms. Safilios-Rothschild brings these insights from social science to bear on the problems women face in their roles as change agents in the struggle for equality between the sexes.

I. INTRODUCTION

Conflict is the basic process leading toward the redefinition of sex roles and the breakdown of sex discrimination. A 'dialectic' process between men and women as opposite social groups is necessary if radical social changes are to take place. Whenever in a society the conflict confrontations between men and women cease too soon, the process of radical change also stops too soon, unless other relevant and helpful types of conflict confrontations can be created. In this chapter we shall examine two very different societal models of sex role change, namely the Swedish and the American models and analyze the macro- and microsociological factors which have been facilitating or hindering the passing and implementation of nonsexist legislation and policies. The type and extent of conflict between men and women at the interpersonal as well as the societal level is the crucial factor which differentiates the two models. Then, a conflict theoretical model of sex role change is proposed and a set of hypotheses are posited which lead to the examination of the conditions and strategies through which conflict may shift from that between men and women to conflict between different types of groups of men and women. Specific strategies of different types of conflict confrontations (suggested by existing research) are spelled out at the individual and societal level which can facilitate sex role changes and the formulation and implementation of nonsexist social policy.

II. TWO DIFFERENT MODELS

A. The Swedish Non-Confrontation Model

In Sweden, legislation and social policies that brought about some radical redefinitions in men's roles (especially the father role) were passed by the late 1960s. The lack of conflict confrontation, however, made it possible for powerful groups such as the Swedish medical establishment to impose conservative and largely sexist legislations and policies in crucial areas, such as abortion, by placing final decision-making in the hands of physicians, rather than in the hands of the women involved. In January 1974, after many years of discussion, a new abortion law was passed that leaves the decision entirely up to the woman. The success in passing legislation aimed at redefining men's and women's roles and eradicating sex role stereotypes in Sweden, despite the lack of conflict confrontation, is due to a number of reasons, the most important being:

(1) Some intellectual and some powerful men were involved in the sex role debate from the start and some men, including congressmen and politicians, such as the ex-Prime Minister Palme, have been instrumental in passing legislation aimed at breaking down sexism and sex discrimination. As a direct consequence of those factors, the sex role debate was viewed never as a women's movement potentially threatening to men. It was not an angry suffragette movement but instead, a humanitarian 'discussion' led by men and women.[1] Women were not viewed as fighting against men and thus the conflict — whenever it occurred — was not seen as one involving men against women but rather as some men and women with more radical orientations against more traditional men and women.

(2) In a society like Sweden, in which humanitarian and egalitarian ideologies have been not merely rhetorical but historically influential in shaping legislation, social policy and programs, the ideology concerning equality between men and women was met with hardly any conflict.[2] It was not, therefore, surprising that it was relatively easy to pass legislation representing extensions of the egalitarian ideology. These prevailing societal values have tended to tone down even potential conflict between more and less radical groups of men and women. Legislation, however, cannot reach or modify sexism in all of its subtle and pervasive ramifications, although it can indirectly affect many areas. In the absence of continuous conflict confrontations, structural and institutional discrimination may be replaced by subtle, informal discrimination. Such subtle, informal sex discrimination takes place at the interpersonal and the implementation level. This type of discrimination determines to a considerable extent men's and women's ability and interest in taking on 'new' or 'sex-inappropriate' options, even when the structure and legislation allow them.

The 'Group-8', a radical feminist group in Sweden, has focussed on women's rights to control their own bodies, both in terms of medical treatment and abortion. Group-8 has attempted to provide the necessary conflict confrontations by raising new issues and questions. The need for such a radical feminist group to appear in a society which has thoroughly accepted the idea of sex equality clearly underlines the crucial importance of conflict for social change to be continuous and complete (Safilios-Rothschild, 1974).

III. THE AMERICAN MODEL OF CONFRONTATION BETWEEN MEN AND WOMEN

The model provided by American society stands in sharp contrast to the Swedish experience. It is important to examine closely the American women's liberation movement, since it represents the major alternative to the Swedish model of social change in the sex stratification system via ideological movements.

In the American model, the initial stages of the Women's Movement were laden with emotion and especially with hostility against men, who were cast as oppressors. For women living in the US, such a psychological catharsis was necessary before they could think and act rationally. But, most importantly, this beginning set the stage for continuous and open conflict confrontations between men and women.

As soon as American women became aware of the prevailing sex stratification system, they began a continuing rebellion against the endless mechanisms and processes used to maintain and reinforce the system. From the moment that women sought to reject and transform their subordinate position, the stage was set for social conflict in Coser's terms. Coser defines social conflict as 'a form of group relationship (or interaction) involving a struggle over the rewards or resources of a society or over social values, in which the conflicting parties attempt to neutralize or injure each other' (Coser, 1956).

There is little doubt that American women have started to struggle competitively with men over jobs, promotions, raises, money, prestige, power. And there is considerable evidence that many men fight against affirmative action for women in general, as well as individual competent women, because of the increased competition over scarce resources. This competition is acutely felt at a time of high unemployment and hiring 'freezes'. The impact of this competition is felt particularly by the most vulnerable men, namely those less intelligent and less competent, as recent research has shown (Komarovsky, 1976; Safilios-Rothschild, 1974; Bayer, 1975).

While some major nonsexist legislation concerning education, employment and equal pay has been passed in the United States, it has predominantly focussed on expanding women's options and redefining women's roles. This legislation only indirectly affects (but does not facilitate) men's roles. Most probably because of a lack of endorsement of the liberation ideology by most men (especially as it affects their own roles), major legislation facilitating the redefinition of men's roles and expanding their options (such as those passed in Sweden regarding the universal legitimation of part-time work and the potential equal sharing of the *parental* leave by mothers and fathers) has yet to be passed in the US. The continuing conflict confrontations between men and women, however, have been helpful in the implementation of non-sexist legislation and social policies.

IV. A CONFLICT THEORETICAL MODEL

In proposing a conflict theoretical model, the extent and nature of conflict between men and women can be hypothesized as follows:

(1) The lesser the degree of spatial and social segregation between men and women (in occupations, education, sports, and other leisure and private spheres), the higher the probability of conflict, at least during the early stages of desegregation.

(2) The higher the degree of women's collective consciousness of discrimination, the higher the degree of confrontation with men, at the interpersonal level, as well as at a structural level through militancy and organized action.

(3) The more women tend to reject the vicarious model of achievement (Lipman-Blumen and Leavitt, 1976), the more they expect from men. That is, in addition to status lines (income, prestige, power), women begin to expect love, sex, understanding, and physical attractiveness. And the higher the women's expectations of men, the higher the probability of conflict at the interpersonal level, at least during the early transition stages. The more, on the other hand, women opt for direct achievement (Lipman-Blumen and Leavitt, 1976) (and not through husbands and/or bosses), the higher the conflict between men and women, both at the interpersonal and structural levels.

(4) Because the nature of discrimination against women has been 'paternalistic' rather than 'negative' and openly hostile (as is true for racial, religious, and ethnic discrimination), the onset and nature of conflict are somewhat different from those occurring between other minority-majority groups. With regard to the onset of conflict, in the case of minority groups 'negatively' discriminated against, conflict has always existed even in the absence of a social movement and a high collective consciousness.

(1) The more 'paternalistic and protective' the discrimination,

however, the higher the probability that conflict does not take place before a social movement has begun and consciousness has been raised. Conflict begins the moment women (or disabled or the aged) begin to reject and attempt to remove 'protective' (and restraining) legislation, attitudes, and practice (as evidenced by the ERA).

(2) The more the discrimination is characterized by paternalism, the greater the possibility that a considerable percentage of the minority group, women (or disabled or aged persons) will prefer to maintain and 'hold on' to the protective legislation, policies, and practices that allow them to be dependent upon men (or the corresponding 'majority' members), thereby causing fragmentation of the minority group. Because of this fragmentation, conflict occurs almost as much (in terms of frequency and intensity) among women as it does between men and women. Men capitalize upon this fragmentation, using it to label, and therefore neutralize, the protesting women as 'deviants' and 'rebels' who betray their inherent 'femininity.'

(3) Under certain conditions, the majority group may also become fragmented. For example, as some men are willing to accept and actively endorse the women's liberation movement by siding with women against sexist men, the majority group has also become fragmented. Thus, it can be hypothesized that since such a fragmentation in the ranks of men tends to weaken their uniformly strong and superior position, *the higher the percentage of men who actively espouse an egalitarian ideology with women and who side with women, the less the degree of conflict* between men and women.

(4) A major mechanism by which men attempt to diminish conflict confrontations with women, while simultaneously preventing them from competing with men over scarce resources, is the substitution of subtle, informal discrimination for structural, institutional discrimination. During the transitional stage, therefore, the more open structural discrimination is replaced by subtle, informal discrimination, the greater the reduction in conflict at the societal level between men and women and the more the conflict remains at the interpersonal level and becomes an individuated phenomenon (Bernard, 1976). Because of this individuation process, women's newly gained collective consciousness cannot help them in coping with the conflictful confrontation with men on the micro-level. Good examples of this are provided by research studies of the effects on a 'solo' woman in psychiatric residence or medical or dental training who cannot be integrated as a regular member of the group no matter what interpersonal strategies

are used. She can only be accepted as a subordinate member who accepts her low position in the sex stratification system (Wolman and Frank, 1975).

V. CHANGE WITHIN AND BEYOND INSTITUTIONAL FRAMEWORKS

The nature and goal of conflict may vary considerably from the consensus-bounded type to the consensus-projecting type. That is, conflict, by and large, may remain within the prescribed institutional framework for conflict in the society and within the norms embodied in those institutions, or it may transcend the routine channels for conflict in the society and attempt to redefine the social order and reach a new, changed social consensus. Women up to now have restricted their militancy and organized action predominantly within the prescribed institutional framework for conflict in American society.

While women have not transcended the routine structural channels for conflict in American society, (a) they have engaged in conflict confrontations at the private, intimate level, a level at which other minority members rarely have been able to confront majority members, since social distance has been the very essence of prejudice and discrimination against them; and (b) some women have attempted to redefine the options and values not only of women, but also of men, so as to erase progressively gender lines. This type of redefinition (especially as it refers to men's options and values and the extinction of gender distinctions and roles) probably represents the most drastic social change attempted by any minority group, since it could lead to a total redefinition of current and potential man-woman relationships and roles.

VI. CHANGE AT THE INDIVIDUAL LEVEL

Changes in some aspects of men's beliefs, attitudes, and behaviors may pass unnoticed because they occur slowly and unevenly. Such change is unpredictable, because it may depend upon the level of interpersonal skill on the part of the women close to these men and a special relationship with them, if it is to take place at all. While this represents a very crucial change, it can hardly be considered an effective strategy for short-range social change. Even if every 'liberated' woman could contribute to the liberation of as few as three or four men from sexism, considerable changes would be forthcoming only in the decade ahead of us. We know very little, however, as to the mechanisms, strategies, and experiences that help adult men break through sexism and feel comfortable in egalitarian relationships with women, breaking through the obsession of dominance and control. Because of this total lack of knowledge, women cannot be effective in bringing about 'planned' change in men. In fact, often they do not know which particular interactions, behaviors, or discussions were the most effective in a continuous process of trial and error.

Some types of conflict confrontations between men and women, especially in some types of relationships vested with considerable affective and esteem feelings (such as marital, love, friendship, and good colleague relationships) may eventually lead to a gradual diminution of interpersonal conflict. As women now increasingly take on work roles such as managers and executives, editors and saleswomen for big publishing companies, cadets in military academies, or team members in competitive sports, new colleagual and friendship roles are emerging that may help ease the man-woman eternal sexually-based conflict (Safilios-Rothschild, 1977a). In some cases, of course, because in the short-range there is considerable transitional conflict, people may settle for little change because they are made to feel anxious by the effect of the ongoing conflict confrontations on the relationship, while others may learn how to manage the necessary conflict involved in a life-long and ever changing dialectic process. A necessary change, therefore, particularly in women's socialization (or resocialization) should involve their ability to manage confrontations without becoming threatened or anxious about generating, intensifying, or perpetuating necessary and focussed conflict. This represents a more radical divergence from the traditional sex role behavior in the case of women than in the case of men, since stereotypically women have had the 'expressive' responsibility of 'smoothing out' conflicts even at the price of continuously yielding, compromising, and sacrificing their autonomy and needs.

VII. CONFRONTATION STRATEGIES FOR MAXIMUM SEX ROLE CHANGE

The application of the conflict theoretical model to the ongoing confrontations between men and women as a result of the women's liberation movement in the United States indicates that these confrontations are presently eroded by several factors: (a) the polarization of some groups in 'hard' antifeminist positions; (b) the official, as well as the substantive, endorsement of the liberation ideology by men mostly with regard to women and less frequently with regard to men; (c) women's fatigue with the continuous confrontations with men at all levels and settings, including the familial and interpersonal levels; and (d) the substitution of structural, formal and open discrimination by more subtle, indirect, and covert discrimination.

Because of these erosive processes, there is danger that the continuation of, and increase in, sex role changes at the individual, the interpersonal and the societal level may slacken, unless new and different types of confrontations can emerge at the societal level. One strategy that can help generate confrontations on a different basis, but which may lead to the formulation of nonsexist social policy and legislation in important areas, is feminist women's active involvement in crucial issues and protest movements other than those specifically related to women. Women should, of course, continue to focus confrontations aimed at passing the necessary legislation to guarantee the equal legal treatment of men and women within the context of all institutions (marriage, work, education and training, law, sports, etc)[3] and continue to protest, fight, and infiltrate the power structure of the established major economic, educational, occupational, political, religious, sport, media, and military institutions. But in addition, women can create new bases for conflict confrontations that may produce and speed up sex role changes and nonsexist legislation and social policies by means of the following strategies:

(1) By joining and assuming leadership positions within the protest movements of different, emerging minority groups which are struggling to gain recognition and express legitimate demands (Dofny, 1976). Disabled women, for example, could play a crucial, powerful role in the emerging 'Crip Lib' movement; American Indian women and older women could do the same.[4] In this way, women would fight for equality and the abolition of stratification systems based on acquired characteristics not as women but as handicapped women or as American

Indian or as old women. Their double or multiple membership of minority groups could help change the focus of confrontations from the 'men-women' one to confrontations regarding the equal validity of different categories of people — *men and women* — with different biological characteristics, strengths, and weaknesses.

Since many women are members of multiple minority groups, this strategy has the advantage that it not only moves the confrontation away from the broad man-woman focus, but also helps liberate society from other 'isms', in addition to sexism. Women can achieve equality and validity as people within the context of a larger humanitarian, societal egalitarian orientation. It must be clarified, however, that this type of strategy can be successful only to the extent that women (disabled, American Indian, and so on) become militant spokespersons, organizers, and activists and obtain power within the minority militant groups. In this way, women may make significant dents in the stratification system, not only as outlined above but also by having power within the minority militant groups. Ultimately, women can officially represent minority groups in institutionalized structural positions, including high elective posts.

(2) By joining and assuming leadership positions in a wide variety of protest movements and groups focussing on issues not specifically linked to sex roles. Such issues include consumer protection, pollution, international trade, the safeguarding of the environment and so on. While it is true that many women have participated in protest movements, especially those concerning the quality of life and the environment, they very seldom have sought or reached high, leadership positions beyond a neighborhood or a small district.

There is a lesson to be learned from the strategy used by Ralph Nader, an unknown consumer, who became a symbol of American consumer needs. Nader was able to become a prominent figure because he entered a controversial area in which initially there were no financial, prestige, or power rewards. He had few competitors for this position. Nader represents an excellent model for women who must find, enter, and dominate comparable domains still accessible and uncompetitive because the rewards are neither obvious, nor certain. These domains and the related rewards must be created by innovative, resourceful women.

VIII. CRISIS AND OPPORTUNITIES FOR ROLE CHANGE

From history we know that societies or groups undergoing serious crises, in which human resources were scarce and desperately needed, recruited women in active, atypical, sex-inappropriate roles. This was more true and intensive, the more serious the crisis and the scarcity of human resources (Lipman-Blumen, 1973). Striking examples are provided by the liberation wars and revolutions of many societies (especially when 'things got tough' and the very survival of the revolution was in danger) such as Algeria, Greece, the underground movements in France and Yugoslavia, the initial anarchist stages of the Russian Revolution, the early persecution stage of Christianity, and so on.

The lesson to be learned from history is that women fare better in terms of access and acceptance in non-established, struggling, marginal or clearly deviant groups, movements, and occupations (Safilios-Rothschild, 1977b). Women, therefore, should capitalize on this tendency. With their newly-gained consciousness, self-confidence, and assertiveness, women should make sure that they are not relegated to secondary, auxilliary positions, particularly as soon as the critical stages of survival are overcome. There is danger (as we know from historical examples), once the movement, group, or occupation moves away from the marginal, 'threatened' status to a more established, 'respectable' position, that women may be entirely thrown out or pushed to the sidelines. At that stage, legislation and policies combating sexism can serve as important tools in aiding women to consolidate their positions, so that their long-term struggles and sacrifices can be rewarded with status, power, and money.

IX. RESEARCH ON THE 'TOKEN WOMAN'

Evidence from recent research suggests that no change takes place as long as women in training groups or high positions remain outstanding exceptions. As long as there is one woman per six to seven men in small groups of medical students or psychiatric residents, she remains marginal, deviant, and threatening to men. She is, therefore, left out and neutralized, while the 'all-male' group remains almost entirely 'intact' in terms of its nature and tone of interaction. The woman often drops out or remains, at best, totally peripheral to the group, unless she is willing to assume a subordinate, 'feminine' position (Wolman and Frank, 1975; Frank, 1975; Frank and Katcher, 1975).

Additional research indicates that hiring one woman professor in an all-male physics or engineering faculty does little to change the 'deviant' status of a woman physicist or engineer. On the contrary, such tokenism tends to underline the individual woman's deviance. In addition, it vests the general image of the woman physicist or engineer with whatever idiosyncratic peculiarities or shortcomings characterize this solo woman (Fox, 1974). Finally, when powerful and prestigious organizations capitulate and hire ONE woman in a high position (sometimes to be in charge of the 'woman's program'), they often deliberately select a 'queen bee' who identifies primarily (if not exclusively) with men, and who will not use her position to engineer social changes.

The implications of these research findings are clear: the image of women in the so-called 'masculine' fields (which usually have higher prestige, pay, and power than the 'feminine' ones) and power positions cannot be normalized until a considerable percentage of women occupy these positions. Otherwise, little progress is possible. In fact, the solo woman may make matters worse by a negative example that deters other women from emulating her and educators and employers from widening the pool of women candidates. The battle over numbers is not an idle one. It is a most meaningful and substantive battle that has still to be won.

X. THE NEED FOR RADICAL CHANGES

When discussing the strategies for abolishing the existing sex stratification system, one must examine the nature of the ultimate social changes desired. Some concern focusses on the extent to which women have the same rights and opportunities as men in all areas of present-day society. Additional concern focusses on the extent to which vital functions traditionally attached to women, such as child care and housework, are granted equal importance with other crucial functions traditionally considered 'masculine' in terms of financial allocations and other rewards.

While these concerns are of great importance, they emphasize primarily equality and redistribution of resources (Wheeler, 1976) and do not raise questions about the nature of the existing structures, institutions, and values which determine the very distribution of resources. We must clarify the fact, that the achievement of equality between men and women does in fact necessitate some radical changes, including redistribution of resources. Other changes include the payment of wages for housework and child care which might help free women from the 'love bondage' that has defined housework and child care as evidence of love, rather than as legitimate work.[5]

Basic questions can and must be raised, however, about the structure of present-day society, the nature of the different institutions, and the prevailing values and assumptions. Even in the absence of any specific ideological criticisms of these structures and values, equality between men and women and the necessary redistribution of resources creates disjointed structures, outdates prevailing values and assumptions, and raises structural problems. The solutions to these problems often require radical structural changes. One example is the radical structural and socio-psychological changes necessary in both occupational and familial institutions to accommodate the spreading dual-work model (Safilios-Rothschild, 1976).

Women, as well as men who increasingly will join their ranks, will have to assess continuously the nature and extent, as well as the consequences, of the confrontation strategies they use to bring about radical sex role changes. Many dynamic forces may continuously tend to diminish and alter the intensity and basis of confrontations as adjustments are made at the societal, the interpersonal and individual levels to tone down and subvert conflict. There will be a continuous tendency for the men in powerful positions to avoid confrontations in areas that either represent radical sex role changes in core power and control domains or in areas that may affect their own personal lives. Special efforts and strategies, therefore, need to be devised so that important areas of sex role change are not circumvented and relevant legislation and social policy can be passed and implemented. Only through a wide range of confrontations can such radical sex role changes be legislated and implemented.

Women theorists and strategists must play a powerful, innovative role in spelling out the theoretical, as well as the practical, aspects of such radical changes. They must be prepared for a continuous process of conflict and negotiation. Therefore, women must learn how to engage successfully in confrontation. They must develop skill in defending their position, disagreeing, negotiating, and reaching satisfactory compromises. Existing and additional research can help identify the most effective methods for developing these skills, as well as the best conditions for their use. Women, as activists in the everyday implementation of 'living' social policy, must not neglect the powerful tool of conflict through confrontation.

NOTES

1. It must be noted, however, that the Swedish society is in general a nonviolent one in which conflict rarely occurs 'in the raw' and, instead, potential conflicts are ventilated within the context of civilized discussions.

2. In fact, Swedish politicians incorporated the ideology of sex role equality in their campaign speeches much as in the US the ideology of freedom and equal opportunity for all has been idealistically incorporated in politicians' platforms and speeches.

3. It could be claimed that the women's liberation movement currently may be at a dangerous standstill at which already there is little collective protest and confrontation, before radical changes have taken place in all types of media and, especially, television. A certain degree of fatigue and indifference already may have set in with potentially deadening effects. Many women are pleased with small 'positive' changes and are willing to settle for them, rather than go on fighting with uncertain results.

4. Actually it is interesting to note that a woman has become one of the leading militant old people in the Grey Panther Movement.

5. Wheeler (1976) makes the important point that many women's occupations are such that it makes it very hard for their occupants to organize and strike because such action would be viewed as cruel, selfish, and irresponsible (e.g., in the case of nurses or teachers) while nobody's humanitarian concerns are touched when male steel workers go on strike! Thus, the 'love and nurturance bondage' of women extends also into their performance as workers.

REFERENCES

BAYER, Alan E., 'Sexist Students in American Colleges: A Descriptive Note,' *Journal of Marriage and the Family*, 37(2) (May, 1975): 391-97.

BERNARD, Jessie, 'Where are We Now? Some Thoughts on the Current Scene,' *Psychology of Women Quarterly*, Vol. 1, No. 1 (1976), 21-37.

COSER, Lewis, *The Functions of Social Conflict* New Yokr: Free Press, 1956.

DOFNY, Jacques 'Personal Communication,' Montreal, Quebec: University of Montreal, 15 December 1976.

FOX, Greer Litton, 'Some Observations and Data on the Availability of Same-Sex Models as a Factor in Undergraduate Career Choice.' Paper presented at the Society for the Study of Social Problems meetings, Montreal, Canada, September 1974.

FRANK, Harold, 'The Socialization of Freshwomen Medical Students.' Paper presented at the American Educational Research Association meetings, Washington, DC, April 1975.

FRANK, Harold and Katcher M.,'Perceptions of Freshwomen Dental and Medical Students by their Freshmen Peers,' in: *Socialization into Professional Roles*, ETS Research Bulletin, Princeton, NJ, December 1975.

KOMAROVSKY, Mirra, *Dilemmas of Masculinity. A Study of College Youth*, New York: W. W. Norton, 1976.

LIPMAN-BLUMEN, Jean, 'Role De-Differentiation as a System Response to Crisis: Occupational and Political Roles of Women,' *Sociological Inquiry*, Vol. 43, no. 2, (April, 1973) pp. 105-29.

LIPMAN-BLUMEN, Jean and Harold J. Leavitt, 'Vicarious and Direct Achievement Patterns in Adulthood,' *The Counseling Psychologist*, Vol. 6, No. 1 (1976).

SAFILIOS-ROTHSCHILD, Constantina, *Women and Social Policy*, Englewood Cliffs, N.J.: Prentice-Hall, 1974.

-- 'Dual Linkages Between the Occupational and Family Systems: A Macrosociological Analysis,' *Signs: Journal of Women in Culture and Society*, Vol. 1 (1976), no. 3, Part 2, pp. 51-60.

-- *Love, Sex and Sex Roles*, Englewood Cliffs, N.J.: Prentice-Hall, Inc., Spectrum Books, 1977a.

-- *Theoretical Model of Sex Discrimination in Education*, Washington, D.C. National Institute of Education, May 1977b.

WHEELER, Susan, 'Libertarian Feminism and Marxism,' *Our Generation*, 11(3) (Summer 1976), 6-12.

WOLMAN, Carol and Hal Frank, 'The Solo Woman in a Professional Peer Group,' *American Journal of Orthopsychiatry*, 45(1) (January 1975): 164-71.

14

POLICY AND WOMEN'S TIME

Jessie Bernard
Pennsylvania State University, USA

When the policy of 'women's two roles' first became legitimized – by the Royal Commission on Population in 1949 in Great Britain and by President Kennedy's establishment of the Commission on the Status of Women in 1961 in the United States – and given research support by Myrdal and Klein in their 1956 book on the subject, it was hailed as freeing women from the old belief that women's only *place was in the home. But the accompanying policy recommendations that went with recognition of women's two roles – provision of services to women to make it possible for them to enter the labor force – were not always fully implemented. Thus, everywhere in industrialized societies, women bear more than their share of the work. They perform their two roles – in the home and in the work place – but men continue to perform only one. The result, well documented by the research, is overload for the working woman. Ms. Bernard's chapter examines four different policy approaches to women's time and argues that there is strong research support for a policy to equalize discretionary time for women. It touches also on the time aspects of homemaking, using pioneer research by Elise Boulding.*

I. EQUALITY OF DISCRETIONARY TIME AS A SOCIAL POLICY ISSUE

Among the several areas in which equality[1] is sought by women – educational opportunities, job opportunities, pay, and the like – it is here suggested that equality of discretionary time is also a legitimate goal of policy. While we are waiting for the elimination of inequalities in the division of labor, an interim move might well be toward the equalization of discretionary time. Not only the kinds of work engaged in by women and men but also the amount of time left over for discretionary use. If both sexes could be guaranteed equal discretionary time, a first step toward equality in other areas might be taken.

A distinction is made between 'discretionary' and 'free' time. Both refer to time not pre-empted by legal or moral or customary role obligations. The concept of discretionary time implies that there are opportunities to use one's own discretion in what to do with it. Among the options available, of course, is the option to add more obligations to one's schedule, thus obliterating the 'free' time altogether. As we shall presently note, this was precisely what happened in the case of some women. As technology and reduced family size made possible more 'free', that is non-pre-empted time for the housewife, many raised their standard of living rather than selecting other uses for the 'free' time. The male 'workaholic' similarly may simply opt to invest his free time in more work. In the case of some of the housewives, such 'free' time became volunteer work with commitments as obligatory as those of any other job. Some found 'free' time boring. Some were led into frivolity, even dissipation. It was this observation no doubt that led the Puritans to the conclusion that the Devil found mischief for idle hands and later critics of the housewife to downgrade her. Still, with all the nuances that have to be taken into account, equality in the availability of discretionary, non-pre-empted time seems a legitimate concern of policy.

Three categories of women will be commented on here: the employed woman; the non-employed woman; and the homemaker. Among these three, the first has less discretionary time than men; the second, has more. The third raises a number of fundamental time-related questions which are only now becoming amenable to scientific scrutiny. It calls for examination of the very concept of 'home' and the time factor involved in the expressive function it is called on to perform. The work of the housewife can be dealt with more easily than that of the homemaker. It can be purchased; homemaking activities are harder to come by.

II. EMPLOYED WOMEN:
INEQUALITY IN DISCRETIONARY TIME

An impressive research corpus documents the inequality between employed men and women in the availability of discretionary time. Although there is a difference of opinion based on ethnographic data with respect to the proportion of total subsistence contributed by women (Aronoff and Crano, 1975; Carroll, 1976; Boulding, 1976),[2] the evidence with respect to sex differences in the allocation of time in present-day societies is unequivocal. It shows beyond doubt that employed women have less non-preempted time at their disposal than men. Long before time-budget studies demonstrated it to us, the folk mind had already observed that although men may have had to work from sun to sun, women's work was never done. Shorter tells us what is was like in Basque country in what he calls 'traditional society.'

> The daily routine of a typical Basque farmwife sets the stage. She rose at 5 a.m., with the sun in summer, in pitch-black darkness in wintertime. Only after she lit the kitchen fire did the men get up...She went to bed towards 11 p.m., some time after her husband (Shorter, 1976: 67).

As a result, predictably

> Men had more disposable time. Male daily routines permitted at least the possibility of bar-sitting several times a week, although not all men did so. In contrast, observers thought farmwives so rushed with their work that virtually no disposable time remained — which is why sociable occasions for women were simultaneously work occasions...(Shorter, 1975: 70).

Time-budget studies from many parts of the world show clearly the deficit employed women suffer in free or discretionary time today. Szalai and his associates have summarized the results of 15 sample surveys carried out in twelve countries (Szalai, 1975).[3] They showed that, overall, employed women had an hour less time daily than employed men on week days and 2.3 hours less on days off (Szalai, 1975, Table 2). Michael Paul Sacks has analyzed time-budget studies of Russian workers over some 50 years. His tables show that women workers enjoy only one third to two thirds as much free time as men. Or, conversely, employed men have a fourth to three-fifths more free time than employed women. Among married men and women workers, men have two to more than three times as much time for self-improvement as do women (Sacks, 1976, Table 5.5). Szalai comments on some of the implications:

> Free time in the sense used here, that is the disposable time remaining after having done all the work and having fulfilled physiological and other personal needs, should not be confused with leisure time...Among the many thousands of employed women...ten percent reported *no* leisure time activities whatsoever on a typical workday, although virtually all employed men reported at least a little...The inordinately small amount of free time at the disposal of employed women...[bears] a heavy responsibility for [employed] women's reduced participation in civic life, in professional training, and education, etc. The implications for women's social advancement and professional career are quite obvious (1975).

Elise Boulding has selected nine samples from the 15 in the work of Szalai and his associates to illustrate the 'remarkable consistence' shown in cross-national studies — France, Poland, the United States, and Soviet Russia. For the average number of minutes per day spent on the mass media (radio, television, movies, reading) and leisure (social conversation, sports, outdoors, entertainment, cultural events, resting), the results for six French cities showed 54 for women, 73 for men; for Torun, Poland, the ratio of 'female' to 'male' free time was 63 to 94; for Pakov, USSR, 61 to 90; and for Jackson, Miss., 64 to 87 (1976).[4]

The greater discretionary time of employed men is achieved by their freedom from work in the household. The traditional division of labor in the household tends to persist almost everywhere that time-budgets have been studied, men spending far less time than women on housework and child care, even on Sundays and days off (Szalai, 1975, Table 2).[5]

Since the trend everywhere seems to be in the direction of increased labor-force participation by married women, the significance of the marked inequality in the availability of discretionary time for employed women seems well worth the attention of policy makers. The corpus of research on working wives and especially of so-called two-career families documents unequivocally the serious overload the women bear (Rapoport and Rapoport, 1971; Holstrom, 1972). Studies of female depression also show that low-income women who must bear both family and work roles tend to be at high risk for depression (Guttentag, 1976). The weight of two roles can be heavy.

In sum, although we all have 24 hours each day, we are not all equal in the amount of time at our disposal. We are not all equally 'time-taxed.' Nor is the spending of our hours equally free.

III. NONEMPLOYED WOMEN: INEQUALITY IN DISCRETIONARY TIME

So far as the time dimension is concerned, the nonemployed housewife is well off. In Szalai's summary of studies in twelve countries, for example, housewives were reported to have an hour more free time daily than employed men and an hour-and-a-half more such time than employed women. True, as Szalai notes, 'as far as housewives are concerned, much of their free time activities and even of their typical leisure activities tend to revolve around the family and the household' — to homemaking activities perhaps — still it is time they choose to use this way.

What, if any, are the policy implications of time inequality which favors the housewife? Should housewives be encouraged to spend more time in the labor force? Is there anything about the situation that calls for policy decisions? Before attempting to deal with policy issues, a glance at the history of the housewife's role is in order.

The history of the housewife as we know her today is not very long. It is only recently with the burgeoning of family history that we are beginning to trace it. True, running a household had been recognized as a worthy occupation from time immemorial. Proverbs in the Old Testament give us a detailed picture of the work women did in running a rather complex household. And we know Xenophon wrote a sort of handbook on the subject for training young wives in their household management duties. We know that there were female castellans or chatelaines in the Middle Ages who ran castles when the men were off to war. And the role of steward who managed the households of large estates was an honorable male occupation until well into the eighteenth century. But for ordinary folk it was not until such amenities as glass for windows, chimneys, and pillows were introduced in the fifteenth century into the hovels, that the role of housewife began to emerge. 'The home became the center of pleasurable activities. To have a wife a home-maker — one that could change into comforts the necessities that man produced — was so much more desirable' (Calhoun, 1917: 38) even in the more humble households.

For many years most of the world's work was centered around the household. We are accustomed to think of the industrial revolution as removing much of this household work out to factories and other work sites. But it might be viewed from the opposite perspective:

> In the old days the home was in the shop or factory. The important things were the looms or the workbench and tools; the home itself was incidental. It was as though everyone lived in a little factory, for when the home was the industrial unit it was as much a small factory as a home (Bernard, 1942, 1973: 518).

Whichever way the change is interpreted, it had wide ramifications. It changed the nature of time.

Pre-modern and modern time

Pre-industrial time differed from industrial time. Pre-industrial time was less rigidly categorical. Household members could move from one kind of activity to another as needed. Leisure or fun could be interspersed throughout the day's tasks. One could lay down the spindle and toss a ball to a child. It might be hard to know where one began and the other ended (Cott, 1977: 58 ff). This freedom contrasted sharply with the time-discipline imposed by work in factories, shops, and other industrial sites:

> Married women's work at home distinguished itself most visibly from men's work, especially as the latter began to depart from the household/farm/ craftshop to separate shops, offices, and factories. The rhythms of adult men's and women's work diverged even as did their places of work...E. P. Thompson has called the dominant characteristic of work in...an agricultural artisanal economy its 'task-orientation,' in contrast to the 'time-discipline' required under industrial capitalism...[In task-oriented patterns] 'social intercourse and labour are intermingled,' Thompson also has pointed out, 'the working day lengthens or contracts according to the task – and there is no great sense of conflict between labour and "passing the time of day". Persons accustomed to time-discipline, however, may consider task-oriented work patterns 'wasteful and lacking in urgency' (Cott, 58-59).

Between 1780 and 1835, a complex of changes transformed a great deal of work from pre-industrial to modern industrial patterns. The changes included: replacement of family production by wage earning;

the replacement of time-discipline and machine regularity for the earlier natural rhythms; and the separation of home and workplace. And, especially, 'the division of "work" from "life"' (Cott: 59). By 1844 Americans had come to organize 'their use of time on an unprecedented scale' (Brown, 1972: 219-20).

The catch in this story is that the time pattern of the housewife's work remained pre-industrial, pre-modern.[6] As such it was both denigrated and idealized:

> Men who had to accept time-discipline and specialized occupations may have begun to observe differences between their own work and that of their wives. Perhaps they focussed on the remaining 'premodern' aspects of women's household work: it was reassuringly comprehensible, because it responded to immediate needs; it represented not strictly 'work' but 'life,' a way of being; and it also looked unsystematized, inefficient, nonurgent...Symbol and remnant of preindustrial work, perhaps the home commanded men's deepest loyalties, but these were loyalties that conflicted with 'modern' forms of employment. To be idealized, yet rejected by men – the object of yearning, and yet of scorn – was the fate of the home-as-workplace. Women's work (indeed women's very character, viewed as essentially conditioned by the home) shared in that simultaneous glorification and devaluation (Cott, 61-62).

The 'glorification' took the form of idealizing the 'homemaker.' The devaluation led to the 'I'm just a housewife' self-denigrating syndrome among women.

The housewife's time and technology

To say that the housewife's work continued to follow the pre-modern pattern does not mean that it was untouched by technology. Or that attempts to rationalize it were not made. Books instructing women in how to perform their household duties efficiently began to appear early in the nineteenth century. Catharine Beecher became the avatar of the cult of domesticity. She designed labor-saving devices and has been credited with the beginnings of household automation (Sklar, 1973: 152). She standardized rules for, among other activities, the timing of meals and hours for rising (Sklar, 1973: 165, 162). Unlike her several predecessors who had written on household management – three out of four of whom were men[7] – she saw the household as performing a fundamental service to nation building.

The successors of Beecher moved increasingly in the direction of 'rationalizing' the housewife's work, applying the same kind of time-discipline patterns to thinking about it as others were applying to industrial work. By the end of the century home economists were beginning to introduce more system and science into household management.[8] Food could be viewed in terms of scientific nutritional standards. Household activities became susceptible to time-and-motion studies similar to those of industrial engineering.[9] Time-budget studies could separate such household activities as food procurement and preparation, cleanliness, care of clothing, and the like. Detergents and other cleaning aids could also be tested objectively.[10] Terms such as 'consumer maintenance' (Bell, 1972) were proposed to indicate the economic work encompassed by the housewife's role (Bernard, 1971) and Kenneth Galbraith came to see the procurement aspects of consumerism as an intrinsic contribution to the economic system (1973).

Despite this taking over of the rationalization concept from modern work patterns, however, there was no way to gloss the fundamental difference. The housewife's work was still pre-modern; it was not under the time-discipline of industrial work. Technology did not have the same impact on the housewife's work as it had on industrial work. Thus the conclusion of studies on the history of the housewife in this country seems to be that although new technologies did, indeed, reduce the amount of labor involved in her work, they did not necessarily reduce the total amount of time invested in it. What were they then doing with their labor-saving appliances? The answer can be sought in Parkinson's law:[11] they were raising the family standard of living (Folsom, 1943; Vanek, 1974; Cowan, 1974). In some cases, over-raising it.[12] Even so, technologies did endow many housewives with a considerable cachet of discretionary time, as indicated in Szalai's summary of time-budget studies.

Toward the end of the nineteenth century, observers of the social scene were beginning to comment on the large amount of time available at least to middle-class housewives. Veblen was analyzing what, among the more affluent, he called the 'vicarious leisure' and 'conspicuous consumption' of women. Ibsen saw them as living in a doll's house. Charlotte Perkins Gilman was labelling the idle wives of even the middle class as, essentially, prostitutes (1898). In a world where women had always been overworked, a new kind of phenomenon was emerging, the housewife with time on her hands.[13] Even when she did, as, indeed, she often did, spend twice as much time on housework as her employed sister (Szalai, 1975). Despite the increasing assaults on the housewife, Myrdal and Klein at midcentury notes — regretfully — how the nineteenth-century ideal of the lady of leisure continued to prevail.

Early seeds of the two-role dilemma

But early in the transition from pre-industrial to industrial work patterns, the housewife was beginning to be caught in a bind. It was during the period between 1780 and 1835 that the market for women's household production became attenuated as commercial markets took over, depriving the housewife of economic rewards for her products. The seeds of the two-role dilemma were thus planted: 'the increasing importance of monetary exchange bore hard on those who needed to replace their former economic contribution of household manufacture with income-producing employment, while meeting their domestic obligations' (Cott, 1977: 45). Many had to enter the labor force. In their role as housewife they still followed the pre-modern time pattern; but in the work force, they were subject to the time-discipline pattern which made no concessions. Although not recognized as something that had come to stay, the women's-two-roles phenomenon was a growing issue in the nineteenth century. On one side was the principle that women's place was in the home, on the other, the fact that many women were shouldering two roles. Nothing could be done about it until the fact had been recognized.

Traditionally, protection of the home was at least officially a basic tenet of policy in the United States. And since 'our home life plainly demands one whole woman at the least to each home, and usually more, it follows that anything which offers to change the position of women threatens to "undermine the home"...and we will have none of it' was the way one feminist expressed the traditional view early in the century (Gilman, 1898: 204). And policy for decades was based on this belief that women's place was indeed in the home. At the turn of the century the so-called Mother's Pensions Laws, which were the prototypes for the aid-to-dependent-children provisions of the Social Security Act of 1935, expressed and sanctioned the belief that the time of women was better spent in the home than in the labor force. The belief gave way only grudgingly and its echo still reverberates in polls, even of college freshmen, presumably an avant garde.[14]

It was not until mid-century that the legitimacy of 'women's two roles' was recognized. In 1949 a British Commission on Population gave official sanction to the outside employment of wives, that is, to the two-role ideology, in a report which stated that 'it would be harmful all round, to the women, the family, and the community, to attempt any restriction of the contribution that women can make to the cultural and economic life of the nation...' A few years later Alva Myrdal and Viola Klein supplied the social-science research undergirding 'women's two roles' (1956). And when John F. Kennedy established his Commission on the Status of Women in 1961 he recognized that it was 'in the national interest to promote the economy, security, and national defense through the most efficient and effective utilization of the skills of all persons' including, of course, women.[15]

But there was a fly in the ointment. Although the British Royal Commission on Population had recommended that 'a deliberate effort...be made to devise adjustments that would render it easier for women to combine motherhood and the care of a home with outside activities'; and although Myrdal and Klein had similarly argued the case for such a policy;[16] and although President Kennedy had charged his Commission on the Status of Women to develop recommendations for 'services which will enable women to continue their role as wives and mothers while making a maximum contribution to the world around them,' the adjustments and recommendations were never adequately implemented. The results of this policy of neglect of the overload of women show up in the time-budget studies noted above. Although 'restrictive laws against women have been generally eliminated and labour-saving devices in the home widely adopted, ... [employed] wives...still work for longer hours than men' (Szalai, 1975). Employed women 'pay' for their two roles in time for study, leisure, and civic participation (Szalai, 1975; Sacks, 1976; Boulding, 1977).

The argument on the side of women's-two-roles challenged the women's-place-is-in-the-home on economic and ethical grounds. Here is the Myrdal-Klein statement:

> Some of our readers may object that our attitude to life, and to women's life in particular, is too utilitarian. Why are you trying, they may ask, to press-gang women into jobs? Why this puritanical attitude towards work as the soul's salvation? Would it not be better to preserve, as long as possible,

the vestiges of a leisured group, or at least a category of people who are able to arrange things in their own time...? To such readers we would like to say two things: Firstly, our modern economy cannot afford, nor can our democratic ideology tolerate, the existence of a large section of the population living by the efforts of others. Whether we like it or not, the leisured class has passed into history...If we want to live in a fairly just, fairly rational society; if we want the living standard of our population to improve and its children be educated; if we want to free old age from the anxieties of dire poverty — we shall all have to contribute according to our best ability.

Secondly, far from preaching a gospel of hard work, we hope for increased leisure so that more people may have a share in the 'good life.'...It is for this reason that we have become convinced that a fairer re-distribution of work and leisure between the sexes is necessary...(1956: 26-27).

This line of argument would have been unthinkable if two centuries of history had not transformed the role of housewife for many women from active producer of goods, not only for the household but also for the market (Cott, 1977), to one primarily of consumer (Galbraith, 1973).

IV POLICY AND FEMALE OVERLOAD

In general, four kinds of policies have been proposed for dealing with women's time.[17] One suggests that we return to household production, going back to pre-modern time. Instead of women leaving the household to enter the time-disciplined industrial work force as Boulding has stated it, we should move 'away from industrial production toward a household-based economy in which men join the women in household production rather than women joining the men in workplaces outside the home...This approach has had exponents continuously since the depression-spawned back-to-the-land movements...' (Boulding, 1977). This is, essentially, a policy of getting rid of women's 'second' role. The chances of general acceptance of such a policy do not seem auspicious.

A second approach lies in the direction of making the housewife role more attractive. Again in Boulding's words, this policy would 'offer stipends to housewives and thus persuade women to "stay in the home"' (1977). This was the policy that led to state Mother's Pension plans early in the century. In addition to stipends, such a policy would seek to give prestige to the traditional housewife role and to persuade women that it would be demeaning to translate the imputed value into a national stipend for housewives' (1977). This approach, Boulding notes, 'has been used for some time in the women's magazines, and is part and parcel of the Feminine Mystique.' Like the first approach, this one seeks to get rid of the 'second' role but in precisely the opposite direction.

A third policy orientation favors the 'second' role. At the most extreme pole, it would get rid of the individual household and hence of housekeeping altogether, and the role designed to engage in it. In the nineteenth century, there were numerous attempts to establish communes and cooperative living arrangements which had such intentions, not necessarily on the grounds of saving women but on the grounds of the wastefulness of separate households, each with its separate fire and garbage pails (Bernard, 1942, 1973: 519). There are some who still favor this policy but it is doubtful it it does much to alleviate the overload of women. Another form of this policy advocates the industrialization of housework, thus relieving women of the housewife role and releasing them for the 'second' role, in the labor force. Ross and Sawhill have seen a trend away from the current household as a distribution-oriented unit in the direction of the household as a mere consumption-oriented unit, with all maintenance and service requirements provided by other specialized agencies, leaving shared consumption alone to the home (1975). Actually, as noted above, such supportive services, though generally recognized as basic if women are to perform two roles, have not been forthcoming. Yet another proposal would discourage the one-role woman with so much time on her hands. One demographer believes the nonemployed wife is a luxury that should be taxed out of existence (Preston, 1972). The nonemployed wife who devotes all her time to the care of her husband is, in fact, a luxury for the man if not for herself. He proposed that there be an earned-income allowance for the earnings of the second earner in a family. 'The effect...would clearly be to reduce the tax burden of two-earner families relative to that of one-earner families.' There is, finally, another form of this policy which seeks to alleviate the strains of the two roles by greater flexibility in the use of time. This form is attracting increasing attention in this country.[18] A broad spectrum of concerned groups are working toward 'Alternative Work Schedules.'[19] The major emphasis, as the name suggests, is on time and work. Newspaper interviews with workers under flexitime systems show a favorable impact on women and their families.[20]

In recent years there has been increasing attention paid not only to the day-by-day or week-by-week allocation of time but also to the allocation of time over longer time units — years, decades, whole life spans. It was in the 1950s that Paul Glick specified the average life course of women in terms of such demographic events as birth, marriage, motherhood, bereavement, and death (1957). Later this demographic approach was supplemented by studies of the work or career aspects of women's lives (Bernard, 1971). The combination of these two approaches raised a number of questions. Why, for example, should educational facilities be beamed only for young people? Why should it not be possible for them to accommodate workers who wish to alternate periods of work with periods of education, or leisure, or whatever? In the case of women, the issue is especially relevant as they begin to think of the allocation of life-time to child-bearing and child-rearing as only one way of using life-time.[21] And they are asking that time allocated to these functions be dealt with no differently from the conscripted soldier's time allocated to military service.

The fourth policy approach is in line with the Myrdal-Klein goal. It seeks increased discretionary time for everyone 'so that more people have a share in the "good life"...a fairer re-distribution of work and leisure between the sexes' (1956: 27).

It should be noted that most of the proposed solutions to the inequality in discretionary time between employed men and women maintain the traditional division of labor and specialization of function between the sexes. Policy is called upon only to make it easier for women to carry their overload. But there is another solution, Boulding notes, which calls for the abolition of not only one of women's two roles but also of all sexual division of labor:

> [Research on time-budget studies] can be used to trigger a movement to abolish domesticity and the gender-based division of labor, releasing women and men equally into the nondomestic work force by providing public facilities for child care and the provision of food; according to this pattern, women and men would share equally in the minor maintenance tasks left in whatever living arrangements they choose... [This] approach, abolishing all gender role concepts and doing away with the household as we now know it, is eloquently advocated by Ann Oakley...(Boulding, 1977).

This extreme solution does not seem to be on the cards at least for the near future. But some relief in the form of more sharing of the domestic role does seem to be within at least hailing distance. Boulding states the case for transcending the extreme gender-based division of labor. She suggests that women may be voting for such an eventuality with their bodies.

> ...there are signals that the worst aspects of the work-load imbalance [between the sexes] are beginning to diminish, though there should be no illusions about the speed with which this will happen...The most likely development over the next few decades is a combination of more maintenance services provided, if not by the state, at least at the neighborhood level, in answer to energy-shortage problems, and an equalization of the remaining work load in the home as women develop the skills to restate the man-woman contract and establish a new reciprocity. A substantial withdrawal of free grants by women from man-woman relationships is certainly taking place in the United States today, as evidenced by the data on withdrawal from marriage and withdrawal from child-bearing by women in this decade (Boulding, 1977).

It is interesting to note in passing that whereas the existence of a large segment of the population 'with time on their hands' was being challenged in the United States, less affluent countries were hoping to be able to achieve it. Thus in 1971 I pointed out that the Soviet press was already expressing a longing for more 'femininity' in women (Bernard, 1971, 82). And Michael Paul Sacks notes that the middle-class woman who could afford to stay home and provide services for her family was a product of affluence which the USSR was only now becoming able to afford. There such a use of women's time was being viewed as highly desirable.

As the time required for housekeeping per se has declined, the emphasis on home-making has come to be emphasized. Housekeeping might not take much time, but serving family members in other ways might. (The sales pitch for labor-saving appliances, for example, came to emphasize that they released more time for child care [Cowan, 1974]. The question then arises, how much time does homemaking — as distinguished from housekeeping or household management — take? How does it affect women's discretionary time? Is it open to expansion or contraction? What should our policy be with respect to it?

V HOMEMAKING TIME

One reason it is so difficult to arrive at suitable policies with respect to women's time is that the housewife's role is so intimately related to the homemaking role, whether the housewife is employed or nonemployed. Whether, that is, the housewife role is her only role or one of two roles. The role of housewife is, indeed, intimately related to the role of homemaker. But they are, nevertheless, distinguishable, and functionally quite different. Housekeeping is, in the Parsons-Bales schema, an instrumental function; homemaking, an expressive one. What constitutes the homemaker's job is not always discernible.

Homemaking is more subtle than housekeeping.[22] It is harder to get a handle on, either conceptually or in measurement terms. Housekeeping is part of the division of labor; paid or not, it is measurable work. Homemaking, on the other hand, cannot be viewed as work; if one has to 'work at' the expressive function it may almost cease to exist. Homemaking is thus conceptually more amorphous than housekeeping. Indeed, the very concept of 'home' is itself amorphous.[23] It is related to but not identical with 'house.' It has to be made. It is not a mechanical product. It did not take Polly Adler to make clear that a house is not a home (1953). Nor Edgar Guest's 'it takes a heap of livin' in a house t' make it home.' Nor the extensive genre of songs proclaiming love of home, the pain of being home-sick, the uniqueness of home, 'be it ever so humble.' It is also related to, but not identical with, the nuclear family. Even unrelated individuals may create a 'home' for themselves. A 'good' family does not necessarily have a good home. The social worker looking for a good foster home will look for more than a 'good' family. The concept 'home' has a strong affective component. The expressive role — usually assigned to women — is intimately involved. The performance of the homemaker role need not involve work in the conventional sense — except when performed by a psychiatrist! — but it does involve time. The homemaker in the expressive role gives generously of her time just listening, reassuring, supporting. Such 'stroking' may often come out of her 'free' time. It does not show up on ordinary time-budget studies but it is no less a charge on her time, and energies. But because she cannot point to many of the human services she has been performing as 'work', she is often at a loss to justify herself.

We cited above the work of Nancy Cott which traced the dichotomizing of housekeeping and homemaking as the housewife's work remained pre-modern but still rooted in vital tasks. As housewife the woman was looked down upon; but as symbol of the old premodern style of living, she was idealized. Women's sphere came to be apotheosized. Ruskin had romanticized the home as the Queen's Garden.[24] Women were the heart of the home. It was their place, their sphere. Not only their place, but their *only* place. It took *all* their time.

One of the major functions of the home as conceptualized early in the nineteenth century was to serve as the restorative antidote to the harsh, competitive outside industrial world then emerging. It dispensed a healing balm that made the struggles tolerable. And, critics have not been slow to point out, it thus shored up the brutalizing industrial system (Bernard, 1974). The home supported the status quo by making it bearable. It soothed the anger of the worker. Cott quotes from an 'Essay on Marriage' published in 1834 which documented the shock-absorbing function of the home.

> ...when his [the worker's] proud heart would resent the language of petty tyrants, 'dressed in a little brief authority,' from whom he receives the scanty remuneration for his daily labors, the thought that she [the homemaker] perhaps may suffer thereby, will calm the tumult of his passions, and bid him struggle on, and find his reward in her sweet tones, and soothing kindness, and the bliss of home is thereby made more apparent (1834: 371).

'The literature of domesticity thus enlisted women in their domestic roles to absorb, palliate, and even to redeem the strain of social and economic transformation...' (Cott: 70).[25]

Exactly what the activities or behaviors are that constitute homemaking as distinguished from housekeeping has not been researched in detail.[26] The dividing line is not clear. The television advertising jingle — 'nothing says lovin' like something from the oven' — illustrates the close relationship between housekeeping and homemaking, as indeed, do other housekeeping 'frills' that show special attention to individual members of the household, such, for example, as preparing their favorite dishes, baking birthday cakes, building shelves for someone's room, and the like.

With such indeterminate boundaries between homemaking and simple housekeeping tasks, is there any time-related aspect to the former? 'What have you been *doing* all day?' the tired husband asks when his wife claims she is worn out upon his return from a hard day at the office. She has been reading to the children, telling them stories, chauffeuring them, pacifying them, amusing them, waiting for deliveries...in brief, performing what Boulding calls human services for all the members of the family. She has been giving time to others that she might have longed to use for herself.

More difficult to conceptualize but basic to the time element is the fact that homemaking may consist not necessarily of *doing* things but of simply being present.[27] 'If married women's occupations no longer predictably consisted of domestic productive activities such as spinning, soap making, or brewing,' Nancy Cott points out, 'nevertheless they were identified with *being at home...*' (1977: 44). An empty house was not a home, either then or thereafter. Someone had to *be* there when any household member returned. The mere presence of someone — usually a woman — was essential. Cott also notes that 'home' became identified with 'retirement' (p. 65). 'In an intriguing development of language usage in the early nineteenth century, "home" became synonymous with "retirement" or "retreat" from the world at large' (p. 57).

It is not generally realized how dependent the world is on the 'stroking' or emotional support supplied by women. We know how damaging withholding it may be for children. But men, deprived of it, suffer also. Erikson, for example, has commented on the need of men for the female presence in the home: 'in some discussions men otherwise not of a sentimental bent insist so strenuously that children need their mothers at home that one cannot help wondering if it is not the husband himself who is the needy person...' (1965: 236).[28] Just being available for 'stroking' takes time, time many women might well long to use elsewhere.

In view of the need for her presence, is discretionary time even possible for a homemaker? Does the fact that her presence is part of homemaking render *all* her time discretionary or *none* of it? Within the home all her time is discretionary in the sense of the discretion permitted to her in the scheduling of her activities. But in another sense, none of it is. For discretionary time is limited by the fact that women are held responsible for other members of the family 24 hours a day, whether or not they are performing any specific kind of work. They are always on call. Thus even when they do have 'time off', they have to be available in an emergency. Their free time is thus always contingent.

We are greatly indebted to Elise Boulding who is doing pioneer work in helping to clarify our thinking on these questions and bring it up to date. She is thinking freshly about homemaking in terms of specific kinds of activities and behaviors — that is, 'tasks' — and using an entirely different set of categories from those dealing with housekeeping activities per se. She conceptualizes them as nurturant, creative, reflective, and recreational rather than in terms of tasks, thus giving a novel and insightful perspective on time usage. She invokes quality of life rather than the more male-oriented concept of efficiency as a criterion in evaluating activities.

> ...a thoughtful critique of how time is used in the family and what services above and beyond maintenance housekeeping are produced, may in the end provide the basis for a more thorough-going examination of the quality of life in American society at large, and result in more adequate quality-of-life indicators to tell us how productive our society [really] is (1977).

Boulding asked her informants — members of ten families who kept week-long time-use records for her — for 'things you do for your family' and 'things you do for yourself' but coding complexities precluded detailed analysis in terms of this variable. All of the ten families she studied were unique in demographic composition so that controlled comparisons are limited. They are, nevertheless, worthy of at least some attention.[29]

Elise Boulding would be the first to decry over-interpretation of the findings of her study, which is as important for its pioneering nature as for its specific results. The interpretation here presented does not necessarily reflect her own.

With respect to the question of equality in discretionary time we cannot speak directly. But if we infer that the activities which I have classified as self-oriented — fun conversation, physical sports, reflection,[30] social life, and spectator activities — come out of free or discretionary time, a rough clue is available. Under this assumption it appears that overall, as in the case of housekeeping, the nonemployed housewives (B/8, B/9) had more such time than the employed women (A/7, C/3), as they did also in the conventional time-budget studies. That is, half (50.1 percent) of the time accounted for in the diaries by the nonemployed mothers was spent in self-oriented activities, not quite half (45.2 percent) in the case of the employed women. Conversely, of course, the nonemployed mothers spent less time, proportionately, than the employed mothers in other-oriented — homemaking — activities (40.0 versus 47.1 percent).

It is fairly easy to think of policies to help women with housekeeping functions or, for that matter, to discourage women from the housewife role by way of taxes or encouraging them by way of subsidies.

But is there any way for policy to influence the homemaking role, for giving employed married women more time for fun, for social life, for television watching, for music-listening? Or have we reached the limits of policy when we reduce the time needed for housekeeping? Perhaps policy could reach the homemaker by way of fathers, by making more home-time available for them?

Fathering-time

More flexible use of time as referred to above would undoubtedly affect not only female but also male time. In the home as well as at work. Flexibility by making more options available could presumably make available more time for father-child relationships. We know children would welcome such a policy; they cherish fathering time. One study of children aged seven to eleven, for example, showed half of them wanting more time with their fathers (Temple University, 1977), while a third wanted more time with mothers. Flexible work time would clear more hours for family trips to the zoo and for other such family activities.

Making more shared hours available for families does not, however, guarantee that fathers would necessarily be willing to take advantage of the opportunity for more home-shared activities. Neither government policy[31] nor plant, agency, store, or other institutional policy can coerce men and women to share more time with one another or with children. Boulding's data support other studies dealing with the small amount of time spent by fathers with their children. Even among men who are willing to share this work the relatively greater pay which men can command for time in the labor force as compared with women makes the substitution of time in the home for time in the labor force an expensive luxury.

Since Boulding's diarists 'were instructed only to write down what they did when they were at home, or what they did away from home that clearly related to household welfare', it is not feasible to compare nonemployed with employed household members. If we compare the three employed fathers selected for discussion here (A7, B2, B9) with the two employed mothers (A7, C3) it appears that the employed mothers invested more accounted-for time than the employed fathers in homemaking activities (an average of 320 minutes per week versus an average of only 195). The employed mothers spent slightly less accounted-for time on self-oriented than on other-oriented activities (45.2, 47.1 percent); the reverse ratios prevailed among the fathers (61.3 percent on self-oriented, 33.6 percent on other-oriented).[32]

Elise Boulding suggests that 'there are signals that the worst aspects of the work-load imbalance [between men and women] are beginning to diminish' but she warns us against 'illusions about the speed with which this will happen.' Rosabeth Kanter in her studies of communal households found that the men were more willing to share the housekeeping work than they were to share the homemaking services, especially with respect to children.

Defections from the home

Boulding's study supported others dealing with the small amount of time spent by fathers with their children. The defection of men from the home is an old problem, not only in the form of desertion, but also in the form of psychological withdrawal from the family. Kenneth Keniston in the 1960s was writing about fathers who devoted time to their work at the expense of their families (Keniston, 1960). Urie Bronfenbrenner has reported that one study of father-infant contact showed an average of only 38 seconds a day of intimate person-to-person interaction (Bronfenbrenner, 1977). Leslie Fiedler has seen the male fleeing from women as a major theme of the American novel (Fiedler, 1962). And although the most impassioned defenders of the home may be men, many are not themselves dedicated to its maintenance as measured by time invested in it. Lionel Tiger, in fact, sees it as uncongenial to the male bond and even advocates provision in all communities for all-male retreats from the home. '...some facilities for men, particularly in suburban areas, could provide a useful counterbalance for men to the heavy emotional and temporal demands of nuclear family life' (Tiger, 1970: 263).[33] One newspaper columnist bemoaned the end of the television football season with the lament that 'this is no time for a man in middle passage to start having to spend Sunday afternoon talking to his wife and children' (Vanocur, 1977). Nor was the situation too different in the Soviet Union: 'asked by a researcher last year to draw their fathers, nearly all of a group of 83 school children placed the male parent on a chair staring at television or on a sofa with a newspaper' (Osnos, 1976). Tom Braden, another American columnist and father of eight, dreams of a time when he reverses roles with his sons and is in a position to exploit them as they now exploit him (Braden, 1977). Art Buchwald notes also the enormous amount of services children demand of their parents (Buchwald, 1977). And at the request of a reader, Ann Landers republishes the anti-parental musings of a good father on a bad day (Landers, 1977). It is by no means clear how policy could reach this reluctance on the part of men to share homemaking services, that is, the expressive role. If many men do not want even to spend time at home with their families, we can hardly look to them to share with their wives the expressive demands of homemaking. Even when, as noted above, more than half of the children reported in a study wished they could have more time with their fathers. When or if the allocation of male time to homemaking becomes a concern of policy makers, it will probably not be justified on the basis of equalizing discretionary time between the sexes. It will probably be couched in terms of the dysfunctional effects of the defection of fathers from their homemaking responsibilities.

The defection of women from the home is more recent and as yet far less extensive. Boulding, as quoted above on the withdrawal 'of free grants by women from man-woman relationships,' believes this female withdrawal solution too costly in homemaking or human services such as those she is studying. 'A renegotiation of the contract [between the sexes] is a more likely outcome once the cost of withdrawal is felt keenly enough...' (Boulding, 1977). What form such a renegotiated contract between the sexes may take is not as yet discernible. Women have not themselves arrived at a consensus as yet. Nor is it clear how policy can be used, once women have worked through their goals. But at least the equalization of discretionary time — however achieved — is a legitimate goal to seek. There is no longer a justification for putting two roles on women and only one on men. There is no longer a justification for 'time-taxing' women so much more heavily than men.

ADDENDUM: TWO MOTHERS

Not in any sense as a basis for generalizing for all employed and non-employed mothers but simply as a basis for raising questions that more extensive research could supply at least partial answers to, two families were selected for more intensive study. These two families had approximately the same structure, that is, both had two children — aged five and six in one case, seven and nine in the other. This age difference, though small, makes a difference in time allocation since in the second family both children were of school age whereas in the first, only one child was. But in the present context another difference was more relevant, namely, in the first (children five and six) the mother was employed outside the home, in the second (children seven and nine), she was not. Since the families differed in at least these two important variables — age of children and the employment status of the mother — it is difficult to assign much interpretive significance to differences in time allocation. Are, for example, the differences reported due to the age of the children so that the allocation of time in the first family can be expected in a year or two to conform to the allocation of time in the second family at the present time? Or is the difference due to the employment status of the first mother so that no change can be anticipated even when the five year old child enters school? The second of these alternatives is assumed here, namely that it is the employment status of the mother rather than the ages of the children which is relevant. Two components of homemaking were selected for comparison, one dealing with children — mothering — and one dealing with adults — supplying emotional support.

Mothering, or time devoted to children. By the end of the eighteenth century 'more than ever before in New England history, the care of children appeared to be mothers' sole work and the work of mothers alone' (Cott, 1977: 46). In the nineteenth century new technologies were 'sold' to women on the grounds that they increased the amount of time available for children (Cowan, 1974). And, *pari passu*, they also strengthened the demands children could make on their time. And Boulding's data show that child-related activities do constitute a large component in the time budget of women with small children.

There has been considerable discussion of the kind of mothering supplied by employed mothers and one of the conclusions frequently arrived at is that it is the quality rather than the quantity of time devoted to the child that counts and that the employed mother tends to make a special effort to compensate in quality for what is lacking in quantity. It is striking, therefore, to note in Table 1 how much more accounted-for time the employed mother, as compared with the non-employed mother — 94 minutes a week versus 42 — devoted to her children (routine child care, story-telling, reading, instruction, helping). And if artistic and handicraft activities are included — as Boulding thinks they probably should be — 112 to 67. (Some of this difference might be balanced by the far greater amount of time devoted to school related activities not included in Table 1 by the nonemployed mothers, 30 minutes versus 3).

The second important time-use for the homemaker has to do with *supplying emotional support.* Since emotional support in the Boulding schema came under the heading of conversation, it probably referred to support of husbands or older sons and daughters. Again, the amount of time devoted to this activity was considerable. And again, the employed woman spent more of her accounted-for time than the nonemployed woman in this activity (42 versus 29 minutes). The nonemployed woman, in brief, had more time for fun, for social life, and for television watching and/or music listening than the employed mother.

There are two ways of viewing the reverse of this. One might say, for example, that the employed mother 'sacrificed' time for fun, social life, television watching and/or music listening on behalf of her homemaking activities. If, however, one takes the time allocation of the nonemployed mother as a standard, then the differences between her and the employed mother may be viewed as a 'discretionary' use of the employed mother's time. She needn't have devoted so much time to mothering activities and emotional support; she may have preferred to do so. Under this assumption, the differences in discretionary time available to the two women diminishes greatly (241 versus 266 minutes). The same cannot be said, however, for the employed mother who was a single parent with two children, five and eight. Even applying the nonemployed mother's time allocation as a standard, the amount of discretionary time was only 197 minutes. She paid for her mothering activities in severely restricted time for fun and reflection. It is understandable that she is especially vulnerable to depression (Guttentag, 1976).

Once again it is emphasized that the comparison here of two mothers does not constitute a basis for generalization and it is not so intended. But it does invite validation or invalidation by standard social science research techniques. Only then could the results serve either activists or policy-makers seeking ways to equalize discretionary time.

NOTES

1. The concept of 'equality' is, strictly speaking, a mathematical one and rests on the assumption of interchangeable units, an assumption rarely valid with human phenomena. For although units of time are objectively and by definition equal, it is a cliché that time is not experientially equal or even equivalent for two individuals. Or, for that matter, the same individual. Some minutes seem to last for hours. Some hours seem to be over in a moment. Some time is fast; some, slow. It flies or it drags. Boring work seems longer than challenging work. And even if units of time are experienced as equal, the results may be quite unequal. Nor is everyone's time of equal value. The value of one's time is often measured in terms of the amount of time one can be called on to wait – for an appointment, for an application, for a reply – or to stand in line. Nor is time today the same as time in the past; technology has greatly changed it. We are told, for example, that the average American spends about an hour a day in travel and that this figure has not changed materially in 200 years (Department of Transportation, 1977). But 200 years ago the traveller had covered a relatively short distance in that hour; today, perhaps fifty miles.

2. The work of Aronoff and Crano was oriented toward testing the Parsons-Bales theory of functional specialization in the family, women being allotted the expressive and men the instrumental. Carroll was controverting the interpretation of the Aronoff-Crano data. Boulding was tracing the history of the familial constraints on women's work roles.

3. Included were adults of 18 to 65 years of age in non-agricultural occupations in: Belgium, Bulgaria, Czechoslovakia, France, Federal Republic of Germany, German Democratic Republic, Hungary, Peru, Poland, United States, Soviet Russia, and Yugoslavia.

4. For 'leisure' alone, as specified in the text, women in Jackson, Miss., averaged four more minutes a day than men. This was the one exception among the samples.

5. The willingness of men to devote time to work in the household seems to vary by class. Thus a study by Judit M. Sas in Hungary found that the proportion of families conforming to the traditional division of labor varied from 25 and 28 percent among professional or executive and upper white-collar workers respectively to 52 and 57 percent among semiskilled and unskilled workers respectively (Szalai, 1976: Table 6). And although the employment status of the wife makes some difference in male contributions of time to household tasks, including child care, the difference is surprisingly slight. A London study, for example, found only 9 percent of husbands of even women employed full-time offering help (Young and Willmott, cited in Szalai, 1976: Table 7). Among nonemployed women, even less.

6. In an analysis of housekeeping I once pointed out the lack of synchrony between the work in the home and work in the outside world (Bernard, 1942: 197, 529-37).

7. The forerunners: Theodore Dwight, *The Father's Book*, 1834; Herman Humphrey, *Domestic Education*, 1840; William Alcott, *Young Housekeeper*,

1838; and Lydia Maria Child, *The American Frugal Housewife,* 1832 (Sklar, 1973: 153).

8. The management component may be somewhat harder to measure quantitatively, but it can be recognized, as when the husband or child can easily prepare a meal if all the ingredients for all the dishes have been planned, shopped for, and placed on the kitchen table.

9. In 1898 the forerunner of the American Home Economics Association appeared as the first of ten so-called Lake Placid Conferences, to become the home economists' professional association in 1908. The concepts of the then-current Taylor system of industrial time-and-motion studies was adopted by many home economists and a rich corpus of studies designed to save the housewife's time and energy resulted. In 1967, the Agricultural Research Service of the US Department of Agriculture published an annotated list of references on Research on Time Spent in Homemaking (62-15, Sept. 1967) containing 29 studies since 1944 alone.

10. Not until about 1920 did the homemaking aspects of the discipline re-emerge, blooming later in departments of child development and family life.

11. Szalai notes that the time women devote to housework tallies with the time men spend at work: 'One of the most curious cross-national findings with regard to housewives' use of time is the fact that they tend to "stretch" their housework more or less in proportion to their husbands' working hours. In social groups and strata where employed men work longer hours, there is a distinct tendency for housewives to put more hours into their own daily housework' (1975).

12. As it became increasingly possible to distinguish the housewife from the homemaking function, treatises and popular books tended to overplay the housewife's work until, finally, housekeeping seemed to overshadow homemaking and women had to be warned against overdoing the housekeeping aspect of their role for the sake of their families. Thus, for example, one book, published in 1870, had this to say about the housekeeper's work: '... As to your "work," a great deal of it is unnecessary. John and the children would be much better without pies, cakes, and doughnuts...Nobody will thank you for turning yourself into a machine. When you drop in your tracks, they will just shovel the earth over you, and get Jerusha Ann somebody to step into your shoes. They won't cry a bit. You never stopped to say a word to them except "get out of my way." To be sure, you were working hard for them all the while, but that won't be remembered. . . If there is more work than you can consistently do, don't do it. . .' (Fern, 1870: 39-40). Compare contemporary advice based on research by Vanek: 'Leave work undone. Unkempt houses may be preferable to losing sleep: (*Comment,* Spring 1976: 5).

13. By the end of the third quarter of the twentieth century, almost three-fifths (57.0 percent of married women, husband present, with no children under 18 were not in the labor force (President's Manpower Report, 1975, Table B-4). Some, of course, were beyond labor-force participation years. But even among married women aged 35 to 54, living with their husbands and with no children under 18, half were not in the labor force. A considerable number were doubtless engaged in voluntary activities and community service programs. A considerable

number were back in school (Astin et al, 1976). Some were probably suffering from boredom. An indeterminate number were women of leisure with time for tennis, golf, theater, shopping, bridge, what-have-you. Some were seeking to become 'Total Women' or achieve 'Fascinating Womanhood.' Some were fighting the equal rights amendment which they feared would deprive them of their privileged position.

14. Not until 1972 did less than half of incoming male college students — presumably among the avant garde — accept the idea that women's activities were best restricted to the home. And a study in Illinois in 1976 showed a large proportion still adhering to the 'women's-place-is-in-the-home' ideology (Huber et al., 1977).

15. At the same time that official recognition of 'women's two roles' was being granted there was a re-emergence of emphasis on homemaking. A period of 'togetherness' began during which critics rebuked women for their 'return to the cave' (Mead, 1962). In the arguments of the opponents of the equal rights amendment there was a strong emphasis on the importance of the homemaking function and a demand for the right to choose it as a life work.

16. Among the specific solutions proposed by Myrdal and Klein, several were time-related: part-time work, extended maternity leave, reduced working hours, increasing open hours by shops (Chapter 9).

17. Not included in the discussion here is the innovative idea proposed by Senator Walter Mondale. He argued that just as legislation establishing federally supported programs be required to supply an environmental impact statement — making clear the probable and predictable results, good or bad, for the environment — of such programs, so also should a family-impact statement be required of all bills establishing federal programs. Granted that it is all but impossible to trace the ramifications of even the simplest programs — let alone judge whether the effects are desirable or at least the best possible trade-off among equivocal effects — the idea is a good one.

18. The concept of 'flexitime' (Flextime, flexible work hours, floating hours) is believed to have had its origin in Germany in 1967 as a method of dealing with traffic jams at a suburban factory and to have been first used in the United States in the early 1970s. An estimated 16,400 government workers in a dozen areas of Washington were working under flexitime rules in 1976 and the numbers were expected to increase under the Carter administration which had promised to support legislation introduced in 1975 to encourage hesitant agencies to introduce it (Causey, 1976). The Women's Equity Action League publishes a directory of agencies that help women find flexitime and part-time jobs, of employers that have implemented flexitime, of the possibilities of flexitime in the professions and a summary of legislation and regulations dealing with the subject, as well as a bibliography on the subject.

19. In March, 1977, there was a National Conference on Alternative Work Schedules in Chicago in which industry leaders, union leaders, representatives of older persons, education leaders, government officials, academic leaders, administrators, and representatives of women's groups participated. Among the financial sponsors were the American Telephone and Telegraph Company, the

Communications Workers of America, General Mills Foundation, Sears Roebuck. And among the cooperating agencies were the Federal Energy Administration and the US Department of Transportation.

20. One woman, for example, worked a four-day week and devoted the other day to babysitting for her daughter (Hadley, 1976). From the point of view of families, the four-day week, if or when it calls for ten-hour work days, as it often does, is not favorable to family life, allotting less time to family more than half of the week. Some of the cases reported were almost story-book in nature. The story of Valda Johnson, 24, mother of two, for example: '...Valda Johnson is both a mother and the head of household, and a flexible work schedule helps her round out both roles...She says that because of the flexible work schedule, and the freedom it offers her to deal with her life, she is a changed woman. "I was a nervous wreck where I worked before, always worrying about being cranky, with being late in the morning, rushing the children. I'd get them up at 4.40 — can you believe that? — so we could be out of there by 5.30. Then it was rush to the sitter's, and then I raced to make the bus so I could be at work before 8. Once I got to work I always had headaches, upset stomachs, there were mistakes in my work and I took a lot of coffee breaks to try to calm down. Even the memory makes her tense. Her words speed up as she tells the tale, then slow down as she relates what life is like for her now that she has a flexible work schedule' (Meyers, 1976).

21. In the last few years I have found myself being consulted by young women in their early or middle thirties facing fundamental life-time allocation decisions. They were deeply involved in their careers or in work for their degrees but felt that if they were ever to have children there was a now-or-never urgency about it. They felt the biological calendar staring them in the face. The years immediately ahead of them were, they felt, crucial to their careers. They were reluctant to withdraw even temporarily, feeling that they would lose so much impetus as to constitute a permanent handicap. This aspect of the allocation of life-time has concerned women for some time. How can child-bearing be incorporated into the total life-span of women. A number of patterns may be sketched.(See, for example, Bernard, 1971, 179ff).

22. Szalai does not accept the distinction between housekeeping and homemaking. According to him, 'homemaker' is a typical American euphemism intended to lend some professional dignity to women's work in the household (1975, Table 4).

23. It has been said that the English language is almost unique in its definition of 'home.' Of the nine definitions in the Oxford dictionary, the oldest (1460) is: 'the place of one's dwelling and nurturing, with its associations' and the next oldest (1548), 'a place, region, or state to which one properly belongs, in which one's affections centre, or where one finds rest, refuge, or satisfaction.' The French translation of 'home' emphasizes the house or dwelling aspect — à la maison, foyer (hearth); the Spanish and Italian use the word for house, 'casa.' In German, 'die Heimat' refers to dwelling place. Szalai, as noted above, did not catch the nuance in the American term 'homemaker.' The history of the concept of 'homemaking' has not, so far as I know, been worked out in detail, although the separation of public and private life has been analyzed historically (Laslett, 1973).

24. 'This is the true nature of home — it is the place of Peace; the shelter, not only from all injury, but from all terror, doubt, and division. In so far as it is not this, it is not home; so far as the anxieties of the outer life penetrate into it, and the inconsistently-minded, unknown, unloved, or hostile society of the outer world is allowed by either husband or wife to cross the threshold, it ceases to be home; it is then only a part of that outer world which you have roofed over, and lighted fire in. But so far as it is a sacred place, a vestal temple, a temple of the hearth... so far it vindicates the name, and fulfills the praise, of home', in Ruskin's words.

25. This concept of the home illustrated the theory of the alienated worker propounded by Marx who in 1844 wrote that 'the worker...feels at ease only outside work, and during work he is outside himself. He is at home when he is not working and when he is working he is not at home'. Recently there has been a re-emphasis on the homemaking function. Again, as in the nineteenth century, the home is touted as a refuge, as a sanctuary, as a place where warmth, understanding, and support perform their healing service away from the hurly-burly of the outside world (Farson, 1969).

26. This does not mean that there is not a great deal of folk or popular recognition of them. A stock situation in theater is one in which a woman transforms a male household into a home by lovingly adding curtains or drapes or ornaments or flowers or what-have-you to soften the general decor and make it more 'homey.' On a more subtle level there is the situation in which a housekeeper performs dozens of loving acts toward all members of the household and transforms their common dwelling place into a home.

27. Such 'being present' may be viewed as a form of 'waiting,' one of Boulding's human services.

28. Erikson identified the home with female 'inner space' (1965: 239). He did not apply the psychoanalytic concept of a return to the womb, but he did see 'the home's protective milieu' as an extension of inner space.

29. Boulding was especially interested in showing the contribution children make to the home. Omitted here are the four families with children over eight and the one family with ages of children not specified.

30. Virginia Woolf, in her essay *A Room of One's Own*, bracketed money and the equivalent of time: 'a woman must have money and a room of her own if she is to write fiction' (p. 4) or, she might well have added, to create in any area or even just to do anything well. She explained the symbolism: '...five hundred a year stands for the power to contemplate,...a lock on the door means the power to think for oneself' (p. 110).

31. Sally Quinn reports on attempts by the Cuban Government to legislate equality in household responsibilities: 'The Family Code...gives the force of law to the division of household labor. Men and women must share the housework and child care equally or one spouse can take the other to court...It is still not totally accepted. Many...have a sense of humor about it and whenever the subject is brought up it elicits smiles, snickers, guffaws... [Wilma Espin, head of the Cuban women's movement understands that] "the law is one thing and the way people live is another. We can't say that in each home there is equality. Tradition is very strong. But we have advanced..."' (Quinn, 1977).

32. Almost as a parenthetical afterthought, Tiger suggests that 'it may be equally desirable to provide similar facilities for females' (1970: 263). Actually,

the provision of refuges for women has become a major concern in some cities. It is of at least tangential interest to note that E. O. Wilson in his tracing of the human biogram found male involvement in parental care to be a general social trait, 'strong' in man and shared with many, though not all, primates (1975: 552). This does not seem to tally with Tiger's interpretations.

33. Almost without exception this defection of women from the homemaking role, in one way or another, is included as contributing to 'the calamitous decline of the American family' (Bronfenbrenner, 1977) as well as to the problems of 'Soviet Families in Trouble' (Osnos, 1976). But increasingly attention is also being paid to paternal disaffection. Not only in the form of desertion — an ancient situation — but also in the form of neglect among even middle-class men. Already in the 1960s Kenneth Keniston was reporting the dysfunctional results of the lack of fathering which the 'alienated youth' he was studying displayed (Keniston, 1965). Men were investing their time in their careers at the expense of time with their families. Some of the consequences of such time deprivation on the family are discussed in Bernard, 1975, Chapter 11).

REFERENCES

ADLER, Polly, *A House is not a Home*, New York: Rinehart, 1963.
ASTIN, Helen S. (ed.), Some Action of Her Own, The Adult Woman and Higher Education, Lexington, Mass.: D. C. Heath & Co., 1976.
ARONOFF, Joel and William D. Crano, 'A Re-Examination of the Cross-Cultural Principles of Task Segregation and Sex Role Differentiation in the Family,' *American Sociological Review,* 1975, 40, 12-20.
BELL, Carolyn Shaw, 'Employment Policy for a Public Service Economy: Implications for Women', *Social Policy*, Sept./Oct. 1972.
BERNARD, Jessie, *American Family Behavior*. New York: Harper, 1942: Russell & Russell, 1973.
— — *Women and the Public Interest.* Chicago: Aldine, 1971.
— — *The Future of Motherhood.* New York: Penguin, 1974.
— — *The Future of Marriage.* New York: Bantam, 1973.
— — *Women, Wives, Mothers.* Chicago: Aldine, 1975.
BOULDING, Elise, *The Underside of History.* Boulder, Colo.: Westview Press, 1976.
— — 'Familial Constraints on Women's Work Roles,' *Signs*, 1976, 1, 95-118.
— — 'The Human Services Component of Nonmarket Productivity in TenColorado Households.' Paper prepared for the Roundtable on the Economy and Sociology of the Family: The Productive Function of Non-Market Goods and Services in the Family. Royaumont, France, 1977.

BRADEN, Tom, 'Ghost of Christmas (Vacation) Future,' *Washington Post*, 1 January 1977.
BRONFENBRENNER, Urie, 'The Calamitous Decline of the American Family,' *Washington Post*, 2 January 1977.
BROWN, Richard D., 'Modernization and the Modern Personality in Early America, 1600-1865,' *Journal Interdisciplinary History*, 1972, 2, 219-20.
BUCHWALD, Art, 'Home Sweet Hotel,' *Washington Post*, 6 January 1977.
CALHOUN, Arthur Wallace, *A Social History of the American Family from Colonial Times to the Present*, Cleveland, Ohio: The Arthur H. Clark Co., 1917-1919.
CARROLL, Michael, 'On Aronoff and Crano's Re-examination of the Cross-cultural Principles of Task Segregation and Sex Role Differentiation in the Nuclear Family,' *American Sociological Review*, 1976, 41, 1075-1072.
CAUSEY, Mike, 'More Flexitime Due,' *Washington Post*, 21 December 1976.
COLEMAN, William T., Jr., *National Transportation Trends & Choices to the Year 2000*. Washington: Department of Transportation, 1977.
COTT, Nancy *The Bonds of Womanhood*. New Haven: Yale University Press, 1977.
COWAN, Ruth Schwartz, 'A Case Study of Technological and Social Change: The Washing Machine and the Working Wife,' In Mary Bartman and Lois W. Banner, eds., *Clio's Consciousness Raised*. New York: Harper Torchbook, 1974, 245-53.
CRANE, William D., see Joel Aronoff.
DEPARTMENT OF TRANSPORTATION, see William T. Coleman, Jr.
DEPARTMENT OF AGRICULTURE, *Research on Time Spent in Homemaking*. Washington: Government Printing Office, Sept., 1967 (ARS 62-15).
ERIKSON, Erik, 'Concluding Remarks,' in Jacquelyn A. Mattfeld and Carol G. Van Aken, eds., *Women and the Scientific Professions*. Cambridge, Mass.' MIT Press, 1965.
FARSON, Richard E., 'Behavioral Science Predicts and Projects,' in Elinor P. Zaki, ed., *The Future of the Family*. New York: Family Service Association of America, 1969.
FIEDLER, Leslie, *Love and Death in the American Novel*. New York: Meridian Press, 1962.
FOLSOM, Joseph K., *The Family and Democratic Society*. New York: Wiley, 1943.
GALBRAITH, John Kenneth, 'Economics of the American Housewife,' *Atlantic Monthly*, 1973, 232, 78-83.
GILMAN, Charlotte Perkins, *Women and Economics*. New York: Harper Torchbooks, 1966.
GLICK, Paul C., *American Families*. New York: Wiley, 1957.
GUTTENTAG, Marcia et al, *Sex Differences in the Utilization of Publicly Supported Health Facilities: The Puzzle of Depression* (Draft Report, 1976).
HADLEY, James, 'Workers Test Flexibility in Montgomery,' *Washington Post*, 3 August 1976.
HOLMSTROM, Linda Llytle, *The Two-Career Family*. Cambridge, Mass.: Schenkman, 1972.
HUBER, Joan, Cynthia Rexroat, and Glenna Spitze, *ERA in Illinois: A Crucible*

of Opinion on Women's Status. Urbana-Champaign: University of Illinois, 1977.
KENISTON, Kenneth, *The Uncommitted.* New York: Delta, 1965.
KLEIN, Viola, see Alva Myrdal.
LANDERS, Ann, *Washington Post,* 3 January 1977.
LASLETT, Barbara, 'The Family as a Public and Private Institution,' *Journal Marriage and the Family,* 1973, 35, 430ff.
MEAD, Margaret, 'Introduction,' in Beverly Benner Cassara, ed., *American Women: The Changing Image.* Boston: Beacon Press, 1962.
MEYERS, Robert, 'Workers Banish Time Clock,' *Washington Post,* 3 August 1976.
MYRDAL, Alva and Viola Klein, *Women's Two Roles.* London: Routledge and Kegan Paul, 1956, 1962.
OSNOS, Peter, 'Soviet Families in Trouble,' *Washington Post,* 3 October 1976.
PRESTON, Samuel H., 'Female Employment Policy and Fertility'. Research paper prepared for *Population and the American Future,* Report of the Commission on Population Growth and the American Future. New York: New American Library, 1972.
QUINN, Sally, 'Wilma Espin: First Lady of the Cuban Revolution,' *Washington Post,* 26 March 1977.
RAPOPORT, Rhona and Robert Rapoport, *Dual-Career Families.* London: Penguin, 1971.
RAPOPORT, Robert, see Rhona Rapoport.
REXROAT, Cynthia, see Joan Huber.
ROSS, Heather L. and Isabel V. Sawhill, *Time of Transition, the Growth of Families Headed by Women,* Washington, D.C.: The Urban Institute, 1975.
RUSKIN, John, *Of Queens' Gardens.* Section 68 in *Works,* Vol. 8, p. 122.
SACKS, Michael Paul, *Women's Work in Soviet Russia.* New York: Preager, 1976.
SHORTER, Edward, *The Making of the Modern Family.* New York: Basic Books, 1975.
SKLAR, Katharine Kish, *Catharine Beecher, A Study in American Domesticity.* New Haven, Conn.: Yale University Press, 1973.
SPITZE, Glenna, see Joan Huber.
SZALAI, Alexander, 'Women's Time: Women in the Light of Contemporary Time-Budget Research,' in Guy Streatfeild, ed., *Women and the Future.* Guildford, Surrey: IFC Science and Technology Press, 1975; Binghamton, NY: Center for Integration Studies, 1975.
TEMPLE UNIVERSITY INSTITUTE FOR SURVEY RESEARCH, study of children's fears reported in *Washington Post,* 2 March, 1977.
TIGER, Lionel, *Men in Groups.* New York: Vintage Books, 1970.
VANEK, Joanne, 'Time Spent in Housework,' *Scientific American,* 1974, 231, 116-20.
VANOCUR, Sander, 'Post-Playoff Depression,' *Washington Post,* 12 January 1977.
WILSON, E. O., *Sociobiology, The New Synthesis.* Cambridge, Mass.: Belknap-Harvard, 1975.
WOOLF, Virginia, *A Room of One's Own.* New York: A Harbinger Book, 1957.

IV
UNRESOLVED ISSUES:
A Look to the Future

15

EDUCATIONAL POLICY FOR WOMEN:
A Look Ahead

Virginia Y. Trotter
University of Georgia, USA

Ms. Trotter turns her attention to a major policy concern in all parts of the world, among developing as well as among other countries, namely the education of women. The specific nature of the issues may vary from one part of the world to another, but the general problems are the same: the costs to individuals, economies, and societies of the educational discrimination against women. Ms. Trotter shows that such discrimination is unfair not only to women but to men as well, a fact recognized in the IWY Conference in Mexico. She emphasizes also that improvement in the education of women cannot wait until arbitrary levels of development have been reached; education is itself an intrinsic sine qua non of development. Despite the results of innovations reported in the chapter on Sweden, Ms. Trotter believes the Swedish experience as well as the burgeoning research on women's studies elsewhere can help other countries in their efforts to improve the education of women. The experience of the United States – both successful and unsuccessful – can also be helpful elsewhere.

We see the gap between what is and what might be as the only source of power in the world (John Plott).

Women today, richly diverse in their cultural heritage, bear in common the problem of sex discrimination in education. Such discrimination is

---

With the help of Candice B. Conn, U.S. Dept. of Health, Education, and Welfare.

an affront to basic social justice in countries presuming to be democratic and it is also a matter of economic importance in all countries feeling the effects of limited economies and shrinking resources. The results of such discrimination are far-reaching. On a personal level, it tends to impede the development of individual potential and to limit the participation of women in decisions that affect their lives. On an economic level, it brings financial hardship to families. In addition, it wastes talents that would undoubtedly contribute to the growth and prosperity of each nation.

This problem is, of course, greatest in countries that assign limited roles to women and erect barriers against their movement into areas of activity traditionally reserved for men. But even in the United States, a country expressly dedicated to the goal of equal educational opportunity, disturbing inequities persist. These inequities inevitably affect the economic status of women. Research data reveal that, despite massive changes in the lives of contemporary women, despite their increased forays into non-traditional careers, the average female worker earns forty percent less than the average male worker. The salary of the average female college graduate is roughly equivalent to that of the average male high-school drop-out.[1] Instead of furnishing the means to overcome such patterns of sex discrimination, however, the American educational system reinforces them by treating boys and girls in terms of separate expectations and values.

Since a woman's career choice and commitment are related strongly to her level of educational achievement, this trend in educational attitudes must be halted at all its levels, from primary through graduate school. Research studies over the past decade have revealed a complex combination of factors that reinforce discriminatory notions and prevent the full participation of women in higher education. Not the least of these are female self-conceptions influenced by the entrenched beliefs of society regarding women. Such studies are of immense help both to policymakers and to the increasingly cooperative body of women (and men) who seek to resolve problems of discrimination on a worldwide scale. This chapter will discuss, first of all, the encouraging international efforts to overcome sexism in education and suggest improvements in educational policy based upon successful policies in countries around the world. It will then examine specific patterns of sex discrimination in American education, as indicated by recent research, and suggest means of resolving the critical issues facing women in education.

Before discussing the problems of sexism in an international context, two preliminary realizations are essential. First, dissimilarities among women, created by race, class, family, and religion, are even greater than those between men and women. Women throughout the world have different goals and, often within the same country, differing priorities. While sex discrimination in education is a common problem, it manifests itself in a variety of ways and calls for a variety of solutions. There is no single universal solution. Second, women and men must work together for the development of all human resources and an extension of all human rights. Sex discrimination in education means discrimination against men as well as women, boys as well as girls. It is neither fair nor useful to approach educational policymaking without the awareness that men too have suffered educationally and psychologically from discrimination based on sex-role stereotyping.

MEXICO CITY CONFERENCE

The United Nations' International Women's Year Conference, held in Mexico City in 1975, applied these realizations on an international scale. Members addressed themselves to the urgent challenge voiced by Helvi Sipila, Secretary General of IWY and United Nations Assistant Secretary General for Social Development and Humanitarian Affairs:

> As a group, women remain the most underdeveloped of all human resources; due to lack of opportunities given to them to play an equal role with men in all areas of life, there is the traditional stereotyping of male and female roles. The time is ripe...to extend to women their full human rights. We have the ideas, the energy, and the enthusiasm to do this. All we need now...is the support of all those concerned – which means everyone.

For the first time at any United Nations conference, a world plan of action was adopted unanimously. Relating to the status of women in society, the plan incorporates a resolution on education and training, initiated by the United States and sponsored by a group of twenty-two countries (developed, underdeveloped, and third-world powers) which I had the privilege of chairing. The resolution includes concern for both sexes. It calls for the expansion of education to close gaps between socio-economic groups, to lessen the increasing threat to human welfare, and to eliminate prejudice against women. It affirms that advantages of education should by right be equally available to all people, regardless of sex.

Other strong messages to educational policymakers emerged from the Mexico City conference. Perhaps the strongest was the necessity of starting efforts toward international educational equality *now*, especially in underdeveloped countries. It would be a mistake to impose arbitrary standards of development to be achieved before provisions were made for educational opportunity and access. Since the difficulties of women are related intrinsically to the overriding problems of poverty and population growth in these countries, equal opportunity for quality education can be a positive, decisive factor as developing nations struggle to achieve their potential. Initial efforts, therefore, are crucial to the final result. In addition, Mexico City emphasized the harm of engaging in negative comparisons of educational conditions in various countries. Perceptions must be attuned to the uniqueness of some problems, as well as the commonality of others. Lessons regarding the best and worst of a country's educational system must be shared in an international framework.

For example, both Sweden and Finland have liberal leave systems, which allow women and men to move easily in and out of the work forces as necessary to share family responsibilities. It is mandated by Swedish law that fathers must relinquish part of their work time for care of their children. In 1968, the Swedish Government made a report to the United Nations stating that 'no rapid advancement of women in employment and the professions, politics, trade union activity, etc. is possible as long as men fail to assume that share of the work of the home which falls to them as husbands and fathers.'[2] Since family responsibilities and their impact on women's educational and occupational achievement are critical issues in any program of equal educational opportunity, such a social policy as Sweden's therefore becomes a paradigm for other countries.

In addition, the Scandinavian countries have systems of adult education that are exemplary in many ways. Between thirty and fifty percent of the adult population of these countries takes part in continuing education.[3] As more and more women over the world turn from homemaking to careers, continuing education for women emerges as the wave of the future. It gives them the opportunity to explore new interests and develop their capacities in any number of areas. This movement toward life-long learning is clearly worldwide, and women are a major part of it. In the past few years it has been a significant topic of various international forums, such as the Nineteenth UNESCO General Conference in Nairobi, Kenya, and the United States-Japan Conference on Cultural and Educational Interchange in Tokyo, Japan. Education ministers from all over the world have endorsed international cooperation to promote life-long learning opportunities for both sexes.

LESSONS FROM AROUND THE WORLD

As the world becomes increasingly interdependent, what we learn from Scandinavia, the member nations of UNESCO, and other nations enables us to cope better with our own domestic educational and social problems. Research projects and curricula in women's studies outside the United States continue to enlarge our perspective. A division of the University of Paris has recently begun a three-year trial equivalent of the American PhD in Women's Studies. The Women's Research and Resources Centre opened in London in January 1975. A 'Research Unit on Women's Studies' operates at the Shreemati Nathibai Damodar Thackersey (SNDT) Women's University in Bombay. The History Department of the University of Göteborg has a research project on 'Women in Industrial Society.' These are only a few examples of the international activity spurred in part by International Women's Year. They signal increased dialogue among world citizens working for equal educational opportunity for women and men.

In all efforts, we share an essential goal: to accept the notion of change and expand our perceptions of ourselves as women into an international, world context. We must internationalize our feelings of self and society through the mutual exchange of knowledge and through the development of intercultural understanding. In this sense, we cannot view the initiatives of any one country toward equal educational opportunity for women in a national context alone. Rather, knowledge of how to improve educational options for women should be the 'property' of all nations, for the benefit of all.

In this spirit of cooperation, we can discuss the status of women in United States education, with the hope that information about our program and policies will be of use to all concerned in the worldwide effort to eradicate sex discrimination in education.

RECENT US LEGISLATION

Most significant to this discussion is Title IX of the Education Amendments of 1972, the federal law which states:

> No person in the United States shall, on the basis of sex, be excluded from participation in, be denied the benefits of, or be subject to discrimination under any educational program or activity receiving federal financial assistance.

The object of the law is to eliminate sex discrimination in elementary, secondary, and post-secondary education. The need for Title IX, both in terms of the equity it seeks to guarantee and the institutional practices its regulations either prohibit or require to establish such equity, is clear: women, both as students and employees, have suffered many forms of discrimination in education. Our educational system reinforces discriminatory patterns which affect a child's development of cognitive powers, social skills, and self-concept. Textbooks and instructional materials, segregation by sex in course offerings, teaching and counseling approaches, and teachers themselves (most of whom at the pre-school and elementary school levels are female) convey to the child a structure of reality in which females yield to male achievement and domination. A woman, thus socially and educationally handicapped, is educated for inequality, for a life-long distortion of her potential as a human being.

This pattern continues as a woman enters post-secondary education and the world of work, where the combination of institutional and personal discrimination on the basis of sex becomes intractable for most women. Women faculty members are under represented in relation to the proportion of female advanced-degree holders, and many are underpaid in relation to their male colleagues. Women are also given short shrift in the curriculum of higher education. Policies and procedures are often geared to perpetuate differential treatment of men and women and thus limit the educational opportunities of women.

Title IX prohibits discrimination on the basis of sex (with certain exceptions) in the admission and treatment of students and in employment practices for educational programs and activities which receive federal financial assistance. Though Title IX is the most comprehensive legislation concerning women in education, several other legal mandates are important to the improvement of women's educational and occupational status:

(1) Title IV of the Civil Rights Act of 1964 authorizes the US Office of Education to provide technical assistance and training services to school districts to counteract problems of sex discrimination.

(2) The Women's Educational Equity Act of 1964 provides grant funds to women and minorities in areas where they have been excluded, under-represented, or included only in stereotyped roles.

(3) Title VII of the Civil Rights Act of 1964 (as amended in 1972) provides that it is an unlawful employment practice to refuse to hire or to discharge any individual, or otherwise discriminate against any individual in terms of conditions of employment because of sex (or race, color, religion, or national origin).

(4) Executive Order 11375 (an amendment to Executive Order 11246, which defined the affirmative action policy) prohibits sex discrimination. Compliance is overseen by the Office for Civil Rights in the Department of Health, Education, and Welfare.

(5) The Equal Pay Act, amended to include executive, administrative, and professional employees in colleges and universities, requires employers to pay women wages equal to those of men when they perform jobs requiring equal skill, effort, and responsibility. It is enforced by the Wage-Hour Division of the Department of Labor.

The activity of the Federal Government to end sex discrimination is becoming increasingly positive. It will take, however, a strong commitment not only from the government but also from the states, local school districts, parents, and students to effect real change. None of these legislative provisions can become truly effective until educators and citizens embrace the spirit as well as the letter of the law.

RESEARCH SHEDS LIGHT ON CRITICAL AREAS

Educational policymakers must be aware of the many critical areas where assertive efforts are needed to combat sex bias: employment and curriculum in elementary and secondary education; employment and curriculum in post-secondary education; teacher education; curriculum in pre-school education; enforcement of and compliance with Title IX and Title IV; women in administrative positions at all levels of education; special educational and occupational needs of minority women; the media, including educational television and radio. The difficulty in American education has been not with compiling lists of crucial issues; these issues are apparent to any interested, aware observer. Rather, the problem has been with reaching a consensus on where and how to focus collective energies to resolve these issues. Clearly, educational and social policy must be directed toward affording women the opportunity to pursue quality education and meaningful, productive work. Since research is the indispensable tool of policymakers, it is useful to describe recent developments (rendered clear by statistical data) in the educational and occupational status of American women. These developments may suggest several major areas for directing our energies.

First, the number of women attending post-secondary institutions, both at the undergraduate and graduate levels, is growing. According to preliminary data from the National Center for Educational Statistics (NCES/HEW), 5.2 million women enrolled in institutions of higher learning in the fall of 1976; ten years earlier, half that number had enrolled. More women are receiving Master's degrees, and twice as many are now earning doctorates. Still, women and non-white men attend college in fewer numbers than white men. Attendance also remains too tied to socio-economic status. Statistics reveal that 66 percent of men with high ability and low socio-economic status go to college, whereas only 50 percent of women in the same category enroll. The difference is in large part attributable to stereotypical views of low-income parents who hold separate expectations for their sons and daughters. In addition, Helen S. Astin finds that women more often complete degrees within four years than do men. However, 'the rate of degree completion over time is often higher among men,' since fewer women persist in extended undergraduate degree programs.[4]

Second, statistics indicate that more women are seeking degrees in occupational fields traditionally chosen by men. Astin reports 'a large decrease in the choice of teaching and an increase in the choice of business careers, engineering, law, medicine, and farming and forestry.'[5] This trend will undoubtedly influence hiring practices in government, business, industry, and academia. Though practical considerations of job availability are a large factor in this change, intrinsic motives are clearly very important. Various studies have identified the personality traits that distinguish career-oriented women and have investigated the relation between career aspirations and female self-esteem. Not enough is yet known, however, about the ways in which young girls formulate their conceptions of self and of work. Nor has there been adequate research on the various influences throughout childhood and adolescence that engender aptitudes for certain careers. Recognizing the need to open new options to women, the Education Division of HEW has conducted programs to assist elementary and secondary school counselors in recognizing and changing sex-biased guidance practices. Early discouragement from certain careers too often affects educational choices later.

Third, part-time and continuing education are on the rise. Larger numbers of women beyond the 18-22 age group now attend colleges and universities. Their experience and competencies, however, are too often ignored by traditional credit procedures; their educational programs are too often unconnected to home or work situations; their sense of self-worth is too often undermined by the insensitivity of other students and faculty. They frequently cannot receive useful pre-enrollment counseling to help identify the best possible learning environments for their particular needs. Also, problems of child care commonly hamper their efforts both to enter or graduate from college and to join the workforce. Only one out of ten children of working mothers is accommodated by day-care, nursery, or group facilities.

The work of the Education Division of HEW (and especially that of the Fund for the Improvement of Post-secondary Education) has demonstrated that collegiate institutions must focus on ways to accommodate older women within new or existing programs. Independent counseling services to women, which are 'brokers' for women's needs, have proved highly successful. Departing from the traditional, college-based adult counseling and educational programs, these counseling services do not rely on support from a particular institution; instead, they are free to match student needs with the most appropriate form of post-secondary education or, in some cases, to suggest alternatives to formal education. Face-to-face para-professional counseling is an important part of this service, because the 'personal' touch proves extremely effective in working with older women. With the Fund's support, the Educational Testing Service of Princeton, New Jersey, has also developed methods to help older women who have extensive experience in volunteer and domestic work demonstrate their competencies as a basis for obtaining academic credit. Without this approach, older women typically have spent time learning once again skills or concepts they have already acquired. In the area of financial assistance, the Department of Education (HEW) has substantially increased its Basic Opportunity Grants, many of which go to part-time students. Its Guaranteed Student Loan Program has facilitated access to education for a growing number of middle-income students.

Fourth, despite encouraging numbers of women in non-traditional fields, the distribution of women by occupational classification has changed very little. Differences persist in the jobs preferred and entered by men and women. Astin finds that female job activities 'in rank order are teaching, service to patients, clerical-secretarial, and administrative-managerial...Present statistics suggest that college-educated women still have limited occupational options and receive lower salaries than men.'[6] According to Mary Allen Jolley, 'women workers are equally qualified with men workers in educational attainment' and constitute a significant part of the work force, yet they continue to earn less because of their concentration in low-paying occupations.[7] The majority of women in the labor force are still in jobs considered 'female' — jobs which have traditionally carried low professional status. The reasons, of course, are complex. Research can document the extent of this built-in occupational sex bias and can also suggest reasons for the low career aspirations of many women.

Fifth, despite minimal gains, women generally remain in the lowest ranks of university faculty positions and receive salaries at every academic rank and institutional level lower than those of men. In 1974, women comprised 24 percent of all faculty on 9/10-month contracts. Their number in relation to men declined at the professor, associate professor, and instructor levels and rose at the levels of assistant professor, lecturer, and 'undesignated.' In fact, there were fewer female associate and full professors in 1976 than in 1974. Sixty percent of the men were tenured; 42 percent of the women. Significant differences exist among fields: 10 percent of faculties in anthropology were female, for example, but only 1.5 percent of those in physics.

NEEDED BEHAVIORAL RESEARCH

If women are to achieve their full potential, more will have to be learned about their behavioral patterns. The research agenda of the Education Division of HEW and, more particularly, that of the National Institute of Education (the Division's research arm) reflect this need. There are plans to study why women can enter leadership roles in non-traditional settings and yet encounter difficulty in assuming the same responsibility in traditional settings. Research by Lipman-Blumen and Leavitt into the various motivations and methods (vicarious vs. direct) for achievement will help explain why many women choose less aggressive ways to achieve.[8] Studies will investigate the reasons that women do not accede to leadership positions in education, even though they constitute the majority in that profession. This knowledge may increase our understanding of the same phenomenon in other fields as well. There are plans to determine the effect of the women's movement on the educational achievement of women, on their behavioral patterns after marriage, and on the ways they transform aspirations into achievement. Research must be conducted also on the special educational and occupational problems of minority women.

Finally, the development of non-sexist career education is critical to a thorough research agenda. The Institute has already enjoyed success with a television series on career awareness, as well as with a project on sex-fair guidance and counseling practices. In addition to these planned research projects, much more research on women in education is imperative. Problems of sex discrimination must be approached from the most informed stance possible.

NEEDED EDUCATIONAL POLICY

Educational policymakers have a significant role in creating within our society the state of mind that will foster the growth of equal opportunity for women in education. Most important, they can conceive and articulate goals that will change people's attitudes and bring them together in the pursuit of non-sexist education for all. Although much of the talk and activity over the past several years has concentrated on legal mandates, the future prospects for eliminating sex discrimination in education depend largely on social policy. Merely barring sex discrimination through legislation cannot, as a practical matter, be expected to result in rapid alteration of the deeply-rooted policies and practices of educational institutions. In addition, merely outlawing present and future discrimination cannot, by itself, eliminate the consequences of generations-long discrimination against women and girls in our schools. Educational policymakers have an enormous job to do.

Therefore, individual policymakers, as well as institutions and governments, must act. Their prompt attention may be one of the single most important factors in the effectiveness of efforts toward eradicating discrimination. Policy-makers must act singly and as a united group — internationally — in what surely is one of the great challenges of our time. As policymakers, they have an unparalleled opportunity to effect change. Their roles in giving both women and men the chance to pursue education and careers uniquely suitable to their needs make this opportunity a responsibility.

Women throughout the world must continue the valuable dialogue they have begun. They must listen with a sense of confidence that the short-comings revealed by shared experiences are capable of remedy. If women are not prepared to believe in and to understand their own lives better than do men, they will not have the courage and stamina to change them. As individuals and as world citizens, their time is now.

NOTES

1. US Department of Labor, Women's Bureau, *1975 Handbook on Women Workers*, Bulletin 297. Washington, DC: Government Printing Office, 1975, p. 134.

2. Sawhill, Isabel V., 'Perspectives on Women and Work in America,' *Work and the Quality of Life*. Boston: MIT Press, 1974, p. 22.

3. Ibid.

4. Astin, Helen, 'Women and Work,' pp. 5-6. To be published as 'Patterns of Women's Occupations' in Julia Sherman and Florence Denmark, eds. *Psychology of Women: Future Dimensions of Research*. New York: Psychological Dimensions, in press.

5. Ibid., p. 7.

6. Ibid., p. 15.

7. Jolley, Mary Allen, 'Federal Legislation: Impact on Women's Careers.' Paper presented at the Tenth Anniversary Celebration of the Establishment of the Center for Vocational Education, Ohio State University, Columbus, 18 March, 1975.

8. Lipman-Blumen, Jean and Harold J. Leavitt, 'Vicarious and Direct Achievement Patterns in Adulthood,' *The Counseling Psychologist*, Vol. 6, No. 1, 1976.

16

THE RIGHTS OF WOMEN AND THE ROLE OF INTERNATIONAL LAW

Cecilia Marchand
Diplomatic Academy of Peru, Peru

Most of the papers in this volume have dealt with the situation of women in specific countries and with the policy problems that have to be solved in order to improve the condition of women. The resources available, we have seen, vary from the situation in Sweden, where there seems to be consensus with respect to the goal of equality and an educated female cadre to implement it, to the situation in underdeveloped and developing countries where such consensus may not yet have been achieved and there is only a small number of educated women to work toward achieving it.

Ms. Marchand makes the interesting and novel proposal that women everywhere use a new lever now becoming available to them, namely the growing corpus of international law dealing with human rights. She illustrates her point by reference to the Universal Declaration of Human Rights, the European Declaration of Human Rights, the American Convention on Human Rights and the Pact of San José de Costa Rica, which includes provision for an Interamerican Court which would function as a tribunal where women could bring violations of their human rights to the attention of the world. She also recommends that the several United Nations documents – Declaration on Social Progress and Development (1969), the International Development Strategy (1970), the World Plan of Action (1975), and the Charter of Economic Rights and Duties of States (1974) – be invoked as well.

Ms. Marchand examines both the strengths and weaknesses of international law as an instrument for advancing the status of women. Although its critics complain that international law is simply a set of symbolic gestures, devoid of significant meaning and ignored by both developing and developed countries,

Marchand argues that international law nonetheless has a genuine function. She sees its importance in raising the conscience of nations with regard to women's rights and in offering the possibility of international tribunals before which women may appear to seek redress.

Women's rights should be seen as an integral part of the human rights advocated in recent United States foreign policy. Marchand suggests that in addition to respect for political rights of their citizens, all countries must consider the individual's right to well-being, the right to equality before the law, and to non-discrimination. She emphasizes the connection between these human rights of women and the 'legal and procedural rights of citizens vis-à-vis the State.'

Marchand points to the role of research in explaining the destructive effects of women's economic marginality on national development. Research is proposed as a method for highlighting the necessity of bringing women into the realm of economic forces of production. Marchand's analysis suggests the unique role of international law in ensuring and protecting women's economic, social and political rights.

The issue of women's rights throughout the world affects the lives and well-being not only of the international female population, but of the male population as well, and should be of great concern to both. In a changing world like ours, both men and women should occupy an equal place in the general fields of economic production, cultural creativity, and social organization. This need is present in all societies, developed and underdeveloped, but is highlighted in underdeveloped nations because of the barriers that discrimination against women places in the road to economic and social progress.

Social and economic progress is closely linked with advances made by women. Economic dependence of women, with its consequent unemployment, is a phenomenon of developing societies perpetuated in the political arena, which has been, and still is, a masculine bastion in almost all societies. Consequently, the male decision-makers design social policies that discriminate against women. Without an active and complete integration of women into the total fabric of society, underdeveloped societies will not be able to overcome the condition which impedes their development. Even when the law provides for equal treatment for both sexes, in most underdeveloped societies practice does not conform to this prescription. (Unfortunately this is also a fact in capitalist as well as socialist developed societies, including the post-industrial ones.) This discrepancy between law and practice is translated, in developing societies in particular, through the dependence and marginality of women.

All nations must make a strong international effort to rescue women from marginality and neglect. One of the best tools available in the struggle toward this goal of equality is international law, for international action is the best means by which to highlight the human rights of women as well as men, and thus to exercise pressure on the governments of the different nations.

The detractors of international law say its norms are only symbolic, and that it is utopian to believe that international enforcement is possible. This is true to a certain extent. Under the aegis of international law, vast territories throughout the world have been invaded, nations have been humiliated, and disgraceful conditions have been imposed upon weak peoples. We must also acknowledge that the enforcement power of international law has been so weak that in the arena of international interests it has not prevented the minority of industrialized nations from increasing their wealth while the majority of nations, the developing societies, have become poorer each day. In spite of these failures, however, only international law can guarantee the universal respect of human rights and attain progress in the field of women's human rights by means of the legal ties maintained by nations through their bilateral and multilateral diplomatic relations within international organizations. The agreements maintained among these nations reach the level of international law only after they have been approved and ratified following the procedure established by international rules. This implies that all these agreements have to be respected and enforced in the same way as the internal law of the participating nations.

It is often stated that international conferences, including Mexico's International Women's Year Conference, and the international agreements, declarations and resolutions adopted in them are merely empty, symbolic gestures. There is no denying that many of these documents, whether called resolutions or declarations, are in general symbolic gestures; but it is also true that they tend to create conscience with regard to the condition of women. Unfortunately, the impact of these international agreements is greater in post-industrial developed societies than in developing societies, because the presence of a large proportion of well-educated and politically-active women exerts a significant influence over the decision-makers in their design of social policies. In most developing societies, a large majority of women have not yet acquired a clear consciousness of their role in society. This is attributable to their lack of education, a problem closely linked to the underdevelopment of these societies. Women, less educated than men, if educated at all, are second-class citizens. Unfortunately, therefore, the decision-makers of the Third World attach very little or no importance to the problems of women. Other emergent problems of development attract their attention and have priority. Unless women play an important, aggressive role in politics, their condition in society will not improve. This is a reality in all societies.

International law has so far had practically no impact in shaping social policies designed to improve the condition of women in developing nations. Social structures in these societies have placed women on a secondary level; the women have been traditionally passive, if not indifferent, witnesses to historical developments. Civic and cultural activities have been denied to them. For centuries, women have played a subordinate role. As a result, there has been a notable difference in the social significance of men and women. All these factors have been detrimental to the condition of women as human beings and as members of society, and the nations which perpetuate these conditions have suffered a great decrease in their potential for creativity and work.

Skepticism towards international law regarding these fragmented societies need not lead us to conclude that it is ineffective. International law, through its conferences and agreements, can and does exercise moral pressure and helps to create a conscience with regard to women's rights in developed societies and, to a lesser degree, in the Third World nations. At the same time, international law generates a moral obligation on the part of governments which participate in agreements dealing with women's rights.

In the crusade for human rights, advocated in international agreements such as the Universal Declaration of Human Rights, the European Declaration of Human Rights, the American Convention on Human Rights, and other international agreements, the issue of women's rights should be permanently under consideration. The respect of human rights inevitably requires the observance of norms that recognize and guarantee the political rights of women and their security in the economic, social, and cultural spheres.

Under President Jimmy Carter's inspiration, the United States' current foreign policy is suffused with a spiritual value that was absent until today: the universal respect of human rights. Nevertheless, this policy is circumscribed to the individual rights of people as they relate to the abuse of power by the state. In other words, emphasis has been placed upon the absolute respect of states regarding the political rights of its citizens: the right to life, dignity, liberty and unrestrained expression of ideas. However, other rights advocated by international and regional agreements, such as the right to the well-being of individuals — that is to say, the socio-economic and cultural norms inherent to the progress of human beings — the right to equality in the eyes of the law, and non-discrimination, have not been emphasized.

The belief that human rights are limited to protection of citizens as they relate to the state by legal and procedural rules is narrow and incomplete. It is most important to emphasize with the same doctrinal stress that the concept of human rights is not limited, but multidimensional; that the rights of equality and non-discrimination which protect women are closely related to the legal and procedural rights of citizens vis-à-vis the state.

Human rights are threatened by the permanent existence, in Third World countries in particular, of large proportions of illiterate, unemployed, and discriminated-against women, stricken by poverty and starvation. If developing societies pretend to seek the social and economic goals necessary to overcome their condition, one of the means to success is to include women in the economic process. Of the three stated principles — the right to well-being, to equality and to non-discrimination — the condition of exact equality of both men and women has a special significance that deserves serious analysis and the adoption of joint actions with the purpose of attaining that equality at national and international levels.

Both the Universal Declaration of Human Rights and the Pact of San José de Costa Rica advocate the equal rights of men and women in all levels of human activity; consequently, it is important to find the path through which these norms may be observed and enforced by all nations.

One of the most effective ways to help decision-makers of different nations acquire a conscious realization of the importance of this issue of woman's equality and attain the enforcement, in every nation, of the international rules that advocate the respect of women's rights, would be to emphasize that the human rights issue subsumes the human rights of women. The work of researchers is of the utmost importance here. Their task is one of the best allies of international law in the struggle to develop and disseminate a worldwide enforcement of women's human rights. In the developing societies of the Third World, the work of researchers has demonstrated how the economic marginality of women is a barrier to the process of development, and how significant it would be to integrate women as an accelerating force toward progress. Researchers have proven the grave consequences produced in developing societies by this marginality and how profitable it would be to incorporate women into the ensemble of economic forces of production in those nations.

The American Convention on Human Rights, or Pact of San Jose de Costa Rica, is a major advance in the women's rights movement. The clauses relating to the Interamerican Court of Human Rights are particularly important, despite the fact that it has not yet been enforced throughout the continent because of lack of a sufficient number of ratifications by the member states. This Interamerican Court would have jurisdiction over violations of the fundamental rights of human beings.

Undoubtedly when the Convention is enforced and the Interamerican Court of Human Rights is established, women of the continent will have a tribunal to which they can bring all violations committed with regard to the rights of equality of treatment and opportunity. It is most important to create conscience at national and international levels in order that all American states ratify this convention and enforce it.

The developed nations of the world should create a special fund of economic cooperation, exclusively designed to promote the enforcement of women's human rights and the incorporation of women in the economic life of member states. At the same time, the United Nations, its specialized organs, as well as the regional organizations, should adopt as a permanent issue on the agenda of their annual meetings, the progress attained in the field of women's human rights. Progress in women's rights should include the incorporation of women into the economy, as it is stated in the Declaration of Social Progress and development (1969), in the International Development Strategy for the second United Nations Development Decade (1970) in the World Plan of Action (1975) and in the Charter of Economic Rights and Duties of States (1974).

17

BEYOND EQUALITY

Judith Buber Agassi
Hebrew University, Rehovot, Israel

Ms. Agassi goes beyond policy and asks the fundamental value question, the answers to which determine the strategy for women to follow. She specifies six possible goals women might work toward: (1) accept the status quo, but seek fairer distribution of both choice and low-level jobs; (3) seek self-realization outside of the productive system; (4) concentrate on eliminating discrimination rather than on socialist revolution; (5) separatism. and (6) work for a fair share of high-level jobs and then join with men in the fight against the structure which produces the low-level jobs. She rebuts the first five, although she does see some room for a limited amount of separatism in all-female work organizations. The final goal she hopes women will seek is a restructuring of the productive system, so that the disagreable roles can be eliminated. Not only for elite women, but for all women; and not only for women, but for both sexes. Like Safilios-Rothschild, she sees room for a coalition with men in working for social-role and sex-role changes. Unlike Blumberg, the author stresses the inequality inherent in the structure which produces high- and low level jobs no less than the inequality inherent in the sexual allocation of these positions.

Let us agree that all discrimination, overt or covert, against women in work and employment should be eliminated. Let us also agree that one of the factors contributing to the inferiority of women regarding pay and status is the unequal distribution of women across the occupational spectrum and their segregation even in the same occupation and the same work organization. Also, that this unequal distribution constitutes a form of covert discrimination particularly difficult to combat. I do not wish to enter here into the important discussion concerning ways and means for fighting discrimination since they have been discussed in other chapters of this book. Rather, my purpose here is to clarify the goal of the fight.

Is the goal merely to obtain for women their proportional share of pay, of social benefits, of status and of power? Will that do for a goal? Is not a better goal to gain satisfying work-roles for women, not only for a few, but for the many? The question is not whether, all things being equal, a satisfactory job is better than a low quality one. The question is, rather, why in fact, so few writers about the cause of women even discuss making the aim of the women's movement that of raising the quality of women's working life. At least six possible attitudes which preclude this can be found in the literature and conduct of the current women's movement.

(1) There are those who accept the status quo of the division of labor in all respects except the current discrimination against women, where the status quo means that jobs are sharply divided into manual, clerical, professional and managerial, and most manual and clerical jobs, and even some professional and managerial ones, are low on diversity, initiative, autonomy and responsibility. It follows that women should take their share of the choice jobs, as well as their share of the poor jobs (and nothing can be done about the poor quality of these).

(2) There are those who assume that only women, due to discrimination, have low quality jobs; hence, the mere overcoming of discrimination will by itself also remove low quality jobs. The underlying rationale suggests that, because men are at the top of the economy, they cause the low quality of jobs, when women will be at the top, things will greatly improve.

(3) There are those who think that better quality jobs are indeed desirable, but impossible because technological development continually increases the robotization of jobs. Thus, to achieve self-realization women should concentrate on activities outside employment.

(4) There are those who think that the present organization of work and division of labor are bad and produce low quality jobs. This situation can be changed only by a socialist revolution. Women should not wait for the revolution in their fight against discrimination, and either should concentrate on this fight alone, or on both this fight and the

revolution. (Those who advocate only the fight for the revolution are excluded here by the opening of this chapter.)

(5) There are those who think that the male establishment, or the male economic establishment, is of such poor quality that women should opt out of it altogether. Those who support this position suggest women can do this by living off the leavings of the economy or by becoming separatists in the world of work, i.e., by building up separate women's work organizations.

(6) The most important opponents of the proposal to combine the struggle against discrimination with a struggle for the raising of the quality of women's work-roles are those who concede both the desirability and the feasibility of both goals, but propose to take them one at a time. It follows that women should first attain equality, of both pay and status, that is, gain their proper share of both high quality jobs and low quality jobs; only then should men and women join forces to enhance the quality of the working life of the many.

I shall try to criticize each of the six positions outlined here. I shall try to refute the claim that the goal of enhancing the quality of the working life of women is not feasible; given that it is feasible, I shall try to show that the claim that it would better be postponed is highly counter-productive. I shall argue that it will be easier to achieve equality while improving quality than while neglecting it for the time being. I shall argue further that some branches of the economy will allow for equality only on condition that the quality of the jobs in question be changed. Finally, I confess I consider only the sixth of the above opinions worth debating, since all other five assume it worthwhile to get an equal share of the good and the bad — a goal I consider not really as worth fighting for as the goal of improving considerably the lot of many working people, including many men and more women.

(1) Let us consider the attitude of accepting the status quo. This means the status quo regarding the current hierarchy, bureaucracy, and impersonality of most work organizations, the current rigid division of work into manual, clerical, professional, and managerial, and the current division between those who draw up the plans and those who carry them out — except regarding the inequality of women in their access to the better jobs, in pay and in benefits. In defense of this view, one might wish to argue that discrimination against women is so great an impediment, that fighting it should have top priority to the exclusion of wider issues. But this defense misses its mark; for the view that there are other, wider issues is not the defense of the

status quo, but the sixth view that will be discussed later on.

Contrary to this view, I wish to maintain that today there really no longer exists a status quo in the world of work, since this world is in a state of turmoil. Working men and women increasingly are rebelling against the failure of the majority of jobs to suit the aspirations of their occupants. The failure is most serious among the lower status jobs, but by no means absent from the higher status ones, including professional and managerial jobs. It is not as if women might shake the status quo; it is already shaken out of any stability, and the only open question is, which way will the division of labor work in the near future? It will assuredly be different, but it may well be less, rather than more, satisfactory. The outcome may depend on the effort invested or not invested by those concerned with the cause of women.

(2) Let us consider the attitude of hoping that the elimination of discrimination will have, as a by-product, the elimination of low-quality jobs, at least for women, perhaps because men are not as good as women at management. It is hardly worth saying that at present not only most women, but also most men, have low quality jobs and that this makes it most improbable that the mere elimination of the unfair distribution of quality jobs will solve either problems specific to working women, or those pertaining to the working life of both sexes. Really this attitude is hardly more than the failure to sort out the causes of the ills of the working life of women, particularly of ills specific to women, as opposed to those shared by the majority of the working population of both sexes.

(3) Let us then consider the technological determinism of those who note the ills of the low quality of the majority of jobs, but see nothing that can be done to prevent its worsening. Technological determinism is popular among many intellectuals, both those connected with, and those remote from, the struggle against the discrimination of women. Ample empirical evidence supports it. In the past, many technological developments that were expected to enhance the quality of working life and lighten the burden of workers often resulted in: (1) the 'deskilling' of artisan and skilled industrial jobs; (2) mass unemployment; and (3) the creation of many new, inferior, semi-skilled, machine-tending and assembly jobs.

Yet all this was during the stage of technological progress leading to industrial mass-manufacture. The present, higher stage of technological progress, that of automation, may result either in further 'deskilling' and robotization or in facilitation of the design of entirely new and much more varied and flexible jobs. It all depends on human planning for job redesign, and so is not at all predetermined.

(4) Let us now consider the socialist revolutionaries. As I said, we shall ignore those who claim that, since only the revolution will eliminate injustice, we should forget about any specific cause of any maltreated group and fight for the revolution alone. There are those who, like Karl Marx, are convinced of the futility of any struggle for any specific cause within the system, yet, nevertheless, advocate such struggles as educational for future revolutionaries and as radicalizing the struggling frustrated groups. These, too, I shall not discuss now. There remain, then, those who select the cause of equality for women, leaving all other causes, including the cause of the enhancement of the quality of working life, to the period after the revolution.

There is a certain arbitrariness about this attitude. It is much more systematic to support no specific cause until the revolution, or to support all specific causes, merely as means to the end of revolutionizing the masses. But why should we accept the cause of equality of women, yet postpone all other causes, including the cause of the enhancement of the quality of working life?

Moreover, the view that a change in ownership will, by itself, result in a more humane division of labor has been refuted by the experience of all socialist societies to date. Even those who extol the Yugoslav experience of Worker's Councils as a success in such an effort to create a more humane division of labor must admit this refutation. For the Yugoslav experience, if successful, indicates that an effort supplementary to the change of ownership is required, and when it is absent the humanization fails to appear. For my part, I consider the Yugoslav experience hardly relevant to the enhancement of the quality of the work-life of the Yugoslav worker. This is true despite even the fact that the Yugoslav experience involves the introduction of some measure of decentralization within the system of state-capitalism and, thus, is an obvious improvement upon the Russian system.

Since the revolution itself, then, does not solve the problem, it does not make much sense to postpone its solution until the revolution. Women's jobs need improvement now, and the way to do so should be devised now.

(5) Let us consider, then, the separatist attitude. The idea of women living off the leavings of the male economy, yet separately from it, is probably untenable (as was the similar idea of the youth culture and even of the black separatists) and can be neglected here. Yet the idea

of establishing viable all-women work organizations is a different matter. There exist already all-women organizations, work-shops, construction-teams, coffee-houses, banks, and newspapers. While most of these aim at serving the special needs of women clients better than the established competition, most also go beyond the idea of enabling a few women to attain positions of power. They attempt to develop new forms of economic and work organization based on new forms of division of labor to enable all women participants to lead more satisfying work-lives. These organizations are usually not very large, and many of them are owned and/or operated cooperatively.

For my part, I see merit in these experiments, not as solutions to the problem of enhancing the quality of the work-lives of women in general, but as solutions for some and as models for many. The models refute, first and foremost, the claim that certain types of enterprise can be viable only on a large scale, and only when run by purely profit-oriented bureaucracies. But as models, they can be emulated by both all-women and mixed groups. And certainly, as far as the struggle for women's equality is concerned, in the transition period these organizations are extremely useful, both in serving women customers better and in giving women entrepreneurs the much-needed initial experience and self-reliance. In brief, separate all-women experiments may be of great value, but separatism is not, thereby, made more feasible.

(6) Finally, let us consider the attitude of first things first. In defense of this attitude, one can say that the goal of equality is simpler and more clear-cut, embedded in broadly accepted democratic ideology, and very urgent. The second aim, by contrast, must be innovative, controversial, and experimental; its success depends on the cooperation of diverse groups, managers, workers and their unions, entrepreneurs and social scientists whose interests are divergent if not actually conflicting. More generally, it is good to order the priorities on goals and not to opt for all or nothing.

The chief argument against this is that the two goals intertwine. To put it in an extreme form, one of the major causes of the inferiority of women in the world of work is not discrimination that can be rectified by mere legal and administrative measures, but the segregation of women in the lowest quality industrial jobs, in certain low quality service and clerical jobs, and in the semi-professions. It is very unrealistic to expect the achievement of the equal distribution of the sexes in these sectors of the occupational spectrum. For example, it is hardly to be expected that in the foreseeable future fifty percent of stitchers in the needle trades will be men. This is true for electronic assemblers, office cleaning workers, typists and keypunchers, telephone operators, and nurses.

Although we know theoretically that segregation depresses not only pay and status, but also the quality (i.e., the content) of most female sex-typed jobs, attempts to eliminate sex-typing in practice are bound to be extremely slow. Efforts to eliminate sex-typing in occupations are so slow that some of the female sex-typed occupations may disappear in Western society as a result of technological innovations or competition from the Third World, before some improvement occurs. What can be done about the situation, however, is radical redesign of these inferior jobs to make them more varied and autonomous. This will more effectively eradicate gross inferiority and may also make men wish to join occupational groups previously marked as inferior and as women's work.

In conclusion, let me address myself to some organizational factors. There is the women's movement which fights discrimination against women in work. And there is the movement for the enhancement of the quality of working life. It would be an error to assume that serving either goal will automatically serve the other. Even if equality could be fully attained without the redesign of jobs, it will not by itself lead to this redesign.

Job-redesign is innovative and must be implemented in one branch after another, and even in one work-organization after another, however, it would be a mistake to assume that the redesign of men's jobs would automatically lead to the redesign of women's jobs. As long as jobs are largely sex-typed, the improvement for one sex may leave the other out in the cold. The fact that men's complaints and demands about their work-life up to now have been better articulated than those of women has directed the attention of those engaged in job redesign preponderantly towards men's jobs. Organizations concerned with the status of women should ascertain what the specific criticisms, desires, and suggestions for the redesign of women's jobs in various occupational groups are. They should consult with engineers and social scientists in developing feasible plans for such redesign, and then demand and fight for such changes. Moreover, the two kinds of movements, for equality of women and quality of working life programs can coordinate and cooperate on diverse projects and levels.

18

THE POLICY PROMISSORY NOTE:
Time to Deliver

Jean Lipman-Blumen
National Institute of Education, USA, and
Jessie Bernard
Pennsylvania State University, USA

Despite the very sensitive political and conceptual issues surrounding sex roles, research on the subject is essential for adequate policy design and decision making. What policies should be created or supported is neither clear nor unequivocal nor easily derivable from common sense, and thus research remains a critical, if underutilized, resource. Policy making with respect to sex roles is mined with ambiguities. Policies designed to achieve one goal may bring about undesirable side effects. Opposite conditions – crisis and stability, homogeneity and heterogeneity – both may favor change.

Even in the face of serious ambiguities and uncertainties, women today are seeking new coalitions – among themselves and with others – in their efforts to bring about change. Men also are being invited to join in these collaborative thrusts. Recognition increasingly is paid to the need for research-based strategies and to the futility of thinking about sex-role policy in one-sided or truncated ways, whether the one side is the world of paid labor or the domestic scene. Increasing complexity in most societies usually means that change in one domain inevitably reverberates and ramifies in many others. And the 'shrinking world' phenomenon suggests that changes within any given society have their effects across societal boundaries.

Most of the thinking about sex role policy has taken place in developed countries; however, more recently attention is being directed to countries in other stages of development. Although cross-national comparisons among women commonly are used to document the relative status of women in different countries, the more trenchant comparison is that between women and men of the same country. Many serious questions regarding the status of women remain to be answered. Perhaps the foremost question is, 'How do we account for the fact that despite variability in economic, political and social structures from one country to another, the status of women is almost invariably below that of men?' In the major effort that remains before us to understand and to improve the status of women in all societies, it is essential that researchers, activists, and policy makers scale the barriers that separate them and work together to forge important and creative policy on sex roles.

I STAGES IN THE POLICY/RESEARCH RELATIONSHIP

During the early stages in the 'development' of a society an inordinate faith may be placed in the potential of 'statistics and numbers' to dictate appropriate social policy. As one American enthusiast proclaimed when the United States was a 'developing' country almost a century and a half ago, now the figures of 'arithmetic,' that is, statistics, would take the place of rhetorical figures of speech in determining policy (Hine, 1848: 398). Social science research today is sparking similar expectations in some currently 'developing' countries where the use of research is urged by social scientists and often also by policy makers and activists as well. With time, however, it gradually becomes clear that statistics and numbers do not provide instant or infallible social-policy solutions. We begin to recognize that our enthusiast's belief was a vain dream, for the dialectic between social science research and social policy has, as this book has shown, a peculiar, though not totally predictable, course. Research, again as shown in this volume, does not automatically supply the answers to policy questions.

The same research results, for example, may move one policy maker to immediate action; they may leave another unmoved. Different groups set different criteria for the validity or relevance of evidence for their concerns. The processes and traditions of research and policy, furthermore, are markedly divergent, often constituting countervailing forces. Also, differences in purpose, values, culture, and training become exaggerated by the lack of communication among researchers, activists, and policy makers, each group tending to dismiss the other as 'missing the point.' Policy makers, for example, decry the often painfully laborious search for understanding that characterizes the research enterprise. Researchers denigrate the 'political' aspect of policy formulation and activism that skims the surface of social issues, applying over-simplified remedies where more in-depth approaches are desperately needed. Activists deplore the footdragging and perceived temerity of policy makers and researchers alike. Such drawbacks are particularly salient in an area as fraught with emotion as that of new sex roles where the relationship between social science research and social policy is especially intricate. Our misleading familiarity with the seemingly straightforward roles of women and men tends to obscure the need for scientific treatment of the issues.

Nevertheless, despite all these recognized limitations to the use of social science research for policy makers and activists, this book is, in effect, a testimonial to the belief that research does — or can and should — play a fundamental part in the process of policy making with respect even to sex roles. In brief, to the belief that neither a 'developing' nor 'developed' country can afford to neglect the contribution which research can offer.

We begin — and end — with the special problems and potentials of women in sex role change. In between, we deal with the disparity between theoretical rights and actual discrimination against women, with the ambiguities of policy vis-a-vis women which render them subject to manipulation, with the objective conditions that make for change or impede it, with possible coalitions and strategies available to women, with the different programs called for in different countries according to the differing statuses that prevail, and with legitimate policy research now needed. No claim is made for exhaustive treatment of all the problems that arise in applying social science research to policy making and activism, but the discussion here does provide a beginning.

II SPECIAL PROBLEMS WITH SEX ROLE POLICY

The special vulnerability of sex roles to political and conceptual difficulties is a reflection of the larger struggle surrounding sex roles, since sex role changes cannot come about without some wrenching. Neither sex can escape some trauma in the process, men in the relinquishment of privilege, and women in the malaise and anxiety so many feel when they engage in confrontation. Deliberate efforts to change things even remotely connected to the structure of sex roles can evoke impassioned responses from individuals who have constructed their lives around very specific sex role definitions. Since sex roles are at the heart of social existence — touching, as they do, our lives as family members, workers, consumers, religious believers, and citizens — to change them is to change the very fabric of our social lives.

Further, because sex roles constitute the intimate armature of our lives, policy makers, activists, and researchers all approach sex roles with a developed — often entrenched — viewpoint. Past changes in sex roles tend to be pressed into the dim recesses of memory marked 'history'. Thus, attempts to develop social policy that would alter this previously 'undisturbed' central definition of social life inevitably meet with strong resistance. Since virtually all stratification systems place the roles of women in the lower half of every social stratum, it is not surprising that most men would try to preserve the status quo, whereas with awakened consciousness most women would seek, through social policy, to equalize their share of resources. Still, as long as women allow men to make policy with respect to women's roles and status, they invite exploitation. Policy making has so long been assumed to be part of the male role that, short of confrontation, it is often impossible to challenge this assumption.

A key theme running through this volume is that policies dealing with changing sex roles are neither self-generating, nor self-implementing. Such policies are not derivable from 'common sense.' Nor, because they are dealing with change, can the formulators of policy rely on the past. There are few reliable precedents to call upon for dealing with the sex role changes now in process everywhere. There is no body of experience to guide the policy maker trying to shape or control the changes. The chapters here, in effect, document why. But they do not, like the naive enthusiast cited earlier, express faith in the figures of 'arithmetic.' Research is itself a strategic ploy, not a *deus ex machina*.

III DISPARITIES IN PRINCIPLES, LAW, AND REALITY

One of the most salient points that strikes the reader of this volume is the disparity between principle and reality, as well as between law and reality. Everywhere, in developed as in developing countries, the norms — social, legal, religious — pertaining to sex roles are far beyond the actuality. Laws are passed, rights are guaranteed, equality is mandated. But the structural aspects of society, that is our institutions and the customs and codes that legitimate them, in many instances have actually been used to preserve the unequal divisions based on sex. Thus, inequalities, discrimination, even oppression, remain. This dissonance between norm and behavior is, of course, not a new phenomenon (Merton, 1957; Bernard, 1942, 1949, 1962). An impressive research corpus on 'deviance' documents it. Formal aspects of discrimination arise from these structural arrangements and are buttressed by more subtle, informal types of discrimination. As Bernard (1976) and Safilios-Rothschild have argued, when formal discrimination practices seemingly give way, the more subtle forms remain — and may grow stronger.

That there is such a lag between the enactment of laws and their implementation is discouraging. It may even become demoralizing as the disparity continues. Such disappointment need not, however, lead to abandonment of the effort. It is a great step forward when the laws are passed, when the principles they embody are legitimized. Laws put on record a goal, a promise, a recognition of the validity of the idea of equality. The values they represent can be appealed to. International law, as Marchand suggests, is particularly important in this regard. The real challenge becomes one of devising ways to actualize such goals as embodied in law. Research should be available to help in this process. The promissory note that laws have embodied begs delivery now.

IV POLICY AMBIGUITIES AND MANIPULATION

It is clear from even a cursory reading of the pages of this volume that what *should* be the policy with respect to sex roles, particularly the roles of women, is far from clear and unequivocal. This social policy ambiguity is increased by the fact that women have multiple roles. Such ambiguity leaves women uniquely vulnerable to manipulative exploitation. History is replete with examples of how women have been manipulated — both formally and informally — to serve societal 'needs' as defined by men. Social policy has been one of the strongest formal instruments to shape women's behavior, and often their attitudes and expectations, to conform to the changing definitions of social need. Women's fertility behavior and related occupational patterns have been the objects of influence and control by formal social policy, as Mazumdar indicates.

If policy is designed to encourage women to enter the labor force, family planning information is made available, and the almost inevitable concomitant is a decline in the fertility rate. Baude, Scott, and Es-Said have documented how social policy has controlled women's labor force participation by opening and closing the spigots of family planning information and measures. Labor force policies have added further constraints or inducements, as the socio-economic and political conditions have shifted. In countries where policy is designed to encourage the birth rate, it often results in serious population pressure on scarce economic resources. When policy attempts to foster both women's labor force and maternal roles, it results in serious overload for women, as the Bernard chapter (14) argues. What policy should seek is the best 'mix' in the use of women's time and energies. To achieve such an optimum 'mix' will certainly tax all our research and policy resources.

It is, we add parenthetically, one of the acute ironies of sex role stereotypes that women are pictured as 'manipulative,' when, in fact, they have been the objects of broad scale manipulation. One key to this irony is the recognition that because women historically have been manipulated on the macrosociological and macroeconomic levels, often, their only structural recourse has been reciprocal manipulation at the microsociological, economic, and psychological levels.

Control of resources, including money, their own labor, and physical beings, which would release them from manipulation has been beyond the reach of most women in most societies. In those cultures and in those historical periods where *some* women have had such control over resources, those women have managed to improve their own lives — but not necessarily the lives of their sisters who lack similar control.

V CONDITIONS FOR CHANGE: CRISIS AND STABILITY

It is another major irony of sex role history that two seemingly opposite social conditions alter the control equation and provide a climate conducive to sex role policy changes: crisis and stability. In crisis periods, such as wars, natural catastrophes, and periods of severe labor shortage, the strictures on sex roles have been at least partially relieved by direct and indirect policy decisions (Lipman-Blumen, 1973, 1975, 1977). In crisis periods, stratification systems begin to weaken, and social policies reallocate and redirect resources in efforts to deal with the emergency. In both world wars, women's roles were transformed dramatically.

While the extreme changes evident at the peak of crisis may diminish after the situation is resolved, the residual permanent changes become the new baseline for sex role divisions and policy decisions (Lipman-Blumen, 1973). Commonly there are only stuttering growth and change in sex roles until the next major crisis provokes a new spurt of sex role advances. Clearly crisis is one avenue to sex role change. But although smaller residual changes usually persist, dramatic and extreme crisis-induced changes in women's family and work roles often are relatively short-lived.

Other, seemingly opposite social conditions also tend to promote steady — if less dramatic — sex role changes through social policy. More gradual changes in sex roles may come about through extended periods of stability — or political continuity. Long periods of political continuity create the possibility for clearly enunciated social policy promulgated by policy makers who can set clear goals, specify the means for implementing these goals, and remain in power long enough to ensure their fulfillment, as Baude reports. But, paradoxically, extended periods of political continuity do not always work in this way. Detailed research could offer us better understanding of why political continuity leads to progressive social policy on sex roles in one time and place and repressive sex role policies in others. Israel, Sweden, and the Soviet Union (Dodge, 1966; Lapidus, 1976) provide compelling individual examples of social policy directed toward altering sex roles and the social conditions that encouraged and inhibited the proposed changes.

Political continuity clearly was *one* crucial ingredient in the relative success Sweden has achieved in creating sex role equality. As Baude suggests, there was a 45-year period of continuity in social policy under a single political party, the Social Democrats. During their 45-year tenure, the Social Democrats set explicit goals which they were able to transform into public policy, with cooperation from other major political parties.

It becomes apparent that periods of crisis and periods of stability each offer their own unique opportunities for changes in sex roles. Crisis creates the possibility for stark, dramatic, extreme advances. The temporary abrogation of formal and informal restrictions encourages women to enter roles in industry, government, and academia previously inaccessible to them. Crisis creates a high water mark of change which partially recedes with the return to a more stable period. But the receding currents of crises leave clear traces of previously unimagined sex role possibilities.

Stability and continuity offer the opportunity for more incremental, steady sex role changes. The new baseline, left by the ebb tide of crisis, may become codified into law. But new and dramatic changes in social structure — and its basic units of roles — usually must await the next surge of crisis.

VI MORE CONDITIONS FOR CHANGE: HOMOGENEITY AND HETEROGENEITY

Homogeneous and heterogeneous societies create distinct challenges for policy makers. They require different strategies for change. Although homogeneity may be linked to traditional attitudes and practices, when shifts occur, they commonly affect the entire society which is accustomed to making consensual decisions. This possibility is enhanced by the common link between homogeneity and limited size in social structures, including entire societies.

Sweden is an example of a situation in which relative homogeneity and limited size of a society aided concerted and deliberate sex role equalization through social policy based on social science knowledge. Unlike more heterogeneous and larger societies, where political consensus may require a dilution of the demands of competing groups with contradictory needs, Sweden's relative homogeneity and workable size contributed to the development of agreement on underlying values and necessary policy measures.

This does not preclude the possibility of disparities in opinion even in relatively homogeneous societies. As homogeneous societies develop and change, different segments may change at different rates, and their attitudes and customs may undergo shifts more rapidly and decisively than other parts of a relatively homogeneous society. Baude's analysis cites clear instances of some unsolved problems (for example, the difficulty in redistributing women in the work force, despite various school reform measures) that can be attributed to the resistant, traditional attitudes of the general society, despite the 'contemporary' views of policy makers and activists. As Sweden faces increasing heterogeneity, presumably Swedish policy makers will feel the press of conflicting demands from divergent constituencies. The recent Swedish election may be a harbinger of increasing divergence and heterogeneity.

Heterogeneity, in its turn, allows *other* possibilities for change in social policy on sex roles (as well as other issues). Heterogeneous societies, almost by definition, are large and complex. Different groups, accepting different values and representing different interests and traditions, compete for control — over resources, policy, and their own lives. Such cultural pluralism permits the acceptance of different explanatory models developed within the social sciences (Sanday, 1970). Social policy may be used as a weapon, as well as an instrument, in the struggle among constituencies competing for control.

But the very fact of heterogeneity allows for political manoeuvering, particularly in the interstices of a complex social structure. Politically astute constituencies, regardless of their size, can influence social policy, often imposing their own policy inclinations on groups larger, but less politically organized and sophisticated, than themselves. The anti-abortion groups in the United States offer a recent example of how small, articulate subgroups within a larger heterogeneous society can use the very factors of size and heterogeneity to press their cause and impose their political demands on larger segments of the population who do not share their viewpoint. It is particularly noteworthy that despite the fact that every opinion poll taken in the United States in recent years suggests that a majority of the population favors unrestricted access to abortion, the anti-abortion faction has been able to create and change legislation, delay congressional appropriations, and raise the right to abortion to a key issue in a national election. In this major struggle over women's right to decide whether or not to undertake or enlarge their maternal role, social and medical research has been used to bolster both sides. Research findings have been used, abused, or neglected — as the moment warranted — as ammunition in the development of social policy on this and other issues.

Other groups have focussed on the questions of educational policy for women. They see educational policy as an equally important and increasingly sensitive area of concern, particularly in heterogeneous societies where social class, racial and ethnic differences have complicated women's demands for equal educational — and inextricable occupational — opportunities. In the United States, for example, politically astute activists have articulated a vast range of questions on elementary, secondary, post-secondary, vocational, professional, and athletic education. These interest groups bring to bear a sophisticated understanding of social policy and social structure which allows them to cope with the difficulties of creating social change for women in a society characterized by great size and heterogeneity.

VII UNLIKELY COLLABORATORS: NEW COALITIONS

Despite the fact that women often represent more than half the population, historical and cross-cultural obstacles in the way of engaging in large-scale political efforts have impeded the equalization of their roles in many societies. More recently, with women's awareness of the possibilities for social action, particularly through organized efforts of the feminist movement, new coalitions are emerging. Politically sophisticated women have recognized the need to organize themselves and to seek coalitions with women of every social class, race, ethnicity, generation, and religious group. The Houston IWY Conference was an example of this recognition.

The step from recognition to realization of this need for coalitions among women — generically called 'sisterhood' — is more difficult than first appears. As the analysts of women's issues have amply demonstrated, women historically have been separated from each other by the strong divisions among the classes, races, generations, ethnic, and religious groups. In addition, their allegiance has been tied to their families, to their children, and to their husbands. Women's family and sexual roles have bound them to men in ways that have made it difficult, if not often impossible, for them to speak for their own needs. But gradually coalitions among women of different groups are taking shape and gaining strength.

In addition to coalitions among women's groups, there is a growing spate of coalitions between women's groups and other groups within the society — civil rights, trade union, other minority groups. The growing concern for 'human rights' underscores the commonalities between women and other interest groups. The call for human dignity highlights the great potential for alliances among women's groups and other segments of the society to develop social policy that eliminates discrimination and inequities with regard to sex, race, ethnicity, age, and occupational roles.

Another factor contributing to the acceptance of social policy as a legitimate means of eliminating sex role inequities is the participation of high level male political leaders in the sex-role debate and social policy initiatives, as both Baude and Safilios-Rothschild note. The collaboration of women and men in the redesign of Swedish and Israeli society helped raise the issue of sex-role equality to one of national importance. The wholehearted and continuous participation of key male political figures, alongside women, in the sex-role equalization movement may be a necessary condition for avoiding the manipulation of sex roles to conform to political and economic shifts. 'Self-interest rightly understood,' as de Tocqueville reminds us, may encourage the participation in a cause that superficially seems at odds with one's individual interests. As more male political figures recognize the possibilities for improving men's lives when they join the cause of equalizing sex roles, the opportunities for coalitions between women's groups and male political figures will grow. With the appearance of more women in key political roles, the collaboration of men and women as equally influential policy makers hopefully will proliferate.

VIII COMPREHENSIVE SOCIAL POLICY STRATEGY

One natural outgrowth of the emergence of political coalitions on sex roles is the awareness of the need to develop a systematic, comprehensive approach to the many issues subsumed under the general rubric of 'sex roles'. Such a comprehensive strategy necessarily involves first the integration of research from several disciplines, and then the integration of these research findings with social policy on sex roles. Interdisciplinary research efforts are needed to produce the kinds of information on all issues linked to sex roles for direct and indirect policy decisions. It is not enough to work on one aspect of sex roles at a time. The cumulative effect of research-informed social policy on family life, work, housing, transportation, mass media, insurance, taxation, social security, child care, health, fertility, education, foreign policy, energy, and law can go far toward evolving creative solutions to the many difficult issues tied to sex roles.

The discussions in this volume highlight the futility of thinking of policy with respect to sex roles in a one-sided or truncated way. Whatever changes are called for in the work site have reverberations in the domestic scene. The 'two roles' of women must be viewed as aspects of a single life, much as we view the several roles of men. Women seek more input not only into policy dealing with family life, but also into policy dealing with work life. Beyond this, they recognize that both sides of life are knit closely into the issues of housing, transportation, taxation, credit, health and a host of other problems. And they recognize the growing need for them to have their say in, as well as control over, many aspects of their lives. In the family, it is essential that women have their way over the number of children they will have, the timing of these children, and support systems for caring for them. Policy with respect to divorce must take into account the differing contributions women and men make to the family with significant recognition and substantial reward for women's part.

This serious, systematic assessment of women's and men's roles and the adjustment of these roles through social policy must take place simultaneously in many countries. Only in this way can each country develop a coherent and integrated social policy on sex roles. When this process occurs simultaneously in *many* countries, the equalization of sex roles arrived at by the social policy of developed and developing nations ultimately, if laboriously, can be forged into a more meaningful international policy and law.

IX THE STATUS OF WOMEN IN DIFFERENT COUNTRIES

Such a perspective brings us to a sensitive point. It is sometimes alleged that Western women are attempting to impose their values on women everywhere, in developing countries as well as at home. If this were indeed the case, it would be unfortunate. Still, we know that the United Nations does try to propagate the ideals of human rights everywhere, and we know that women's rights are also a legitimate part of human rights.

If is not that women in developing countries should seek to emulate women in Western societies. It is only that in developing countries, no less than elsewhere, the gap between men and women should be narrowed and that social policy should provide the mechanism. It is not that women in the Third World should seek the same goals as women in the West, but that they should seek to approach the rewards available to men in their own societies. And it is here that we see sharply defined one of the many intersections of social policy and research.

Many social science efforts to gauge the relative status of women around the world have resulted in comparisons of literacy, fertility, marriage, and divorce rates in different countries. In addition, cross-national comparisons of educational and occupational patterns have been a major research thrust in attempts to measure women's relative world-wide standing. In formulating policy within national boundaries, policy makers have pointed with embarrassment or pride to the relative position of women within their own society compared to women in other cultures.

While these estimates offer us one slice of reality, they fail to reveal a more important set of facts: women's status relative to the status of men within their own society. After all, it should surprise no one that women living under *differing* sociopolitical and economic conditions represent disparate rates of marriage, divorce, fertility, and literacy, not to mention educational and occupational levels. What should both surprise and concern us is that when we compare men and women living under *identical* political and economic conditions within the same country, the status disparity is significant if not shocking. Thus, Blumberg's argument for social scientists to develop paradigms that highlight the status differentials between men and women in the same country points the way for diagnosing the intervention points amenable to social policy solutions.

Literacy gaps, salary gaps, occupational and educational gaps are some of the more obvious points of disparity between men and women in most countries. One of the important issues in narrowing these gaps between the statuses and roles of men and women has to do with the equalization of discretionary time, as Bernard reminds us. Women have been doing a disproportionate part of the world's work for millennia. The work overlaod can become a particularly serious burden on women in developing and developed societies, particularly if consumer services are not in adequate supply. Health and nutrition of women are affected by the disproportionate allocations of workloads and discretionary time in different societies. Interdisciplinary research can provide the metric for determining the relative contributions and rewards for women and men in each society, and social policy can take the next step to equilibrate the imbalance. Time budget studies must be translated into the language of social policy and economic compensation within both the world of paid work and family work if the omnipresent status gaps between men and women are to shrink. The effects of work overload on women in most societies must be dealt with through improved family, industrial, financial, and health policies. And creative policy solutions — based on meaningful research — must be keyed to the special needs of women in each society.

X LEGITIMATION OF POLICY RESEARCH

If, as this volume argues, research can be a significant adjunct to social policy on sex roles — as well as other issues — why is the marriage between social policy and research rarely consummated? Earlier, we focussed on the miscommunication among research, action, and policy people. We noted that the dialogue among researchers, activists, and policy makers has not included a clear understanding of what research can and cannot do for social policy. But beyond this, the research world has failed to offer legitimation to policy research. The research community *qua* community must acknowledge its stake and obligation in creating an understanding of the strengths and limits of research, as well as in providing policy analysis and policy relevant research with sorely needed professional legitimacy.

The social research community has not recognized its responsibility vis-à-vis social policy. Particularly in non-totalitarian societies, only a small band of researchers has taken social policy as a serious research concern. This indifference to social policy as a legitimate focus of research interest is a reflection of the structure and ethos of the research world, which tends to see its natural habitat as academia. Until recently, the academic community, for reasons that warrant a separate volume, tended to denigrate policy research. The researcher who ventured on to the thin ice of policy research often could not count on returning safely to the shores of academia. In addition, the policy community offered no alternative haven. Policy research was a treacherous adventure for most researchers, with little or no reward from either the world of research or that of social policy.

To compound the problem, social scientists who took sex roles as their subject struggled for recognition in the research world. In part, this situation arose because women predominated in this research area. As in other fields where women predominate, their overrepresentation affected the status of this professional specialty. But the low status contaminated male researchers as well and discouraged their further entry into the field of sex role studies.

This no-win situation for policy-oriented researchers reduces the likelihood of a growing cadre of researchers applying their knowledge and skills to social policy questions. The fewer the researchers involved in social policy work, the more difficult the communication among researchers, activists, and policy people. The confusion about research simply grows, and the probability of effective collaboration among social policy makers, researchers, and activists diminishes.

A social policy/research community which legitimates and rewards this crucial undertaking is sorely needed. Without recognition and encouragement for researchers to undertake this difficult task, we shall continue to founder on the turbulence of ad hoc solutions to the problems that emanate from and complicate sex roles. While educational and economic reforms have much to contribute, research and social policy must be used in a deliberate, systematic, multifaceted approach to equalize sex roles. Legitimation of this activity is crucial to its growth and effectiveness.

XI SPECIAL ROLES OF WOMEN

What, we may ask, is the special role of women in this formidable task? The answer is simultaneously simple and complex. On a simple level, they must, as they already have begun to do, take a greater part in fashioning their world — as activists, researchers, and policy makers. On a more complex level, their participation in all of these activities must be developed at the highest levels of responsibility. This is no simple task. It is not merely a matter of wanting or willing. Women are confronted with centuries of tradition that impede their efforts, as the Es-Said chapter demonstrates. They must find new ways of attacking these problems, despite entrenched opposition.

Women researchers in many countries already have taken the lead in pursuing policy-relevant sex role research. They have developed new research strategies for sharpening our perspective on the multiple roles of women and men. The current feminist research has opened new vistas, provided important insights on sex roles. At a time when the universities are declining, the burgeoning growth of women's studies centers around the world is testimony to the viability and recognized need for these new research approaches. Women as researchers are redefining appropriate and legitimate research issues and methodologies. Feminist researchers have called attention to the serious inequalities women face at home, at work, in the political, economic, and social arenas. They have provided serious analyses and new paradigms for understanding the problems that can be addressed by social policy remedies. Feminist researchers, in the course of these efforts, have begun to create a support group for both female and male researchers who would tackle policy research on sex roles. Their example eventually may bestow legitimacy on policy-relevant research in general.

Women as activists and policy makers confront analogous problems. They face the challenge of reconceptualizing and legitimating political roles to provide new strengths and options for the larger society. As policy makers and voters, they have played a redemptive role, as Bernard suggests. Feminist activists and policy makers have begun to reject the authoritarian, elitist hierarchies which have characterized the social institutions of many societies. Women traditionally have been seen as the culture-bearers; now they must accept the challenge of becoming culture-changers. As voters and political leaders, they increasingly will face the opportunities to act as change agents — not only on the microlevel of everyday interpersonal behavior which has been their traditional baliwick, but also on the macrolevel of formal institutional decision-making from which they no longer can be barred.

In undertaking these new challenges, women need not transform themselves into distorted imitations of their male political predecessors and colleagues. Feminists' recognition of the inadequacies of the world created by males goaded their demand for policies that would alter inequitable sex roles. A recreation and reformulation of sex roles and the entwined social structure now must be undertaken by feminist policy makers who acknowledge that their special strengths and skills offer unique possibilities for creating meaningful change.

For centuries, women have been told that their tasks within the family were the most difficult and important responsibilities in society. We would be surprised, indeed, if women, schooled at dealing with life's most important tasks, were unable to translate their hard-earned gains to the broader, but not necessarily more complex or difficult, arenas of the world beyond the hearth. Women from many cultures, as citizens, activists, researchers, and policy makers can help create social policy solutions that ensure the equality of sex roles requisite to the full development of women and men in all societies.

REFERENCES

BERNARD, Jessie, *American Family Behavior,* Chapter 7, 'Explanation and Evaluation of Nonconformity', pp. 182-207. New York: Harper Brothers, 1942.

-- *American Community Behavior,* Part 4, "Disorganization and Dissociation", pp. 457-555. New York: Dryden Press, 1949.

-- *American Community Behavior,* (revised edition), Chapter 27, 'Community Dissociation', pp. 406-21. New York: Holt, Rinehart, & Winston, 1962.

-- 'Where Are We Now? Some Thoughts on the Current Scene,' *Psychology of Women Quarterly,* Vol. 1, No. 1, 1976, pp. 21-37.

DODGE, Norton T., *Women in the Soviet Economy,* Baltimore, Md.: The Johns Hopkins Press, 1966.

HINE, L. A., 'A General Statistical Society for the United States', *The Merchants' Magazine,* Vol. 18 (1848), p. 398.

LAPIDUS, Gail Warshofsky, 'Occupational Segregation and Public Policy: A Comparative Analysis of American and Soviet Patterns', in Martha Blaxall and Barbara Reagan, *Women and the Workplace,* Chicago, Ill.: University of Chicago Press, 1976.

LIPMAN-BLUMEN, Jean, 'Role De-Differentiation as a System Response to Crisis: Occupational and Political Roles of Women', *Sociological Inquiry,* Vol. 43, No. 2, 1973, pp. 105-29.

-- 'A Crisis Framework Applied to Macrosociological Family Changes: Marriage, Divorce, and Occupational Trends Associated with World War II', *Journal of Marriage and the Family,* November 1975, pp. 889-902.

-- 'A Crisis Perspective on Divorce and Role Change,' Chapter 10 in Jane Roberts Chapman and Margaret Gates, eds., *Women Into Wives: The Legal and Economic Impact of Marriage,* Sage Yearbooks in Women's Policy Studies, Vol. 2, pp. 233-58. Beverly Hills, Calif.: Sage Publications, 1977.

MERTON, Robert K., *Social Theory and Social Structure.* Pp. 18, 343-45. New York: Free Press, 1957.
SANDAY, Peggy R., 'The Relevance of Anthropology for US Domestic Social Policy.' Paper presented at the American Anthropological Association Meeting, San Diego, California, November 1970.

SUBJECT INDEX

Abortion laws: Eastern Europe, 180, 181-182, 183-184, 191, 195*n*; India, 259; Norway, 215, 219; Sweden, 157, 174, 288, 289; United States, 285*n*, 371. *See also* Birth control; Fertility
Abortion, physiological side effects of, 184, 195-196*n*
Abn Hanifeh theological order, 230
Activists, 21-24, 78, 365, 372, 377-379
Adult education, in Scandinavian countries, 154, 340-341
Affirmative action, 57, 135*n*, 150-152 male opposition to (U.S.), 290
Africa: child care, 96-97; crude birth rates, 88; education, 91-92; female labor force, 92, 93; fertility rates, 89; literacy rates, 90-91; market women, 125; marriage, 87; modernization's influence on sex roles, 85; university enrollments, 92
Age: childbearing, 89; distribution in labor force by (Jordan), 243; marriage, 87-88, 94, 95, 97-98, 230-231
Agrarian societies, women in, 121-122, 128, 137*n*, 228-229
Agriculture, women in (Czechoslovakia), 188
All-women organizations, 357, 360
Allegiances, women's, 372
Allowances. *See* Child allowances; Family allowances
Alternative Work Schedules (U.S.), 314, 328-329*n*
Arab National Union, 228
Argentina, median education in, 91

Asia: child care, 96-97; literacy rates, 90-91; marriage, 87; median educational attainment, 91; secondary school enrollments, 92; university enrollments, 92
Automation, 358

Basic Opportunity Grants (U.S.), 346
Basque country, 305
Bedouin women, 11, 118, 229
Bhadralog, 263, 266*n*
Birth control, 32, 88-90, 98, 184; India, 258-261; Norway, 205-206, 219; Sweden, 156-157, 162, 174-175; United States, 285*n*, 316. *See also* Abortion; Fertility
Birth order of siblings, 35
Birth rates, crude, 88, 104-107, 189; as indicator of women's status, 88-90, 94, 95. *See also* Fertility; *and specific country*, e.g. Czechoslovakia; Finland; Pakistan; etc.
Breast feeding vs. bottle feeding, 96-97, 122
Bulgaria: abortion and birth rates, 182; female labor force participation, 181, 183; fertility, 177; motherhood encouraged in, 190-191

Cambodia, female labor force in, 93
Canada, female labor force in, 93
Change: conditions for, 368-372; transitional periods of, 57-59; women as agents for, 287-301, 378-379.

381

See also Education; Equality; Family patterns; Labor force participation; Role transformation
Child allowances: Eastern Europe, 184, 189-190; Norway, 201, 204, 205, 207, 219; Sweden, 146, 148
Child care: female labor force participation and, 186; nutrition and, 96-97; payment for, 299. See also specific country or region, e.g. Africa; Eastern Europe; Norway, Sweden; etc.
Child-care centers. See Day-care centers
Child care salary (Norway), 208-209
Child marriage (India), 253
Child support payments (Sweden), 147-148
Childbearing: age for, 89; economic development levels and, 86, 88-90
Childrearing, 122-123; leaves of absence for, 99, 158-160, 184, 215-216, 220, 340; male participation in, 99, 129, 162
Children: aid-to-dependent, 311; learning of sex roles by, 50-51. See also Child care
Children's rights, 10-11; Norway, 215
Chile, marriage age in, 87
Chotolog, 266n
Citizen's Advisory Council on the Status of Women (CACSW), 65, 79n
Civil Rights Act (1964), 343
Civil service employment (Sweden), 150-151
Coalitions, 363, 365, 372-373
Co-educational classrooms, 24-25, 38n
Cohort research, 52
Colombia, median education in, 91
Commission on the Operation of the Senate, 66-67
Communal societies, 127-128, 138n
Communes, 314
Communist Party (France), 271-272
Community service. See Volunteer work
Conflict confrontation: in sex role change, 287-288, 290-301; strategies of, 295-296
Congress, U.S., internal research support agencies, 67-68, 79n
Congressional Budget Office (CBO), 67-68
Congressional Fellows program, 69
Congressional Resource Service (CRS), 67-68
Consultants, scientific: difficulties of, 28-29; to federal government, 66, 69-70
Continuing education, 340-341, 345
Contraception. See Birth control
Cooperative living arrangements, 314
Counseling services (United States), 345
Crisis, as condition for change, 181, 369-370
Cross-cultural research, 7-8, 9, 13-14, 52-53, 57, 362-363, 374-376; on discretionary time, 305-312, 326-327n; on indicators of women's status, 83-112; on female participation in labor force, 52, 120-123, 137n; on political participation, 284n
Cuba, 330n
Cultivation. See Horticultural societies
Cultural pluralism. See Heterogeneous societies
Czechoslovakia: abortions and birth rates, 182, 184; child care, 185-186; female labor force participation, 183, 185, 186, 192, 196n; fertility rate, 89, 184, 189; housework hours, 182; population changes, 180; protective legislation in, 187; social policy on women's status in, 178

Dahomey, fertility rates in, 89
Daughters, of highly-educated women, 35
Day-care centers: cross-national studies of, 53; employer-provided, 238; equality, and need for, 222-223; as socializing institutions,

Subject Index

218, 220; *See also under name of country or region*, e.g. Jordan; Norway; Sweden; etc.
Death rates, 86
Decision-makers. *See* Policy makers
Declaration of Human Rights (U.N.), 10, 349
Democratic ideology, 360
Depression, discretionary time inequalities and, 306
Desertion, male, 322-323, 331*n*
Development. *See* Economic development
Discretionary time: cross-cultural research on, 305-312, 326-327*n*; of homemakers, 319-321; household tasks and, 177, 190, 233-235, 305-325, 326-331*n*, 374; inequalities in, 12, 303-304, 305-313, 315, 326-329*n*, 375-376; of mothers, 324-325; pre-modern vs. modern, 308-309; social policy and, 303-333
Discrimination: concept of, 49-50; covert, subtle, 289, 292, 295, 356; cross-cultural, 7-8, 9, 13-14, 52-53, 57, 362-363, 374-376; in education, 154, 165, 174, 337-346; legislation against (Sweden), 146-175, 289; (United States), 24, 38*n*, 50, 57, 59*n*, 63-73, 79*n*, 285*n*, 290-291, 292, 342-343, 347; legislation against vs. reality of, 8, 366-367; paternalistic, 291-292; strategy to eliminate, 355-361
Divorce laws and rates: Eastern Europe, 180, 184; India, 252; Jordan, 230-231; Norway, 204, 209; Sweden, 158, 170
Domesticity, cult of, 309-311

East Slovak Iron Works (Czechoslovakia), 196 *n*
Eastern Europe, 11, 177-197; abortion laws, 180, 181-182, 183-184, 191, 195*n*; birth rates, 181-182, 189; child care, 184, 189-190; day-care centers, 182, 185-186, 189, 191; divorce, 180, 184; female labor force participation, 93, 177, 180-183, 186, 187, 191-193, 196*n*; fertility policies, 183-184, 189; household tasks, 181, 182, 189, 193, 197*n*; housing shortage, 181-182; labor shortage in postwar, 180-181; maternity leaves, 184; population policies, 183-184, 195*n*; protective legislation, 187; vocational training, 187-188, 196*n*. *See also specific countries*, e.g. Czechoslovakia; Hungary; Soviet Union; etc.
Economic development: agrarian base of, 121-122; education and, 12-13, 134-135, 225; female labor force and levels of, 93, 121, 138*n*; fertility and, 88-90, 94, 95, 98, 124-125, 137*n*; sex role equalization and, 83-112, 163; women's status and, 83-112, 138*n*, 163, 180-181, 257-258, 350-352. *See also specific country*, e.g. France; India; Norway; etc.
Economic power: females' relative, 114-115, 117-119, 128-130, 131-132, 135-136*n*, 137-138*n*, 338, 368; kinship arrangements and, 124, 126-127, 128; road to female, 120-128, 129; social relations of production and, 127-128; strategic indispensability factors, 124-126
Ecuador, median education in, 91
Education: co-ed classrooms, 24-25, 38*n*; continuing, 340-341, 345; discrimination in, 154, 165, 174, 337-347; economic development and, 12-13, 134-135; equal access to opportunities in, 24-25, 165, 285*n*, 340; female enrollment trends, 91-92, 108-110; (Jordan), 231-232; (United States), 92, 344-346; fertility and, 97; financial assistance by (U.S.) government for, 345-346; as indicator of women's status, 90-92, 94, 95, 134-135, 230-231; for inequality, 342; labor force participation and,

97, 233; leadership in, 347; levels of women in world, 108-110; lifelong, 340-341, 345; median attainment, 91, 110; part-time (U.S.), 345, 346; policy for women, 96-98, 337-348; retraining courses (Sweden), 149-150; role in changing sex roles, 145-146, 152-154; role in development process, 12-13, 134-135, 225; secondary school enrollments, 91-92, 108-110; social consequences of spread of (Jordan), 232; time allocated to, 315, 329*n*; university enrollment trends, 92, 108-110, 344-346. *See also* Literacy; Vocational training; *and specific country*, e.g. France; India; United States, etc.

Education Division (HEW), 345-346

Educational Amendments (1972), 59*n*, 79*n*, 342

Educational Testing Service, 345

Effecting Social Change for Women (Federation of Organizations for Professional Women), 78

Egalitarianism, 129; male supporters of, 292, 294. *See also* Equality; Sweden

Elites. *See* Leadership roles; Power

Emigration. *See* Rural to urban migrations; Talent drain emigration

Emotional support, provided by women, 319, 325. *See also* Homemaking activities.

Employed women, 304; inequality in discretionary time, 305-307. *See also* Labor force participation; Mothers, employed

Employment. *See* Labor force participation; Occupations; Part-time employment

England: discretionary time inequalities, 326*n*; female labor force, 92, 312; peasants, 126

Equal Pay Act, 59*n*, 343

Equal pay goal (United States), 346

Equal pay legislation (Sweden) 150, 165; (United States), 59*n*, 343

Equal rights. *See* Human rights

Equal rights amendment: opposition to, 328*n*; political participation and, 281-282, 284-285*n;* protective legislation and, 9

Equality: concept of, 326*n*; conflict confrontation as way to, 287-288, 290-301; creating, 4-5, 8, 9, 11, 164 171-172; day-care centers as necessary condition for, 222-223; of discretionary time. *See* Discretionary time; economic development and, 83-112, 138*n*, 163, 180-181, 257-258, 350-352; goal of, 11-13, 355-356, 357, 360-361; in known societies, 116; male participation in debate on sex role, 155-156, 162-163, 287-289, 300*n*, 373; in 'morals and manners,' 115; in occupational world, 93, 99-100, 114-115, 118-119, 135-136*n*, 147, 150-151, 346, 355-361 (*see also* Labor force participation); planning for, 133-135; predicting relative, 113-138; in property ownership and control, 99-100; in school vs. outside reality, 165; simultaneous international work toward, 374; social issues and public actions affecting women's, 172-175; socialist guarantees of, 180; in socialist societies, 177, 190-191, 193, 356, 359; strategies to achieve, 295-298, 355-361, 366. *See also* Female-male comparisons; Human rights; Women's status

Equality grants, to employers (Sweden), 151

Ethnographic Atlas (Murdock), 121-122, 136-137*n*

Europe: female labor force, 92-93; marriage, 87. *See also* Eastern Europe; *and under name of country*, e.g. France; Norway; Sweden; etc.

Evolutionary-economic determinism, of female status, 85

Subject Index

Executive Branch (U.S.), as user of research, 63-66
Executive Orders 11246 and 11375 (U.S.), 59*n*, 64, 65, 343

Fact finding, 45
Faculty (United States), 346
Fair Credit Billing Act (U.S.), 69
Family: functions of (Norway), 211, 222; image of, 219; theory of functional specialization in, 326*n*
Family allowances (Eastern Europe), 184
Family law (Sweden), 157-158, 167-170
Family patterns, 42, 44; India, 42, 44, 261-265; Jordan, 230-233; Norway, 199-224; Sweden, 146-147, 162-163, 166-168, 340, 369
Family planning policy. *See* Birth control; Fertility
Family Rights, Law of (Jordan, 1951), 230
Family therapy, 211, 218-221
Fathering time, 321-322
Father's responsibilities, 340
Father's rights: Norway, 215-216, 220; Sweden, 158-159, 170, 175
Federal Republic of Germany: child care, 186; female labor force participation, 186; marriage age, 87
Female-male comparisons, 9-10, 113-138, 338, 375-376. *See also* Women's status
Female roles: alternatives to traditional, 86; in family, 99; history of, 12; manipulation of, 40, 46, 367-368; multiplicity of, 177, 190, 233-235, 311-313, 374; research on. *See* Research; traditional, 86, 87-90; (India), 251-253, 257-258; (Jordan), 228-229, 233-234. *See also* Family patterns; Household tasks; Labor force participation; Motherhood; Mothers
Feminist activities, 289, 378. *See also* Activists
Fertility: economic development and, 88-90, 94, 95, 98, 124-125, 137*n*;

education and, 97; labor force participation and, 99, 177, 368; as indicator of women's status, 88-90, 94, 95, 134-135, 226; nonmarital, 90, 104-107, 210; rates, 88, 104-107, 189; social policy influence on, 98, 189, 368 (*see also under name of country*, e.g. Bulgaria; India; Sweden; etc.). *See also* Birth control; *and specific country*, e.g. India; Hungary; etc.
Fifth Republic (France), 271, 272-275
Finland: crude birth rates, 88; female labor force, 92; liberal work leaves, 340
Flexitime systems, 314, 321, 328*n*
Folk Pension system (Norway), 199, 201, 206
Food supply, female contributions to, 120-123, 137*n*, 138*n*
Foraging societies, women in, 121, 122, 127, 129
Force, uses of, 117-118, 129, 131-132
France, 12, 53, 269-278; child care, 186; Communist Party, 271-272; day-care centers, 53; discretionary time inequalities, 306; economic development, 273; educational policy, 270, 276; female labor force participation, 186, 269-270, 276; marriage age, 87; political participation, 269-275; university education, 92, 270
Free time, 304. *See also* Discretionary time
Full employment goal (Norway), 199, 201, 203-204
Functional drainage/renewal of family (Norway), 199, 206, 218-221, 223
Fund for the Improvement of Post-Secondary Education (U.S.), 345

Galton's problem, 136*n*
German Democratic Republic, 191-194; child care, 186; female labor force participation, 183, 186, 191-193; living standard, 194*n*; population losses, 180, 191; sex

imbalance, 180; sex role patterns, 177
Germany, West. *See* Federal Republic of Germany
Goals, 355-361
Government, 1-2, 62-73, 150-151, 345-346. *See also under name of country*, e.g. Bulgaria; Japan; Sweden; etc.
Government Accounting Office (GAO), 67-68
Greece, marriage age in, 87
Grey Panther Movement (U.S.), 300*n*
Gross National Product, correlation with women's status, 94, 95, 96-99
Group-8 (Sweden), 289
Guaranteed Student Loan Program (U.S.), 346

HEW. Education Division, 345-346
Health care services and systems: Norway, 201, 205, 207, 214, 218; Sweden, 146, 147, 167; United States, 285*n*
Heterogeneous societies, 21-22, 370-372. *See also* United States
Hindu women, 265*n*
Home: concept of, 317-318, 319, 329*n*, 330*n*; defections from, 322-323; functions of, 318, 330*n*; protection of, as basic U.S. policy, 311-313, 328*n*
Home economics professional association, 327*n*
Homemakers, 304; discretionary time of, 319-321
Homemaking activities, 307, 329*n*, 330*n*; household tasks vs., 317-321, 322, 327*n*, 329*n*, 330*n*; idealizing of, 309, 316, 317-318; male involvement in, 322-323; time required for, 316-323
Homogeneous societies, 370-371. *See also* Sweden
Hormonal factors, 136*n*
Horticultural societies, women in, 121, 122, 137*n*

Household tasks: discretionary time inequalities and, 305-325, 326-331*n*; elimination of, 314; excessive attention to, 310, 327*n*; homemaking activities vs., 317-321, 322, 327*n*, 329*n*, 330*n*; male participation in, 129; management of, 309-311, 326-327*n*; payment for, 299; time patterns of, 181, 182, 189, 193, 197*n*, 308-311, 316-323, 326*n*, 327*n*; 'two roles' of women and, 177, 190, 233-235, 311-313, 374
Housewives, 304; discretionary time inequalities, 307-313; history of role of, 307-311; as reserve army, 125; role change from producer to consumer, 313, 314; self-denigrating syndrome of, 309; stipends to, 313-314; time and technology of, 309-311; with time on their hands, 310-311, 327-328*n*; 'two-role' dilemma of employed, 177, 190, 233-235, 311-313, 374; volunteer work of, 304, 327-328*n*
'Housewives' wage (Norway), 208-209
Housing programs: Norway, 201, 204, 205; Sweden, 145, 146-148, 166-167, 173
Housing shortage (Eastern Europe), 181-182
Human Relations Area Files (HRAF), 130, 138*n*
Human rights: of children, 10-11, 215; U.N. Declaration on, 10, 349; women's rights in context of, 9, 10, 349-354, 374-376
Human services, women's provision of, 317, 318-319, 323
Humanist issues, women's involvement with, 282
Humanitarian ideologies: and love/nurturance bondage of women, 300*n*; Sweden, 289
Hungary: abortions and birth rate in, 88, 182, 184, 195*n*; child care, 186; discretionary time inequalities, 326*n*; female labor force

participation, 181, 183, 186; fertility rates, 89, 189

Illegitimate births. *See* Nonmarital fertility
Illness, family policy on (Norway), 206
Impact analysis: of research, 61-73, 76-79; of social policy, 54-56, 76
Income disparity, between men and women, 114-115, 117-119, 131-132, 135-136*n*, 207, 338, 368
Income redistribution, family policy and, (Norway) 204-205
Income tax: joint vs. individual (Sweden), 154-155, 165-166, 167-168, 171, 174; (Jordan), 226
India, 249-266; abortion laws, 259; birth control, 258-261; divorce, 252; economic development, 250-265; education, 92, 252; family patterns, 42, 44, 261-265; family policy, 258-261; female labor force participation, 92, 93, 99, 252-253, 255-258, 262-264; fertility policy in, 12, 36-37, 98, 249-266; legislation for sex-equality in, 255-256; literacy, 252; marriage, 252, 255; political participation, 253-255, 266*n*; population policies, 258-261; professional women, 256-258; secondary school enrollments, 92; social class biases, 249, 250-252, 263, 266*n*; sterilization programs, 259, 261; women's rights, 254-255
Individuation of the family, 200, 218, 219
Industrial sector, women's employment in (Jordan), 236, 240
Industrial societies: reserve army of housewives in, 125; time in, 308-311; women in, 122
Industrialization. *See* Economic development
Infant mortality: bottle vs. breast feeding and, 96; impact of reduced, 55
Inflation, 208

Interamerican Court of Human Rights, 354
Interdepartmental Task Force on Women (U.S.), 79*n*
Interdisciplinary research, 53-54, 373-374, 376
Intern and Fellows programs (U.S.), 69
International law, 349-354
International Women's Year, 43, 59*n*, 65, 79*n*, 114, 116, 190, 225-226, 238, 339-341
International Year of the Child (1979), 10-11
Intervention points, in social processes, 12-14, 50-51, 57
Intimazation, of the family, 219
Ireland, marriage age in, 88
Iroquois: relative economic power of women, 118; sexual equality among, 116
Islamic societies: female labor force in, 93; literacy rates in, 90-91; marriage in, 87; median educational attainment, 91; secondary school enrollments, 92
Israel, 11-12, 53, 369; child care, 186; female labor force participation, 186; marriage, 87; university enrollments, 92; women's status, 127-128
Italy, marriage age in, 88

Jamaica: female labor force, 92; marriage rate, 87; median education, 91
Japan: female labor force, 92; fertility rates, 89; marriage age, 88; sex role patterns, 177
Job redesigning, 359, 361
Jordan, 225-248; Bedouins in, 11, 118, 229; day-care centers, 238; discrimination, 226; divorce, 230-231; economic development, 225; female labor force participation, 225, 227, 233-239, 240-248; guardianship of children, 230-231; historical and political background, 227-228; income tax,

226; labor legislation, 237-238; leadership roles, 227; marriage, 230-231; political participation, 228; professional women, 236, 241; rural to urban migration, 225, 230; self-employed women, 235, 236, 241, 242; social change, 230-233; traditional role of women, 228-229, 234, 237; vocational training, 233
Judicial Branch (U.S.), 70-73

Kibbutz, 127-128
Kinship: government aid to individuals and, 218; and women's economic power, 126-127, 128
Koran, on treatment of women, 226
Kuikuru, 127
!Kung Bushmen, 116, 129

Labor: reproducing, *see* Reproductive sphere; sexual division of, 131, 137-138*n*, 252, 306, 315-316, 356, 357-358; socialist view of, 178, 194*n*
Labor force participation: child care and, 186; control of technical expertise and, 125; cross-cultural research on, 120-123, 137*n*; discretionary time and. *See* Discretionary time; economic development level and, 93, 121, 138*n*; and economic power, 120-130; education of women and, 97, 233; equality in, 93, 99-100, 114-115, 118-119, 135-136*n*, 147, 150-151, 346, 355-361; fertility rates and, 99, 177, 368; on flexitime schedules, 314, 328-329*n*; full employment goal (Norway), 199, 201, 203-204; history of female, 120-123; income tax and (Sweden), 154-155, 165-166, 167-168, 171, 174; as indicator of women's status, 92-93, 94, 95, 134-135, 368; labor demand vs. sex-specific supply and, 122-123; marginal workers, 166; of mothers, 32, 99, 162, 169, 177, 190-191, 208, 234-235; and overload for women, 306, 312, 313-316, 328-329*n*, 368, 375-376; planning for women increased, 96-100, 368; quality of, 356-361; rates of, 92-93, 111-112, 148-149, 183, 192-193; recruitment for, 180-181; redesign of jobs, 359, 361; relative income of male/female, 114-115, 117-119, 131-132, 135-136*n*, 338, 368; research on, 49, 50; social policy influence on, 145-175, 177-197, 225-248, 368; substitutability at the margin of female, 124-125; time discipline imposed by, 308-309, 311; women's status and, 92-93, 94, 95, 134-135, 245-246, 368. *See also* Occupations; Part-time employment; 'Two-roles' of women; *and specific country or region*, e.g. Africa; Eastern Europe; Finland; etc.
Labor legislation, protective, 291-292; Eastern Europe, 187; India, 255-256; Jordan, 237-238; Sweden, 147; United States, 9, 43, 71-72
Labor market: cross-cultural comparisons of distribution of women in, 52; strategic indispensability factors in, 124-126
Labor Party (Norway), 201, 206, 208, 210
Labor unions (Sweden), 150, 159, 160, 162, 166
Language, 277-278
Latin America: education, 91; female labor force, 92, 93; literacy rates, 90-91; marriage, 87; median educational attainment, 91; university enrollments, 92. *See also specific country*, e.g. Argentina; Chile; Venezuela, etc.
Leadership roles, research on, 58, 346-347; (Jordan), 227; (United States), 295-296, 300*n*
League of Women Voters, 281, 284*n*
Leaves of absence (maternity and childrearing), 99, 158-160, 184, 215-216, 220, 340

Subject Index

Legislation, disparity between reality and, 8, 165, 366-367. *See also* Discrimination — legislation against; Labor legislation, protective; *and specific country*, e.g. India; Sweden; etc.
Legislative Branch (U.S.), as user of research, 66-70
Legislative Reorganization Act (U.S.), 67, 68
Legitimacy, societal 'principle of,' 90
Leisure class, 313, 328*n*
Leisure time. *See* Discretionary time
Liberia, secondary school enrollments, 92
Libya, secondary school enrollments, 92
The Life and Work of Women (Dahlström), 155-156
Life-long learning, 340-341, 345
Life options: list of, 119, 133; organization of, 164, 170-171; relative female/male, 118-119, 129, 131-132. *See also* Quality of life
Life-time allocation decisions, 315, 329*n*
Literacy, 108-110; Africa, 90-91; India, 252; Islamic societies, 90-91; Latin America, 90-91; and women's status, 13, 90-91, 96-97, 375
Life expectancy rates, 86
Love and nurturance bondage, of women, 299, 300*n*

Machismo, 282
Male bias, in social policy design, 42-43, 177-178, 179, 194, 350, 366
Male-female comparisons, 9-10, 113-138, 375-376. *See also* Womens' Status
Male roles: changes in, 10, 288, 290-291, 293-294; in family, 99, 129, 162; in labor market, 152; research on, 53-54, 156; in sex-role debate, 155-156, 162-163, 287-289, 300*n*, 373
Male supremacy, ideology of, 129-130

Mali, secondary school enrollments in, 92
Manipulation of women, 40, 46, 367-368
Marginal labor supply, women as, 166
Marriage: age, 87-88, 94, 95, 97-98, 230-231; in agrarian society, 229; as indicator of women's status, 87-88, 94, 95, 97-98; quantity and timing of, 102-103. *See also* Family patterns; *and specific country*, e.g. India; Norway; etc.
Mass media, role of, 43
Maternal deprivation, 185-186
Maternity care (Sweden), 146
Maternity leaves. *See* Leaves of absence
Mathematics, study of, 32
Mbuti Pygmies, 116, 129
Medical insurance (Sweden), 147
Mexico City Conference (1975), 339-341
Middle Eastern societies: female labor force in, 93; history of, 121
Migration. *See* Rural to urban migrations; Talent drain emigration
Military service, leaves of absence, 99
Minority groups: coalitions between women's groups and, 372-373; leadership of, 295-296
Modernization: sex role stereotyping increased by, 99; and women's status, 85, 251
Motherhood: redemptive function of, 280, 284*n*; as womanhood, 88, 191
Mothering time, 324-325
Mothers, employed: implications of, 32; reduced fertility of, 99, 177; social acceptance of, 99, 162, 169, 208, 234-235; socialist attitudes, 190-191; time devoted to children, 324-325; traditional views, 234. *See also* Labor force participation
Mother's Pensions Laws (U.S), 311, 313
Muller v. Oregon, 71-72

Namibia, sexual equality in, 116

National Commission on the Observance of International Women's Year (U.S.), 65
National Institute of Education (U.S.) 346
Nepal: female labor force in, 92, 93; secondary school enrollments in, 92
Netherlands, female labor force in, 93
New Zealand, female labor force in, 93
Nicaragua, median education in, 91
Nonemployed mothers, time devoted to children, 324-325
Nonemployed wives, taxation of, 314
Nonemployed women, 304; discretionary time inequalities of, 307-313
Nonmarital fertility, 90, 104-107, 210
Norway, 199-224; abortion laws, 215, 219; analysis of family policy in, 217-221; birth control, 205-206, 219; child care, 200, 204-206, 212-216, 220; day-care centers, 208-209, 212, 214, 218, 220, 222-223; divorce, 204, 209; economic development, 199, 201, 203-204; family patterns, 199-224; family policy (1945-1970), 203-209; (1970s), 210-221; female labor force participation, 207-209; full employment goal, 199, 201, 203-204; health care services, 201, 205, 207, 214, 218; housing programs, 201, 204, 205; marriage, 88, 207, 209, 210, 219; maternity leaves, 215-216, 220; reproductive sphere as government responsibility, 204-206, 213-216, 217, 221, 224n; social insurance systems, 205, 218, 221; social problems, 201-202, 211; social security system, 201, 206; standard of living, 204-205
Nuptiality. *See* Marriage
Nursery schools (Sweden), 147. *See also* Day-care centers
Occupations: prestige scores of, 118-119; women seeking degrees in traditionally male, 344-345. *See also* Labor force participation
Of Woman Born (Rich), 74
Office of Technology Assessment (U.S.), 67-68
Old age, 98, 206
Oppression of women, family institution contributions to, 221-223
Overload, women's, 306, 312, 313-316, 323, 328-329n, 368, 375-376. *See also* Discretionary time; 'Two-roles' of women

Pakistan: crude birth rates, 88; secondary school enrollments, 92
Palestinian refugees, 233
Paraguay, median education in, 91
Parent-child relationships, research on, 58
Parental insurance system (Sweden), 158-160, 169, 170, 174
Parson-Bales theory of functional specialization in the family, 326n
Part-time education (United States), 345, 346
Part-time employment, 99; Jordan, 247-248; Eastern Europe, 181; Sweden, 149, 151, 165, 166, 173, 195n; United States, 328n
Paternalism, 291-292
Peasants, 124-126, 137n
Personal Status Law (Jordan, 1976), 230-231
Philippines, sexual equality among Tasaday in, 116, 129, 136n, 138n
Poland: abortion, 182; day care, 185, 186; discretionary time inequalities, 306; female labor force participation, 183; fertility rates, 89; war dead, 180
Policy. *See* Social policy
Policy makers: level of understanding of social phenomena, 25, 42-44; male bias of, 42-43, 177-178, 179, 194, 350, 366; and research, 3-5, 7-14, 17-60, 62-72, 83-112, 363-380; in Third World, 350-353;

traditions of, 23-25; women as, 9-10, 100, 279-286
Political continuity, 146, 369
Political participation, cross-cultural data on, 284*n*. *See also specific countries*, e.g., France; India; United States; etc.
Political power, relative female/male, 117, 129, 131
Politicians, personal views on women's roles, 168-169
Politics: in policy-making process, 20-22, 365-366, 373-374; in research process, 39-40, 46-47, 75, 77
Popular Republican Movement (France), 271-272
Population: socialist 'law' governing, 182, 195*n*; traditional roles and over-, 86. *See also* Birth rates; Fertility; *and specific countries and regions*, e.g. Eastern Europe; India; etc.
Portugal, marriage age in, 88
Power: differential male/female, 10, 117-119; of force in female life options, 117-118, 129, 131-132; women's 'poker chips' of, 128-130. *See also* Economic power; Political power
Pre-industrial societies, 121, 137*n*; substitutability at the margin in, 125; time in, 308-309
Preschool teachers, male (Sweden), 152
Preschools (Sweden), 169. *See also* Day-care centers
President's Commission on the Status of Women (U.S.), 64-65
President's Task Force on Women's Rights and Responsibilities (U.S.), 65
Primates, 129
Privatization, of the family, 219-220
Privilege, power and, 117-119
Production: changes in sphere of, 199, 201-202, 217, 222, 223*n*, 224*n*; concentration of (Norway), 210-211, 217; restructuring of system of, 355, 360-361; social relations of, 127-128
Production, participation in. *See* Labor force participation
Productivity, national. *See* Gross National Product
Professional women, 93, 112; India, 256-258; Jordan, 236, 241
Prohibition amendment, 284*n*
Property: equality in ownership and control, 99-100; socialist view of private, 179
Prostitution: idleness of middle class wives as, 310; migration, urban slums, and, 98, 257
Protective legislation. *See* Labor legislation, protective
Protest movements, leadership of, 295-296
Prussia, East, peasants in, 126
Psychology of Women Quarterly, 77
Public administration. *See* Services sector

Quality of life, demographic indicators and, 94-100
Quality of working life, 356-361

Rape, 285*n*
Rashomon, 17*n*
Recruitment, 180-181
Redemptive function, 279-283
Reproductive sphere, 202-203, 210, 223-224*n*; government responsibility for (Norway), 204-206, 213-216, 217, 221, 224*n*
Research: abuses of, 39-40, 44-48; analytical, 49-51, 57; applied, 48-49; basic, 48-49; 'big business' aspects of, 40, 46-47; cohort studies, 52; conceptualization of, 8; cost-benefit analysis of policy implications of, 31-32; cross-sectional, 51; data gathering methods, 107*n*; descriptive, 49-51; evaluating, 27-28; 75-76; fact finding, 45; follow-up of same subject population, 51; government role in, 1-2, 62-73; impact points

for, 61-73, 76-79; implementation of findings of, 30-37, 73-79; interdisciplinary, 53-54, 373-374, 376; international activity in, 341; intervention-oriented, 12-13, 50-51, 57; 'irrelevance' of, 25-26; legitimation of policy, 376-377; longitudinal, 51, 57; misunderstandings of, 17-60, 48-49, 364-365; misuses of, 39-40, 44-48, 371; political problems of, 39-40, 46-47; politically useful, 75, 77; predictive power of, 45; reporting of, 26-27; role in social policy development, 1-5, 7-14, 17-60, 62-72, 83-112, 363-380; strategies, 48-56; as strategy, 366; time required for, 51; traditions of, 23-25, 364-365; useful, 73-79, 133-135; users of policy-relevant, 62-73. *See also* Cross-cultural research; *and specific topics*, e.g. Discretionary time; Labor force participation; Women's status; etc.
Researchers: as consultants, 28-30; model for relationship between activists and, 78; women, 42, 377-379
Resources, control of. *See* Economic power
Retraining courses (Sweden), 149-150
Revolution. *See* Socialist societies
Role transformation, 10-11. *See also* Change; Equality; Sex roles
Romania: abortion and birth rates in, 182, 183-184; female labor force participation, 183; living standard, 194*n*; population changes, 180
Rural to urban migrations: marriage patterns upset by, 98; Jordan, 225, 230; Sweden (1950s-1960s), 148
Russia. *See* Soviet Union
Rwala Bedouin, 118

Saudi Arabia, relative sexual equality in, 116
School children (Sweden), 146-148, 164-165
School desegregation, research on, and court decisions, 72

Schools. *See* Education
Scotland, female labor force in, 92
Secondary schools, female enrollment trends in, 91-92, 108-110
Segregation, of women workers, 355-356, 360-361
Self-employed women (Jordan), 235, 236, 241, 242
Separatism, in work world, 357, 359-360
Services sector: Eastern Europe, 181; India, 257; Jordan, 236, 240
Sex education (Sweden), 153
Sex role equality. *See* Equality
Sex role patterns: Eastern Europe, 177-197; India, 249-266; Jordan, 225-248; Norway, 199-224; Sweden, 145-175, 287, 288-289; United States, 290-291. *See also* Family patterns
Sex role stereotypes, 339, 368; in vocational guidance, 154, 165, 174, 338; children's learning of, 50-51; debate over (Sweden), 155-156, 162-163, 167, 170, 171-172; economic development and. *See* Economic development; education and, 145-146, 152-154; research on. *See* Research; transformation of, 10-11, 57-59, 287-301, 368-372, 378-379; vulnerability to political and conceptual difficulties, 365-366. *See also* Female roles; Male roles
Sex Roles, 77
Sex stratification, 9-10, 113-138, 375-376; conflict confrontations to change, 287-288, 290-301; economic power and, 117-132; history of, 9, 86, 121-122, 125; paradigm of, 116-117; theory of, 133-142
Sexual behavior, research on, 54
Sexual Politics (Millett), 74
Single mothers (Sweden), 157
'Sisterhood.' *See* Coalitions
Slaves, 131
Social class: biases in India, 249, 250-252, 263, 266*n*; relative sexual

Subject Index

equality and, 128, 136n, 224n
Social conflict, 290. *See also* Conflict confrontation
Social Democratic Government (Norway), 201, 202, 209, 223
Social Democratic Party (Sweden), 146, 149, 152, 159-160, 163, 167, 369
Social engineer, 36
Social insurance systems: Norway, 205, 218-221; Sweden, 147-148, 164
Social phenomena, overestimation of understanding of, 42-44
Social policy: ad hoc formulation of, 20-21, 377; ambiguities of, 367-368; delivering on promise of, 363-380; demographic indicators used in formulation of, 94-100; difficulties from research perspective, 39-60; discretionary time and, 303-333; example of research relevant to, 83-112; family and. *See* Family patterns; functions of, 178-179; homogeneity or heterogeneity of society and its, 21-22, 370-372; impact analysis of proposed, 54-56, 62-72, 76; implementation of research findings through, 30-37; international law and, 349-354; male-designed, 42-43, 177-178, 179, 194, 350, 366; manipulation of women through, 40, 46, 367-368; and overload of women's time, 306, 312, 313-316, 328-329n, 368; relative economic power and implications for, 133-135; research's role in developing, 3-5, 7-14, 17-60, 62-72, 83-112, 363-380; socialist view of, 178-179; as substitution policy for traditional solutions, 220-221; women as agents of change in, 287-301, 378-379. *See also* Female roles; Male roles; Policy makers; *and specific countries*, e.g., India; Norway; etc.
Social problems (Norway), 201-202, 211

Social processes: intervention points in, 12-13, 50-51, 57; research on, 50
Social science. *See* Research
Social security systems: Norway, 201, 206; United States, 285n, 311
Social welfare system (Sweden), 146-148
Socialist Party (France), 272, 274
Socialist societies: equality and sexism in, 177, 179, 190-191, 193, 356, 359; female labor force participation, 93, 177, 180-183, 186, 187, 191-193, 196n; on labor, 178, 194n; marriage, 87; university enrollments, 92. *See also specific country*, e.g. Bulgaria; German Democratic Republic; Soviet Union; etc.
Sociobiology, 285n, 331n
Soviet Union: abortion laws, 181-182; child care, 185-186; discretionary time inequalities, 305-306; fathering, 322; female labor force participation, 183, 186; labor shortage estimates, 186, 196n; relative sexual equality, 116, 305-306; sex role responsibilities, 177, 190; social policy and sex roles, 369; war dead, 180; women's time in, 305-306, 316
Spain, marriage age in, 88
Spatial visualization skills, 51
Stability, as condition for change, 369-370
Standard of living: equality in (Norway), 204-205; housewives' role in raising, 310, 327n. *See also* Quality of life
Status. *See* Power; Women's status
Status-prestige complex, 118
Sterilization programs, 36; India, 259, 261
Strategies, 355-361; conflict confrontation, 295-298; research, 48-56, 366
Substitutability at the margin, of women and peasants, 124-126
Substitution policy (Norway), 220

Success, women's alleged fear of, 25, 76-77
Suffrage, women's. *See* Political participation; Women's rights
Suicide, lack of contraceptives and, 184
Sweden, 10, 11, 21, 52, 53, 145-175; abortion laws, 157, 174, 288, 289; adult education, 154, 340-341; affirmative action programs, 150-152; birth control, 156-157, 162, 174-175; child care, 146-148, 151, 158-161, 164, 165, 173-174, 186; childrearing, 158-160; civil service employment, 150-151; crude birth rates, 88; day-care centers, 147, 160-161, 164, 165, 167, 168-169, 173-174; divorce laws, 158, 170; education, 146-148, 152-154, 164-165, 169, 171, 174; egalitarian ideology, 289; family law, 157-158, 167-170; family patterns, 146-147, 162-163, 166-168, 340, 369; female labor force participation, 147, 148-153, 159, 160, 162, 166, 186, 195*n*; feminist activities, 289; fertility rates, 89; health care services, 146, 147, 167; as homogeneous society, 370-371; housing, 146-148, 166-167, 173; income tax, 154-155, 165-166, 167-168, 171, 174; labor legislation, 147; labor market policy, 149-153, 166, 171, 172; labor unions, 150, 159, 160, 162, 166; legislation against discrimination, 146-175, 289; marriage, 88, 147, 157-158, 169, 170; parental insurance system, 158-160, 169, 170, 174; political continuity, 146, 369; relative sexual equality, 116, 147, 340; retraining programs, 149-150; secondary schools, 153-154; sex role debate, 155-156, 162-163, 287-289, 300*n*, 373; sex roles and education in, 152-154, 340; social insurance system, 147-148, 164; social legislation, 145-175, 340, 369; social welfare system, 146-148; university education, 146, 152-153, 154; workday hours, 151, 159-160
Switzerland, marriage age in, 88
Syria, secondary school enrollments in, 92

Taiwan, female labor force in, 93
Talent drain emigration, from Jordan, 226-227
Tasaday, 116, 129, 136*n*, 138*n*
Task-orientation, of non-industrial work, 308-309
Taxation: on childless persons (Romania), 184; of nonemployed wife, 314. *See also* Income tax
Teachers (Jordan), 244-245
Technical courses. *See* Vocational training
Technological determinism, in quality of working life, 356, 358-359
Textbooks: Swedish, 153; United States, 342
Textile technology industry, women in (Czechoslovakia), 196*n*
Third world, 13, 375. *See also* Africa; Latin America
Time, 303-331; allocation of, 315, 329*n*; flexible use of, 314, 328*n*; homemaking requirements for, 316-323; in industrial societies and before, 308-311; mothering, 324-325; patterns of household tasks, 181-182, 189, 193, 308-311, 316-323, 326*n*, 327*n*; policies dealing with, 313-316, 328*n*; required for research, 51. *See also* Discretionary time; Overload, women's; 'Two-roles' of women
Title IX, 38*n*, 59*n*, 63-64, 79*n*, 342
Token woman, research on, 297-298
Trade unions. *See* Labor unions
Training programs. *See* Vocational training
Transitions, 57-59
Transportation (Sweden), 173
Tunisia, fertility rate in, 88-89

Subject Index

Two-career family, discretionary time inequalities in, 306
'Two-roles' of women, 177, 190, 233-235, 311-313, 323, 374. *See also* Discretionary times; Household tasks; Labor force participation; Overload, women's

Underemployment, of women, 166
Unemployment (Norway), 201
United Nations, 10, 84, 339, 349, 374
United States: abortion laws, 285*n*, 371; affirmative action programs, 135*n*, 290; birth control, 285*n*, 316; child care, 186; Congressional research support agencies, 67-68, 79*n*; counseling services, 345; discretionary time inequalities, 306; education, 92, 341, 342-346, 371-372; female labor force participation, 92, 93, 186, 311-313, 327-328*n*, 346; health care services, 285*n*; as heterogeneous society, 371-372; labor legislation, 9, 43, 71-72; leadership roles, 295-296, 300*n*; legislation against discrimination, 24, 38*n*, 50, 57, 59*n*, 63-73, 79*n*, 285*n*, 290-291, 292, 342-343, 347; marriage in, 87, 316; political participation in, 279-286; policy to protect home, 311-313, 328*n*; research and policy-making in, 61-81; social security system, 285*n*, 311; 'two-role' dilemma in, 311-313; university education, 92, 342-346; women's rights, 281-283; 284-285*n*; women's status, 114-115, 135-136*n*, 342-346
University education, female enrollment trends, 92, 108-110, 344-346. *See also specific countries*, e.g., France; Sweden; United States; etc.
Unmarried persons, as political pressure group (Norway), 205
Urban women, in Jordan and Arab world, 229
Urbanization, causing changes in family structure (Jordan), 230-231. *See also* Rural to urban migrations
Uruguay, median education in, 91
U.S.S.R. *See* Soviet Union

Variety, behavioral, 84, 88-90, 94, 116
Venezuela: female labor force in, 93; fertility rates in, 89
Vicarious-achievement pattern, 282, 291, 347
Village women: India, 255; Jordan, 228-229
Vocational guidance, sex role stereotypes in, 154, 165, 174, 338
Vocational training, 97-99, 233; Eastern Europe, 187-188, 196*n*; Jordan, 233; Sweden, 148
Volunteer work, 340, 327-328*n*

Wages, relative male/female, 114-115, 117-119, 131-132, 135-136*n*, 207, 338, 368
Waiting, as human service, 318-319, 330*n*
Welfare societies. *See* Norway
Wellesley College Conference (1976), 5*n*
Wifebeating, 118, 131
Womanhood, motherhood as, 88, 191
Women: family policy as policy for (Norway), 207-209; heterogeneity of, 21-22
Women and Madness (Chesler), 74
Women's Bureau (U.S.), 63-64
Women's Educational Equity Act (U.S., 1964), 343
Women's Equity Action League (U.S.), 328*n*
Women's liberation movement (U.S.), 116, 290-291, 292, 295, 300*n*
Women's Research Program (U.S.), 4-5
Women's rights, in human rights context, 9, 10, 349-354, 374-376
Women's roles. *See* Female roles
Women's status: compared with men's, 9-10, 113-138, 375-376; cor-

relation analysis of measures of, 94, 95; cross-cultural research on indicators of, 83-112; demographic indicators of, 83-112; in different countries, 374-376 (*see also* Cross cultural research; *and specific country*); diversity and variation in, 9-10, 84, 88-90, 94, 116, 375-376; economic development and, 83-112, 138*n*, 180-181, 257-258, 350-352; education and, 90-92, 94, 95, 134-135; employment outside home or farm and, 92-93, 94, 95, 134-135, 245-246, 368 (*see also* Labor force participation); fertility as indicator of, 88-90, 94, 95, 134-135, 226; Gross National Product and, 94, 95, 96-99; history of, 9, 86, 121-122, 125; improving, 363-380; international law to advance, 349-354; literacy and, 13, 90-91, 94, 95; marriage and, 87-88, 94, 95, 97-98; measuring, 9, 83-112, 113-138, 375-376; nonmarital fertility and, 90; paradigm for prediction of, 113-142; relative economic power and, 113-142, 338, 368; socialist view of, 177, 179, 190-191, 193, 356, 359; theoretical issues, 84-85, 114-115; world plan of action on, 339-340. *See also* indicators of, e.g., Discretionary time; Economic power; Education; Fertility; Labor force participation; Sex stratification; *and under names of countries*, e.g., India; Jordan; Norway; etc.

Women's studies, centers and programs of, 75-76, 378

Work. *See* Household tasks; Labor force participation; Occupations

Workday hours: Eastern Europe, 181; Norway, 216; Sweden, 151, 159-160, 164, 170-171, 173

Workers' rights. *See* Labor unions

Working conditions (Sweden), 150, 162, 172-173

Working women. *See* Household tasks; Labor force participation; Mothers, employed

World War I and II, and transformation of women's roles, 369

World War II, population losses of, 180

Yugoslavia: marriage age, 88; Worker's Councils, 359

Zaire, sexual equality in, 116

AUTHOR INDEX

Agassi, J. B., 11-12, 355-361, 381
Akugawa, R., 17*n*
Allan, V., 65
American Political Science Association, 69
Aronoff, J., 122, 305
Astin, H. S., 328*n*, 344, 346

Bales, R., 120
Baude, A., 10, 11, 22, 145-175, 368, 369, 370-371, 381
Bauerova, J., 194-195
Beecher, C., 309
Bell, C. S., 310
Berelson, B., 55
Berger, M., 72
Bernard, J., 3-5, 8, 12, 279-286, 292, 303-333, 363-380, 381
Berry, M., 1-2
Birdsall, N., 134
Blake, J., 119
Blumberg, R. L., 9, 45, 113-142, 375, 381
Boserup, E., 13, 88, 134, 138*n*
Boulding, E., 7-14, 136*n*, 283-284, 305, 306, 312-325 *passim*, 326*n*, 330*n*, 381
Braden, T., 322-323
Brandeis, L. B., 43, 71-72
Brock, W., 69
Bronfenbrenner, U., 322, 331*n*
Brown, J. K., 116, 122
Brown, J. S., 78
Brown, R. D., 309
Buchwald, A., 323
Burns, A., 65

Calhoun, A. W., 308
Carden, M. L., 283
Carroll, M., 305, 326*n*
Carter, J., 64, 79*n*, 352
Caplan, N., 63, 73
Causey, M., 328
Chaney, E., 134
Chester, P., 74
Childe, V. G., 121
Clark, K., 72
Cohen, D. K., 72, 73
Collins, R., 129, 132
Conlin, E. R., 79*n*
Conn, C. B., 337*n*
Constantini, E., 281, 282
Coser, L., 290
Cott, N., 308-309, 311, 313, 317-319, 324
Cowan, R. S., 310, 316, 324
Craik, K. H., 281, 282
Crain, R. L., 73
Crans, W. D., 122, 305, 326*n*
Cronin, T. E., 63, 64, 66

Dahlström, E., 145-146, 155-156
David, H. P., 195*n*
Davis, K., 119
De Gaulle, C., 271, 273
D'Estaing, G., 274-275
DeTocqueville, A., 70, 373
DeVore, I., 121
Dixon, R., 134
Dodge, N. T., 369
Dofny, J., 295
Douglas, W. O., 73
Du Granrut, C., 12, 269-278, 382

Duverger, M., 279

Ehrlich, H. J., 136n
Engels, F., 179, 194n
Enke, S., 134
Erikson, E., 319, 330n
Es-Said, N. T., 11, 225-248, 377, 382

Farson, R. E., 330n
Federation of Organizations for Professional Women, 78
Fernandez, C. A., II, 116
Fick, I., 197
Fiedler, L., 322
Firestone, S., 132
Folsom, J. K., 310
Ford, G., 65
Fox, G. L., 298
Frank, H., 293, 298
Frankfurter, F., 70
Freeman, J., 64, 69, 280, 281
Fritchey, C., 282

Galbraith, J. K., 310, 313
Gandhi, M., 254-255, 259
Germain, A., 134
Gilman, C. P., 310, 311
Giroud, F., 275
Glick, P., 315
Goldberg, S., 136n
Goldmark, J., 71
Goldschmidt, W., 121
Gough, K., 127
Green, E., 68, 69
Greenberg, S. D., 63, 64, 66
Gronseth, E., 200, 208
Guttentag, M., 306, 325

Hadley, J., 329
Hammond, S., 68
Harlan, Justice, 73
Hartley, S. F., 9, 83-112, 382
Hassan, Crown Prince, 226, 238
Henriksen, H. ve, 199-224, 382
Herzberg, F., 37
Hess, R. D., 280
Hine, L. A., 364

Holmstrom, L. M., 306
Holter, H., 12, 199-224, 285n, 382
Howe, J. W., 280
Huber, J., 328n
Hussein, King, 228

Ibsen, H., 310
International Sociological Association, 3-4, 7

Johnson, L. B., 64, 65
Jolley, M. A., 346

Kanter, R., 322
Katcher, M., 298
Keniston, K., 322
Kennedy, J. F., 64, 312
Khayri, M. O., 246
Klein, V., 311, 312-313, 315, 328n
Knudsen, D. D., 85, 135n
Komarovsky, M., 18, 73
Kotasek, A., 196
Kraditor, A. S., 280
Kreinberg, N., 32

Lamphere, L., 129
Landers, A., 323
Landman, L. C., 37
Lapidus, G. W., 369
Laslett, B., 329n
Leavitt, H. J., 34, 282, 291, 347
Leavitt, R. R., 127
Lee, R. B., 121
LeGuin, U., 11
Leibowitz, L., 129
Lenski, G. E., 117, 121
Lenski, J., 121
Liljeström, R., 42
Lipman-Blumen, J., 3-5, 8, 17-60, 73, 181, 282, 291, 297, 347, 363-380, 382
Lipset, S. M., 282
Lynch, F., 116

McMillan, L., 61n
Marchand, C., 9, 349-354, 383
Markus, M., 189-190

Author Index

Marx, K., 171, 179, 255, 330n, 359
Maslow, A. H., 37
Mazumdar, V., 12, 249-266, 368, 383
Meyers, R., 329
Michaelson, E. J., 121
Michel, A., 7
Miller, J. B., 284n
Millett, K., 74
Mondale, W., 328n
Mosher, C., 68
Murdock, G. P., 121, 124, 136n, 138n
Murphy, I. L., 18
Myrdal, A., 42, 164, 311, 312-313, 315, 328n
Myrdal, G., 91

Nadar, R., 296
Nasir, S., 245
National Institute of Education, 4
National Science Board, 73
Nehru, J., 255-256
Nixon, R. M., 64, 65

Oakley, A., 315
Oboler, R. E., 125
Oppenheimer, V. K., 123
Osnos, P., 322, 331n

Parsons, T., 120
Paul, B., 33, 36
Peterson, E., 64
Platt, J., 283
Pleck, J. H., 53
Plott, J., 337
Pompidou, G., 272, 273
Preston, S. H., 314
Provost, C., 123

Quinn, S., 330n

Radvanová, S., 194n
Rapoport, Rhona, 306
Rapoport, Robert, 306
Reinhardt, H. H., 126
Rich, A., 74
Rivlin, A., 33, 62, 68, 76
Rosaldo, M. Z., 129

Rosen, J., 146n
Rosen, P. L., 70, 71, 73
Ross, H. L., 314
Ruskin, J., 318, 330n
Russ, J., 11

Sacks, M. P., 305-306, 312, 316
Safilios-Rothschild, C., 10, 12, 85, 136n, 287-301, 383
Sanday, P. R., 120, 371
Sandler, B., 68
Sas, J. M., 326n
Sawhill, I. V., 314
Schlegal, A., 126
Scott, H., 11, 22, 46, 58, 177-197, 383
Sells, L., 32
Shorter, E., 305
Sipes, R. G., 134
Sipila, H., 339
Sklar, K. K., 309
Special Commission on the Social Sciences, 73
Spiro, M. E., 128
Stack, C. B., 128
Stinchcombe, A. L., 125
Strasburg, G. L., 8-9, 25, 29-30, 61-81, 383
Sullerot, E., 42, 86n
Szalai, A., 305-307, 310, 311, 312, 326n, 327n, 329n

Tangri, S. S., 8-9, 25, 29-30, 61-81, 383
Tavris, C., 76
Terrell, K., 118
Thompson, E. P., 308
Tiger, L., 284n, 322, 330-331n
Tinker, I., 138n
Torney, J. V., 280
Treiman, D. J., 118
Trotter, V. Y., 9, 24, 337-348, 383-384

Van Allen, J., 85
Van den Berghe, P., 85
Vanek, J., 310, 327n
Vanocur, S., 322

Veblen, T., 310
Viel, S., 275

Ware, H., 134
Warren, E., 70
Weber, M., 117
Weiss, J., 72, 74-75, 77
Weiss, L. A., 73
Wheeler, S., 299, 300*n*
White, B., 71
Whiting, B., 122
Wilber, G., 85

Williamson, N., 98
Wilson, E. O., 285*n*, 331*n*
Wolfe, E., 72
Wolman, C., 293, 298
Woolf, V., 330*n*
Woolsey, S. H., 22, 53

Youssef, N. H., 9, 83-112, 384

Ziegler, P., 126

NOTES ON CONTRIBUTORS

Judith Buber Agassi of the Hebrew University of Jerusalem, is author of *Mass Media in Indonesia* (1969) and 'The Worker and the Media' (*European Journal of Sociology,* Spring 1970).

Annika Baude has been involved with sex role and family questions since 1962 and is currently working for the National Board of Health and Welfare in Stockholm. She has promoted and contributed to the English edition of *The Changing Roles of Men and Women* (London, 1967; Boston, 1971).

Jessie Bernard is Research Scholar Honoris Causa at Pennsylvania State University. In the last few years she has written extensively in the area of marriage, family, community, and women. Among her recent books are: *Women and the Public Interest* (1971), *The Future of Marriage* (1973), *The Future of Motherhood* (1974), and *Women, Wives, Mothers* (1975).

Rae Lesser Blumberg is Acting Associate Professor in the Department of Sociology at the University of California, San Diego. She has published numerous articles dealing with cross-cultural paradigms of sexual stratification, the interrelationship of economic factors, female status and fertility, societal complexity and familial complexity, ethnicity and extended families, and has written on education, family, urban ecology and political economy in developing countries. She has written a book, *Stratification: Socioeconomic and Sexual Inequality* (1978), and is working on another detailing her theory-testing research on women's relative economic power as a primary determinant of their status and life options in comparison to the men of their groups.

Elise Boulding is Professor of Sociology at Dartmouth College, Hanover, New Hampshire, USA, having been previously Professor of Sociology at the University of Colorado and Project Director at the Institute of Behavioral Science. She was associated with the founding of the Research Committee for the Study of Sex Roles in Society of the ISA. She is author of *Handbook of International Data on Women, Women in the Twentieth Century World,* and *Underside of History.*

Claude du Granrut is Deputy Director, Labor Department of the French Government. She is also a member of the Committee on Women's Work and Director of Studies at the Paris Institute of Political Studies. From 1971-77 she was General Secretary of the Women's Work Committee.

Nimra Tannous Es-Said has since 1967 been Assistant Executive Secretary to the Supreme Ministerial Committee for the Relief of Displaced Persons in Jordan. Dr Es-Said has devoted most of her research to women in traditional male-oriented societies and frequently publishes articles in local and other Arab journals.

Shirley Foster Hartley is Professor of Sociology at California State University, Hayward. She is Associate Editor of *Contemporary Sociology* and has published *Population: Quantity vs. Quality* (1972) and *Illegitimacy* (1975) as well as numerous articles on population, illegitimacy, and women.

Hildur ve Henriksen is a Researcher at the Institute of Sociology of the University of Bergen. Her current project is the relationship between girls' social class background and their views on family life, education and work.

Harriet Holter is Professor Social Psychology at the University of Oslo and a member of the Royal Norwegian Academy of Science. She is currently working as a Research Supervisor for the Norwegian Research Council for Social Science and the Humanities. Her research in recent years has combined sociological and psychological perspectives and has been concentrated on industrial relations and work life, sex roles, and the family and social policy. She has published *Sex Roles and Social Structure* (1970) and numerous articles.

Jean Lipman-Blumen is Assistant Director of the National Institute of Education, Department of Health, Education and Welfare, Washington, DC. She is also a Senior Research Associate and Director of the Women's Research Program. Dr. Lipman-Blumen is currently on special assignment to President Carter's Domestic Policy Staff. She has published extensively on sex roles and society.

Cecilia Marchand is Professor of International Law at the Diplomatic Academy of Peru.

Vina Mazumdar is an historian and political scientist by profession and has served as Member-Secretary of the Committee on the Status of Women in India. She is currently Director of the sponsored research programme of Women's Studies of the Indian Council of Social Science Research, New Delhi. She has contributed extensively to academic journals and official publications in India.

Constantina Safilios-Rothschild is Professor of Sociology at the University of California at Santa Barbara. She is the author of *Toward the Sociology of Women; Women and Social Policy; Love, Sex and Sex Roles;* and many articles on the status of women cross-culturally; power and family dynamics; sex role socialization and sex discrimination; and sexuality and birth control.

Hilda Scott is a journalist and writer who lived and worked in Czechoslovakia from 1949 to 1973, specializing in women's and medical subjects. She now resides in Vienna, where she is associated with a research group studying social problems. She is a member of the editorial advisory board of *Women's Studies International Quarterly,* and is author of *Does Socialism Liberate Women? Experiences from Eastern Europe* (Boston, 1974), published in the United Kingdom as *Women and Socialism* (London, 1976) and a number of articles.

Georgia Strasburg is a Research Psychologist with the US Commission on Civil Rights and a doctoral candidate in social psychology at Howard University. Her research is concentrated on group dynamics, with a special interest in political process. She has consulted widely to small groups, in clinical and applied settings.

Sandra Schwartz Tangri is Director of Research at the US Commission on Civil Rights. Her primary research interests are in social change, sex roles, psychology of women, fertility, population planning, personality, and sex and race relations. She is joint editor of *Women and Achievement: Social and Motivational Analyses* (1975) and *New Perspectives on Women: Journal of Social Issues* (1972), among other publications.

Virginia Yapp Trotter is Vice President for Academic Affairs at the University of Georgia. She was from 1974-77 Assistant Secretary for Education at the Department of Health, Education and Welfare, Washington, DC. Dr Trotter's main interest is in Home Economics, on which she has published extensively in US journals.

Nadia H. Youssef is Visiting Associate Professor of Sociology at the University of Southern California, and a Research Associate at the International Center for Research on Women in Washington, DC. Her major interests are in social demography, comparative sociology, women in development, the family, the social consequences of industrialization, sociological theory, social organization, and social change. Dr. Youssef has contributed extensively on these subjects to books and journals.

NOTES

NOTES

NOTES

NOTES